Section 36
A Wyoming Journey From Then and Now

by
Greg A. Garton

To Pat
Hope you enjoy the book
Greg Garton

authorHOUSE™

1663 LIBERTY DRIVE, SUITE 200
BLOOMINGTON, INDIANA 47403
(800) 839-8640
WWW.AUTHORHOUSE.COM

First published by AuthorHouse 04/27/05

ISBN: 1-4208-3942-X (sc)
ISBN: 1-4208-3941-1 (dj)

Library of Congress Control Number: 2005902386

Printed in the United States of America
Bloomington, Indiana

This book is printed on acid-free paper.

This book is dedicated to my wife Kathleen who has loved me in past lives, and again in this one, spanning the lifetimes with sunflowers.

Acknowledgments

When I was a young boy growing up on my ranch home in the Laramie Range of the Rocky Mountains there weren't the vast arrays of entertainment available to the young people of today. Game machines, computers and other electronic gadgets weren't invented yet and once night came my family gathered together to play cards, read, or tell stories. My parents, and their parents, and their parents before them accumulated a large library of hardbound books that were shelved in bookcases arranged in every room. I was drawn to these stories that helped relieve the feelings of loneliness and isolation. When I read, I could travel anywhere and to any time the stories led. Sometimes I feel sad for many of the youth today who are trapped in this time, and need someone or something else to entertain them.

My favorite authors were Zane Grey, Gene Stratton Porter, Edgar Rice Burroughs and of course Louis L'Amour. Through these writers I learned that a good story was always worth retelling, and that there was honor in doing the right thing. Their descriptions of the land and the depth of characterization transported me to their settings. Powerful stuff indeed. I can only hope that one day, my descriptions and characters will take someone else to a different time and place.

Section 36 is a work of fiction, pure and simple. What I have tried to do is to interweave my characters with historical events and historical figures of the past that did live, love, and die trying to make their country a better place. Through them I wrote what I imagined their thoughts, feelings and desires were. Men like Manuel Lisa, Andrew Henry, and William Ashley truly were giants of their time, and without men like these our country would never have achieved its full potential. Many great historians have written biographies of these and other early pioneers of the frontier and I recommend that you take time to research and read their histories.

The descriptions of the country through which my heroes and villains travel are real. For the last three years I walked, rode, and floated through these places from St. Genevieve to the high rugged crags of Laramie Peak. A city, a mountain range, geological time periods, and a river bear honor to Jacques La Ramie who was one of the first white men to live freely in this land and I took special care to accurately depict this part of Wyoming.

Several historians have written excellent histories of Wyoming and the trails along the Platte River and her larger sisters. <u>Footprints on the Frontier: Saga of the La Ramie Region of Wyoming</u>, by Virginia Cole Trenholm, is perhaps the best and although now a rare book is one that should be read by anyone interested in Wyoming history. <u>The Mississippi Valley Frontier</u> by John Anthony Caruso, and <u>The Great Platte River Road</u> by Merrill J. Mattes are also excellent. No matter what region of this great country in which we live, there are exciting historical events that occurred there, and by reading, and researching the past, our homelands come alive. I thank these people for the hours of research they conducted and for making history come alive for me.

I would also like to thank my mother Thelma for instilling in me a love for reading and my boys Travis and Tyrell for their hours of patience through this project, and especially my wife Kathy who made this trip with me. I also owe a large debt to Elizabeth Scicluna and Pat Mitchell who continually tried to keep me from mixing my gerunds with my dangling participles. Thanks gals.

Greg A. Garton

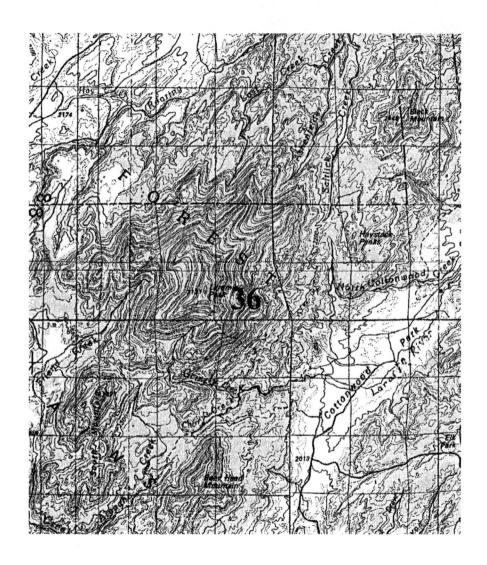

Chapter 1
The Wasp

The Earth knoweth not its name;
Only the Maker who mouldeth it from clay.
No other master's yoke will she own,
though fire and water it abides,
and even time does it defy.
Earth to Earth, Ashes to Ashes.
Into her bosom she will take all things and holdeth there
To change their form and keep them dear.

Carrigan watched the first wasp of the spring circle in slow, lazy arcs, bouncing against the ceiling tiles. The wasp seemed assured that something of great value was hidden behind each tile, and then, frustrated by that section of spotted asbestos surface, he would ineffectively bounce against another one. Was he seeking a way out of the room or was he fulfilling some quest against the broad expanse of suspended ceiling? Ten feet away a cool breeze flowed into the doorway from the hall, half filled with the squirming young bodies of the uneducated, who wandered the corridors for endless hours. It would have been a very short flight for the wasp into the hallway. There, a much broader expanse of ceiling beckoned, along with a path to freedom through the orange double doors at the end of the hall. But alas, did the wasp not want larger fields of explorations, did he not want the freedom of the green grass and the sunshine, or did he simply not know the portal was there? Perhaps the decision was too much, routine and futility were easier, more comfortable, more known.

Carrigan's eyes shifted to the other features of the room, which he could describe in detail, even with his eyes closed. His eyes gazed about the room--there was a ceiling vent (which once upon a time had circulated cigarette smoke from the small room), round tables (strangely oaken, when all else in the room was chrome and plastic), the rows of ephemera and books (from which the daily lesson plans were derived). Routine echoed from every book and paper, pointlessness from every glazed eye of every student who failed to grasp spoken facts that never even remotely connected with their vision of future lives. Unlike the wasp, the kids knew where the doorway was, they could envision the sunshine and breezes that flowed outside, but even this difference seemed small because they uselessly bounced against the ceilings in their lives, never knowing or caring what lay beyond their understanding. Perhaps the students also felt some treasure was waiting for them if they continued to follow their routine of doing nothing for long periods of time. They consistently set very low goals for themselves and continually failed to achieve them.

Deferred gratification, the words kept emerging into his thoughts. Adolescent Psych, or perhaps Societal Trends, Carrigan couldn't remember where he first heard the term, sometime early in his college career. Deferred gratification was the ability to put aside immediate pleasure, and work toward a higher or future goal. The words illuminated in his consciousness, almost framed in Greek letters, which was fitting because it was 'Greek' to his students.

They deferred nothing. Shared everything. Except learning. Inhalants, purchased always in the color of white (because white paint was cheaper) were sprayed into plastic sacks and passed around the group to huff. Cigarettes were puffed and passed until the stench of the burning filter made even the coolest of the group discard it on the littered sidewalk.

At night, hurried sex amid the evergreens of the campus, or quickly completed on the outside benches was a shared behavior among the sad-eyed children. Immediately after completion, the girls were sure they were engaged and could begin to feel the love they never received at home, while the boys only wanted to disengage, to find their friends and hint at the details of their coupling. Carrigan watched the aftermath of this routine daily in his classroom and desperately wanted to tell the girls they reminded him of the cigarette butts which lay discarded upon the sidewalk, having provided only a momentary fix for an insolvable problem. Perhaps the huffed paint destroyed their capacity to see the prospect of escape from their small little rooms. Or just maybe the nightly release of bodily fluids drained their desire to fly through those double orange doors and into the worlds of learning.

It was April, Carrigan reflected, usually a good month. Shakespeare was born in April, wars in foreign jungles ended in April, and baby calves were born in April. Few things in life were more worth watching than the wobbly progress of a newborn calf making a triumphant appearance into his world. First, the back legs straightened, and the rump arose only to fall, tangled in its mother's afterbirth. Undaunted, the rump arose again, then one foreleg. From this triangular position the world was surveyed. Unlimited possibilities were all that was foreseen. Suddenly noticed, the other front leg gained movement and the baby calf arose to the soft moos of its mother. The calf could feel its mother's rough tongue bringing warmth to all parts of his body, and the calf felt the natural desire to seek nourishment from the swollen teats beneath the mother's belly. Carrigan sadly conceded that perhaps the best part of his day was the drive into the school past the meadows where these newborns raced like the wind, only to swerve and buck and jump, enjoying the vitality of their bodies. Maybe their play was just to cause consternation in the herd and push the buttons of annoyance within their mothers, which all young animals love to do.

Carrigan began to realize that like the wasp's journey across the white ceiling, he too was beginning another phase of his journey; one that had began forty-something years ago. He reckoned he also foresaw a world of unlimited possibilities, but from these possibilities, the years narrowed the choices, mutually excluding things left undone, which would now never be accomplished. He would never be rich. The teaching field, years in the future, would probably provide a very lucrative income. Young college graduates these days were avoiding teaching professions like the plague, and who could blame them. Signing bonuses, complete benefits and starting salaries at close to six figures in the IT field totally decimated the ranks of young teachers. Almost the entire teaching staff here at Lakota High School was his age or older, marking their time day by day, until years of service and age equaled the golden number-85--and the sweet release of retirement beckoned them away from the routine of the school.

The careers of this cadre of teachers began in promise twenty-five years ago. Wyoming salaries were attractive then, and so were the recreational opportunities. Spouses were garnered and through the years homes purchased, children raised, and the two salary incomes provided for the responsibilities of these baby boom educators. Over the year cars were paid for, as were the houses, and summers and weekends on the streams and hunting in the mountains provided benefits to their lives. On these terms, the teaching salary was enough. What it wasn't enough for today was a young family that was just starting out and had to pay for transportation, housing, food, and daycare, along with a few luxuries like utilities and insurance. Carrigan chuckled when he envisioned a day ten years in the future when twenty-five of thirty certified teachers suddenly retired. Perhaps then the administrators, school boards, and community would realize they were getting a good bang for their buck. The mere thought of a first year teacher, if one could be found, trying to engage his students in learning chased away the vapors of dark thoughts Carrigan allowed to creep into his head. He even envisioned a first day conversation between "New Teacher", as he quickly named him, and one of his veteran students going something like this.

"Now class, please complete the three basic math problems on the sheet before you and we will go over them when you are done," New Teacher said.

"Why?" replied the Veteran Student.

New Teacher countering, "Well, it is important that the first graded assignment of the year be a good one, so work carefully."

The Veteran Student's lips gave the briefest twist of a smile anticipating the coming exchange. He carefully began the game.

"Well, I don't care much about grades; my dad says I don't need to know this math stuff."

"Think about your future, you will need a good education to get a job in this world," replied the teacher.

"I already got a job digging fence posts this summer, I don't need to solve equations to dig fence posts, and it pays good too," answered the veteran student. "Anybody that does this worksheet is a complete fucking idiot."

"I did the worksheets like this and now I have an education, and a better job than digging holes," answered the New Teacher, "and I achieved this by doing my schoolwork, and please don't use profanity in the classroom."

"There you go," said the student, "you got your answer."

"Are you deliberately defying me, young man?" New Teacher said.

Veteran Student appeared to consider this question and then coughed deeply, bringing up a large ball of phlegm from his throat; he rolled it around in his mouth for a moment, enjoying the spotlight, and then spit the glob onto the floor at New Teacher's feet.

"Nope, you called yourself the fucking idiot, I didn't have anything to do with it," he said.

The ball of phlegm commingled with the carpet fibers and seemed to settle slightly. New Teacher stared at it in horrified fascination. He appeared mesmerized by the light reflecting off the glistening glob and the way the particles of tobacco enclosed in the globule seemed suspended, weightless in the gelatinous mucous.

With howls of laughter from the other students, New Teacher, now screaming despite his college training in classroom discipline which carefully taught him not to, continually repeats, **"OUT, OUT, GET OUT, GET OUT OF MY ROOM."**

"I kinda like it in here; maybe you should be the one to get out, Teach."

As New Teacher flees the room in search of some authoritative figure that will listen to him, Veteran Student lights up the last Camel cigarette from his pack and passes it to the other students to take a hit. The sharp bite of the tobacco stings his throat this early in the morning but helps to deepen his sense of power and pleasure from establishing his command of the room. After the principals sort out the problems they are having from the other twenty-five classrooms, he will jokingly apologize for coughing in the classroom, using great detail to tell how sick he had become, and sincerely explain to the principal that the teacher refused to help him with his math. All thirty-two other students in the class will solemnly acknowledge this to be the sole and absolute truth. The principal will then note in a file that New Teacher needs work in classroom management.

The end of class bell pushes the fantasy from Carrigan's head, and the students bolt from the prisons of plastic, so startling the wasp he injures his wing by banging it too hard against the ceiling. This collision causes the wasp to bounce in circles in the far corner of the room, instead of inspecting the ceiling as he had been doing. My wings have been clipped a little bit too, murmured Carrigan, as he followed the students into the hallway.

Second period planning. Carrigan was usually glad when his second period was planning. First period and his black thoughts weighted his limbs with weariness this morning. He needed a chance to stretch, gaze longingly at the rays of sunlight streaming from the outside, and refill his coffee cup for the third time this morning. The teacher's lounge was halfway down the hall, and he whistled as he dodged the flying bodies running the length to its door. He tried unsuccessfully to avoid listening to the shrill shrieking of the freshman girls, as their current flavor of the week pulled their hair, slapped their rounding cheeks, or in some other inappropriate way gave the young girls the attention they so desperately needed. How many, he wondered, would join the stale, used butts lying on the sidewalk outside the door?

Entering through the lounge door, he was blindsided by the volume of sound emanating from the room. It cascaded around him higher in decibel than the shrillness in the hall, momentarily stunning him and causing him to pause. Mentally plugging his ears and refocusing he saw Jenny Albright, the music teacher, vibrating like the tardy bell that was now going off. Jenny was one of those types of women who hit age fifty and stayed there. She had gained no weight, nor lost any in the last twenty years, and thanks to Clairol, her hair had not changed color; neither had her clothing. Mousy always came to mind when Carrigan looked at her. The nondescript gray dress, a gay color for her, swirled and leapt around her body as she screamed and shook her finger at Chuck Attenby, the physical education teacher. Carrigan didn't believe he had ever seen a redder face than Jenny's. Sprays of saliva punctuated every finger shaking she aimed in Attenby's direction.

"Goddamn you to hell, you fat bastard," screamed Jenny. "You sorry ass excuse for a teacher. For twenty years you have done nothing but try to embarrass and humiliate me, and this time you've gone too far. This time I'm going to kick your butt clear out of school, and you're going to have to find some other game to play."

Damn, thought Carrigan, there hasn't been a morning this interesting for a long time. Resisting an urge for self-survival, Carrigan took his eyes off Jenny to cast a quick glance toward the object of her verbal assault. Chuck sat wide-eyed on a tabletop trying to consider his options. The screaming from Jenny made it extremely hard for Chuck to concentrate; hell, most things made it hard for Chuck to concentrate. Chuck was most at home telling war stories from a bar stool, with his audience surrounding him. Chuck tolerated the school day, the students, and the principal's semi-annual attempts to try and get him to write and perform standards by which to teach his physical education classes. For twenty years, his students ran ten laps in the gym, cheated their way through twenty pushups, and then participated in whatever activity required the least amount of his supervision. Chuck's somewhat corpulent figure expanded over the recent years, but Carrigan knew the vast reservoir of powerful muscle that overlaid Chuck's frame. Even at fifty-two, Chuck could easily bench-press three hundred fifty pounds numerous times and move with deceptive quickness for his size. Carrigan could vouch for that after Chuck snatched him off a stool and threw him over the bar past a very startled barmaid one time several years ago. Carrigan never was quite sure what he said to piss the big man off so badly that evening, but now he always sat several stools away when they were drinking together. Distance and head starts were never bad things.

Chuck was diligently trying to bite the inside of cheeks to keep from laughing as Jenny's tirade continued unabated.

"You're filthy, you stink, you ruined my purse, I could have been poisoned, my makeup case is ruined and you just sit there like the smart ass you are," Jenny ranted.

Chuck bit harder on his cheeks and considered his chances of making it past Jenny into the hallway outside. About that time he noticed Carrigan standing in the doorway and realized that Jenny would probably get in two or three good licks before he could get past both her and Carrigan. Maybe the window, he thought; no, that wasn't any good. What if he got stuck and gave Jenny unlimited access to whatever part of his posterior was still hanging inside. Chuck gave up and resigned himself to take the abuse. He shoved his huge hands deeper under his armpits, ducked his head, and reflected on last Friday's turn of events that landed him in this situation.

Friday there had been a staff luncheon for the teachers during the noon hour. The principal must have tapped some previously unfound fund and parted with money enough to buy five roasted chickens, along with potato salad, pork and beans, and chips. A dollar tip to Shawn, a junior who looked like a weasel, or maybe he was a weasel masquerading as a junior, and the student council pop machine was jimmied open so the teachers could wash down the feast with cans of caffeine free Pepsi. Most of the staff finished their meals and returned to the classrooms leaving only Chuck and Jenny sitting at a table. All in all, the free lunch lifted the staff's spirits enough to allow them to finish the afternoon with some semblance of decorum and effort. After making sure there were no more edible portions left on the last chicken carcass, Chuck being overcome with a feeling of adventure, stuffed the chicken carcass inside the large purse that Jenny carried with her at all times for twenty years.

This was a purse lover's purse. Made entirely of leather, it had one time been richly hand tooled with a little saddle on top, with deep swirls of leatherworking, and dark lacing. The purse would probably hold more than a fifty-pound potato sack, which was the reason that Jenny's left shoulder always drooped four inches below her right one. No one knew why she carried the strap of the purse always on her left shoulder. Jenny too must have been feeling good about the dinner because she left her purse laying on the floor next to her table as she escorted her plastic plate back to the container of pork and beans for an uncharacteristic second helping. Chuck couldn't help himself; in went the chicken, pushed snugly all the way to the bottom. All good things come at a price, and now Chuck was paying it, a small one indeed when measured against the amount of mileage Chuck could gain be retelling the events. Weakened and exhausted by her outburst, Jenny finally stopped talking although her jaw continued to move; the bright red color slowly drained from her face, and with a glare, she squared her shoulders, well, at least she attempted, and marched past Carrigan into the hallway.

"Jesus, she was pissed," said Chuck.

"My God, Chuck," said Carrigan, "what on earth did you do to wind her up this time?"

By this time Chuck completely lost control and tears of laughter were streaming down his face.

"Jenny never found the chicken I put in her purse last Friday after lunch until she was in the grocery store this morning buying bagels for her class," Chuck finally explained after catching his breath. "She went to pay for the bagels and out came the greasy chicken bones. God, would I have loved to be at that checkout stand this morning. I can't stand it, I'm turning my kids loose and going over to find out who was clerking this morning. Can you imagine the look on the clerk's face when Jenny tried to pay for bagels with a chicken carcass?"

Carrigan immediately felt sorry for Jenny as he imagined the humiliation she must have experienced in the store. The story would soon spread to the local coffee shops and the beauty salons. Nothing worth telling, and much that was, circulated Rockville's population of five thousand in an amazingly short period of time. The kids would be merciless for the next several weeks. Maybe Chuck went too far this time, but it was funny. Carrigan immediately began to imagine Jenny trying to clean the inside of her purse of the carrion-like chicken grease. Looking on the bright side, perhaps she found items that were missing for many years. He sincerely hoped that if Jenny did continue to again pack the saddlebag around, he wouldn't start laughing when he saw her.

By this time Chuck was struck with another paroxysm of laughter, and in this condition was not suitable company to bullshit with, so Carrigan left the lounge to return to his classroom, caffeine fix in hand, and finish his notes for his reading class after lunch. Sitting at his desk he remembered the wasp, but a close inspection of the ceiling tiles revealed nothing. Perhaps the injured wing regenerated and the wasp availed itself of the opportunity to flee the room into the spring sunshine beckoning outside. If only Carrigan could do the same.

As he tried to decide the grading scale for the rubric on the short story his students wrote, Carrigan sipped his coffee and licked the last remaining bits of chocolate off his fingers from a week old Chocodile he found lying in his desk drawer. He never had been a picky eater, other than fast food, and outside of the crème filling being slightly sour tasting, and the cake covering being chewy, the Chocodile really hit the spot.

The story his classes read was "The Lady or the Tiger", which dealt with a young man choosing a door in a gladiator-style arena. If the young man chose wisely, a beautiful maiden would emerge from the door, and he would be married in a grand festivity. If he chose wrong, a vicious tiger would emerge and watching his grisly death would thrill the crowd. The complicating factor was his illicit love affair with the Emperor's daughter, which brought about this situation in the first place. They loved each other with a deep and ferocious love. Just before choosing a door the young man stole a quick glance at his former lover in the coliseum, and she pointed toward a door. Did she want him to choose that door which would enable him to marry some other virginal maiden; or did she wish him dead since she couldn't have him? The other problem dealt with the fact that he did not know if her indication meant the door was dangerous or safe.

Carrigan always had students write an ending to this classic fable. This ending helped him determine how they felt about their own lives. Most of the boys assumed that the maiden would want her lover safe and with another woman, while the girls usually ended the story by providing the tiger with lunch. Both sexes were always astonished by the endings when read in class.

On a deeper level, Carrigan believed that students usually wrote the endings based somewhat on their belief in fate. Did they believe that life happened to them; or did they believe that life was what each made it? Unfortunately, most of his students in this basic reading class felt they had no power in their lives, and what would be, would be. The previous day the students read the story and wrote their endings; today he would have them grade their writing based on the rubric he was just finishing.

One student in particular wrote a story ending that brought satisfaction to his soul. Sherri Jones was an eighteen-year-old sophomore who Carrigan had been working with all year. She took several years off from high school to pursue her career of immediate satisfaction and probably single-handedly raised the stock price in several tobacco and condom companies. Her caustic wit and portrayed toughness, drove away most of the classmates her own age. Sheri's source of living previously came from older construction workers in town with whom she slept and from whom she stole. Up until her eighteenth birthday, she dared her one-night stands to report her to the police on theft charges. She quickly pointed out to them, how could they report they were having sex with a underage girl when the money was stolen? At eighteen and considered an adult, she was deprived of this source of income.

Sherri was of medium height and wolf thin with warrior breasts, high and proud. Her favorite attire was a tank top that covered these breasts

9

only if she stood very still. As she was in constant motion, she drove the boys in the room to distraction by showing the top half when she was leaning over or the bottom half when she was leaning back. Her lean muscled stomach and slim hips barely supported the denim jeans that Carrigan was sure were her only pair. Carrigan finally gave up trying to change the attire and kept a tee shirt in the room for her to wear so his male students could concentrate. After a full month of constant argument in which Sherri would state she didn't need the shirt because the boys shouldn't be looking at what they couldn't have, Sherri would finally walk in, put on the tee shirt, and sit down.

Her story ending provided Carrigan with the hope that perhaps after seven months of mouthing platitudes about taking charge of your own life and not making bad choices, she saw that she could achieve almost anything in life she wanted. She became a voracious reader, and Carrigan kept shoving material at her. Classics, magazines, and biographies of successful women made up a large part of his reading list for her. They even worked out a plan for her to take a GED test this spring and follow with junior college in the fall. Due to her now limited income and her high scores on the ACT test, a Pell Grant was assured, and doors were opening in her world. Her ending to the story stated that the young man shouldn't open either door, but instead he should fight his way out of the Coliseum, snatch the princess from the stands and escape into the countryside. Here they could start a family and flee from the fate in which they were currently placed. Although not technically within the bounds of the assignment, Carrigan was changing the rubric by increasing the points for creativity thereby allowing her to receive a high grade on the paper and reinforce his months of work.

The schedule of classes in Lakota High School was composed of four class periods a day. Each teacher taught three periods and supposedly used the free period for planning lessons. Some days Carrigan tolerated the small classroom better than others. Days offering the promise of spring sunshine and warm temperatures were tougher on him than those in which the cold winter winds sifted snow through even the smallest cracks of the brick exterior. If only there was a window to allow him to see what he was missing. Instead, he owned four off-white walls and a doorway. The advantage lay in being able to close the door when he was teaching, effectively eliminating distractions from the outside world. His students needed very little excuse to daydream, and with a window, nothing would be accomplished during the class period. Carrigan made up for this claustrophobia by frequent trips to the hallway to gaze longingly down the long corridor and through the mesh paned windows toward freedom.

He finished altering the rubric, and anticipated the wry smile that Sherri would give him when she graded her assignment based on his new criteria. Very few things escaped her. The last few minutes of his planning period were occupied by removing several layers of paperwork from his desk. These layers were usually transposed onto other layers somewhere else in the room, but today Carrigan took a little extra time and actually filed some of them in the general area of their right location. Several hundred thin trees actually found their way into the trashcan. Janitors hated it when they had to empty the trash cans, but tonight Carrigan observed they would earn their money, not that they didn't every day.

The work of janitor was a daily round of sameness--vacuuming the same floors, emptying the same trash cans, continually cleaning up after kids who gave no thought to spitting chewing tobacco in the urinals, spilling pop, candy, and their lunches on every available square inch of floor in the school. The students were always ready with a cutting insult or remark if the janitors ever chastised them. These remarks usually included something about loser, and screw you; you're not my parent. Occasionally, the limit would be reached and something of value to the student would disappear out of their lockers such as alcohol or marijuana, or maybe their new Columbia coat would be used to clean a toilet.

Carrigan's favorite example of innate cunning was when the school board hired a behavior expert last year to provide recommendations on how to keep the girls' restrooms clean. The girls loved to buy outlandish shades of lipstick and then kiss the mirrors leaving "lip prints" behind. This soon expanded to the white walls of the bathroom. Every night the janitors were expected to clean the mirrors. The behavior expert, who received in one day the monthly wage of a janitor, explained that the girls were just finding their quality world, establishing boundaries. Addressing their inner needs through student council programs could solve the problems. This was implemented by the school board, passed to the administrators, and imposed upon the teachers to sponsor these needs-fulfilling programs. The expected outcome was not achieved, the problem worsened, and girls began writing the names of the boys they conquered next to their daily lip prints.

Finally having her fill, Sally Redding, the head janitor with twenty years of bathroom cleaning experience persuaded the principal to let her work just one day shift. At the end of first period, she entered the girl's bathroom as the young nubiles were marking their favorite territory. She smiled nicely exposing her missing front teeth, dipped her slimiest mop into the un-flushed toilet and began washing the mirrors above the sink

11

with the mop. Twenty freshman girls fled the bathroom gagging as they went. Needless to say the problem never reappeared, and Sally claimed it was the only day shift she ever worked.

Second period ended allowing Carrigan the chance to escape the room. Hunger crawled slowly in his stomach. The stale Chocodile just wasn't enough. He usually avoided the student-served lunches, but today he decided to try it. Walking briskly he entered the lunchroom and saw that special education students were behind the lunch counter.

"Hi, Mr. Carrigan," shouted Tina Marsh. "Does you want some soup today? "

Carrigan replied with his usual answer. "You mean, 'Do I want some soup today?'"

"That's what I sez," Tina replied.

He could see that this conversation was going nowhere in a hurry so he smiled nicely and nodded. Finally, the department of health harassed the special education teacher so much that the serving students were actually wearing plastic gloves with which to handle the food. The problem was that Tina dipped Carrigan's bowl into the soup pot up to her wrist to fill the bowl. Next week the students were going to work on using utensils. Cream of potato today, Carrigan observed, as white rivulets ran down Tina's limb seeking the expanse of curly hair under her arm. She smiled as she took his money with the same soupy hand, imprinting milk mustaches on the two George Washingtons. She shoved the money in the box, and hurried back quickly to serve Trisha Collingworth, the new English teacher. Trisha must have suddenly remembered an appointment because she scuttled out of line scattering English papers from her portfolio behind her as she headed for the door. Undaunted, Tina used the same plastic gloved hand to help Carrigan pick them up, and she chased after Ms. Collingworth waving papers, cream of potato soup, plastic glove and all.

"I guess Ms. Collingworth wasn't hungry today," said Carrigan to the special education teacher.

Heading for the staff table in the lunchroom, Carrigan noticed that both Chuck and Jenny were already seated there. Both were gazing steadfastly down at their brown bag lunches. Carrigan imagined that they were seated the maximum possible distance away from each other, which were polar opposites at the round table. He almost felt the torment of their decision making process when they took their seats. They could have crowded in with kids at the student tables foregoing the pleasure of each other's company or take positions at the staff table. Hatred aside, it was better to face the devil you knew than swim in the deep blue sea you didn't. Carrigan sat with Chuck and Jenny at the staff table. He provided most of the conversation as Jenny was still fuming over the chicken incident. Thankfully, Chuck never said a word and lunch passed without the fight resuming. Carrigan glanced quickly about, but no sign of the leather purse could be seen, and Jenny's shoulder already seemed to be a little straighter.

After lunch, Carrigan watched the students file into his classroom nodding his head with the obligatory nods and hellos to each student. Carrigan always addressed them by mister or miss and expected the same courtesy from them. Thirty students filed past him, but none had Sherri's swagger. He waited a few minutes before taking roll. Only three gone today, two of whom he had only saw twice this whole year and Sherri. Feeling a sense of foreboding, Carrigan used his ritual salutation.

"Good afternoon, students."

"How's it hanging, Mr. Carrigan?" came the reply.

"Today we, or I should say you, will grade your writing assignments," Carrigan said.

"Aw hell," came a response from the first row, "why don't you just give us all A's and be done with it? Hey, where's Sherri? We got nothing to look at today."

The student was quickly answered by calls of perv, or sicko from the girls of the room, who were really quite glad Sherri wasn't here. Dawn Mason, an extremely fat girl in the back of the class raised her hand.

"Yes Dawn?" Carrigan said.

"Didn't you hear, Mr. C.? Sherri left town."

"No, I didn't hear," Carrigan replied.

"Ya, she rolled some fat cat welder from the rail yard last night. My mom works at dispatch, and the cops say she kicked shit out of this guy and took his whole paycheck and his car. They tried to catch her at her parent's house, but when the cops got there, she was long gone."

"Dawn, haven't we talked about passing on rumors before, and how people can get hurt when rumors are spread?"

"Ain't no rumor, Mr. C., and besides, the only one that got hurt was that stiff dick welder!"

"Enough Dawn, let's mind our own business, and get to work grading your papers."

Most of the papers were written with the endings Carrigan predicted, with the boys lamenting that they couldn't believe what a bad bunch of bitches the girls were, and how they were never going to trust a girl again. The poor guy in the story trusted a woman once and look what happened, a tiger ate him. Nope they weren't going to trust women any more, not at

13

least until after school. No one scored well in the creative category of the rubric. The standard answer was, when it's your time to go, it's your time to go. Carrigan couldn't but help feel a sense of loss and could only hope that Sherri stole enough money from her last score to run a long ways away from Wyoming. She would probably be okay, as she possessed a natural survivor's instinct, but she could have been so much more. Maybe it was true; maybe, just maybe, fate does play a role.

Third period turned into fourth and the endless game of kids trying to do nothing, and teachers trying to stay sane played out, just as with the hunter and the prey. Carrigan never quite knew which he was. The fourth period bell elicited the usual frenzied rush for the door and slowly the dust settled, the hallway grew quieter and still Carrigan couldn't push the thoughts of Sherri's crime from his mind. He had no doubt that it was true; student rumors always contained a foundation in truth. He lifted his eyes to the teaching diploma on the wall. The paper in the cheap frame proclaimed that James T. Carrigan was certified to teach in the State of Wyoming; beyond that the gold stickers announced endorsements in social studies, math, reading, and coaching. Jack-of-all-trades and master of none, his father's words came flooding back to him.

He could remember that conversation with his father as if it were yesterday. Twenty-five years ago Carrigan graduated from college and entered the police academy. He was certain law enforcement was his calling. His father told him law enforcement was not suited for college graduates and he should attend law school if that was his area of interest. Law was interesting, but seventeen years of school, and the completion of his master's degree left Carrigan with an extreme distaste for more of the hallowed halls of higher learning. Upon completion of the police academy, he was hired by a city south of Rockville, and his journey of trying to understand human behavior began.

Five years and one shift later, all of which occurred between the hours of eleven p.m. and nine a.m. left him feeling trapped, stymied, so law enforcement was left behind. After these 1,041 midnight shifts Carrigan decided to follow a different path on his journey.

During the half-decade run of darkness, the city that employed him was experiencing a phase of real growth caused by the building of a new power plant. A quiet population of 23,000 people suddenly swelled to twice that number in the course of a year. Housing for the workforce was nonexistent, bars were filled to overflowing nightly, and the usual recreational vocations of single, working men flowed within the city after the sun went down.

Whores, pimps, and purveyors of drugs of all color, types, and varieties followed them, mingling nightly in the bars and trailer camps that choked the edges of town. Shifts changed at the plant every twelve hours, and just at the stroke of midnight the camps and bars would empty only to be replaced by the second wave. Even the whores and dealers operated on this schedule. Twelve on and twelve off. At fifty dollars a pop, two pops an hour, most of the attractive working girls could turn a thousand dollars a night. Lines of coke became a substitute for currency and dealers traded ounces for paychecks. Vehicles were purchased using the white release and more banging headboards were paid for with drugs than money. The girls didn't have to wait for the stores to open to spend their revenue.

The time of night that Carrigan hated the most was three in the morning. Some of the workmen either accrued women while in town or brought wives and families with them. The usual arrangement was for the family, consisting of a young woman with a child from a previous entanglement, a natural child by the man she was living with, and of course, her means of support--the plant worker. The worker arrived in the bars at midnight, drank, used, or fucked furiously for three hours, and then weaved his serpentine way home to the little woman waiting in the castle. And a magnificent castle it was! The trailer seldom was larger than ten feet wide by twenty-four feet long. Mamma had been cooped up in the mansion since her man went to work fifteen hours earlier. She was smart enough to count hours, and he should have been home three hours ago, but of course, he wasn't. Upon his entering the door, the verbal altercation would start and escalate into punches and blood shortly thereafter. Carrigan and his other patrol units answered fifty of these calls a night for 1,041 nights.

Police units would arrive, then began the task of trying to sort the address out among the thousands of travel trailers. Each officer would try to separate the fighting parties, usually making an adult hold a crying child as they talked to the police. Carrigan firmly believed it was harder for the drunken worker to hit him if the man was holding a screaming infant. Here, routine was your friend. If ambulances were needed, as often were, someone was going to jail for the night, and social services would be called to care for the children.

Most of the time a severe threatening was all the impetuous needed to reunite mamma and papa, and the police could clear the scene. Carrigan gingerly felt the lump of scar tissue behind his right ear remembering the time his vigilance momentarily waned. He arrived on the scene of a domestic disturbance only to find a very large man punching a very small, very naked woman in the face. He and his partner immediately realized they needed backup, and having secured this, they attempted to handle the disturbance and rescue the semi-conscious woman. By this point in his career, three years, Carrigan entertained a healthy distrust for rookie police officers, and tonight he was training one. Jose Flores. Jose was five feet, two and one-third inches tall. If you didn't believe it, just ask him. The John Wayne syndrome ran deep in Jose's Mexican blood; and he always carried sap gloves, police baton, pepper spray, and of course, sunglasses.

Jose's greatest wish was to always work day shift so he could wear his sunglasses--deep dark reflecting ones, which covered the quick beady eyes.

"Pleeze Sergeant, I can learn training so much more wheen the sun shines," he would announce to the scheduling officer.

Carrigan wondered what he did to deserve such a fate to train this young federalé.

Jose grunted as he struck the man across the back full force with his police baton. The desired effect was not achieved, and Lurch turned his head slowly to look at the banty policeman. Carrigan knew they were in deep shit and sinking fast. Within three strides, he was at full speed. When he hit Lurch with the point of his shoulder, not even Lurch could maintain his perch atop the woman. Wrapping his forearm across the man's throat, Carrigan locked his hands and pulled for all that he was worth. Jose, sensing victory, now clung to Lurch's leg like a Chihuahua in heat. Slowly, Carrigan could feel the man's immense strength departing and Lurch's body began to convulse for lack of oxygen. As Lurch passed out, his bladder and bowels released covering the 'Chihuahua' still attached to his leg.

"Fucking gringo, fucking son-of-a-beetch," screamed Jose.

Carrigan began to suspect he had more problems now, other than 300 pounds of plant worker jerking like a rodeo bull. Now that he choked out Lurch, he would probably have to provide CPR to get him breathing. He was trying to decide whether to start CPR first or cuff Lurch. He finally decided to cuff him; the probability of live brain cells was minimal due to the lack of oxygen and the abundance of alcohol.

"No gringo sheets on me," said Jose having released the feces covered leg.

Jose's pepper spray can exploded into Carrigan's face. Lurch's head suddenly drooped as Jose squeezed off the canister, and Carrigan caught the full blast, instantly blinding both of Carrigan's eyes. He quickly rolled off of Lurch and staggered to his feet. He could hear the sounds of his backup sirens screaming as they pulled to the scene. Finally, his vision cleared enough for him to see Jose dancing around the prone form of

Lurch kicking him in the ribs, screaming in Spanish something about broken sunglasses.

Two other officers used flexible plastic strips to cuff Lurch, as ordinary handcuffs wouldn't start to go around his post-like wrists. Fortunately, enough of the pepper spray had gotten in Lurch's throat bringing him, coughing and puking, back to consciousness. Carrigan then tried to focus on the now standing form of the naked woman. He began to wish his vision hadn't come back so soon. She was covered in blood, Lurch's evacuations, grass, dirt and other assorted particulates. Carrigan deferentially averted his gaze and turned toward the car to find a bottle of water to wash out his eyes. He took one step when his ear exploded in pain, bright lights within his head flashed, and he slumped to the ground. Amid the shouts from the other officers, he remembered hearing the woman screaming.

"No fucking pig hurts my man and gets away with it."

The other officers, all except Jose who was on extended suspension, greeted Carrigan warmly upon his release from the hospital. They gave him, as a present, the small garden troll, thrown by a very small, very naked, very dirty, and very angry woman. The troll was gaily painted in blues and reds and appeared to have slim lips, which curled into a slight smirk. Carrigan still kept the troll on the mantle of his fireplace. The troll never gave any indication whether he liked or disliked his new home better that the hardscrabble rock garden from which he was plucked and hurled because of a woman's anger. Carrigan's head still hurt sometimes. Maybe the male students were right; you never could trust a woman.

Jack of all, and master of none. His father hit the nail on the head. During his careers Carrigan had been a police officer, social worker, ranch hand, carpenter, and now a teacher. None of these occupations provided him with all of the answers for which he searched. The task would have been made considerably easier if he even knew what it was that he was looking for. There was no possibility of retracing his steps down those dusty roads now, even if he wanted to. He enjoyed teaching for the present, and perhaps somewhere in those sad eyes of his students he would find what he was missing in his life.

Remembering suddenly the school board meeting tonight, he quickly checked the time. The clock informed him, that with haste, he could grab a bite to eat prior to the meeting. Long since having sworn off any form of fast food, Carrigan mentally listed his options as he strode from the school building toward the familiarity of his 1979 Ford pickup truck. Someday he should repaint the old gal. Internally, the transmission, chassis, and engine were immaculate. She had been a consistent traveling partner with Carrigan for the last twenty-two years, and he continued to maintain and drive her daily to and from the school. Something about her style and durability linked Carrigan to her, and the mere thought of the newer vehicles, with their false toughness, caused him to refuse all offers for her sale. Seated high in the cab, he gunned her engine to life, then idled back to allow the lifters a chance to lubricate before shifting her smoothly out of the parking lot and down the avenue toward dinner.

Carrigan's dislike of fast food dealt more with the sameness of the establishments than with their quality. All of the franchises reminded him of his classroom as they gleamed in their plastic and chrome. No, Carrigan's dinner of choice was the h'orderves served nightly at Ben's Bar and Burgers. Here, for the price of a beer, a man could feast on tacos, hot chicken wings, burritos, buffalo burgers and sometimes mushrooms. Well, never mushrooms. He distrusted mushrooms as he distrusted himself, always comparing them to his role in life. He often stated that the school district kept him in the dark and fed him bullshit just like a mushroom. Anything that grew and fed from the bowels of others shouldn't be served with beer. After numerous rounds being served, Carrigan invariable announced to the bar the reasons he never ate mushrooms.

Cocking his head and affecting his best Irish brogue he would state,
Ah, Mary with hair of red, me first wife died from eating mushrooms.
Katie with the lilting bosoms and second to share with me the wedded bliss,
also died from eating mushrooms and a fine lass she was, too.
And my third wife, Shaleen, with eyes of green, died,
bless her Irish soul, because she wouldn't eat the mushrooms.

Tonight, fortunately, the bar food was tiny egg rolls served with hot mustard. Several platefuls later and with one large mug of Fat Tire beer to quench the hot mustard, Carrigan felt revived enough to observe the bar and its customers. Chuck Attenby was seated on his throne in the rear of the bar engaging several bar patrons with his recent conquest of Jenny's purse. Carrigan was sure the story was growing by leaps and bounds with every telling. The patrons were roaring right along with Chuck as he described the store clerks reaction to the rotting chicken bones. Perhaps they enjoyed Chuck's company and conversation, or maybe they were hoping that he would buy the next round of drinks, so they paid close attention, laughing when he did.

Carrigan hoped it was the company they enjoyed, because getting Chuck to buy a round was a near impossibility. In earlier times, Chuck had a habit of carrying a very worn $100 bill around in his wallet. Invariably when it was his turn to buy Chuck would present the barmaid with the 'Ben Franklin' when the drinks arrived. She never had cash to change that large of bill on her drink tray. Someone else would ante up for the drinks, and Chuck would replace the bill in his wallet for his next evening of reveling. Tiring of this game early in their drinking career, Carrigan kept five twenties in reserve in the far recesses of his wallet. When the tattered hundred appeared, and the bar maid again explained she couldn't break the bill, Carrigan, with a flourish, produced the five twenties, slapped them in Chuck's hand, and quickly pocketed the hundred.

Chuck obligingly bought the round of drinks after a long slow look at Carrigan. Chuck's eyes washed to a lighter shade of gray when Carrigan made the exchange and Carrigan always believed this was one of the primary factors in Chuck shot putting him over the bar several months later.

Deciding not to join the storytelling in the rear, Carrigan retreated from his barstool and left Ben's headed for the school board meeting. Fortified by the food and drink Carrigan stopped to enjoy the gathering dusk. Somewhere coming from the west, he could feel the spring breeze blowing off the snow pack in the mountains. The chilly breeze reminded him that the cold stillness of winter was not yet over and Wyoming could hold many surprises this time of year.

The thickly adorned walls quickly absorbed the murmuring of the small crowd already in the boardroom. The audience's chairs were arranged neatly in rows as if to ascribe order to the room and precision to the process, which was about to begin. Their slim plastic legs and unpadded surfaces did not attempt to mask their uncomfortable nature, almost as if proclaiming, "sit ye here, but tarry not long." At a cautious distance in front of the first row of these chairs sat a semicircular expanse of desk area spreading its influence from wall to wall with only a small opening in the middle to allow access. The chairs behind this were deeply upholstered, with padded arms, noiseless casters, and raised to make their occupant appear possessing in stature. These chairs were for the board members. The lighting in the room, directed toward the plastic chairs, vaguely resembled the spotlights in a police interview room. Reflections did not penetrate the desk area, leaving this end of the room almost in shadow.

Carrigan took his seat in the last row of the room. This served the double purposes of anonymity and ease of escape. At times, school board members floundered in answering questions from their constituency. It was at these times they used the glare of the spotlight to look for teachers in the audience who could bring about further light on the subject at hand. Carrigan hated to be called upon to save a bureaucrat from squirming. He answered, usually in "educationalese" and with the broadest use of generalities. This hopefully prevented the school board member from retaliating against him and gave the question asker an answer that required several days to decipher. The back row gave him some measure of security from being recognized by the podium. At other times, the meetings dragged on for hours over the smallest of details concerning the color of roofs for new school buildings or the availability of keys for teacher aides. Within two steps he could be out the door and into the protection of the night, only to nod sagely the next morning about what good input went into the board decisions the night before.

The major agenda for this evening's meeting dealt with the RIF policy as it was being implemented in this district. RIF was an educational acronym for reduction in force. When reduced enrollment, lack of funding, (and or) general dislike of a tenured teacher by administration reared its head in the district, the board always reviewed its policy to insure the least possible chance of litigation against its board members. The head had been raised in the form of Wesley James, the vocational science teacher. Vocational science was an elective class at Lakota High, which meant it was not required for graduation. Students signed up for the class after they completed the required two years of biology and needed filler material to flush out their class schedules to appease parents.

Mr. James had a history of not grading too toughly, allowing students a reasonable amount of roaming time, and requiring projects instead of lengthy papers. He taught four sections of this class and two sections of wildlife management. The problems arose during scheduling this year when edicts from on high were dictated by the state department of education, mandating that all high school students would be required to complete one year of chemistry. With a limited number of class offerings during any given day, students were forced to enroll in chemistry and desert the comfortable security of vocational science. This drove the number of students in three of Mr. James' classes below the working standard of ten students per class. When the number of students sank to below ten, the class was usually dropped, and the teacher was assigned to teach a different class.

Here came the rub; Mr. James was not certified to teach chemistry, and even the most ambitious attempts at summer classes would not make him so. His students in wildlife management could be distributed among the other teachers; science teachers with chemistry certifications could be assigned chemistry classes at a reduced rate during their planning periods. Presto, Mr. James could be reduced in force. The only ways a tenured teacher could be fired were by this mechanism, or gross evidence of misconduct, the dreaded Section 36 of Wyoming Education Law. Mr. James, although not of ministerial quality, certainly did not meet the misconduct standards, so RIF was the only available avenue for the school board to remove him. This $40,000 in salary saved, plus miscellaneous benefits, minus the bone thrown to the other science teachers, would replenish the dwindling school board travel fund. This fund diminished over the past several years due to the necessity of using it to buy schoolbooks. Parents finally convinced the board that twenty-five-year-old science books were beyond salvaging.

Recommendations from principals could have saved this RIF policy from happening, but Mr. James dared to question last year's scheduling process, and the cavalry charge by the administration was probably not forthcoming this year. All in all, Mr. James' situation met all three categories for the board to review the policy, remove the teacher, and begin the protection of their comfortably seated backsides.

The board chairman called the meeting to order, and the usual bill-paying, minute -reading agenda was followed. The only item of interest in the early going of the meeting for Carrigan was a tongue lashing by Big Reed Lansing. Mr. Lansing was the board's newest elected member. In an effort to appear informed, he actually read the list of bills submitted by the transportation department for payment by the board. When he came to the line items detailing the amount of work subcontracted to local garages for school bus repair, he felt here was a point on which to make the assembled voters proud of him. With a noticeable puffing up, like that of an adder, he addressed the head of transportation, Jimmy Sickle.

"Mr. Sickle, why haven't you arranged for any of your mechanics to take training in repairing diesel buses? This is the reason we, as a board, appointed you; to take these measures to insure the district can repair its own vehicles. If you can't handle the job, perhaps we as a board should find someone who can."

Carrigan immediately felt empathy for Jimmy because he was so sarcastically addressed during the meeting of the school board. As Carrigan raised his eyes to observe the effect of the serpent's strike on Jimmy, he was surprised by the broad smile on Jimmy's face as he answered the charges.

"Well, Big Reed," score one for Jimmy, thought Carrigan when he heard Jimmy's lack of the use of Mr., "the reason we don't send our mechanics to diesel school is that we don't have any diesel busses in the district."

The room exploded in laughter. Carrigan noted two immediate effects on Big Reed. He noticeable reddened and quickly deflated, almost wilting into the soft padding of the chair. Perhaps he wished his padded chair were not so elevated now.

"We can't work on the transmissions of the busses we have, because at the last board meeting you turned down our request for a new garage hoist to lift the big busses. That is why we take them to the local garages for repair," continued Jimmy.

This completed the destruction of the board's newest member; even with repeated gaveling by the board chairman, the room took several minutes to quiet down. Carrigan was somewhat surprised when, after the completion of new business, the chairman announced that this year they were going into executive session to discuss the board policy on RIF. This departed from the customary procedure and did not bode well for Mr. James. Executive session meant the board would discuss the matter in private, and their thoughts would not be available to the general public. Nor would the public assembled have even the slightest chance to speak on Mr. James' behalf. Carrigan had been debating with himself on what he would say when the issue came up. Although far from a close friend of Mr. James, the man had taught here twenty-one years, and in Carrigan's opinion, did at least an average job with some very tough students. The board's decision left Carrigan with a feeling of relief at not having to defend the man's job, but also brought about the disquieting effect of removing his last vestige of respect for this board's notion of duty and fairness.

Realizing the session might last anywhere from one to three hours, Carrigan yielded to the urge to leave. The unpadded chair increased Carrigan's weariness deep in his bones. Tomorrow he would think about writing a letter to the board supporting Mr. James, and maybe even leaking a copy of it to the local scandal rag of a newspaper. This might bring some pressure to bear on the board causing them to rethink any decisions they made during the executive session tonight.

With a few quick goodbyes to some of his seatmates, Carrigan slipped out of the door from his preplanned position and gained the relief of the early spring night. Just as he was about to unlock his pickup door, he remembered that he promised to write a letter of recommendation for a graduating senior girl in one of his classes. He always cautioned his students, when they requested a letter from him, that he was brutally honest in reference letters. He would then ask them if they were sure they wanted a letter. He was well known in the school for typing such statements in reference letters as, "This student, may with time, overcome her innate laziness."

The girl smiled and replied in the affirmative. She was sure of herself with good reason; Carrigan would provide her with a well-written reference. She continually did the required work in school and always pushed for a little more. She possessed looks, intelligence, and a ready smile that assured everyone she was capable of accomplishing anything she started. She possessed what Carrigan called "Curb Appeal." Her lifelong dream was to become an archeologist after graduating from college, and she wished to discover the mysteries of some ancient civilization through their fossilized records. Carrigan owned an amateur interest in archeology himself, so they held discourse on this subject numerous times during the last year. Her transcript she provided him, to help guide the letter, was still lying on his desk in the classroom building, and he would need to retrieve it tonight. This would provide an outline for his reference letter. With a sigh, Carrigan pulled back the key from the pickup's door and trudged the block to the now darkened classroom building, which housed his windowless cubicle. He was pleased with himself when in less than ten minutes, and five layers; he found the transcript on his desk.

How different, he thought, were the lives of the two young women he would be writing about tonight. First, there was the need to write a brief report of Sherri's standing in his class, and the story that he heard today from the other student about her robbery and flight to avoid arrest. This report would be given to the school counselor and filed away should a juvenile institution ever need this to continue her schooling in a more confined setting. He would then write a reference letter for a budding archeologist to help her gain admission in to some prestigious institution of higher learning. Did she choose this future for herself though her actions, or was even this positive outcome preordained?

Problems of depth were best not thought about on this night and Carrigan moved to turn the light out. As he reached for the switch, he heard a rapid buzzing sound followed by stillness. Peering suspiciously at the light switch, he reached slowly for it again, expecting a discharge of electricity. Confirming his suspicions of the light switch's malevolent intent, he again heard a buzzing sound when his finger touched the outlet plate. This time, however, he realized that the buzzing emanated from the floor near his feet. Blinking twice, he looked downward toward the stained brown stripes, which constituted the carpeting in his room. There, almost indistinguishable from the worn coloration, he saw a wasp lying on the carpet. As Carrigan watched, the wasp fluttered his wings again. This caused the now familiar buzzing sound. With the satisfaction of performing his last act, the wasp quit attempting to move his wings and lay still. The broken wing deteriorated into worse injuries when the wasp continued to batter against the ceiling. Broken and dealt a deathblow, the wasp had fallen to the floor, there to expend his last reserve of energy. Carrigan wondered if the wasp was satisfied with his short career of ceiling exploration. The wasp died never reaching the open portal to the sunshine and warm breezes; perhaps some of God's creatures were meant to fulfill only certain roles. Carrigan hoped the wasp wasn't sorry that he never achieved his full potential and made his way into the world. Death without remorse was bearable. With that, Carrigan turned off the light, locked the door, and walked slowly on the new path of his journey, toward his old Ford pickup and the road home.

Chapter 2
The Boy

Joshua Timenaux Coural bolted upright from his sleeping robes, his eyes probing the darkness around him. The same dream from previous nights returned to him, early in the hours of the spring morning. Joshua switched his gaze to the remaining embers of the campfire, built to reflect heat to the bottom of his robes. Red-hot ashes were still discernable in the darkened coals, red-hot cinders just like the eyes that pursued him in his dreams. It wasn't the eyes that disturbed Joshua's slumber, it was the teeth. Huge teeth that could penetrate a man's chest, severing him in half. This was the third time the dream had come, each vision more detailed than the last. Long, clawed feet, directed by red and glowing eyes reached out to spear and ensnare him. That was it, Joshua thought, no more sleeping tonight.

Joshua saw a drawing of an animal once, in a book back in Missouri, and he heard that creatures like them lived in the lowlands of Florida, but they didn't look at all like the varmint in his dreams. They didn't walk on two legs, they didn't have heads the size of buffalo, and they didn't pursue him in his dreams at night. What ever it was, he wished it would go away. Maybe, it wasn't a dream, but actually was out there in the night, waiting.

Beating the stiffness from his limbs Joshua climbed out from beneath his buffalo robes to feed the fire. He hoped there was enough sticks close at hand, because he sure wasn't going to hunt for them in the nearby forest. Not with his vision of those teeth. No Sirree! Joshua pushed the wood deeper into the flame and set his hide bowl on the rock circle around the fire. As long as the hide bowl retained water, it wouldn't burn, and the water inside would serve to mix some aspen tea, to warm his insides.

Suddenly remembering his horses, Joshua turned quickly, knocking the bowl into his just growing embers, causing the fire to hiss angrily at him.

"Gol darnit," he exclaimed.

The horses, standing hip shod, the heads bowed in slumber, did not respond to the exclamation. Joshua's eyes lingered on the big horse, his large head nodding, the small eyes closed, offering no indication of the loneliness that must lie within. Feeling particularly chagrined, Joshua crawled back under the cold robes, forced his eyes shut, and shifted his body to avoid the lump under his blanket, an irritation that had plagued him all during the night. If the ground weren't so frozen he would have taken his knife, dug out that lump and flung it into the darkness. Maybe he would hit one of those old red eyes, and teach that critter a thing or two about disturbing the slumber of an honest man.

Tomorrow, he thought, tomorrow I'm going to get rid of that lump for good. But for now he curled tighter in a ball and drifted restlessly back to sleep, jerking sharply when the red eyes in the darkness shifted in his direction. Finally relaxing, the varmints in the darkness of his dreams allowed Joshua to drift into a deeper sleep, sending him back to his home on gentler currents than those that brought him to this rocky, timbered hillside.

Joshua was born in Missouri in 1775, in a small, French-populated settlement of St. Genevieve. His father was a French lead miner lured from Illinois to the frontier outpost by rumors of exorbitant wages being paid to men with his skills.

The mining of Galena, or lead glance, was becoming a thriving business in this area. Large masses had been discovered underground and the mineral with metallic luster was mined to fuel the growing need for lead in the St. Louis area. Once processed, other substances such as copper, gold, and arsenic in small quantities could be extracted. These deposits also contained high concentrations of silver and the extraction of silver was the reason Joshua's father was hired. He learned the skill from craftsmen during his apprenticeship in Canada before coming to the territories.

St. Louis, a day's boat journey to the north, was a growing area but held little appeal for the older Coural. Joshua still could visualize the house built by his father. His boyhood in the house held such fond memories and sad sorrows, that he doubted he would ever return. The house of his parents was adjacent to his best friend's, Jacques Bolduc. Mr. Bolduc, Jacques' father, had been in St. Genevieve several years now and was instrumental in establishing the growing lead industry located southwest of the settlement. Bolduc also recently began selling lots within the town and opened a merchant store for the miners to purchase goods. The land that Joshua's father built upon was purchased from Bolduc.

The two boys were inseparable from an early age. Both sets of parents realized this fact and treated each of the boys as if they were brothers. Throughout the long summer days the boys played near the Mississippi River on the Le Grand Champ Field. Joshua's parents' house was built upon seasoned timber logs buried deep into the rich dark river soil. Perpendicular logs were then laid between these supports. Joshua could still remember the stockade fence between the houses. Hours were spent pretending they were Indians sneaking stealthily over the stockade, ambushing whoever lay within. Once inside the fence the boys would steal beneath the hip roof covering the expanse of the porch, and then rush, Indian-style, through the doorway into the open beam interior, screaming war cries as they went. Joshua's Creole mother would always smile, but never submit to their requests to scalp and torture her. She would gently chastise the boys in her soft natured Creole way and then return to cooking and attending the food on the river-rock chimney rising from the center of the house.

Tragedy struck the Coural household early in Joshua's ninth year. His father left for a week to instruct in the building of a new smelting furnace for lead, several miles inland from Le Grand Champ Field. Joshua begged to go, but citing the necessity of someone to watch over Mere Coural, his father insisted the boy stay home. In the early hours of a warm April morning, Joshua awoke to find water pouring through the lower sill of his bedroom window. The leaded, bubbled windowpanes exploded inward from the force of the rising water. The water was dirty and brown, thickened with vegetation. Falling twice, on the mud slickened board floors of his room; Joshua attempted to make the doorway into the main room of the house.

"Ma Mere, Ma Mere," he cried choking from the foul water filling his mouth as he again slipped into the ooze. "Attention, Deluge, l'eau nous ommene partons!"

Fighting his way into the grand room against the strong current of the water as it washed through his house, Joshua saw his mother clinging to the rock chimney of the central fireplace. Half swimming, half running, he splashed his way to her, the flagstones here providing better footing than in the bedroom. Finally reaching her, they clasped each other closely. The terrified look on his mother's face frightened Joshua worse than the cold water flowing around him. Joshua could feel his legs beginning to float from beneath him as the flood waters climbed higher on the gray, stone chimney. In all of his years he had never seen water even close to the front steps of his house, now all windows poured with the dirty brown torrent as it rushed into the house. The predominance of windows on the riverside allowed more water to enter the house than there was room for it to escape through the arched doorway on the far side. This had the effect of actually making the water level higher in the house than it was in the rapidly expanding river. As the river raced along, it sent high plumes of spray over the roof of the house where it met the corner posts driven deep into the earth. The rushing flood hitting the house sounded as if winter winds were driving through the logs and the roaring continued to escalate in volume. Clinging together, they were forced to climb higher on the chimney to keep from swirling away with the current. Fearing the house would soon be totally filled; his mother grasped Joshua by the hair forcing his cheek away from the rough stone of the chimney. She pointed toward the water pouring out of the door on the far side of the house and screamed at Joshua that they must go now.

"Nagons avec le courant, we must swim--*NOW*," she shouted into his ear.

"J'ai peur, Je ne peux pa…, I am afraid to go," he shouted back. He could see the river waves slapping angrily at the exposed beams of the ceiling. If they tried to swim they would be trapped against the ceiling by the force of the current and would be unable to swim downward to the door opening.

"Maintenant on y va, mon enfant," and she forced his hands away from their grip on the rough stones urging him to go.

Instantly the current raised and lifted them toward the roof. Joshua slammed against the rough beams of the ceiling, knocking the breath from his slender body. His mother clung tightly to her son, as she tried to grasp the rough undersides of the boards that composed the ceiling in the great room. The water had now risen enough that both of them were being buffeted against the roof, their feet were forced against the sides of the house where the ceiling joined the wall supports. Even this air space was rapidly diminishing.

"Plongons, Plong…," she screamed in his ear, the water cutting off the last of the word, "dive."

Drawing a deep breath he kicked his feet off the ceiling and plunged straight downward into the murky depths. The rushing force of the water angled his dive so that he scraped his face on the rough walls of the house and fighting desperately Joshua crawled back up the surface of the wall, clawing toward light and air. Scant inches of air space remained at the top of the ceiling and here Joshua found his mother still clinging to the roof supports.

"Encore, mon enfant, plongez, encore," she shouted at him. "Dive again my child."

"Vite, allez-," he shouted back. "We must go quickly."

"Aide-toi, et le ciel t'aidera," and turning loose from the ceiling she used both hands to push his head back into the water.

Liquid rushed through his nose. Fighting the urge to raise again, Joshua could feel his mother's body struggling downward beside him. Again he was forced against the wall, this time he used his hands to pull himself downward. Through the muddy water he could see a wooden bench suddenly explode past him through the doorway of the house. Then the whirlpool had him. Spinning like a top, Joshua was sucked through the doorway. His lungs bursting, Joshua felt the exhilaration of freedom when his body again slammed against the stockade fence outside of the house. His vision tunneling before he blacked out, Joshua looked backward toward the doorway. Through the muddy water he could not see the form of his mother anywhere. Darkness claimed his vision as Joshua felt the fence give away and he began to float upward.

Awareness came slowly back to Joshua. The warm spring sun was shining on his face and his feet dangled below the rough boards he was lying on. Every inch of his body hurt, and the right side of Joshua's face felt as if it were on fire. He quickly withdrew his hand after touching his cheek. The raw flesh burned as if branded. Turning his head slowly Joshua felt tree leaves fluttering lightly against the top of his head. Looking downward he was startled to see his feet were hanging off of a portion of his own fence. Twenty feet below, turgid brown water flowed slowly around the tree in which he was suspended.

"Ma Mere, Ma Mere," he called only to be answered by the flow of the water as it journeyed on to the Gulf of Mexico.

By the next morning Joshua's fevered and slashed body was taken from the stockade fence, and lowered into a waiting bull boat to be returned to St. Genevieve by river bargemen. After two days of searching, his father found Joshua in a makeshift hospital located on the highest portion of ground in the settlement of St. Genevieve. The Mississippi claimed an untold number of lives that early spring morning as the rushing water from the Missouri River upstream cascaded into the Mississippi and together deluged St. Genevieve with their fury and wrath.

Joshua's father found the crushed body of his Creole wife still in the house he built. Respecting her wishes the senior Coural wrapped her in blankets and placed his wife within the huge funeral pyre built along the edges of the river she loved. For two days his father sat beside her, bringing fresh fuel to the fire when it burned low, until all that remained was a mounded pile of ashes. The April winds then carried these ashes in swirling gusts out to float upon the crests of the brown water steadily flowing to the sea. Joshua cried softly for his mother when he recovered from the fever racking his body. The raw skin on the side of Joshua's face slowly scabbed and began to heal providing him with a constant reminder of her love. He vowed to never speak French again. Thirty-five years later he held fast to the vow made beside that great flowing river.

Dawn gusted with a hard wind blowing down the canyon Joshua chose as a campsite. Already a heavy mist filled the air as the frigid gale was turned into a fog that made the campsite a ghostly gray. He rubbed the ribbed flesh along the side of his face and stretched his back to alleviate the cramping from sleeping on the hard ground. Joshua remembered the glowing red eyes of the night before, but the gentle thoughts of his mother chased away any fear. Climbing from beneath the robes, Joshua began the process of restarting the fire for breakfast. This time he checked the horses first, and satisfied with their unconcerned, nonchalant appearance, Joshua crumbled the broken piece of pemmican into a hide vessel. This morning he would need all the strength he could garner. Spotted Owl, his adopted Indian son, should be arriving soon with the other packhorse and they could begin to load the furs from the cave, before they started on the long journey to the rendezvous. Such a long ways had he already come. Remembrance came easily into his mind as he thought back along the course of events that had brought him to these rugged Wyoming mountains.

The journey was contemplated three years before in 1817, and finally began last summer with high spirits and a shared comradeship. Nothing else could Joshua ask for, more than his face pointed toward the west, and the restless energy bundled within the powerful shoulders of the horse that was between his knees. Joshua felt blessed that he could share the trip with Jacque La Ramie. La Ramie traveled this country for the previous seven years and understood the nuances and dangers that constituted the great natural wonder they were about to enter. La Ramie learned of this jump off place from his conversation with Robert Stuart, an agent for the Astor Fur Company. La Ramie received the description of the convergence of the Platte River and the river Stuart called The Arapohay, and realized immediately this was a natural meeting spot for God's creatures.

Stuart explained that he volunteered to transport the fur company dispatches on a return trip from Oregon and carry them to St. Louis and the parent company. Stuart left Astoria situated in Oregon on the Columbia River, in the early summer of 1812. Seeking speed for the company dispatches, he followed the traditional route back to Three Forks. Stuart then dropped far more southward than the westward bound party of Astorians had traveled to reach the Oregon coast. Along with a small group of men, Stuart descended southward along the Gallatin

River. Almost dying from starvation while crossing the Grand Tetons in December of that year, Stuart built a cabin and with his men managed to stave off starvation, waiting out the early snows. They continued traveling in January of 1813, working always southward until they found a crossing over the great sheath of mountain curving downward from the Tetons. This Southern Pass, although still high in the mountains, was lower and gentler in slope than any pass the Astorians used before. Stuart's band survived an attack in the Sweetwater country from Blackfeet Indians and followed this sweet water river across the mountain plains until they met the curving arch of the Great Platte River. In the spring while following the Great Platte River, Stuart came across a river leading back to the southwest. He believed this to be the Arapohay or South Platte River about which the friendly Indian tribes told him.

Using knowledge gained from Stuart, La Ramie traveled extensively throughout the region. So vast was La Ramie's knowledge now of this country and the northern Platte area, that General William H. Ashley, who was organizing the Rocky Mountain Fur Company, hired La Ramie to organize trapping parties. All of La Ramie's men would follow him through hell--and often had.

Joshua met many of these grizzled veterans, including Jedediah S. Smith, Jim Fitzpatrick, Hugh Glass, and young Jim Bridger, while in La Ramie's company or at Fort Lisa. La Ramie arranged rendezvous for the trappers, and when the spring snows released their grip on the mountains, the trappers met where the two rivers joined for the rendezvous. There, at the confluence of the Platte and the Arapohay, would gather Indians of mixed tribes, La Ramie's mountain men, and a supply train from New Fort Lisa. Between the days of fighting and drinking, beaver pelts were swapped for bangles, beads, booze, and supplies to permit survival in the rugged country for another year. Sometimes the mountain men would accompany the supply train eastward after the rendezvous, and at other times the buckskin veterans would vanish like ghosts, accompanying the Indians back to their camps near the headwaters of the Arapohay. Joshua was the trader that brought the supplies to these rugged individuals when they met at rendezvous.

Viewed from the rendezvous site, the westward mountains appeared to extend from horizon to horizon, and in the very middle of this range sat the triangular dimension of a lofty peak. La Ramie laughed at Joshua's astonishment when Joshua first saw the mountain and assured him that Blue Peak, as La Ramie called it, was not even the tallest in this range. Joshua could tell, from La Ramie's description of Blue Peak, that it captured La Ramie's imagination also. Stuart told La Ramie this mountain was over 10,000 feet high as it lifted itself through the wisps of early summer clouds dotting the sky.

Joshua first met La Ramie when he led the pack trains from Fort Lisa and bartered with the Indians and mountain men. Joshua understood that the goods he traded for were often gathered at the expense of the mountain men's lives, and Joshua always dealt fairly, even with the Indians.

It was because of this fairness in trading and Joshua's love of the country, that La Ramie invited Joshua to visit the rugged splendor from which came the prime beaver pelts. Arrangements for their supplies were agreed upon and with his arrival at the rendezvous in 1820, Joshua stored his provisions deep within the limestone cave awaiting La Ramie's appearance. Joshua's second in command would escort the pack train home, while Joshua would at last experience the majestic splendor of the far Blue Mountain, this time as a trapper.

Joshua eagerly anticipated the coming rendezvous. He ordered the men to stake tents in the area adjacent the vee formed by the flowing streams of the two great rivers. Ropes were strung from riverbank to riverbank joining each end of the tents to a different river, marking the traders fur claim to both streams, from which flowed the lifeblood of their trade. This allowed a defensible position in guard of the trade goods and horses, and also provided a floating escape route down the river, should it ever be needed. Past experiences with water left Joshua distrusting the flowing brown surge, but the strong currents of the river could rapidly separate his company from approaching danger. With ten armed men this may have been overprotective, however Joshua's previous experience taught him that anything was possible when Indians, trappers and alcohol mixed during the weeklong rendezvous.

The packs were neatly arranged in rows, tempting even the curious magpies watching from the surrounding trees. Bolts of material were unfurled to lie across the tops, gaily displaying their potent lure that trolled for the trade of Indian squaws. From the corners were hung the beads and bangles. So attractive were the glittering advertisements, that when woven with the native materials of the Indian life, they served as proud adornments for the fierce warriors. Trading materials such as whiskey and gunpowder were cached in the soft sand to prevent early temptations. These being the staple of Indian trade, they must be rationed and apportioned with the accuracy of gold to insure a full week's activity. The currency to purchase the pews was wrapped securely around Joshua's waist, there to stay until exchanged for the pelts destined for the return trip back to Fort Lisa. No advertisement was made of this currency cache and the slim bulk added little to Joshua's powerful frame.

The first arrivals were a small band of Shoshone Indians, slowly dragging their way southward on the western side of the Platte River. Kills-Crowe, a distinguished chief, rode in the front. Three younger Shoshone braves raced circles around the white haired leader shouting and displaying their horsemanship. Kills-Crowe seemed content with his pace as the pony's slow plodding kicked up spurts of early summer dust with each reluctant step. Following closely behind were two other travois-ladened ponies beside which walked the squaws, their buckskin dresses reflecting the sun where bright bone beads were attached. One small child sat aboard the travois on the first horse. He was the designated fly chaser and was proud of this position. He swatted the river flies buzzing around the rear haunches of the pony with determination and vigor of the future warrior he would become. Even if no flies landed, the boy continued to swish his willow stick in warning that no one should challenge the grandson of Kills-Crowe, Shoshone warrior. Joshua watched in interest as they set up camp a quarter mile distant, choosing to remain apart from his men, isolated yet visually within the mix.

During the next several days many of the free trappers arrived and built their camps stretching westward from Joshua's front tents. Some consisted of little more than rings of stones, while others sported notched willow frames with brightly painted skin coverings. Other camps of Indians, laden with plews for trade began to dot the plain and smoke from the evening fires hung low in the air of the muggy river bottom. The sound of neighing horses and the throaty gurgled laughter of the eastern tribes floated across the water. On the northeastern side of the Platte a small band of Blackfeet warriors established a camp. Extreme in austerity, no squaws were discernable among the warriors; several times Joshua saw the braves riding far down stream on the opposite side of the river as if searching for provisions.

La Ramie and Joshua greeted each other with firm handshakes. As is often the case with men of strength and self confidence, either would have been embarrassed to show displays of emotion, even though the friendship between them had deepened over the years. Smiling, Joshua tried to pull from La Ramie the story of his previous winter's sabbatical but La Ramie, with his natural reticence, said very little of the last year.

"Deep snows last year, them old beavers grew fur so thick and rich that the traps couldn't hold them tight. I found one big grizzly sow that had plum choked to death trying to swaller a beaver. Once she got him in her mouth the fur waz so thick that it swelled up an' choked her to death. Good deal for me, I pryed that beaver outer her throat, took off his coat and let

33

him go for us to catch next year. That grizzly coat I borrowed from Mrs. Sow, kept me warm all winter."

Joshua smiled to himself, imagining the real story behind the bear jacket.

Rendezvous tradition dictated that Joshua ring an iron bell when time for the trading arrived. The bell, forged and rusted, was hung from the limb of a huge, broadleaf cottonwood tree on the first year of the rendezvous and was left for future gatherings. Joshua removed the clapper at the end of last season and packed it eastward, returning it this year. Hooking in the clapper, he pulled mightily on the leathern rope lead, setting the bell to pealing up and down the riversides announcing to one and all that the rendezvous had begun.

Up came the whiskey from the sanded graves, dark and rich in hue. The first pelts began to arrive from the trappers to be exchanged for the raw alcohol flavored with chewing tobacco, red peppers, molasses and hickory gum. Unlike the traders for Astor's Company, Joshua never cut the alcohol with river water as the week went on. Unscrupulous traders, knowing the trappers would be uncaring after the drinking began, added water to extend the whiskey supply. More money for the company coffers; but not Joshua, he treated all honestly.

A few of the trappers quickly mingled with the native people, trading firewater for the Indian pelts. The trappers always tried to barter for more pelts than the raw liquid cost them from Joshua, adding these pews to their own cache. The Indians soon learned that, although the traders were sharp, they received a much better deal bartering directly with them rather than the trappers.

The next several days, fierce hatreds put aside, the Indians and trappers shouted and staggered among the camps together. The more sober participants gambled and engaged in athletic contests. Knives and hatchets were thrown at any stationary target that availed itself. Knowing this, no one stood to watch in that area, not being naturally desirous of feeling the bite of cold steel. Mountain men raced horses past posts set in the ground. While the horses ran full speed the trappers attempted to hit their wooden foes by firing pistols. Three posts were set for them to gallop by, and each post was to receive two balls. Loaded pistols were to be exchanged hand to hand while riding which required tremendous coordination. La Ramie seldom lost this game. Foot races were popular entertainments and Joshua amazed the trappers and Indians with his foot speed. The previous year no one at the rendezvous could best him. The heavy labor spent as a youth layered his buttocks and thighs with sprinter's quickness and bets against him were impossible to find. The drunken trappers offered up other participants, in hopes of furthering the game against native foes. Wrestling matches would go on for hours with the loser finally quitting, returning to the shaded hide wickiups to quench their thirst with more whiskey.

After several days, trading would begin in earnest. Indians traded beaver pelts for gunpowder, lead and shot, and of course, more whiskey. Four prime pelts would buy an Indian rifle. Its 'Brown Bess' design was garishly decorated with gleaming metal tacks much admired by the young braves. Many of the doe-eyed squaws watched patiently as the men traded first; disinterested in the long rifles, they gazed upon the fabric and beads so brightly arrayed on the robes, hoping favors would be granted them. Many trappers recognized that fact and traded pelts for the cloth goods, only to be exchanged later with the squaws for the particular favors only the women could grant. Every night, buffaloes with two humps grunted and groaned, straining and bucking together on the banks of the Arapohay. Trappers often negotiated with the young women not yet covered in beads, knowing they would be the first, hoping for a chance at fresh meat.

One squaw in particular, a Crowe named Screaming Bear, flowed with yards of material and dangled beads from every limb. She was the daughter of Komseka-Kinahyop and known for her conquests and coups. Although aging and thickening now, she still owned the bright sentinel looks of her father, a much-feared warrior. Her own man, dead ten years, drowned in the spring floods along the Platte. Screaming Bear enjoyed the variety of life and took no other permanently as her man. She liked the spontaneity of coupling with many warriors, drawing their strength deep into her loins. She must have become quite accomplished judging from the stores of her trade goods. At night, her naming became evident, as shrill 'AiYee's' reverberated from the cliffs, rapidly increasing in frequency until slain by the long drawn wail of Crowe victory. The next day more beads would adorn her stout figure and rounded breasts, accentuated by the short, deerskin frock which advertised delights beneath as she bent to gather firewood.

The trappers also traded for moulds and powder but scoffed at the cheaply made Indian rifles, preferring instead sugar, salt, and beans. These three items seldom lasted the entire trapping season, and starved for these tastes, the trappers dealt furs rapidly in the staple's acquirement. Metal objects such as traps, pans, and ovens were also replaced. Lost from the hardships of the year, these were necessary for life itself and greatly valued. The smart trappers placed credit with Joshua's company to guard against future years of hardship, much like money in a bank. The week went well and huge bundles of pews were gathered and banded. Joshua stored these strapped bundles behind the tents, constantly guarding them against theft and disappearance. Left alone, the furs would soon vanish only to be traded again for more bottles of fiery brew.

On the last day of trading, as the final cache of whiskey was unearthed, the Blackfeet warriors stoically rode across the river, eyeing the rifles and gunpowder. Their leader, with hawk eyes and a fresh scalp dangling from his waist, finally motioned the last warrior across the river. The Blackfoot arrived with a horse in tow. Throwing the rope of the still dripping mount at Joshua's feet, the pock-faced warrior in the lead brokenly addressed Joshua.

"Plenty fur, good altime, want whiskey, powder."

Joshua already attached the name of this warrior to the distinctive face several days earlier and knew that he was trading with Lame Wolf, a proud and fierce fighter of the Blackfeet tribe.

"Where get pelts, Lame Wolf?" asked Joshua.

Frowning from the use of his name, robbing him of power, Lame Wolf gazed slowly the length of the trader before replying. "Came Lame Wolf in a dream. Lame Wolf mighty. Ride the bitter woods two days travel, beside the great pool, Lame Wolf provides for the needs of his people. Need whiskey to dream again. You take horse, pelts. Give Lame Wolf whiskey, fire powder. Need many silent bees and fire hammers."

Joshua inspected the pelts adorning the pony. The horse was saddled, and the saddle bore the makers stamp of Louis Ostere of St. Louis. Splashed across the cantle were dark stains, still slick on the leather. Ropes attached the furs. Two half hitches were rigged through the circingle on the front of the saddle, looped back around the cantle and ran through the far side rigging before being double diamonded over the furs. Joshua was sure no Indian tied these knots.

"Lame Wolf dreams well, perhaps too well," said Joshua.

Scowling again, but not understanding the meaning, the Indian again signed the signal for trade.

Knowing further discussion would be useless, Joshua spread a blanket upon the ground. On this he set a small cask of whiskey, the remaining two rifles, two casks of gunpowder, three oil boxes of striking flints and steels, and a heavy sack of lead balls.

"All much gone," said Joshua, "end rendezvous, follow water home."

Lame Wolf carefully looked in Joshua's face, then flung his hand toward a Hudson blanket marked with bright red and blue stripes.

"Bright wool skins, too," said Lame Wolf indicating the thick Hudson blanket folded at Joshua's feet.

Joshua looked down toward the folded blanket. Three times Night Wind, the eldest daughter of Kills-Crowe, had passed by the trading tents.

Three times she knelt and brought the soft edges of the blanket up to the cheek of her sculptured copper face. Lack of pelts was the only barrier that kept Night Wind from trading for the blanket that obviously caught her eye. Other squaws bartered furiously with Joshua, but his price stayed firm, as did his resolve not to dicker on the blanket so coveted by Night Wind.

"Blanket already gone," said Joshua, "bad medicine to trade what is already promised."

"Many pelt; two rifles not enough."

Slowly reaching inside his left boot, Joshua removed a small silver flask in which he carried a more discriminating brand of whiskey, for snakebite as he always told himself.

"Much powerful firewater, make many dreams, now we trade."

Casting one last glance at the brightly striped blanket, Lame Wolf nodded his assent. The deal was struck and with whooping war cries the braves gathered the goods and at full speed, plunged into the river swimming upstream to the far shore. Joshua led the newly acquired horse back to the tents, wondering at the fate of the poor trapper whose blood was sacrificed to complete the trade. Refusing the trade would only have angered the Indians, and not regained the property. He would talk to La Ramie before adding these to the pelts in the company's bundles. Perhaps the rightful owner's heirs could be found.

Decision made, Joshua walked through the milling trappers and Indians until he found the camp of Kills-Crowe. Seated near the opening flap of the teepee sat Night Wind. Her eyes promptly brightened when she saw Joshua carrying the Hudson blanket and then quickly she cast her eyes downward again. She was wearing a white buckskin dress with lacings on each side exposing only hints at the soft brown skin that lay within. Around her neck was a hair pipe, or necklace, adorned with bone beads about four inches long interwoven with red and amber trade beads. Long, raven-black hair flowed over her shoulder and cascaded down upon her lap.

"Damn blanket, no good, no one wants. Maybe it will keep the daughter of Kills-Crowe warm; I don't have room to take it."

Night Wind looked quickly up again, searching for treachery in his eyes, but seeing none, quickly shook her head saying no. "I am only a spirit woman; I don't have pews to trade."

"Next year bring me one of those," said Joshua indicating the beaded par fleche she was sewing. The bag bore painted geometric designs and was brightly dyed. Bone beads were threaded along the edge highlighting the beautiful pattern.

"Only a bag, nothing more?"

Joshua nodded, and laid the blanket at her feet. Smiling he walked off. Perhaps he would never see the bag next year, but maybe he would. Indians had a profound sense of honor, and once a deal was struck they kept their end.

That night Shrieking Bear again sang to the moon. After the crescendo and wail, the night was still again until Joshua heard a louder voice raised in rage coming from the riverbank near Shrieking Bear's favored spot. This voice was answered by a woman's voice raised in anger and fury sounding like a battle cry. Rousing three of his men, Joshua and his tent-mates grabbed their rifles and ran stocking-footed toward the sandbank from where the voices were coming. Upon his arrival Joshua observed a large group of trappers already there, brandishing aloft pine torches. The glow from the torches flickered out across the water and illuminated the slim body of Night Wind, standing knee deep in the swirling current, her doeskin dress slashed and hanging from her slender body. Her left breast, hip and leg were bare, and a long scratch ran down the inside of her thigh slowly oozing dark red in the torchlight. Mud smears darkened the erect, coffee-colored nipple as her chest heaved. Night Wind backhanded the blood trickling from her nose and mouth. Her war cry had ceased, but fire still leapt from Night Wind's eyes, which never shifted from the crouched form of the man in front of her. Floating gently, bobbing on the current was a striped blanket the middle of which she held clutched in her left hand. Her right hand owned a knife, held low and ready. The bone handle rested on her inner leg showing the pathway to the dark triangle of womanhood between the slim hips. Wickedly the blade reflected the confrontation in the flickering glow of the river sands. Night Wind's intense gaze focused only on the swarthy form of Lame Wolf crouched in front of her, holding the other end of the contested blanket. The scene played on until in the growing stillness, Joshua heard the distinctive cocking of a hammer, drawn to full readiness by La Ramie. Four more times the sound was repeated as Joshua and his men also readied their rifles. The barrels never wavered as La Ramie spoke.

"That's one squaw that doesn't want to trade any of her possessions, Lame Wolf, although I admit her wares are mighty tempting. I might be of mind to make an offer myself if I was younger. Now Shrieking Bear there," said La Ramie, indicating the aptly named squaw watching the scene with the other trappers, "she would trade you out of anything you have, and you wouldn't have to cut her up to do it. Vamoose now, and let us sleep, morning comes early."

Although not understanding the words, the cocking sound of the S hammers on the rifles left no chance of misunderstanding their meaning.

Slowly straightening, Lame Wolf threw his end of the blanket into the water's rolling eddy. Amidst the shouts from the trappers, Lame Wolf strode swiftly off, his back stiff from lost pride, across the sandbar and down the streambed into the dark stand of cottonwoods. The laughing continued to follow Lame Wolf's progress, though no one there doubted La Ramie earned a life long enemy that evening. Quickly looking around, Shrieking Bear followed after Lame Wolf into the trees.

The fire now dwindled in Night Wind's eyes; she cast a small smile toward La Ramie and the traders, and quickly folded the wet blanket against her thighs. Attempting to secure the slashed dress, she sheathed the knife and walked rapidly, unembarrassed with her head held high, upstream toward the waiting camp of her father. Every trapper among the group quickly calculated whether they still had anything of value Night Wind might trade for, worth the price of removing the mud from her fiercely pouting breast as she hurried by.

Morning broke with trappers and Indians spreading to the four winds of heaven, perhaps never to see each other again. In the summer, La Ramie was sending two groups of men north of these rivers to follow the Platte until it reached the flowing waters of the Sweetwater, and then southward to scout for new rendezvous sites deeper in the heart of the mountains. Using Stuart's description, these men, as all explorers before them, needed little urging to view what always lay beyond the next mountain. La Ramie and Joshua were heading more due west to encircle the Blue Mountain. Lame Wolf and his braves weren't seen again as Joshua helped pack the furs on the waiting caravan for the long journey back to Fort Lisa and then on to St. Louis.

At last the caravan of pelts was headed east, his mission fulfilled, Joshua was ready to travel the mountains of his own dreams. Accompanying La Ramie, they were riding toward it, Blue Mountain, the one that seemed to hold the answers for that which Joshua searched, and release the mystery that called deep in his soul.

The first day of the journey proved immediately frustrating. Each trapper was responsible for his own mount and a packhorse to carry the necessary supplies they would need until the rendezvous next spring. La Ramie planned to travel north following the Platte River, crossing into the Cottonwood country to the north of Blue Mountain. From there he explained they would circle back south surrounding this lofty peak and reach the high summer plains where an ample amount of jerked buffalo meat could be laid in. Here the Arapohay narrowed and La Ramie would finish work on his cabin to provide accommodations for the long winter of trapping.

The packhorses were sulky under their heavy load of sugar, salt, coffee, beans, flour and bacon. The traps, hanging on long chains across the packs, swung wildly when the horses trotted, causing the animals to snort and jump with the least provocation. As the rendezvous was held between the two rivers, the men were obliged to cross back over the Platte thoroughly wetting the men and horses. Shivering from the light breeze, Joshua followed La Ramie's horse, a dark bay with mean eyes and a huge roman head, up the high embankment from the river valley onto a flat plateau. Here Joshua could see some of the vast length of the Platte as she snaked, curling and bending northward, skirting the eastern edge of the Blue Mountains. Joshua's horse, a piebald with one white sock and eye, was smaller than La Ramie's horse, but deeply built and well muscled. After several miles' travel on the plateau, horses and riders found their rhythm, and settled into it, grinding out the miles ahead of them.

As the sun lowered from the middle of the clear blue sky, they rode past circular wells dug deep into the hard rock surfaces. La Ramie explained these diggings where not done by white men, nor were they the work of Indians. The elders, with whom he had spoken, said legends handed down told a story of men who lived before the birth of Old Man Coyote. They dug here to obtain tools from the white quartz. These tools, imbued with special powers, cut large blocks of stone. This stone was used to make high mountains far to the south beyond the edge of light. From the tops of these mountains, the hanging road of stars could be reached.

La Ramie began to explain the peculiarity of the Indian tribes in this area. "While at Rendezvous, Sioux, Blackfeet, Arapahoe, Crowe, and Shoshone Indians may mix with the trappers; but many were actually death enemies and a constant state of warfare existed among them."

La Ramie's reputation among these Indians was as a man of peace. He dealt fairly with all of the tribes he could, and either out-fought or out-ran the ones he couldn't out-fight. The Platte area, although not an ancestral home to any of the tribes, was a vast resource of hunting grounds for many of them. As alliances shifted, and the strength of Indian groups fluctuated, the small bands moved to different areas.

The introduction of horses from the Spanish further aided these nomadic peoples in following game. The reliance on the buffalo, deer, and antelope also ensured that none of these tribes would travel or live in large groups unless the chiefs called tribal councils.

These Indian tribes valued bravery and ability. They often tortured themselves and fasted in order to suffer hallucinations that would reveal a personal guardian spirit for their protection in the hunt and in battle. Most tribes believed in the many myths handed down to them from their pre-horse days. Some elements of these beliefs were widespread--the ability of old man coyote to trick, the bear to overpower, and the buffalo to provide for and persevere. All tribes held a belief of Manitou, the pervasive spirit. The Sun was the supreme God, from whom all sustenance came.

"How have you managed to trade with them and still keep your hair?" Joshua asked.

"Well, one or two men ain't much of a threat to Indians," La Ramie replied in his rambling vernacular.

"Respect is probably what they value most. Take for instance that snake," said La Ramie motioning to the companion of Eve, belly-walking quickly into the brush. "We could kill him if we wanted to, but while we was throwing rocks at him he would find some hole to hide in. Then we would hafta find a stick and try and dig him out. All this time he would be buzzin an' striking at us. The horses would be going crazy pulling on the reins and trying to run away. Maybe we'd find a stick and run it down in the hole messing up that snake something fierce, then maybe you'd stick your hand down in there to try and steal the rattle off Mr. Snake's tail for a souvenir to prove how brave you was, and quicker than a catamount, Mr. Snake would fang you cause they always lays their heads right behind their tail to try and trick ya. You'd scream, turn loose your horse, he'd run off, and your hand would swell bigger than your head. You'd either have to chase your horse or cut your hand, maybe you'd die and maybe you wouldn't, dependin' on what I did first, but either way Mr. Snake would still be in that hole just lookin' out. All this fuss, just to cause him some grief. Indians are kind of like this. If they respect you, they usually don't try and kill you because, like Mr. Snake, you might be more trouble than the souvenir of your hair was worth. It's easier just to ride on."

Joshua quickly gave up the any thoughts of killing the snake that was angrily buzzing at them from the stunted sagebrush. Although he hated snakes with a passion, it just didn't seem worth it now. The rest of the day the two men traveled northward skirting the deep draws that ran down to the Platte River. As evening approached, La Ramie's horse snorted and shied when a flock of sage grouse exploded under the horse's nose. The birds flew a short distance and then landed, beginning to peck among the sagebrush for their supper. Stepping from his horse, La Ramie drew his ornate Fincher shotgun from the doeskin scabbard that hung under his left leg. Throwing the reins to Joshua, he walked slowly toward the birds. The report of the shotgun re-startled the covey except for two young sage chickens flopping in the red clay soil. While attempting to finish their supper, they inadvertently provided it for the trappers. At the base of a small stand of stunted evergreens, La Ramie built a fire. After cleaning and dressing the birds, he quickly smeared the two chickens with mud made from the red earth and canteen water. Joshua pushed a tin of coffee nearer the flames of the evening blaze. He then unpacked the horses, picketing them in the tall grass inside the circle of trees. Upon returning, Joshua observed how La Ramie dug a hole burying the red-hot coals from the fire into it before laying the mud-encrusted chickens in this prairie oven. La Ramie covered the hole with the remaining coals, fed the flames more wood and stirred the coffee now bubbling on the rocks.

Sipping the coffee and relaxing on the ground sheets of buffalo hide, the two men talked of the country and what lay ahead of them tomorrow. "If you was to listen real close," La Ramie said, "somewhere in the wind just north of here, the canyon spirits will sing you songs all night long. There is a deep canyon there that boils and roils like this coffee. I always enjoy looking down in the canyon, but never cared to climb down into the bottom. The Indians believe that the spirits of dead warriors live there, chanting of their victories at night. Sometimes the Indians know of what they sez; we'll ride by there in the morning. Don't do no good to go messin' near Indian haunts late a night."

Leaving Joshua to reflect on these statements, La Ramie stirred the fire with the tip of his Arkansas Toothpick (an evil looking serrated knife), speared the chickens, and laid them on a flat rock nearby. Reversing the blade in his hand so to use the handle of the knife, La Ramie struck the baked mud covering. The mud broke in pieces revealing the steaming meat within. Washed down with gulps of hot coffee and the last of the loaves of bread from the rendezvous, the two men feasted well. Later looking at the bright rotation of stars far above his head, Joshua thought he could hear a chanting sound on the wind blowing from the canyon.

Morning packing started the routine with which Joshua would become well accustomed in the days to come. The trail horses were saddled first, giving them time to blow their held breath. The mean eyed bay was especially tricky. Flattening his ears he would squint his eyes further and draw in deep draughts of air. He learned early in his life that by doing this, the cinch would not be as tight when he breathed out. La Ramie played along with the game; snugging the cinch and then whistling a retort while gazing around as if interested in the landscape. The horses' roman nose would begin to twitch and slowly the bay would let out some air. The eyes would again swing to watch La Ramie still standing there admiring the beauty of some imaginary object. Smiling in his equestrian way, old bay would straighten his ears, fully satisfied the ruse worked; he'd widen his squinty eyes a smidge to expel his long pent up breath. Much to Old Bay's dismay, La Ramie then quickly tightened the cinch the last notch and stepped aboard the now secure saddle. Joshua imagined the bay's feeling of humiliation at being hoisted on his own petard.

Joshua, skilled by years of saddling packhorses, made short work of the packing detail. After combing each horse's back to remove mud and caked on sweat, he next put on the sawbuck lined with wool to protect the back and withers. He checked the breast collar, squared it slightly, and dropped the triangle ring between the horse's front legs to rawhide on the cinch buckle. Joshua's sawbucks were double cinched and experience taught him to only use horses that allowed a tail collar as well. Once satisfied with the buck's position, his closed-top panniers were balanced off the sawbuck, one on each side. The panniers were double-stitched, shrunken buffalo hide with oak frames and ash carry poles. Finishing the load with the tent and ground robes tightly rolled, he secured the top with the alforja strap and backed the tie with double-diamond hitches. Two ropes led from the lead halters, one to his pommel, and one coiled back on the left side of the sawbuck.

Both riders were quieter this morning as La Ramie led them higher through the pines. Joshua could clearly hear the roaring water in the Platte below.

"Seems like the Good Lord just plum got mad at this here old river," La Ramie soliloquized. "Here it was just runnin' fine and wide, not giving its daily thanks to its maker, thinking it was jus' bout the finest river around here. An' lo and behold the Lord decided the river needed a lesson on who was boss and pushed up these here hills. Now the river thinks its no big deal, it just back up gits a run at these hills and over it goes. Now Old River is feeling pretty proud. But a funny thing begins to happen and the rocks she's a running on begin to wash away and the faster old river runs over these rocks the faster they wash away. By now Old River is scared but there ain't no way out of it and pretty soon she just keeps sinking deeper and deeper in those rocks. The more she struggles the harder it is to flow wide and nice, an pretty soon she has to get all narrowed up and foam and splash just to move along. After a while the Lord lets her go, but keeps this canyon here just to remind her she isn't so almighty after all. And every time she flows through here she remembers to thank the Lord cause she don't like getting all squished up. Sometimes when a body is caught in a trap its better just to lie still rather than thrashin' all about and getting' yourself in deeper and deeper."

"Jacque, are all of your stories this long?"

"Nope, just the ones about rivers and snakes and injuns," answered La Ramie.

Noon saw them still gazing down into the angry gorge. Joshua could see the twisting, tormented river bashing itself ever deeper against the canyon wall. He was glad he wasn't in a barge trying to make it through the boulders that foamed white in the water below. With a short break to swallow some dried antelope jerky chased down with water, they slowly began the descent off the high plateau. Here the river widened and slowed as they rode closer to it to avoid the rugged hills on their right. Giant cleavers looked to have chopped with impunity into the earth. Joshua began to wonder why there were draws that ran into draws, sometimes just stopping and going nowhere. It would have taken days to ride through this bizarre landscape. The grass was rich and lush near the river and deer often stared at them, startled from their noon siestas in the shade of the pines. Sometimes they crossed stretches of sand bars leaving darkened potholes where the horse's feet punched into the white granules. Glancing behind, Joshua gazed at their trail across the sand, wondering if he was the first white man to mark this wilderness, to force his will on the nature of this giant land.

Late in the evening they turned the horses into the water of the Platte, and though tired from the long day's ride, the horses swam upstream facing the current, stroking strong to reach the far shore. Joshua could feel the persistent pull of the current, almost pushing his mount sideways; he grabbed huge handfuls of mane to prevent being floated away from the horse. The packhorse lacked the strength of his piebald, and several times Joshua felt the lead rope tighten pulling him backward in the saddle. He urged the trailing pony onward with shouts of encouragement and checked the powerful neck of his horse turning him slightly more upstream. Joshua watched La Ramie's horse, straining to reach the shoreline, neck out, his head and floating tail the only visible reminders that under the water swam the heart of a mountain horse. Slowly finding footing, La Ramie's horse lunged the remaining distance to the far sandy shore, completely jerking the packhorse off his feet, dragging the sliding pony onto the dry shore. Suddenly Joshua felt the piebald scramble for footing. He stopped, allowing the pack animal to catch up, and then emerged beside La Ramie on the shoreline.

From here a rutted trail rose steeply out of the river valley through a tunnel of willows and brush. The riders were forced to lean low on the horses' necks to avoid being swept from the saddle. Joshua smiled as he watched La Ramie's pack animal desperately trying the keep up with the lunging bounds of Old Bay, evidently not wanting to be drug again. They reached the top of the embankment just as the sun vanished from sight; amid the chopped hills they had yet to climb. In the enclosure of huge, rounded boulders the travelers stripped the saddles and packs from the animals, rubbing them with handfuls of the coarse river grass to ease the miles of the day. Both men then fell into their sleeping robes, fire and hot coffee pushed back in their minds, wishing only for rest and warmth to ease the chills and shaking caused by the cold water of the Platte.

Morning drifted into the dry camp of the trappers, dawning with a gray filtered light caused by the drifting haze running down from the slopes of Blue Mountain. For the last two days of hard riding, the mountain seemed no closer than when they left the fork of the rivers. Joshua understood they were skirting the edge, but the sixty miles of northward travel did not rotate the mountain to their view. It appeared the same, squatting among its neighboring peaks almost as if it were turning with them as they traveled, never revealing an unprotected flank. Joshua witnessed pronghorn antelope doing this to face the onslaught of prairie wolves in defense of the young fawns. The does would constantly face the threat slowly turning on their hind legs as the wolves circled looking for an opening to rush in and tear the vulnerable flanks and hamstrings. The antelope's front legs would balance delicately in the air as they turned, waiting the chance to slash downward, the sharp hooves capable of blinding or disfiguring a wolf. Joshua wondered if the Blue Mountain was doing the same to them, always keeping its face toward them, waiting for its chance to slash them if they approached too near.

By the time they were fed and outfitted to ride, the sun's rays were valiantly trying to penetrate the graying gloom that swirled around them. This effort illuminated patchy spots, checker boarding the slowing rising hills of sagebrush they were riding through.

Joshua looked back wistfully peering into the rivers of fog below which he knew disguised the channel of the Platte. From now on, only Blue Mountain would point their course; no longer would the broad flowing waters serve as a beacon to guide their journey. La Ramie led the way; Joshua startled as a deep canyon appeared on his left side. Unconcerned by the drop off, even as the loose shale tumbled and slid beneath the horse's feet, La Ramie worked their path upward not leaving the canyon lip for several miles, at last turning northward away from the chasm below. Relieved by the improved trail, Joshua tried to peer into the mist before them, imagining a constant danger was lying, hidden by the vapor, waiting for its chance to attack.

Jolted by suddenly running into the back of La Ramie's halted horse, Joshua looked up to see the guide's eyes peering intently at the swirl of clouds in front of them. Shifting his gaze to look also, Joshua imagined he saw movement as the fog shifted in form. Looking closely now the mist changed shape, growing shaggy and horned only to return to the gray wetness of its former appearance.

"Injun haunts," whispered Joshua.

"Quiet," came the terse reply.

Joshua's back began to ache from the frozen position and his horse sidestepped with impatience. The sunlit square of the checkerboard suddenly appeared again and the cloud turned back into hide and hair--hide and hair with curved horns reaching skyward, framing the coal black eyes and nose. Vapor rose from the nostrils as the apparition snorted disapproval and suddenly swung sideways exposing a broad side mounted by lighter brown hair scaling a huge hump.

"Buffalo," Joshua started involuntarily.

"Not just one," whispered La Ramie. "Quick! Swap ends and ride back to the edge of the canyon."

"Nooo, I don't like high places I can fall into."

"You won't like being in the middle of what we're in now," La Ramie replied.

Joshua pulled sharply on the reins guiding the horses back toward the slate edge of the draw. Joshua, now in the lead, almost spurred his horse forward, when the piebald suddenly stopped. Looking past the horse's head Joshua saw only air where land was a moment before. Thankful for the pony's insight, he turned to give La Ramie a questioning glance and them mimicked his behavior as La Ramie dismounted to stand beside Old Bay, stroking the horse's neck and rubbing the large roman nose.

"Not a word, not a sound," whispered La Ramie. "Stay in front of your horse not to the side of him; if he goes over turn loose of the reins and let him go."

Wondering why any horse would want to go over the edge into the depths below, the answer arrived in the form of a shaggy brown wall moving in unison downward, following the trail they had just ridden up. Smelling the closeness of the buffaloes, Joshua's horse snorted. Joshua jerked hard down on the bit and grasped the horse's right ear, to pull the head down against his chest. Over the saddle he watched the brown wall continue, sometimes in singles and often in pairs, steam rising from their backs. Fascinated, Joshua lost all track of time. At first the horses shifted, wanting to face the buffalo, but the continued calmness by the mountain men quieted them and the horse's heads lowered and their hindquarters sagged as they realized the wait would continue. The sun completely disappeared from view now but still the wall of moving flesh continued within rope length from the men waiting on the edge. One calf, raced toward them, skidding to a halt, and switching ends, bucked back toward the rolling herd, only to be butted by the large bull he ran into. Bawling, the calf worked his way back into the flow of the herd and disappeared down the trail.

Desperately trying to keep up with the herd, a single old cow limped slowly by, her hindquarters stifled from some injury. The steepness of the trail assuring the river bottom would keep her after she drank. Her great shaggy head swinging massively side-to-side, the dislocation of her hip made it painful going down the trail and impossible for her to follow the herd back up.

As she wandered deeper in the river, the cold flowing water would be a relief to her arthritic joints, and the mud slipping ever higher on her flanks offered balm to the small biting flies. At last sensing the herd leaving, she would attempt to turn and follow. The solace would turn to despair as she realized she possessed not the strength to free herself from the mud. Vainly would she struggle to follow the herd from the river. Exhausted at last, the huge head would droop and the waters of the river would welcome the cow, taking her into its bosom. As the years passed her flesh now rotted and gone, the framework of her bones covered by repeated siltings of the river, would begin the slow process, where Mother Earth reclaimed her own, from bones to rock, a perfect stone memorial that once she was here.

"One place you don't want to be," said La Ramie, "is smack dab in the middle of that much meat. First thing happens is they get nervous trying to go around you, and then they start to run. With this fog no matter how a man tried to get away, you'd get turned catawampus, and down you'd go, either off this edge or ground into the dirt. Them buffaloes knew we were here, but being thirsty, and us being quiet, they weren't bothered none. Wild horses graze among them all the time. Standing beside the horses makes it seem just like we was here natural. Damn, Old Bay was standing on my toe and I didn't want to kick him to get him off."

"How many were there?" asked Joshua.

"Well, I kain't count that high, but the injuns always sez, like blades of grass."

"Enough standing here, I can't look down this edge any more," said Joshua, tugging his horses from the precipice.

La Ramie, with a glare at Old Bay, mounted up also.

"Without them buffaloes, the injuns would be in a heap of trouble," said La Ramie. "They use all parts of them in their lives. The hair and hide they makes robes out of, and they braid the best reins you ever saw. They stretch the guts and use them for lacings, mold the hide into pots, make glue out of the hooves, and drink out of the horns. Most of the meat they dry, keeps them in stew all winter."

"Should we kill some now?" asked Joshua.

"Don't rightly have time to take care of the meat, no use wasting things. We got a lot of hills to climb before we start shootin' buffaloes."

The trail was resumed and the rich yeasty odor of buffalo dung rose around them as they followed the trail up to the high plains waiting above. Stopping only for brief periods to rest the horses the two men continued to climb ever further up the steep slopes, the sweating horses and the pressure within their ears indicating the altitude they were gaining.

Finally the terrain flattened. The sun appeared low over the hills above them, revealing late afternoon. Blue Mountain, finally let down its defense, and turned its watchful gaze elsewhere. Joshua began to make out the rough ridges running down the flanks of the mountain and shades of dark greens blended with the blues. Large expanses of stone walls girdled the mountain like slick amour. The mountain also grew in size, expanding, more dominant, but somehow less ominous.

Mingled in with the sharp turpentine-like smell from the blooming resin weeds, and the pungent dry odor of the sage, Joshua imagined he could also smell smoke. Feeling his sense of smell was awry; he at first saw no indication of fire near them. Aiming for a mounded hill two miles distant, La Ramie pointed toward the grove of evergreens perched atop the hill like a verdant hairpiece. At last Joshua thought he could see a small spiral of smoke rising from the treetops disappearing in the early dusk of the mountain's shadow.

"No cover here," said La Ramie. "We are too much in the open to stay here and these horses stand out like a sore thumb. We might as well ride up and see if they have supper waiting."

"I'm too tired to stop trusting your judgment now," said Joshua, "but just the same I might loosen Miss Hawken and check the priming in case we are in need of her."

Joshua noted that La Ramie removed his long Hall rifle from the scabbard and rode forward with the rifle balanced on top of his thighs. The Hall, a breech-loading flintlock, was unusual for this country. By setting the S hammer on half cock and rolling the frizzen forward, the lever on the lock plate could be slid downward. This enabled the breech and priming pan to be raised. Into the chamber the powder from a paper cartridge could be added, along with the ball. The paper would provide the wadding to insure a true flight for the ball down the barrel and closing the breech seated the round into the chamber. The remaining powder would charge the pan and the rifle was ready to fire. Precision work in a St.

Louis gun shop insured minimal gas leakage from the chamber. The large, .69 caliber was a deterrent to most men it faced, red or white, and Joshua knew that La Ramie could fire the rifle four times in under a minute, twice as fast as his Hawken's rate of fire which was loaded by the muzzle. Including two braces of pistols and the short barreled Model 1816 under Joshua's left leg matching the extra shotgun of La Ramie; the fangs were poised ready to bite any hand attempting to remove their rattles.

With the shadow of dusk growing ever nearer, La Ramie kicked the big horse forward. Even Old Bay seemed apprehensive as they approached the hill and the rising smoke. Was it white trappers stopped for the evening or Blackfeet warriors luring them in to ambush them and count coup? La Ramie angled toward the hillside till he reached the beginning of the rise leading up into the evergreens so desperately trying to make a living on the rocky hillside. He then turned his horse and motioned Joshua to move some distance away from him. Joshua was beginning to feel the tension rising as La Ramie continued to set his horse, patiently waiting. Just as Joshua turned to question the wait, a voice called from the top of a rock outcropping two hundred yards in front of them.

"Ho, ho, ho, La Ramie, you make an old Indian wait too long. Soon it be too dark to shoot you good. My old rifle won't spit the silent bee that far. Come in soon, night time makes my sons afraid of the spirits and they will be shooting each other thinking it is you, come and bring trader. The dog and onions are done and an old man is hungry." "Damn," La Ramie said, "it's old Kills-Crowe; maybe we will get supper tonight."

Feeling slightly silly, Joshua led his horses toward the big boulders and Kills-Crowe standing beside the rocks smiling at them.

He noticed that La Ramie also was working his way up the rocky hillside but angled twenty yards to his right. Cresting the rise Joshua could see a small depression below. A pool of water was in the bottom of the circular depression, reflecting the orange flames from a small fire. Although here in the soft, velvet dusk the fire was clearly visible, once he stepped down in the depression Joshua knew that on the plains outside the lip of the rock circle no sign of a campsite would be evident. Even the smoke would be shielded by the prairie night. From the other side of the bowl Joshua saw La Ramie emerge behind the lowered heads of two, young, Indian boys as they walked in front of him. Seated on a bundle of soft buffalo robes near the fire, Night Wind rocked a young boy in her arms, the same child who so proudly swatted the flies from his Grandfather's horses the first day of the rendezvous. Loosening the cinch on his horse Joshua squatted to wait for La Ramie.

"La Ramie too damn much Indian," remarked Kills-Crowe. "Young braves too damn much white men, they look in fire and no see that sneaky trapper. La Ramie leads them into their own camp. How many horses you steal, La Ramie?"

"No steal horses tonight, Kills-Crowe, all four of yours plus mine are tied in the trees."

"Lone Eagle, guard those horses so no more white Indians sneak up on you tonight. Little Dog, you help your brother; don't embarrass your father any more tonight."

With this, Kills-Crowe limped on down to the fire. Joshua followed the two boys, leading his horses through the hollow and back to the trees where he unsaddled them. The two boys, now grinning, signed to him that they would rub down the horses. Joshua walked back down to the smells of the boiled dog and prairie onions bubbling from the cooking pot simmering above the fire. Darkness reached its apex as Joshua settled beside La Ramie. Hunger caused his stomach to growl harshly, bringing a soft laugh from Night Wind.

"The bear growls loudly tonight," she said.

She ladled his bowl deeply with the rich, brown stew paying careful attention to include large chunks of dog meat. Joshua ate ravenously, pausing only long enough to allow Night Wind to dip another bowl for him from the rapidly diminishing level in the kettle. The dog was tender but possessed a strong flavor, even with the wild onions to mellow the rankness. Pausing at the end of his second bowl, Joshua looked up to find the gazes of La Ramie and Kills-Crowe smiling, watching him eat.

"Why you bring trader with you La Ramie?"

"Not enough buffalo on these plains to feed him. That's why we share your camp," said La Ramie. "My packhorse lightens his load too quickly."

Joshua's face reddened as both men continued to badger him. Finally the conversation moved forward to discussion about the best path north of Blue Mountain. This allowed Joshua the chance to escape the teasing. He rose to his feet intending to rinse the bowl in the shallows of the small pond.

"My work," Night Wind said, taking the bowl from his grasp with her small, calloused hand, the same hand that once held a knife willing to stab Lame Wolf in protection of her honor and the Hudson blanket. He followed her to the water's edge fighting a temptation to hold back her thick folds of hair as she leaned to scrub the bowls in the soft, bottom sands. Perfectly balanced, kneeling, she finished her task and returned to the fire with Joshua following as her obedient dog, probably acting like the one he just finished eating. Feeling embarrassed by his boyish fantasy, he sat down across from La Ramie to listen to their talk. It was evident to Joshua that these two elements of the wilderness were close friends and their paths had crossed many times before. The two young boys came quietly back to the fire; and gathering bowls of the remaining stew served by Night Wind, they trudged back up the slope to lay beside the horses, comforting the ponies with their closeness.

"Spirit Woman serves you well in your old age, Kills-Crowe," said La Ramie.

"Yes," answered Kills-Crowe, "she sees far. At night she flies with the great owl. The wind whispers to her and all creatures on this land she sees. She knows the place and time of my death but won't tell me. 'Not yet, Father' is all she says."

"And your grandson, he grows brave and tall."

"Even from rape and death, from the murder of her relatives by the child-killing Sioux, something to brighten my old days has come. Already he can ride like the wind, outracing his uncles. He has visions like his mother and soon will ride the owl, and murmur to the wind with her."

Joshua now understood her ferocity as she faced down Lame Wolf rather than submit. Like a wounded she-wolf, even when beaten, cut and bleeding, she would die trying to bite her tormentor. The child-killing Sioux must have respected her bravery, letting her live after raping her.

The talk turned to Kills-Crowe's other sons and daughters-in-law. Kills-Crowe explained that he feared Lame Wolf and his marauding band of warriors would attack his tribe at their home, high on the plains of the Blue Mountain. Lame wolf cared not the sex or age of the scalps that graced his coup stick, only that their owners died easily and quickly. Kills-Crowe sent his older sons, and lodge daughters on ahead, trusting in his two youngest and their sister, the vision woman, to bring him safely home.

The miles of the day finally overcoming him, Joshua spread his ground robes across from the glowing coals and the brightly colored blanket where Night Wind and her child lay. The stars above wheeled, clear and bright in the mountain sky. Just as Joshua drifted to sleep he heard the rustle of rushing wings in the night, and felt a breath of cool winds against his cheek, like the rush of air from a bird's wing, blowing down through the pines from the mountain, whispering its secrets below.

Chapter 3
The Land

Tuesdays were always much better than the day they chased after. For some reason the grind was started and the dark clouds never seemed quite as bleak on a Tuesday. Words rattled around in Carrigan's head, something about 'a good start is half done.' Maybe that applied to the days in the week also. The start to this week hadn't been especially promising, considering the school board meeting the previous evening, but today was guaranteed to be brighter. Perhaps, thought Carrigan, he could get through an entire day with no one running away, or robbing someone, and with a little luck he wouldn't get RIFed or have anyone stick a dead chicken carcass in his briefcase. Yes, today was definitely going to be brighter.

Last night his plate was full with writing reference and report letters to the counselors about Sherri's sudden disappearance from this locality and her travels to parts unknown, along with college letters for budding archeologists. Carrigan made a mental note to check with Rudoff, the high school principal, concerning the status of Mr. James. Thinking deeper, he decided that he would start the section of Wyoming history today instead of waiting for next week. He always needed the help of Mr. James when Carrigan was bogged down in all the technical jargon about up thrusts and volcanic activity occurring only in certain eras. Carrigan firmly believed that without written documentation to prove the opposite, volcanoes could happen any time they wanted to, and if he wanted dinosaurs to exist the same time as modern man that was ok, too. Just in case James was a short timer, he better use the science teacher's talents quickly so Carrigan didn't embarrass himself in front of the kids. Mr. James knew the difference between a tectonic plate and a plastic one.

The morning bell rang and in filed the faces of the forlorn, careless and indifferent. Mingled sparingly among these were two or three that might still contain a spark of desire to learn something new or different. 'Teach to all, and maybe one would learn' had always been his motto.

"Morning ladies and gentleman," said Carrigan.

"Hi, Mr. C., are we doing anything today?" came the class response.

"Only if you want to, the only things you have to do is die and sometimes pay taxes."

"But you'll flunk us if we don't do anything," cried the assemblage.

Carrigan's pat answer was then returned. "No, only you can choose to flunk, and everyone has a chance to live their lives by their own choices."

Carrigan long since stopped being bored by this exchange and now accepted it as part of life. It was the duty of the kids to whine and his duty to ignore it.

"All right, grab your shorts and pull down your hats, cause we're going to start learning something about Wyoming history," said Carrigan gleefully, the groaning from the class only goading him on.

"Not another long lecture, Mr. C. Pleeeeeeze," said Fat Dawn who took Carrigan's class every chance she got.

Fat Dawn was an interesting student. Innumerable times she approached Carrigan and wanted to take classes through him to avoid other teachers. Sometimes the counselors allowed this because there was little sense in her taking a basic algebra class three times from the same math teacher and flunking the class each of the three times. Carrigan, upon occasion, was able to teach the material in a different way and get the objective across. When he first came to Lakota High, this caused some turf issues with other teachers, but they soon realized that it helped their classes to get the problem students out, and now they worked well with Carrigan by providing lessons for these kids to be taught in his room. This class that Dawn was in today was a reading class and Fat Dawn was supposed to be in here.

Last year when she was taking algebra from Carrigan, his phone would ring late at night. When he answered, only breathing, well maybe panting, could be heard on the other end. Carrigan tried to listen to Dawn's breathing in class to see if she was the culprit, but matching the sounds proved very difficult. The worst problem was that Dawn thought she was a size five, when actually size eighteen clothes would have been too tight. The size five clothes on her were like band-aids on road kill. They covered the raw parts but didn't help heal the rest of the carcass. When he was grading papers at his desk, she liked to stand close behind him and rub whatever part of her she could, which in her case was considerable, against his back and arms. He gave brief thoughts to telling her he was gay, but decided the fallout from the rumors would be too great. There was no telling who might be gathered around his desk if that story circulated around the school.

Finally he told her that as attractive as she was, he was in a committed relationship with someone else who would be very jealous if she caught Dawn standing that close too him. This seemed to simmer the situation down some and Carrigan was very careful never to get trapped in the room alone with her. At the start of this year she asked him if he was still with someone and Carrigan explained he was. He even added to the lie by saying they met on a blind date, chuckling to himself when he thought of the joke about the blind date. One friend trying to get the other friend to agree to a blind date made the statement that although the prospective girl wasn't particularly attractive, nor did she have vast sums of money, she didn't sweat much for a fat girl.

Unfortunately, Carrigan thought of this joke when Dawn was rubbing herself on him. He never allowed himself to look closely enough to see if it was true about the lack of perspiration. The phone calls stopped, and Carrigan rearranged his desk to prevent students from standing near him. Her behavior this year was appropriate, even if her size of clothing wasn't. Maybe she found her own blind date to tantalize with her fleshy charms.

"Nope, I'm only going to talk for five minutes and then you get a chance. I know all of you are very good at talking, especially you, Dawn, since you manage to do it all day."

Blushing, Dawn decided she was getting the bad end of this exchange and zipped her lip. Carrigan continued with his opening lecture on how the beauties of the geological surroundings, the countryside the kids took for granted everyday, came into being.

> *Well first of all you need to understand that the ages of the earth can be compared to the ages all of you are going through. First a person is a baby and they do kid stuff such as learning to talk, roll over, walk and those sorts of things. Then they are young people and like to participate in riding bikes and hunting frogs, but pretty soon they start enjoying the company of the opposite sex, and before you know it, teenagers arrive.*
>
> *Next comes young adulthood and the young*

people begin to think about getting married. After that they are older than dirt like myself, families are raised and the kids go off to college or start raising families of their own. At last people retire and just do what they want to do. I like to call these four stages the kid stage, the young stage, the middle age stage, and the old stage. Geology is similar to this because it also has four major stages correlating to a person's life with some sub-stages thrown it. You will need to know these four big stages and some of the in-betweens.

The kid stage is called the Pre-Cambrian and this happened about 3 billion to 570 million years ago. The young stage is called the Paleozoic stage and this happened about 570 million years ago to 245 million years ago. The middle age stage was the Mesozoic, which I feel is the most interesting stage, just as it should be in your lives. This period happened about 245 million years ago to 66 million years ago. The last stage, the old age stage, was called the Cenozoic stage and this took place from about 66 million years ago to just recently in geologic time.

There wasn't too much going on in the Pre-Cambrian except for rocks and earth were getting moved all about, and the earth was changing pretty rapidly, every 100 million years or so. Around here things were uplifting all over the place. Most of the living organisms were plants, algae and squishy things.

During the Paleozoic stage fish really flourished. This period lasted 230 million years. There were a vast variety of different kinds of fishes evolving because they had to deal with water for their environment. Also there were deep layers of limestone being deposited in the low places as it settled from the water.

Next came the middle age stage or the Mesozoic, this is when all the reptiles happened along. Dinosaurs were roaming about and the land was covered with heavy vegetation including evergreen trees and even some reptiles were starting to fly instead of walk or swim. This middle age period had three sub periods, broken into the Triassic, Jurassic, and the Cretaceous. These three periods you need to know, write them down. Just like the movie Jurassic Park there were dinosaurs cluttering up the landscape. Sometimes scientists find the fossilized bones of the big creatures that were buried by sediments in the rivers. During the Laramie orogeny of the Cretaceous period, which was a time of uplifting that made the Rocky Mountains, these bones were raised to the surface of the earth and can sometimes be found just under the ground because weathering and erosion has removed the top layers of dirt.

All sorts of factors made the earth around us, particularly in this area of Wyoming. Glaciers played a big part in moving rocks, grinding them up and filling in the holes or basins between the mountains. Caves were made from the limestone that was deposited out of the water, sometimes by chemical actions and sometimes by ice working in the rocks. Wind and water erosion shaped our hills, as did volcanoes especially up by Jackson Hole. Folds bent flat surfaces and wrinkled them, and faults slid rocks up and down, sometimes spreading them apart. This really shaped the heights and roughness of the land around us. There were earthquakes that were really just fault lines moving around.

We are also going to learn about three different types of rocks. These three different types are igneous rocks, sedimentary rocks, and metamorphic rocks. Igneous rocks come from volcanic activity and they can cool off either under the ground or on top of it and are labeled by how much silica they have in them. If they have a high content of silica the rock is called granite or rhyolite, depending on where they cooled.

Devil's Tower, here in Wyoming, is an example of igneous rocks that cooled off inside the ground and then erosion washed the dirt from around the sides, leaving it standing tall and proud. This tower is over 1200 feet high and was hidden under the surface of the earth for a long time until it became exposed. The Indians of the area called it Bear's Lodge, and it is considered a very sacred site for them. Teddy Roosevelt made Devil's Tower area a National Park in 1906.

The Indians of the area claim that Devil's Tower arose because seven sisters were playing with their brother. The brother was pretending to be a bear that was chasing them and an evil spirit, wanting to possess the young Indian maids, perhaps for immoral purposes, took over possession of the brother and turned him into an actual bear. The sisters were terrified and attempted to escape the bear by climbing onto a large tree stump. The great Manitou, or Indian Spirit, taking pity on the girls, caused the stump to grow taller and taller. The higher the bear tried to climb the more the stump grew and the young sisters were saved from their lecherous bear brother. Knowing the girls could never go home, the Manitou then took the girls and made them part of the sky and stars, what the Indians call the Hanging Road to Heaven. The thick grooves caused by the bear's claws can still be seen today. Every time you look at the Big Dipper in the sky you can see the sisters watching their home down below.

Sedimentary rocks were made from rocks that were weathered and worn down and then washed around till they were deposited in places like the Laramie Plains. These plains grow lush grasses in the summer and 200 years ago buffalo beyond counting roamed over these high prairies. Indians from all over Wyoming came to hunt the buffalo for their winter supply of food. In places like Chugwater, some historians believe that buffalo were driven off the tall cliffs in the thousands by the Indians who then used all parts of the buffalo for their everyday life. Supposedly that was how Chugwater received its name. As the buffalo fell from the cliffs they splashed into the creek, making a chugging sound. Who knows, it might be true.

Sedimentary rocks are those rocks like sandstone, limestone, shale and even salts and gypsums. When heat or pressure works on rocks and twists and shapes them, then metamorphic rocks are formed. These are some of the oldest rocks in existence. The earth can heat up slate and make shale, twist around limestone and make marble, and pound on mica till it makes schists, which are pretty common in the mountains of this area. Most of the coal in Wyoming came from the cretaceous period and it was made from all the marshy plants that covered the ground. We will even spend some time talking about the dinosaurs that walked around and a few other early animals. After that we will touch on the first people that came to Wyoming and how they arrived here. Naturally, no discussion of Wyoming will be complete without learning about the Indians, the mountain men, and the early pioneers that came here, settled, homesteaded the land, and made this a great place for us to live. We will wrap it up by talking about how much land the State of Wyoming owns, and what they do with the income from renting this land.

Each township of land in Wyoming has two sections, usually Section 16 and Section 36, which the state rents to private people and then turns the income over to school districts. We may even get into how land is divided into acres, sections, townships and ranges and last but not least we will learn why you need to know this information and how it can help you with your lives.

Now Dawn, and the rest of you, I'm done talking and it is time for all of you to begin learning about Wyoming. This is what I expect. I am going to put you into teams of two and I want you to take a particular section of what we have just discussed and do a twenty-slide presentation for the rest of the class that provides a lot more detail than I just went into. I will even ask Mr. James to come in and provide feedback on your presentations, because he knows a whole bunch more about the land and the time periods than do I. Now if you don't have any questions, the first people who choose their groups receive first choice of a subject area. I need your names, what subject you want to present, and then I will help you find information to complete your PowerPoint presentation.

The room exploded in conversation as the kids tried to find a partner that was more ambitious than them. Carrigan couldn't but help smiling to himself. This activity worked well every year, especially the part where the kids had to teach the rest of the class. He remembered an old teaching mentor explaining to him once that doing and learning by teaching was a far better tool for imparting knowledge than just sitting, listening and taking notes. If he was especially sneaky he might even be able to work in some math without the kids knowing they were learning something about it. Besides that, the kids almost enjoyed doing this lesson as they had some choice in choosing the subject matter and they were allowed to play with the newest technical equipment for their presentations.

The rest of the class period passed quickly as the young people were engaged in the research for their projects and Carrigan found himself moving from one group to another giving them ideas on where and how to find information. The biggest battle he faced was convincing them that information was sometimes much easier to find in books rather than on the Internet. With the vast array of information on the web, finding particular facts could be very frustrating. Sometimes books did a better job of specific organization when they needed to find details. The Net was great, however, for cutting and pasting graphics to be used in the presentations.

Surprised by the bell ringing so quickly, Carrigan paused to reflect on what went well during the class and what he would need to adjust about the plan prior to starting this same lesson for third period. Second period planning would give him a chance to pump the principal for information about Mr. James, and speak to the scapegoat science teacher himself about helping with the class project.

Carefully waiting until the hallway outside quieted down and second period was engaged, Carrigan slipped out of his rectangular cell and trekked across the open space toward the bastion of leadership known as the principal's office. In route, he was almost blindsided by a short girl running like mad to make her next class prior to being counted tardy. They exchanged smiles, but Carrigan knew she had no idea the role he played in her early life. Sissy Gleans, or Curly as the kids called her because of the mass of sandy curled hair that perched atop her bespectacled face, entered into Carrigan's life during his tenure as a Child Abuse Investigator for the State of Wyoming. Once shed of his role as a cop, with a dose of being a ranch foreman thrown in, Carrigan took a position with The Department of Family Services investigating child abuse. His past experience as a law enforcement officer would play a relevant role in trying to put back together the broken families that continually seemed to appear in the small towns and countrysides of Wyoming.

Curly's older brother, Jimmy, was a first grader during Carrigan's second year of work with family services. One day, he received a call from an extremely upset teacher requesting that he immediately come to the elementary school to look at some drawings made by Jimmy, who was one of her students. Hearing the panic in her voice, he left the mounds of paperwork signifying the fifty damaged children, and made the short trip to the school. With trembling hands, the teacher handed him four drawings composed by Jimmy during her art session that day.

The first drawing, etched in childish scrawls, indicated a stick figure with a collar around its neck being tied to what appeared to be a clothesline. Beside the shirts hanging on the clothesline, the stick figure showed a wire running from its neck to the line holding the shirts and from this wire ran short curved lightening bolts with the words 'ouch' printed beside them. The stick figure, doglike on the ground, was labeled 'Jimmy'.

The other three pictures displayed two stick figures drawn by the same artist, but one of the figures was a much larger matchstick man with a huge protruding penis jutting outright from its legs. The smaller figure was impaled on the end of the stick man's male organ. A frown and tears were drawn on the diminutive rounded face of the smaller one. The top of her head was portrayed with locks of curly hair. The word 'daddy' was printed in red beside the large stick figure. Graphic in their simplicity, Carrigan realized the reason for the teacher's call, and understood what the pictures would entail if they were accurate.

Carrigan interviewed the artist in the counselor's office and between playing roles of sternness and compassion, prodded the boy to tell the story behind his artwork. Jimmy related that sometimes Mommy tied him to a clothesline and then Daddy (his stepfather) hooked the electric fence charger to the wire and turned it on. Every 30 seconds the charger would deliver 110 volts of low amperage current into him through the line attached to his neck. This punishment often lasted for several hours, but only occurred if he tried to help his little sister when she was alone with 'Daddy', practicing playing 'Mommy'. He was afraid that he would get the electrical treatment for talking to anyone about this, and didn't want to go home that night though he was worried about his little sister, Sissy, if he didn't. Taking a chance Carrigan called law enforcement, arranged a foster home for Jimmy and gave his detailed notes to a judge for the purpose of obtaining a search warrant at the boy's residence.

By ten that night, with aid of the sheriff's deputies, they found Jimmy's residence. Isolated among thousands of acres of wheat fields, the nearest neighbors twenty miles away, sat a small white clapboard house, stark among the waving fields of amber wheat. The dirt front yard's only remarkable feature was two sagging posts with barbwire running between them serving as a clothesline. Two work shirts, the same color as in Jimmy's picture, hung cerulean upon the line in the moonlight. The ranting parents, Jimmy's mother and stepfather, screaming about the abuse of their constitutional rights, were restrained by the deputies as Carrigan searched the house. Three times he went through the small house, finding evidence of a young child within, but not her actual presence. At last returning to the sty of a master bedroom, he noticed the iron railed double bed sat crookedly against the peeling paint of the wall. Grasping the footboard, he pulled the bed from the wall causing the ply board partition behind the bed to fall open. From within this recess he could see the remnants of a white wool blanket, stained brownish yellow from excrement.

The odor bit his senses, even with the mentholated cream he had pushed up each nostril prior to doing the search. This was a trick he learned early in his career of dealing with the dregs of humanity. When he went into houses that reeked with moral decay, his jar of mentholated cream was his medicine bag against evil spirits trying to steal into his body. Amongst the folds of the blanket a young child stared at him over the tops of skinny knees pulled tight to her chest as a barricade of protection.

The child was rushed to the hospital and additional law enforcement was called in, the small, white house grudgingly giving up its clues to the style of parenting it housed. Step by step, Polaroid pictures taken by the parents showing each rung of Sissy's training in becoming 'Mommy' were found hidden in cracks and crevices, almost as if they were dust covered trophies for a child's album. Mommy had served as the photographer.

The case never went to trial; both parents relinquished parental rights to the children and pleaded to felony child abuse rather than face the charges of rape and sodomy in the courts of the small, rural town. The medical evidence gathered from Sissy's small body, with its scarred orifices, along with the pictorial record of 'sexual training' was overwhelming. Both parents received twenty-year sentences and were still incarcerated in their respective places of abode, Rawlins and Lusk, hopefully receiving the full treatment from their fellow inmates that was reserved for sex offenders who had preyed on children.

Jimmy went to a foster family in a nearby town, and when last Carrigan checked, completed high school and was working in the oil fields. Sissy was still living with foster parents here in Rockville, and bore little resemblance to the small child Carrigan pulled from the hole in the wall. Her next few years were filled with labels such as attention deficit disorder, mental retardation, and behavior disordered, as she was passed from foster home to foster home. These people who offered abodes for foster children were horrified when she hid in closets and wrote her parents names with feces from her own body as her ink of choice. As she aged, she attempted to sexually molest animals and would insert candles deep within her own body or coyingly attempt to touch the genital areas of her foster parents.

Long years passed before she found a foster home that convinced her of their love and protection, and provided the consistency and discipline, that allowed her mind to heal. Carrigan's appeal to a juvenile court assured she would attend a specialized school during her grade school years, specialized because it was filled with caring professionals and therapists, and was paid for by the local school district. This was the straw that broke the camel's back and the school district hired Carrigan away from Family Services to teach troubled youth for them. It was cheaper to pay him as an employee, rather than to pay for the children he convinced the courts to place at the school's expense.

In high school Sissy was an excellent student, participated in sports and showed the immature adolescence of all other girls her age. Mission accomplished, the scars were hidden if not removed. He was glad she didn't remember who he was.

Exchanging comments with the school secretaries guarding Jan Rudolf's door, Carrigan entered the office in hopes of engaging Rudolf in conversation concerning the board meeting last night. Principal Rudolf sat behind his desk, both hands propping his gleaming bald head, his eyes cast downward upon the newspaper lying open before him.

"Morning, Rudy," was Carrigan's opening salvo.

Slowly Rudolf raised his eyes, squinting somewhat to observe who was entering his domain. Before answering, Rudolf lowered his eyes back to the paper in front of him.

"Go away, Carrigan. I don't want to listen to you today."

"Why, when all I bring is cheer to this foreign land, am I so poorly treated?" asked Carrigan.

"Because you're just like a vulture, you only come around when you smell carrion."

"I just wanted to know whether to loan Mr. James my suitcase or not," said Carrigan straight faced.

"None of your damn business; go find some kids to teach."

"Come on, Rudy, what's going on?"

"James is gone at the end of the year; they're cutting all of his sections. He's done, RIFfed, out of here, and so am I; now go prey upon some other poor soul."

"What did you do, finally try to protect him and they bounced you too?"

Looking up again, Rudolf turned the paper around for Carrigan to read. There centered in the middle of the page was a picture showing a school car, a Lakota High School car. Behind the driver's steering wheel was a picture of Mr. Rudolf, his baldhead reflecting dully in the candid shot, locked tightly in an embrace with a woman owning much longer and darker hair than the short blonde curls belonging to his wife, Marge. Their lips were matched, and gauging from the hollowness of their cheeks, their tongues were thrusting deeply. Rudolf's left hand was sunken beneath the open buttons of the woman's blouse. Her eyes, set far apart in the tilted head, were closed, turned blindly upward. Even closed, Carrigan could tell those were the eyes of Trisha Collingworth, the new language arts teacher who was not partial to potato soup. The caption on the picture read--'Jan Rudolf, Lakota High School Principal, providing training to his staff.'

The article then rambled on about the declining morals in the schools and how school prayer would bring the voice of God back to our classrooms.

"Jesus Christ, Jan," said Carrigan softly, "how long has this been going on?"

"Too long, Carrigan, too long. Now get out of here so I can call Marge before the paper is delivered to our door."

Quietly Carrigan left the office, pulling the door shut behind him.

"Hold all calls for Jan," he told the secretaries, "he's not feeling well this morning and just needs some time before you start shoveling any problems his way. If you get any discipline complaints in, push them off to me this period or to Chuck next period, he has planning then."

With that, Carrigan went in search of Mr. James to request his help. Perhaps the school board did Mr. James a favor by forcing him out. This school teaching was starting to get more complicated the longer he was in it, thought Carrigan. The basest of human emotions--lust, revenge, and greed--seemed to continually play a recurring theme in the lives of people around him. Carrigan existed in this world long enough to know not to judge any other person's behavior. Like his father always said, 'Don't sit in judgment of your fellow travelers on this earth until you have walked a mile or two in their moccasins.'

Jan's wife, Marge, certainly wasn't any sexual goddess but then neither were many other women her age, and Marge would be crushed when she read the headlines. It's just plain amazing, thought Carrigan, the extent to which other people don't think about the amount of pain they can cause to those closest in their lives.

Carrigan found Mr. James packing boxes in the science building. The room always tingled with a funny smell, no matter what type of incense the teacher burned or air freshener he used. It was somewhere between the smell of dead cats bathed in embalming fluid, dry phosphorus burning, decayed rotting plant matter, and locker room sweat fighting each other for dominance. Mixed together the odors were truly unique and Carrigan decided he would be in a constant state of nausea if he taught there all day; it was bad enough just to visit the room for a short while.

"Mr. James, sorry to interrupt your class, but I need some help again this year," said Carrigan trying to hold his breath against the noxious perfumed odor hanging in the air.

"Hey Carrigan," James replied, "you ain't interrupting a helluva lot, just those four seniors, who haven't done shit all year and are now trying to sweet talk me out of a passing grade."

The seniors in question glanced up at Carrigan, smiled, and returned to their conversations about who was boffing whom these days.

"I'm doing that Wyoming thing again this year and we should start having presentations about Monday of next week. May I use you again to help be a resource person for us? My 'inclining, reclining and anticlining' aren't any better this year than they were last time."

"As long as you don't expect me to find any 'faults'," said James, playing into the role.

"Na, the kids quake in their shoes when I grade them," said Carrigan finally cracking his straight face. "Seriously," he continued, "I would really appreciate it. Now what's all this shit about you not coming back next year?"

"Right as rain," replied James, "and you know, I was really upset last night, but the longer I think about it, I'm looking forward to leaving. My wife still has a good job at the plant, five more years and I can take retirement and there are a lot of places around here that I wouldn't mind checking out. My mom left me some money and her house when she died last year and the old Bronco is paid for. Beer money and fishing supplies are about all I need, and I won't have to put up with this shit any more. The resource district has been after me to do some independent water testing for them and so have the real estate companies. Hell, I can even fish and take water samples at the same time, it's going to be all right."

Carrigan could detect no sense of bitterness, and after offering to write letters or attempt work actions against the decision, Carrigan wasn't surprised when James turned down the offers for collegial support. It was almost as if once the decision that he wasn't going to be here next year was made, Mr. James felt relief. James said he could farm out his kids a couple of class periods next week and he would stroll into Carrigan's room to help him and the kids with the presentations.

Carrigan glanced up toward the warm spring sunshine, thankful to be leaving the smell behind, and gauged it was almost noon. He couldn't remember which student group was serving lunch today, but the morning was going so smoothly he decided not to tempt the fates. It had been several weeks since he experienced a good grease attack, and he decided to drive down to the local diner for a hamburger and fries. Not the type you received from the 'choke and pukes', but a real 'pounder' on a homemade bun, with lots of fresh onions, pickles slices, tomatoes, and fries, fresh cooked, dripping with fat. Damn he thought, that really sounds good today. The diner wasn't filled to capacity when Carrigan slid onto a stool and smiled at the girl behind the counter.

"Hi Tracie," he said, "I thought you were working at Andy's Burgers."

"Nope, Mr. C., the tips there sucked and Andy played too much grab ass, if you know what I mean," smiled Tracie.

"Well, give me a half pound deluxe with lots of onions and fries and a big lemonade, and hurry a little will ya, third period comes pretty quick?" said Carrigan.

"Sure thing, Mr. C. Do you want it rare?"

"Yep, wipe its nose and run it by, Tracie. Thanks."

Tracie was a past student who got knocked up by the football team her sophomore year and now was the mother of the cutest six-year-old quarterback Carrigan had ever seen. She fell for the old I'll-still-love-you-tomorrow routine. The play continued to work until she became pregnant and then the boys went on defense and no one claimed responsibility. Carrigan didn't even think she knew which member of the team scored in her backfield. The result, a little girl named Katie, played in a youth team that Carrigan coached, and she could throw better and run faster than any of the boys her age. Tracie tried coming back to school after she gave birth to her daughter, but daycare was hard to find since she wasn't receiving any income, and she found little in common with the other students. Tracie was a hard worker, often holding down two jobs, one to eat on and the other to pay the babysitter, and Carrigan always admired her determination. He helped her study when she completed her GED Tests, and steered her toward taking night classes through the local college nearby. Tracie really wanted to be a Vet. Tech. and in one more year she would have her associate of arts degree in veterinary technology, and the first leg up on getting a better job for herself and her Katie. Several local ne're-do-wells, were always trying to provide Katie with a brother or sister, but Tracie steered clear of them and Carrigan heard she was dating a professor at the junior college. Time to grow up, that's all some of them need he thought, and even though she made some poor choices earlier in her life, Tracie seemed to be traveling down the right trail now.

The ground beef arrived, served still steaming on the heavy crock platter. A separate plate was needed to hold the small mountain of French fries, which Carrigan smothered in ketchup and salsa. He ate quickly, licking the grease from his fingers and then washed it all down with the last gulp of the lemonade, fresh squeezed with the seeds still floating in the glass. Sometimes it just didn't get much better than this. Looking at the neon clock ticking away his moments of freedom, Carrigan left $10 by his plate and snatched two cinnamon toothpicks from the holder by the door. A fiver was too much of a tip to leave, but Tracie would use it toward Katie and Carrigan didn't mind donating toward those kinds of causes. As he was leaving the diner he nodded to three farmers who had just entered the restaurant and were seating themselves in a booth by the door.

"Hey, Carrigan," said the oldest of the group, his thumbs hooked smugly in the straps of his bib overalls. "What the hell you teaching up at that high school? Seems to me it's something we all wished we were learning. Maybe next week you can get your picture in the paper."

Carrigan thought briefly of removing the smugness from the farmer's tobacco stained teeth, but pushed the thought away, and instead replied simply. "Hell, I didn't know you good ol' boys could read the newspaper. Have you been taking home study courses?" He was well out the door before the farmers, looking at each other, finally understood his answer.

The burger didn't set quite so well when he thought about the coming phone conversation between Jan and Marge. There just wasn't any easy way to get through that, and both would also have to endure the snide remarks and staring glances from the community and the school. Yup, thought Carrigan, we all have to live by the choices we make, the problem was, those closest to us also had to live by them, even if they didn't have a part in the deciding.

Carrigan slid the '79 back into his parking place near the rear of the school. The best part about this pickup was that everyone knew she belonged to him, and that the old girl was far more capable of handing out damage than she was at receiving it. The students always parked several cars away so the heavy bumpers on the pickup and her high swinging doors didn't dent the sides of their new, foreign imports. Gertrude, the name that just seemed to fit the pickup, paid little attention to the dents and dings of life, and her heavily steeled frame and body panels had little to fear from her herd members in the parking lot. There was a rumor around the school that Carrigan once drove completely over the top of a small car that had the audacity to run into his front bumper in the middle of an intersection. Carrigan never denied the rumor because it always served to keep his parking place open, and besides, the story was true.

The changes were made in his lesson plans as the third period students began filing in the door, still stuffing down the last gulps of Surge and chocolate that were the main courses of their luncheon plate. This class was the most challenging of the day, and Carrigan always prepared for something to go wrong, because it usually did. It was a big reading class, filled mostly with people who didn't read, either because they didn't want to or couldn't. He also would be forced to endure another helping of Fat Dawn. The schedule claimed she was taking a social studies class she flunked last year but Fat Dawn often needed two class periods to finish her lessons in reading. Also enrolled were Becky Lansing, Big Reed's daughter, and then, of course, there was Tommy.

Why was it that Carrigan always noticed the kids that were just a little different from their classmates, the ones who could but wouldn't, the ones who shouldn't but did anyway, or the ones who might be but never were.

Tommy was one of those. What the heck was 'one of those' anyway, he thought. When Tommy was a freshman his hair was spiked and colored, no one knew what shade of the rainbow might appear above his serious face from day to day. Silver chains hung in profusion from belt loop to pocket, restraining him, perhaps from himself. Slender in build, the sagging pants hung low and baggy on his slim form, threatening any minute to fall completely to his ankles, and would have except for the constant hoisting he performed. Stairs were difficult barricades for Tommy; each leg must be swung sideways to achieve elevation, the low hanging crotch forbidding the climbing motion. Tommy's eyes rarely held indications of mirth; they were deep pools of dull brown, and no assault into his quality world seemed to cause change. Carrigan was one of the few teachers who did not label him as a future dropout by the end of Tommy's freshman year. Upon reaching sixteen, those who had been his classmates were academically of junior standing, while Tommy was still being enrolled in freshman classes. These classes he amused by playing the role of prankster and resident bad boy. His association of friends changed from the maturing students his age, to the 'outback' crowd, anyone with a cigarette for the day. The chains were not as evident; the hair was cropped close to the skull now, and black emerged as the color of choice in clothing. The eyes, however, never changed, remaining darkened pools of pain looking inward. By seventeen the close-cropped hair lengthened to butch, uncolored and dirty, his associations grew rougher and younger. The fan club dwindled to the twelve-year-old male 'wanna bes' and several young, hard-faced girls capable of fulfilling his needs for smokes. He tried sex with these girls but his few fumbling attempts resulted in a wilting failure on his part, causing the young vixens to giggle wildly when discussing him with their friends. He hated the way the other young girls would wiggle their little fingers at him when they walked by, they were only stupid fag bitches anyhow he thought.

The bad boy pantomime during class was stale now, not even the freshman found him amusing. Teachers removed him, sometimes forcibly, at their first chance, depriving him of the audience he craved. The eyes continued unchanging, dull, humorless, and murky. They darkened even more as the jocks sought him out in the hallways to practice 'locker buffing' as they called it. Slammed against the metal doors by the athletically chosen, they would slide him down the rows of steel until stopped by unsympathetic teachers, or till his rage escalated to the level which scared even the jocks.

As an aging leader of the out-backs, so named by teachers because of their chosen location for nicotine inhaling, Tommy railed vague threats against the stupidity of school and its inhabitants. His young followers encircled him, followed his every mood, their young faces nodding sagely in agreement with Tommy's protestations. His first thoughts of getting even, which came to him in November, dealt with stealing a tank and smashing it through the double orange doors, destroying everything in his path.

"Cool, go for it man," urged on the boys between classes.

Tommy changed his desire for revenge toward something more achievable, tanks being hard to come by; his thoughts turned toward fire.

"Yeah dude, burn the fucking school down, yeah man," they agreed.

Christmas Eve a Molitoff cocktail was hurled against the windows of the high school building. The double strength glass warded off the fiery attempt and merely blackening the window as the gasoline burned itself out. Prestige points were gained amongst the disillusioned, but no one squealed to authorities about the fire thrower. In March, an alley cat, hunting among the school dumpsters failed to recognize his peril as a noose tightened over its head. Choking and hissing, the cat was dragged over the limb of a large pine tree marking the school entrance. For half an hour Tommy watched the twisting shape dislodging showers of pinecones and needles as it fought against the wire necktie, at last succumbing and hanging lifeless like a banner proclaiming pain and mistreatment. The janitors removed the feline body and decided not to inform administration; perhaps the school's neighbors didn't like cats. Toward the end of school, the last ointment from the cat's death had been smeared on Tommy's soul, and a new balm was needed. Carrigan knew little of Tommy's day-to-day life, only that he was one of those kids, and that try as he might, reading class offered little to Tommy.

Computers were a bright spot in Tommy's life. Through the high-speed connections he found web sites advertising thoughts that he felt. Worlds of scientific explanations were revealed, especially those that explained cordite, ammonium fertilizer, fuel oil, black powder, and timers. At home, the broken TV offered little stimulation, but the printed web pages from the school printer were read and re-read and then hidden under his bed. His father long ago gave up paternal thoughts about Tommy, but did pay the rent and sometimes brought home food between his long road trips as a big rig trucker. His mother found freedom running far away from Tommy and his father. She was somewhere in Vegas working in a casino. Free school lunches and stolen brown bags provided most of the nutritional requirements for Tommy. It was the lack of emotional factors and stimulation that left him close to starvation. Having read <u>Peter Pan</u> as a little boy, Tommy felt he fit the role perfectly; he was the chosen one to guide the lost boys. Thoughts of sinking the 'pirate ship' continually played across his mind.

Becky Lansing was Tommy's one significant tie to Lakota High School, and had been ever since she transferred here for the start of this semester. Becky was in Carrigan's afternoon reading class along with Tommy. Carrigan liked to believe it was the variety of reading material rather than Becky's slim, long legs that brought Tommy to class; either way Tommy came and read, discussed and looked at Becky, although not always in that order. Becky's mother continually reminded Carrigan, during parent teacher meetings, that Becky was deprived of oxygen during her first few minutes of life, and this deprivation left the young girl in a child-like state in many areas. Perhaps she believed Carrigan could fix this defect.

Becky would nod and smile, and read energetically whatever material was presented to her, but seldom gained meaning from the printed word. From grade to grade, through other schools she advanced, smiling and nodding, showing rows of bright teeth. She often dressed closer to her mental age than her actual accrual of years, which were fifteen. White, low-cut blouses, sometimes decorated with cartoon characters and short pleated skirts that exposed the long tan legs running clear down to the sandaled feet with painted toenails were common vestments for her. Becky was a cheerleader, her smile and looks guaranteeing the position even if she couldn't remember the cheers. Deep down she was aware that she wasn't bright, but when she smiled no one seemed to care. Lusted after by the athletes, she was popular among the boys who always dreamed of going out with her until they did. She was included among the snobbish cliqués of the girls because of the followings of male admiration she attracted and thus she graced the halls of Lakota High. Sometimes she let boys touch her, but never in places her mother said were dirty. She knew what happened then, her mother had shown her on her Barbie Dolls. She really didn't like to be alone with boys anyway, much preferring the company of girls where she didn't have to listen so hard to try and understand what they were saying.

Tommy was about out of ideas to get her attention. He begged her to go out back with him and smoke between classes, but she just smiled and said no. He tried showing her how tough and brave he was, but again she smiled and turned her head away. She didn't smoke, didn't screw, didn't drink or use drugs. Tommy just couldn't figure out what her fix was but he kept coming to reading class just in case she changed her mind about his favorite subjects.

Becky did introduce some variety into Tommy's life. At night when Tommy was home in bed, the empty house offering little in the way of family, Tommy would take out the pictures of explosive devices. He could feel himself growing hard and powerful as he imagined building a bomb. Not like when he was with those dumb junior high bitches, but really potent. The bigger the bomb he imagined, the harder he would become, his hand motion moving faster and faster until at last his device went off. Becky's picture in her cheerleading uniform, pasted against the peeling, stained wallpaper, offered some change in this routine, as he imagined exploding into her, deep between those long brown legs, forever wiping the childish smile from her face. Sometimes he tried to determine which turned him on the most. Bombs or Becky, it was a hard choice.

Carrigan went through his same lesson plans in this class talking about how the landforms in Wyoming came about until he arrived at the part about the volcanoes in Jackson Hole.

"Mr. C.," said Becky excitedly, waving her arm in the air, "Daddy and I built a volcano once for science fair and it went off and everything, and the judges said I did real good."

"That's nice, Becky," replied Mr. C.

"Can I do that again? My Daddy can help me, can I, can I?"

"Well, we're really going to do projects that have more to do with this area, and there wasn't much volcanic activity around here."

"Please, I will read about them and everything."

"OK," said Carrigan giving in. Becky might get something out of this, at least the other kids wouldn't whine because they got stuck with her in a class project.

"Yo, Mr. C.," said Tommy jumping into the conversation. "How about me doing volcanoes, too. I kinda like to watch them spurt their hot juice all over the place?"

"Lava, Tommy, lava is the word, and if you jerk my chain you're going to visit the hallway today."

"No, Mr. C., I wasn't trying to be smart-ass, I promise I won't give you any shit, just let me do this volcano thing, OK?"

"All right you two, you can make a small model of a volcano, but there is much more required. You will need to put together a twenty-slide PowerPoint presentation about volcanoes, where they were active in Wyoming, and how they create landforms. Can you do that?"

"Sure, Mr. C., we can do that, can't we, Becky?"

Becky just smiled. The rest of the class was paired into teams to take various epochs and make presentations on the landforms found around the Laramie Mountain Range. Carrigan noted, after the bell, Tommy was arranging a time to meet Becky in the school library. This should be interesting, thought Carrigan; maybe this is the spark Tommy needs to actually do something in school other than just breathe the air. The briefest sensation of danger breathed across the back of his neck. Tommy and the daughter of Big Reed, school board member--it was surely a pairing that would make an interesting volcano.

It was evidently perfect timing for Tommy as he was returned to the school after ditching fourth hour. Grabbing Becky, just at the end of third hour, he arranged to meet her in the school library to plan building the volcano and gathering material for the presentation. Fourth period he would skip class to go home, change his clothes and maybe even steal some of his father's aftershave. At last, here was his big chance with Becky and he was going to make the most of it. He tried to remember all of the things he wouldn't do--no swearing, no flipping people off, and he would try not to stare down her blouse at her firm young tits, just waiting to be held. Jesus, he thought, she never even wears a bra. Well, he wouldn't look much, just if she acted like she wanted him to.

He just smiled as he walked past the black-shirted students lighting up for their afternoon fix following their release from school for the day. He even resisted the temptation to take a drag from the proffered Camel. The smoke would taste good but he wasn't taken any chances, not after he just used half a tube on the old toothbrush he found under the sink in his house.

"You guys just go ahead and smoke your brains out," Tommy said. "I have to go meet Becky for a date."

"Yeah, sure," said the runt of the litter, "you got a date with Becky, Becky one hand you mean."

"Remind me to beat the shit out of you when I get done," said Tommy, quickly removing the smiles from the faces of the boys.

Tommy sauntered into the library and sat down at the smallest table in the room.

The minutes ticked by and still Becky didn't show, most of the kids in the hallways left for their homes; gathered in groups of twos and threes, they departed from the school leaving the confines behind them as they planned activities for the afternoon, and still Becky didn't show. Finally even the librarians were getting ready to go home and Tommy finally accepted that Becky wasn't going to arrive. Heedless of his snarls and threats that he would get even if they didn't leave him alone, the librarians

72

escorted him out of the library and through the double doors, locking the doors behind him. By now Tommy was fuming. Five blocks he marched away from the school, to the nearest telephone hanging on the outside wall of the local Quick Mart. He didn't know where Becky lived but when he found her dad's name in the book, he would know which house held the traitorous bitch. The further he walked the deeper his anger swelled. Fucking bitch, he thought, nobody stands up Tommy Columbo. Goddamn slut is going to pay for this.

By the time he arrived at the telephone his anger had cooled, cooled into a deep recess far inside him, cooled into a simmering hatred. Gaining control of his anger, he searched the yellow pages and found the ad for Lansing's Drug Store, inside the frame of the add was a line of script, for emergencies call 1800-Big-Reed (244-7333). He dialed the toll free number that required no change from his pocket and when Big Reed answered he calmly asked for Becky.

"Who's calling please?" asked Big Reed.

"Mr. Lansing, this is Tommy Columbo. Becky and I were planning to work on a history project today after school, and she didn't show up at the library. I was worried and just wanted to check and make sure she was OK."

"Just a minute, Tommy, I'll put her on the phone," Big Reed's statements sounding more like an order than a request.

Tommy waited as he heard muffled voices through the receiver, and finally a childish voice said, "Hi Tommy, Mommy forgot to tell me I had to go to cheerleading practice this afternoon. I was going to tell you tomorrow that I couldn't go to the library. I'm all done now. You can come over to my house if you want to, Daddy can't help us tonight, but Mommy is home and she knows how to turn on the computer. We live at 3434 Birch Lane."

Almost taken aback by her simplicity, Tommy felt his anger relaxing. "Sure," he said, "I had some things to do myself. What if I stop by around 7 o'clock?"

Tommy could almost feel the nodding head and see the smile on the other end as the line went dead. She sure doesn't say much thought Tommy.

He should have known which house it was, the big white one with the tall pillars in front, right beside the third hole of the golf course. Tommy didn't usually cruise this part of town. The cops got all pissy when he and the boys even went near the golf course. By seven he was ringing the front door bell and Mrs. Lansing was letting him into the house, telling him how nice it was for him to come over, and would he like some cookies while he and Becky were working. Becky smiled at them when they entered the kitchen. She was sitting at the kitchen table, her long, brown legs drawn up under her chin, the wave of blonde hair spilling down over her shoulders framing the words "PEPPERDINE" on her sweatshirt. Her attire was changed little except her cheerleading shorts were shorter, bright white against the copper of her legs, and she switched the sandals for Scooby Dooby Do slippers that stared suspiciously at Tommy when he entered the room. The strangeness continued as Mrs. Lansing offered Tommy a seat at the kitchen table, a spotless and shinning centerpiece among the gleaming stainless steel of the kitchen. Tommy wasn't even sure what some of the appliances were, but they looked important and professional. Becky sat at the table across from Tommy eating and smiling as Mrs. Lansing opened up a laptop, plugged it into the phone jack on the counter and then hustled off to some other room in the house, doubtlessly to buff more of the furniture.

This scene here in the track lighted kitchen might as well have been the moon, Tommy thought, as he realized he was at a loss for words. He tried to find the reservoir of anger deep inside him, but was unable to swim in that direction. Somehow this setting and Becky's freckled face completely threw him off his stride. Maybe this was the way other kids lived, in big white houses on golf courses, in homes that mothers fed you cookies, but the environment was too sterile, too alien for Tommy. The kitchen he was in, Becky's kitchen, was bigger than his house.

"Here is the way I see it," said Tommy finally, his voice almost seeming to echo among the Radar ranges and Frigidares. "I will write the script about the volcanoes up in Jackson Hole, if you will find some pictures and put them on PowerPoint. I think the hard drive is going out of my laptop computer. Then I can give you the text and you can type them in your computer and save them on your Zip. All we have to do then is load the Zip at school and presto we have a picture show. I'm taking a metals class in school so I will build the form of the model volcano. Then if you and your dad can bring home some of the stuff from his store that we need for the project, we can make a real cool volcano that will spur…. Er… flow all over the place, and even Mr. C. will have to give us a good grade."

"That sounds fun," said Becky. "Do you want some milk or anything?"

"No thanks," replied Tommy, "I'm trying to quit."

Becky smiled, and then more seriously said, "Oh, I'm sorry. I shouldn't have asked you."

"It's OK," grinned Tommy. "Now that this project is all planned out do you want to watch a movie or something?"

"I can't, Tommy. Daddy says I can only watch the TV on the weekends."

"Hey, me too, man; our folks are just alike. Maybe we can get together this weekend and watch some, you could come to my house."

"Thanks Tommy, that sounds like fun, but the cheerleaders are coming over and we get to have a pajama party."

At a loss for any other opening, Tommy just sat there and watched Becky eat the rest of her cookies. The Nickelodeon screen saver of the forgotten laptop whirred quietly as she ate one at a time; carefully twisting them apart, and then licking the cream from the inside, before nibbling the outside in tiny little bites. Tommy began to realize that maybe Becky wasn't like any other girl he had known. Maybe she hadn't stood him up, all in all things weren't going too badly for a first date. She hadn't said that she wouldn't go out with him, just that she couldn't this weekend. Slow and easy were the words that kept running through his mind.

"Well, alrighty then," Tommy laughed, "I need to get home before my Mom and Dad begin to worry about me. Hey, would it be all right if I use your bathroom before I go?"

"OK," said Becky, frowning at the disobedient Oreo that broke in two as she was trying to twist it apart. "There is one right by the front door. I will tell Mommy that you have to go. Do you want her to drive you home?"

"No," said Tommy quickly, "I really like the exercise, besides Dad told me to walk by a house just down the street that is for sale, we are thinking of buying it."

"OK," smiled Becky as she finally finished her cookie before showing Tommy the doorway down the hall, "I'll tell Mommy and be right back."

Tommy watched the swish of her hips as she went in search of Mommy. Jesus, he thought, has she got a tight ass or what? In the bathroom the gleam was the same, except in the color white instead of stainless steel. Tommy was careful to lift the seat and took dead aim to avoid any yellowing splashes on the pallid carpeting. With a final shake and an adjustment, needed after watching Becky eat the cookies, he noticed the Barbie Dolls on the lip of the bathtub, their long tanned legs protruding from the miniature shorts, acting for all the world as if they were perched next to their own private swimming pool.

Without thinking he picked one of the dolls up, thrusting it down into the back pocket of his pants and then he tugged his shirt over the top, checking in the mirror to make sure the doll didn't show. Becky and Mommy were waiting for him when he opened the door to leave the bathroom. Becky hugged Mommy tightly as she waved to him goodnight and both women smiled goodbyes as he walked down the curved stone walkway. He heard the front door shut behind him and the feeling that this was all a dream came flooding through his consciousness. Did people really act and live like this? Barbie and Tommy took the long way home, stopping at several holes on the golf course to break the flagsticks and scratch the words, 'cops are pricks' with their sharpened ends on #4 and #5 greens. Nope, it wasn't a bad first date after all.

Carrigan also was feeling that the day hadn't been too bad. In fact, with only a couple weeks left to the end of school, he almost felt buoyed by the shortness of the remaining year. Most of his classes would be doing presentations, and he could concentrate on cleaning his room, perhaps even filing some of the neglected documents that were scattered about his room. His house in town seemed to welcome him home and he was glad that he remembered there were three beers left in the refrigerator. His favorite TV show was on tonight, and while he was watching this show, maybe he would start unpacking some of his fishing supplies. A trip to the mountains this coming weekend might be just the tonic to kick start him out of the doldrums he was feeling of late.

Maybe he would run up to a piece of ground he purchased last year from an old German moon shiner who Carrigan visited at the senior citizen home. He'd met the old German when Carrigan made continual vigils to sit beside the senior Carrigan's bedside and hold his father's hand as his aging parent lay dying from cancer. The old German would come into the room during those nights and regale him with tales from the old days, the old days when Laramie Peak cast its mountainous blue shadow across the land, and the river running from the far blue sources sparkled and murmured forgotten tales and adventures. Carrigan loved the land and was fortunate to have bought a section--640 acres--that abutted a section of state land, School Section 36, because it doubled his access to the river running through it.

Chapter 4
The Meadow

The morning broke early, evidenced by only the faintest light seeping into the eastern sky. La Ramie knelt by the small rocked fire, slowly adding twigs and cones, urging it back to life. Kills-Crowe and the boys weren't in sight. Night Wind sat on a log by the small pond twisting a rawhide string around the braids of her long hair. The wraps were beaded on each end and from a piece of fur in the middle hung two owl feathers. When finished, the long braids fell down her back, as straight as the spine upon which they lay. The beaded ends of the rawhide and the two feathers crossed her chest coming to rest over her heart, floating and bouncing as she walked back to the fire. Smiling at Joshua, she quickly set to frying small balls of cornmeal in the kettle of remaining dog fat, and heated a small tin of water into which she crumbled bitterroot leaves. The tea quickly boiled in the awakened fire and she dropped the cornballs in the popping grease.

"Two canyons north," she said, "by the trail of the short waterfall, we can ride past the shadow of Blue Mountain to Elk Ridge."

"That canyon is much rougher and harder to travel than the first draw with the bitter cottonwoods. Kills-Crowe thinks it will be easier to pull the travois," answered La Ramie.

"Easier is not always better," she replied, a quick smile disarming any sharpness to her words.

"Waterfall Canyon it is then," concluded La Ramie.

Joshua was surprised that La Ramie gave in so easily. He watched her as she moved away and started her morning chores. Remembering the sound of the owl wings in the darkness, he wondered if Night Wind knew something they didn't.

"Kills-Crowe and I," said La Ramie to Joshua, "decided the best way to reach the great buffalo plain was travelin' together, 'round the base of Blue Mountain. Without his older sons for protection, our rifles and his make the odds better for all. Both canyons lead to the snows of Elk Ridge two days ride. Night Wind, she's strange sometimes, but I never knowed when she was wrong."

Joshua nodded, anticipating the view of Blue Mountain up close. He just finished sipping his tea when Kills-Crowe and the boys walked down the slope. Together they ate the hot cornballs that sizzled in their mouths, finished the tea, drowning the fire before packing the horses for the morning's journey.

Heading due north again, the mounted horses quickly covered the distance across the remaining flat plain. Behind them, the hillock where they spent the night shrank and then disappeared from sight as they began to enter an area of rolling hills. Gone were the deep waves of sagebrush, shining silver in the morning light, and the earth was turning redder like the cleavered hills on the other side of the Platte. The smell of cedar was heavy in the air and by late morning indicated by the sun's climb into the sky, they were sitting on the edge of a steep canyon. The bottom, half a mile below them, was thick and green with foliage swaying in the early summer breeze. Hawks circled high in the sky, soaring on unfelt currents, searching for signs of movement below indicating lunch was near at hand. La Ramie took the lead here, turning back westward again along the rim, which wound its way toward small masses of hills, heavily forested with trees, over which Blue Mountain peeked its head. After several miles he stopped, stood in his stirrups looking down into the canyon. Wheeling his horse around, he rode back past the group, and plunging directly into a thick stand of cedar, he disappeared from sight.

"Well, are you comin' or not?" floated La Ramie's voice through the cedar.

Night Wind was the next to go through the foliage followed by the boys. Joshua brought up the rear. Once through the clinging brush, Joshua found they were angling down into the canyon on a narrow game trail that switched back on itself twice before ending in the bottom and continuing through the canopy of trees.

"This here leads on up to Elk Ridge," said La Ramie.

"An old man should travel trails that are smooth," agreed Kills-Crowe.

No word in response came from Night Wind as she slid from her horse, loosening the cinch, allowing him to drink his fill of the water running in the bottom of the canyon. The two men looked at each other, grinned,

78

and then found places deep enough to allow their horses to drink also. All three boys were soon off running through the water, splashing and laughing when Spotted Owl slipped and fell in the wet mud. Scowling, he emerged, mud-speckled, only to begin throwing rocks at the bigger boys he couldn't keep up with.

"How like a man to pout when he doesn't get his way," she observed.

Returning to his mother's side, Spotted Owl refused even to glance toward the other two boys who were making faces at him from behind the thick trunks of the cottonwood trees. This, his ninth summer would be one of turmoil.

"Spotted Owl," said Joshua, "suppose you could lead my packhorse for a while. My arm is plumb tuckered out from dragging this beast, and if I don't rest my shoulder it might plumb fall off."

Casting a swift glance at the breadth of Joshua's shoulder and the hard muscles that bulged his woolen shirt, Night Wind didn't think it would fall off anytime soon, but was amazed at the bright grin that appeared on Spotted Owl's face.

"Now don't lose him, guard him with your life; this whole trip ain't no good if we don't have our supplies," finished Joshua.

Quickly leaping astride his pony, Spotted Owl accepted the rope lead from Joshua. Now, sitting proudly, the young Indian led the packhorse across the stream, following closely behind La Ramie, up the winding trail on the other side.

Although fairly flat, the next ten miles led their way through dense clumps of cedar trees and the red earth turned to gray shale, brittle and sharp under the horses' hooves. By noon the path chosen by La Ramie sloped downward, gently at first, and then rapidly increased in steepness until once more they sat before a clear running stream, faster and wider than the last. Here the trees were older and twisted; fallen logs lay intermingled like matchsticks crossing and re-crossing the stream. This brush, too, was bright green, but instead of cottonwoods, the ground close to the water was shrouded with willow clumps. To their left the water ran between two, high, canyon walls and then rounded back, the sharp ramparts closing out the rest of the creek from their view. Resting their horses again, the small band drank the clear water and finished handfuls of the remaining cornballs. The dog grease, cold and rancid, was bitter to Joshua's taste. Spotted Owl never released his charge on the lead rope while the horses drank and spoke sharply to the pony when he lagged after the group turned westward toward the base of Blue Mountain, now hidden by the ragged, shale cliffs.

Twice that afternoon La Ramie pointed to animals high on the canyon walls. Following his motion Joshua could see mountain sheep moving against the backdrop of large boulders and felled timber. The lead ram stopped only momentarily to gaze downward at them in the canyon below, and then hooking the flanks of the ewes, he hustled them over the top. The second time the sheep came into view, the canyon twisted itself deeper and the aspens were growing taller, more mature, and thicker in their groves. On this occasion the ram casually jumped between two, rock perches, appearing not to notice the chasm of air below him. As if showing his courage, he turned back to face the ewes, stamping hard on the shale shelf below his feet. Obediently the ewes also made the jump, single file, each waiting her turn. Butting them together again, the ram sniffed the tails of each ewe, then raising his head, arched his neck proclaiming his right.

"Manitou made all the same," said Night Wind.

"And how is that?" asked Joshua, as he paused his horse beside her, letting him drink from the stream while watching the sheep high above.

"Once the ewes submit to the ram, he always expects to lead them, telling them where and when they can go, butting them with his horns, and demanding to mount them whenever he wants."

"But he is bigger and stronger, is that not the way of all animals?"

"Only those who cannot know trust and love. Would not the grasses grow and the rivers run without him? Is he not the first always to run from danger?"

Confused by the direction of the conversation, Joshua made the prudent decision to stay quiet and watched as the sheep again moved over the next ridge.

"Soon we will come to the waterfalls and there we make camp for the night. La Ramie knows of this place well. That ram would provide our evening's meal. But like his kind, he stays well out of reach. The last of the dog tonight unless the mighty hunters among us can find something," said Night Wind in her soft, musical voice.

Joshua estimated the distance to where the sheep were standing, and realized that even his long barreled Hawken would not reach that distance. Even worse it would be if he shot and missed with Night Wind watching. La Ramie rode past them, nodded and then urged Old Bay on as he stepped over the deadfall littering the canyon floor. Following the stream upward, Joshua let his horse pause and then fell in behind Night Wind as she rode next to Kills-Crowe and Spotted Owl, the horses of the youngest and oldest laden with the travois carrying provisions. Behind him Joshua could hear the soft voices of the two boys, Lone Eagle and Little Dog. Grudgingly the miles fell behind them and it began to darken within the canyon walls, as the bulwark hid the progress of the sun toward its nightly bed.

The piebald jumped from the quick cascade of rocks sliding down the talus slope waking Joshua from his reverie. He quickly cast his eyes upward toward the edge of the rim they were riding under. Not seeing the source of the small rockslide, his peripheral vision just glimpsed the white feet of moving animals, which had caused the cascade of stones. Spurring hard ahead, he flashed past Night Wind and the others. Forward toward the rock countenance in front, he raced into what appeared to be a box canyon. The aspen leaves splashed across the top of his blue cap warning him to duck just in time as the branch whipped across the side of his face. Leaning low on the horse's neck, he went onward. The wall of stone miraculously yawned an opening as he approached. The horse exploded through a thick stand of chokecherries, jumping the dead log guarding the far side of the summer bounty. Berries rattled off his hands and arms as he pulled the Hawken from her scabbard, fighting to slow the piebald's charge, both reins in his left hand. Stepping from the iron stirrup, his right leg sweeping the rump of the horse, he jerked hard down on the reins and settled the rifle across the saddle. The creek that turned and twisted in front of him was now empty; the only sound was the pounding of blood in his ears and the hard breathing of the horse as he scanned, first the brush in front of him, and then the steep hillside rising from the tangled undergrowth. Looking back sharply to his right he searched what he could of the other hillside, the thick bushes weaving in front of his sight obstructed the view.

Nothing. Only the 'haws' of a magpie perched atop the stick nest forty yards in front of him. Suddenly the black wings of the bird took flight and Joshua saw the ram, followed by three ewes digging hard, throwing a shower of small rocks from beneath their feet as they ran up the slope to the crest above. Running flat out now, the big sheep laid his massive curls far back on the pumping shoulders and went straight for the top. His nose reached for the rim, outdistancing the ewes to the crest.

Estimating the range, which was quickly increasing, Joshua flipped up the second rear sight, snapping it against the lower, fixed one, and pulled back on the front trigger setting the spring. This calculated move settled the front ramp across the nose of the ram and squared itself across the shallow sight-notch through which Joshua was aiming. His finger pull continued back to the second trigger. The Hawken cracked and the billowing powder momentarily hid his view. Even the smoke could not obstruct the hollow sound echoing to Joshua's ears as the ball struck flesh and the curled horns of the ram slammed hard into the hillside. Stopping, confused, the three ewes looked tentatively at the leader, seeing the rivulet of blood racing down the hillside wetting the earth as it came. With one more look backward at Joshua, the ewes bounded past their silent male, over the hill, their white rumps a final statement.

The adrenalin was still pumping when La Ramie rode up; Joshua smiled crookedly, "Night Wind said we had to eat more dog tonight if we didn't get fresh meat, and hound doesn't set well with me."

"That was as good a shot as I've seen in some time," said La Ramie. "Remind me not to run straight away from you if you're hungry. Now the work begins."

If Night Wind was impressed, she didn't show it. She quickly ordered the boys to cut a gambol from an aspen limb upon which to hang the sheep. Once the men finished dragging it down the hillside, La Ramie helped Joshua gut the ram in the cold water of the creek bottom, being careful to save the heart and liver. Inserting the gambol through the broken ends of the sheep's hock tendons, they raised the carcass into a quakie tree by pulling heavily on the rawhide rope attached to the gambol. Chasing the men away, Night Wind began skinning the animal, carefully cutting only hide. Joshua and La Ramie helped Kills-Crowe and Spotted Owl pick hatfuls of the wine colored chokecherries while the other boys provided tension on the hide to help Night Wind's quick knife strokes. Making short work of the job, she then de-boned the meat wrapping it in wetted hide and lashed it to the travois. Traveling upstream once again, they headed for La Ramie's waterfall. The boys amused themselves by throwing berries and chattering about the distance of Joshua's shot. Finally the falls were reached and all thoughts turned to breaking out camp, picketing the horses, and starting the evening meal.

The thick, sheep liver, dripping with yellow fat, roasted on willow sticks as the travelers relaxed around the evening fire. Almost an amphitheatre, the canyon here appeared rounded and hushed. Spring water gushed downward over hardened rocks, reforming into a deep pool before racing on through the canyon. After replenishing strength gained from the organs of the ram, La Ramie grasped a burning brand from the fire and motioned Joshua to follow him. Edging between the cascade and the rock wall forming the falls, La Ramie disappeared behind the water, the brand's glow absent now in the night. Following close behind, Joshua felt the spray of mist before smelling the interior of the dry, musty cave behind the cold torrent. The ceiling was tall enough for him to stand upright, and the torch revealed a sanded, interior floor. Turning in a circle he studied the granite walls and their richly painted surfaces. Here were drawings of men and beasts, some unknown to Joshua. Elephants with

hair, and pumas with long fangs were painted on the rock. Newer drawings overlaid some of these paintings, showing diamond-shaped buildings, and sacrifices running red with blood. Cut deep into the granite was a date-
-1537. Broken shards of pottery littered the floor and slumped against the wall were a metal helmet and breastplate, holding little more than a powdered skeleton.

Astonished, Joshua looked to La Ramie for explanation.

"Sometimes we think that us'n was the first," said La Ramie. "This makes lie of that. He was Spanish," indicating the skeleton, "and the pottery is older than him. Who knows whether them other paintings are true, but I've seen some strange happenins' my own self. If these walls could talk, we might learn wondrous things of the people and animals that walked the earth before us."

"What was he doing here I wonder?" asked Joshua.

"Don't rightly know, but my mom used to tell me about two men named Pizarro, and Cortez. They was Spanish soldiers who went all over hunting gold, mite be this is as far as they got. None of us knows when it's our time, 'cepting maybe Night Wind."

They disturbed nothing. Returning to the fire, Joshua understood why La Ramie liked this spot. It made a man think deep about a lot of things. If a person didn't have a family, children, and someone who loved him, who would know or care if death came in some isolated wilderness? Who would carry on his name?

The boys, especially Spotted Owl, were still filled with pent up energy, and they soon included Joshua in their game. Spotted Owl stole his worn, blue hat, and squealing with delight, began tossing it to the other boys, playing keep-away. As soon as Joshua would catch one, the thief would toss the hat high in the air to another one of his conspirators. In short time, all were laughing and wrestling in the soft sand. Night Wind, still young at heart, joined in the game, grinning with pleasure when she could avoid Joshua. Catching her just before she threw his hat, she was astonished at the ease with which he lifted her high in the air, his gentle hands strong as iron bands around her waist. She found herself wishing for those hands to touch her in other places, so she quickly left the game to return to the fire.

That night, with the horses close, every one slept around the fire, the summer air still cold this deep in the mountains. Night Wind dreamed restlessly, disturbed by her earlier feelings. Unsure why a white man who made her child laugh, possessing the strength of a bear, could make her feel like a doe in heat, flushed and warm. The owl was late to hunt tonight, and her dreams were blurred and unclear.

The face drifted slowly into her vision, cold and unblinking. Particles of ice clung to the beard, the nose was frozen, the features still and lifeless, the lapping of the water caused the only movement focusing in and out of her sight. The blue wool hat was still pulled far down over the ears, protecting them from the icy currents that seeped into the lifeless body. The eyes so hard but kind, were filming over, pupils dilated to pinpoints seeing only the clear pane before them. Pulled tight to the chest, palms upward as if in supplication, the hands pushed against the barrier that held them, unable to reach and stretch toward the light. And then, slowly sinking, the face drifted deeper into the harsh blue depths; farther from view, the frozen stream washing clean the memory of the image from her mind.

The next morning the party again rose early, and continued up the draw before the first rays of the sun gained access to the canyon. By noon the head of the canyon was in sight, as Elk Ridge loomed square in front of them, snow still sculpting the high crags. Reaching the base of the massive ridge, a decision needed to be made concerning which drainage to follow upward. From these sources the creek was made, flowing downward to the Spanish Falls, then onward to the Platte. As if feeling the sound rather than hearing it, Night Wind turned to view the canyon lip which tumbled down into the valley of the cottonwoods, several miles to the south. This lip also adjoined Elk Ridge, but runoff from the southern hills was funneled down that draw, never reaching the canyon they were in. Dark shapes emerged from the lower valley and then disappeared into the thick timber of Elk Ridge. Were these shapes only elk, which liked the high altitude of this huge landform, or were they horses, running hard into the cover of the trees? The distance being too far to tell made her unsure, but her inner voice knew it was horses.

Joshua and La Ramie listened closely when she told them of what she had seen and felt, neither man doubted her feelings, nor the danger they might portend. Leaving everyone else there, Joshua and La Ramie rode southward to the thick cottonwood draw, the tracks would tell the tale, be they elk or horses.

Following the head of the cottonwood draw back downstream felt unnatural to both trappers and the horses reflected the riders' tensions. Although the banks of the stream were bright and airy, without brush, a tangible feeling of fatality hung in the air.

"I'm starting to act as strange as Night Wind," thought Joshua.

La Ramie beside him, rode alert, glancing down often at the soft loam and then worked both sides of the canyon walls with his gaze. Turning the rock corner, they rode upon a large patch of wild strawberries. An open canopy above allowed sunlight to fall to earth bathing the bedding plants that spread from stream to canyon wall. The plants' outer edges hung green with fruit, but in the center the berries turned crimson, low against the ground. Across this area ran horse tracks that churned and trampled the unharvested abundance. In this dirt trail, the berries flattened by the passage of the horses, dripped juice, dark, red, and sticky in the afternoon sun. Flies and wasps droned, buzzing among the broken shells of fruit, trying to recover salvageable nectar within the desecrated vegetation.

The soft ground, yielding as a grave, offered up few clues except the hoof prints of mounts, moving fast, uncaring of this oasis of life. The breeze suddenly freshened in their faces, and another smell entered the canyon walls. Thicker, heavier, the stench of death, mingling with the aroma of crushed berries cloyingly sweet, gagging their senses. Dismounting, both men secured their horses to a fallen log, and taking separate sides of the stream, moved cautiously down the ravine. The ripe berries stained Joshua's moccasins, as he moved silently through the plants. Easing his rifle over the jam of logs and flood debris in front of him, Joshua looked down into the canyon, steep and eroded from past floods. He searched the rocks below, the putrid smell urgent and close. His eyes focused on a lone pine tree directly beneath him, alien among the thickets of cottonwoods and aspen. From its stranglehold on the steep slope, the tree, victim of a mudslide during the last high water, jutted horizontally over a small pool of water formed by the slide. Partial roots sticking straight in the air, its lower bows brushing the water, swaying slightly with the current, the tree kept its stranglehold on the earth. Swaying also--the body of Shrieking Bear--hung, naked, mutilated, alone.

Turning his head sideways, Joshua looked to La Ramie, noting that the trapper had already witnessed Shrieking Bear's grisly corpse, and now was searching the living slopes further down the canyon, tree by tree. At last satisfied, La Ramie arose, clambering over the debris and walking slowly, waving his arms scattering the feasting ravens. The scalped corpse appeared to stare down the canyon with sightless, empty sockets, its trailing intestines from the gaping stomach wound, floated gently in the small pool of water beneath it. The hands, breasts, and nose were sliced off and showed bone, gleaming white beneath the flesh. Cutting the rawhide thongs holding her blackened, swollen feet raised to the sun, they lowered the body, heavy and slick from the afternoon heat. Removing the final insult, Joshua pulled the sharpened pine branch from between her thighs, throwing it far away.

That night in the canyon of the cottonwoods, Shrieking Bear, daughter of Komseka-Kinahyop, brave warrior of the Crowe, was laid to rest between two aspen trees high in the fluttering silver leaves. Night Wind, Spirit Daughter and Vision Woman of the Shoshone, planned the burial, singing softly the death song as she prepared the body, unaffected by the grotesqueness. She had come quickly after Joshua returned to inform her of the murder. La Ramie stayed with the body, guarding Shrieking Bear's spirit until Night Wind arrived to give it peace. Wrapped in the fresh hide of a mountain sheep to help steer the way along the steep cliffs of the hanging stars, the large curls of the ram's horns protected her, lest some spirit steal her soul. Wrapped tightly on her bed of cottonwood poles, with gut strings taken from the ram, her burial altar proclaimed she died bravely, unafraid, enduring the insults ravaged on her lifeless corpse. Only the brave were so mutilated to prevent them seeking revenge from the spirit world. Blinded, the spirit could not see the face of its attackers, and without hands no weapon could she wield. No spirit children would be born from her ravaged womb to avenge their mother's death. The forms that Night Wind saw earlier were definitely horses.

Returning to camp near the head of the other canyon chosen by Night Wind, no words were spoken, and sleep did not come easily until late in the night's darkest hours. Everyone in the group knew what death was like at the hands of the Blackfeet, especially from Lame Wolf with his twisted hatred for the loss of face given him during the Rendezvous. Whether Shrieking Bear went with Lame Wolf willingly and later tried to leave, or whether she was abducted, her grisly end was the same.

Twice Lame Wolf set the jaws of his trap for La Ramie. At the head of the drainage providing a straight route to the top of Elk Ridge where huge boulders lay, he waited beside the only trail leading through them. Throughout the night he stayed with the other young warriors, listening intently to the night. No sound of approaching horses, reached the ears of the wolves in hiding, until Lame Wolf himself rode carefully down the draw to find tracks indicating the failed trap and the different route the travelers had taken. Again, on the very top of Elk Ridge through a portal of rock and stone, narrow enough to scrape both stirrups of the rider, Lame Wolf planned his ambush. The long afternoon waned, and Kills-Crowe riding with the hated Whites did not appear. Lame Wolf wet his lips, thinking of the firm young thighs riding Night Wind's painted horse. Long would she pleasure him before she died. This time his knife would cut deeper. By nightfall he knew they were not coming, the Vision Woman steering their course away from him. One young warrior, smirking at Lame Wolf's loss of face, died with his smile on the end of the pock-faced warrior's blade. Crumbled, he lay on the trail, alone as the others in the pack followed Lame Wolf down the ridge. This time there would be no chance for escape. Elk Ridge sloped hard south, to the very flanks of Blue Mountain. The only approach, a flat plateau bounded on one side by soaring sheer cliff walls, on the other the depths plunged downward into a main flowing source of the Arapohay. Through this meadow, all must travel, unless with wings they flew. Desire for a quick kill made Lame Wolf discard this option at first, but now it was all that remained. The size of the meadow made the ambush harder to plan. More than a mile was it in depth and half that wide.

Seven now numbered the braves in Lame Wolf's band. Hardened, seasoned, their only thoughts were of coup. Perhaps Lame Wolf too quickly killed the squealing squaw, but now one more this way would come. Soon. Spreading his pack among the trees on the far side of the meadow, Lame Wolf made sure their tracks through the marshy grass led only on the south side, marking the way of danger for La Ramie. Avoiding this path would bring him to the jaws of death on the north side and deliver up the fresh young meat. It was on the north side that Lame Wolf lay in wait.

With the moon still in the West, from the canyon rode La Ramie and his fellow travelers, moving in the dark, quietly while the wolf still slept. The moonlight guided their way up the steep drainage, deeper into the heart of Elk Ridge. Daylight appeared and La Ramie forced the group out of the drainage, sliding, climbing onto the ridge beside them. The morning progress was lost, but the direction of their travel was changed and predictability now meant death. Along the ridge the travel was slow; constantly they had to find pathways through the tangled timber and rocks. When darkness came still they rode on passing far above the easier trail through the huge boulders below. By the stroke of midnight they stopped and on this high promontory camped, still and dark among the trees.

As night first fell, Spotted Owl sagged upon his horse, strength gone. He vainly tried to hold on but lost the battle to his dreams. Sweeping him aboard the piebald, Joshua folded him beneath his coat and continued onward, the riderless pony following.

"I'll take him," whispered Night Wind, but only received a quiet sign from Joshua. His head lying against Joshua's chest, the boy dozed fitfully until they stopped. Retrieving her child at last, her hands brushed feather soft against the hard flanks of Joshua, causing him to look down quickly into her face. Darkness hid her intent. Morning came too quickly; the trappers scouted all sides before pushing the tired horses on. Ten miles extra they traveled, choosing to ride down and across the deep arroyos instead of passing through the narrow rock sides of the passage above them. Again the night came and they stopped well back in the trees from a vast park over which they must pass. With light tomorrow, they would carefully search the area before venturing into the open, unprotected from view. They slept the night, close together, taking turns on watch. La Ramie awakened Joshua for the last watch before dawn. Upon arising he found the edge of a Hudson blanket thrown across his shoulders, under which Night Wind and Spotted Owl were curled tight to his back for warmth.

Dawn still hid far behind them in the east as Joshua and La Ramie searched the meadow and the trees beyond for any evidence of awaiting danger.

"I'm thinking I don't like this, not with the woman and the kids," said La Ramie still gazing out across the meadow.

"The horse tracks there skirt the edge and cross this meadow on the south side near the river. Why did they go clear down there?" asked Joshua.

"Maybe so they weren't in the open so much, and maybe to leave us a sign."

Joshua began to feel the question forming in La Ramie's mind. Should they cross the meadow in the middle, or skirt either side. If so, which side?

"I'm thinking maybe we should go clear on the north side against the rock face, I don't like following behind those tracks, what if they double back on their trail?" Joshua's questions reflected the doubt in his own mind.

La Ramie finally answered with conviction. "Well, it doesn't do any good worrying over it, we gotta get across. Kills-Crowe, Night Wind, and the boys will cross right in the middle. That way they can make a run to either side if need be. I'll ride to the north of them and you take the south. That way either one of us can provide covering fire if we need to. Lone Eagle can handle a rifle pretty well, and Kills-Crowe has counted coup more than one time in his life. Check your priming on your pistols, too."

The decision was explained to Kills-Crowe and the group started across the meadow, walking the horses slowly out of the trees. The travois were discarded and the horses repacked. They would need speed now. They rode single file, Kills-Crowe in the lead, gray head high, searching the wind. His eyes cast on the distant tree line from which the danger would come. Behind him rode Lone Eagle, the Indian rifle longer than him, at full cock. Little Dog and Spotted Owl came next, their young eyes aware of the danger; they tried hard to imitate intonations of the singing coming from Kills-Crowe's lips. In a song older than the Shoshone language itself, Kills-Crowe readied for battle.

Thank you Old Manitou for this fine day to die.
The sun warms my back.
The earth nourishes my spirit.
Let me be brave.

Behind the boys rode Night Wind, her painted pony smelled the lush green grass of the meadow and wanted to run. She checked him hard. Danger swirled all around. She cast a quick look toward Joshua far to her left, what if something happened to him now that she allowed herself to feel? No fear did she feel for herself, only for Spotted Owl, so young, so brave. Her talons would be sharp should anyone attempt him harm. Upon reaching the middle of the meadow she was sure the trees held danger, she could feel it, palpable in the air. She rode closer to Spotted Owl ready to pull his horse, fleeing from the enemy, or if need be sending her child on, and turning to face the threat.

La Ramie, riding on the north, kicked his horse on. Surprised, the big bay jumped and pushed harder through the tall grass. By reaching the trees ahead of Kills-Crowe, he could check for safety and then swing south through the trees to wait for them. Both pistols rode in small scabbards over the withers of his horse, his left leg covered his Hall rifle, and the shotgun rode across his lap. Should he meet Lame Wolf, it would be close fighting, personal.

Lame Wolf and two warriors, Hunting Elk and Dance Walker, Lame Wolf's nephew, waited just inside the edge of trees watching La Ramie's horse quickly closing the distance. Two others Lame Wolf sent to the southern edge of the meadow in case La Ramie followed his tracks on that edge. The remaining three in his pack were mounted, deep behind trees in the center, waiting for Kills-Crowe as he approached. He must kill La Ramie quickly before that idiot Winking Eye beat him to the girl. She was his, Lame Wolf's, to take first. The others could have the old man, children, and the trader. He looked forward to hearing Trader scream long into the day. La Ramie must die quick, no chances would he take with the trapper. He was too tough, too smart. Looking behind him, Lame Wolf could see his nephew holding the long rifle without support.

"Stupid bastard child of a whore," he mumbled to himself, "does he not know to rest it on the tree? Look at the way the barrel goes around, he won't be able to…"

The explosion blasted past Lame Wolf's face, ringing loud in his ears. He felt the hot beads of gunpowder sting his cheek as a young sapling in front of him fell, halved by the ball's flight.

"My eyes," he thought, "my dog of a nephew has blinded and

deafened me." Tears streaming down his face, he rubbed his eyes hard, then looked up to see if La Ramie was close enough to shoot, the hot gases still blurring his vision.

The huge head of a horse was close on him as the animal's barrel chest knocked him sprawling hard against a tree, his rifle flying from his hand into the brush. More shots rang out from further down the line, echoed and re-echoed in the trees, not looking behind him he ran. Hard. Not even ducking the branches whipping his face, he must get away. He would check later, if La Ramie was dead he would walk out of the woods to claim his prize, if not there was always later. Let his nephew face La Ramie now, maybe he would be lucky. If not, it was a good day to die for his nephew. If La Ramie didn't kill him, he would cut the life out of the bastard dog himself.

La Ramie saw the puff of smoke before he heard the report, he waited expecting to feel the round hitting his chest. Nothing came. Leaning low he spurred the bay and charged the smoke before it reloaded. Pulling the reins high to his throat he checked the medicine bag, it was still there, this was not his time. The words 'cowards die many times, the brave but once' ran through his mind. Entering the trees, he felt the thud as Bay struck Buckskin flinging it from his shoulder, more than one he thought, the smoke was from straight ahead. Then he saw a young Blackfoot warrior, eyes wide still staring at the betraying rifle in his hands, the shotgun exploded in La Ramie grasp, and from this range literally severed the Indian's body in twain chasing the guts high into the brush. Sliding from his horse he clawed the pistols from their holsters and dived to the ground expecting more fire. Hollow sounding shots echoed further to the south. Kills-Crowe was under attack also.

Hunting Elk clung close to the bark of the large, pine tree. He heard the rifle explosion, too soon, before La Ramie was in range. He also saw Lame Wolf running like a rabbit holding his eyes, maybe he was shot, and maybe he was a coward. No matter, he, Hunting Elk, would take the hair of La Ramie. He should shoot the big horse, and then La Ramie would come out of hiding. Looking around the tree to see if the horse was still there, he peered carefully in the thick brush. Where was that whiteface dog? Come out and fight like a man. He would eat the horse after shooting the trapper. He slowly raised his rifle, aiming between the small mean eyes. He heard the report, not realizing that he fired. He didn't. Blood filled his mouth and something struck him in the throat, something hot and burning. Smoke floated from the brush at the big horse's feet. The dog eater had shot him. Rapidly losing strength, his life's blood pulsing from the neck wound, he struggled to raise the rifle, he must shoot. The ball from La Ramie's second pistol smashed through his lips, splintering teeth, driving them deep into the roof of his mouth, ripping out his tongue and cheek before continuing on to shatter the neck bones. Hunting Elk felt his body slacken and unable to stop from falling, or even sing his death song, he slumped to the ground.

La Ramie quickly primed and loaded both pistols sticking them within his bright red sash. He returned to Old Bay who was dancing nervously, the smell of blood heavy in the closed confines of the trees. Drawing the Hall, he picked up the shotgun and slid it in its scabbard. Securing the bay, he ran toward the last sound of shots, how many more he wondered?

Kills-Crowe stopped his chanting when he saw the puff of smoke from the trees in front of La Ramie, the sound reached him seconds later and he smiled with satisfaction when the big horse far on his right never faltered.

"Quickly my sons," he said, "ride like the wind away from the wolf in the north, take Night Wind and follow Joshua into the trees."

Night Wind, Spotted Owl and Little Dog needed no further evidence of danger. Their horses were running low and fast, mud flying past their ears angling a course to intercept Joshua on their left. Lone Eagle stayed and a smile broke upon Kills-Crowe's lips when he heard the nervous song behind him.

Thank you Old Manitou for this fine day to die.
The sun warms my back.
The earth nourishes my spirit.
Let me be brave.

Knowing their prey would come no closer, Winking Eye and two more braves burst from the trees. Shrill, fierce yells accompanied their charge. Kills-Crowe dropped the reins of both packhorses rather than fight to control them.

"Dismount my son, and let your pony fly, the rifle is too heavy. Wait until the hot breath of the horse blows on your face before firing. This day you will count coup. Look into the eyes of your enemy and be not afraid."

Kills-Crowe then reined hard right and raced sideways away from Lone Eagle, causing two of the Blackfeet riders to change course to intercept him. Urgently he rode for ten beats of his heart before he reined in to face his adversaries. Distance from Lone Eagle had been gained. Then he charged, his war cry high and piercing in the morning air. As they met in the field of green, Kills-Crowe swerved so both warriors could not fire on him at once, shooting his rifle across his lap toward the mass of the rider and horse now beside him. The heavy slug glanced off the shoulder of the Blackfoot horse and traveled on into the Blackfoot's groin. Giving a high-pitched cry of pain, the wounded horse reared, throwing his injured rider. Satisfaction settled deep in Kills-Crowe's heart as he raced back toward Lone Eagle.

Blood lust now filled Winking Eye's vision. Small and dark the boy lay on the ground in front of him hiding like a mouse in the grass. What honor it would be to smash the mouse's head counting coup with his rife. One more jump and he would be there, his nervous eye fluttering rapidly now testifying to his name.

The recoil from the big rifle nearly broke Lone Eagle's shoulder, as he lay flat on the ground. After pulling the trigger he rolled, releasing the empty gun, too scared to see the result of his shot. Over and over he rolled until the sharp hoof of the riderless horse trapped his hand as it raced over him. Free again, he quickly stood drawing his knife. Twelve summers had he lived, and now he would die fighting. Winking Eye lay on the ground in front of him, jerking his death dance. A small, blackened hole was etched upon his chest.

Proud was Kills-Crowe when he saw the Blackfoot warrior blown from his horse by Lone Eagle's shot. Pain clutched his chest when he feared Lone Eagle had waited too long. For the moment his son was safe, but the pain in his chest continued as he raised his hand feeling the blood, slick and hot. He never felt the bullet that caught him from behind, shot by the last Blackfoot. Slowly he slid from his horse to the cool grass. He felt the hoof beats through the ground, he must rise; Lone Eagle needed him now. The pain rushed through him, goading him to stand. His right arm numb, he looked down to see he was holding his empty rifle. He heard the horse now, pounding close. Spinning hard, he swung the rifle, one-handed by the barrel, wincing as he felt the ligament tear from his knee. Above him the stone hammer was descending, searching for his head. The barrel of the rifle met the rising front foreleg of the horse, breaking both and slamming Kills-Crowe to the ground again. Three-legged, the horse fell head first, somersaulting forward; the Blackfoot warrior flew far out in front of the horse, landing hard. One more shot did Kills-Crowe hear, as La Ramie fired from the trees, killing the Blackfoot brave when the warrior staggered to his feet in front of Kills-Crowe.

Joshua too, heard the first rifle crack, and turned immediately to search for Night Wind. Toward him she flew, followed by Spotted Owl and Little

Dog. Relief flooded his chest until he realized they were angling in front him, closer to the trees than he was. Pumping hard he raced to put himself between the dark green boughs and Night Wind. The piebald closed the distance in huge chunks, catching up with Night Wind fifty yards before the forest edge, their horses colliding as they attempted to slow in the wet grass.

"Take the boys," she cried, "I must help my father!"

"No," said Joshua, his own guilt weighing heavily on him. "La Ramie is there. We must keep the boys safe. Follow me!"

Her head lowered, anger flashed in her eyes, but she knew he was right.

Prairie Dog, Blackfoot warrior, and his brother, watched the trader ride toward them. The fighting in the middle of the meadow was not going well, and they failed to hear Lame Wolf's howl of victory when he killed La Ramie. Worse yet the Vision Woman, the one that made Lame Wolf lose face three times, joined the trader with her pups. Silently they withdrew, the medicine was not strong enough today.

With a look, Joshua demanded Night Wind to stay after they were out of sight in the trees. Drawing his short-barreled rifle, he handed it to Little Dog. Riding north up the tree line, a last shot echoed to his ears as the middle of the meadow came into view. Riding back out to the edge of the meadow he saw Kills-Crowe lying where he had fallen. La Ramie was standing between himself and Kills-Crowe, pointing a pistol toward the ground. Joshua saw the puff of white before he heard the report and the wounded Blackfoot screamed no more. No quarter was asked or given in the mountains. The battle of Elk Ridge was over, silence and blood mixing on the green grass of the mountain park.

Returning to Night Wind, Joshua helped her gather the strayed horses, and with mercy put down the horse that Kills-Crowe struck with his rifle. Lone Eagle took the scalp of Winking Eye before shedding tears over Kills-Crowe. Until he grasped the greased hair of his enemy did he realize the little finger of his right hand was missing, cut off by the sharp hoof of a horse. La Ramie and Joshua helped Night Wind bury Kills-Crowe in a rock cairn just over the south edge of the meadow, looking down into the river canyon. As she chanted her soft song for the departed spirit, Joshua thought of the words he remembered from poem from William Cullen Bryant.

The all-beholding sun shall see no more
In all his course; nor yet in the cold ground,
Where thy pale form was laid, with many tears,
Nor in the embrace of ocean, shall exist Thy image.
Earth, that nourished thee, shall claim
Thy growth, to be resolved to earth again,
And, lost each human trace, surrendering up
Thine individual being, shalt thou go
To mix forever with the elements...

Yet not to thine eternal resting place
Shalt thou retire alone, nor couldst thou wish
Couch more magnificent. Thou shalt lie down
With patriarchs of the infant world-with kings,
The powerful of the earth-the wise, the good,
Fair forms, and hoary seers of ages past,
All in one mighty sepulcher. The hills
Rock-ribbed and ancient as the sun, -the vales
Stretching in pensive quietness between
The venerable woods-rivers that move
In majesty.

Looking at the young Indian boys trying so hard to be brave, Joshua remembered burying his father on the banks of the Mississippi two short years after losing his mother, and felt the pain of sorrow for Lone Eagle and Little Dog, alone like once was he.

The wind blew cold and chill that morning of his father's funeral, knocking up small whitecaps on the great flowing river that ran beside Joshua's home. The death of his father came as no surprise to anyone in St. Genevieve, except perhaps for Joshua. During the years after the death of his Creole wife, Joshua's father steadily beat a path between working long hours and the rough taverns serving raw, corn liquor. Neither remedy served to ease the pain caused by the death of his wife. The only result was his rapidly declining health. His memory became faulty and for days he would appear confused, barely knowing even who Joshua was. Whether it was lead or alcohol poisoning no one knew for sure, although the long years in the lead mining profession certainly took its effect. Many men from all walks of life intoned the final funeral passages before Monsieur Coral was buried, vaulted in hardened granite, above the marshy ground of the lowland river town. As they solemnly struck the funeral chimes to waft a friend and brother home, Joshua never realized how many friends his father had as they came to offer their last respects. Many of them, clad in white gloves out of respect of the senior Coral, laid sprigs of evergreen on the marble resting place, to represent the soul's lasting life in the kingdom of God. Joshua sat huddled; unaware of the townspeople passing by until he felt the soft gloved hand of a woman, resting gently on his small shoulder. The undersized, tearstained face observed the elegantly black-gowned figure of Justine Barent.

Justine lived in a small, stone house, situated behind the boarding house in St. Genevieve, located close to the docks. It was the only stone house and almost served as a small oasis in the frontier town. The mortar holding the stones of the house together were like Justine herself, as she was a unifying factor for the rough border settlement of miners and river men. Perhaps originally the stone building was erected for the service to God, but Justine and the two young ladies living with her, used the premises for servicing men, the hardened men who often found no other white women within a fifty miles radius.

Without a word, Justine took Joshua by the hand and turned him to her, hugging him deeply into her yielding figure. Joshua relinquished after months of being strong, the burgeoning man in him retreated to the child he still was.

"Joshua," she said, her voice husky with emotion, "I promised your father that should anything happen to him, you always would have food and warmth under my roof. Your father and I have become close friends during the last two years and several times he protected and aided me. You are old enough to know that some people here in this town do not approve of me, but if you will consent, I will keep the promise I made to your father."

Still numb, the death of his mother returning to his mind, Joshua could merely nod and that night slept in the house of Justine, built, maintained, and paid for by the rough and tumble men that plied their trade along the banks of the Mississippi and in the lead and saltpetre mines beneath the earth. Thinking back on it, Joshua did not know to this day how old Justine was. The lines around her soft eyes were fine, and her hands, when she played the spinet, gave no hints of the age of their owner. Her body, the source of her fame, was simply a soft place to be held against. It was not until Joshua was older that he realized the bosom that comforted him, held so many others for passion. The years etched in Justine's face fell away when Joshua would return home in the evenings to recount the stories he heard on the river each day.

Justine arranged, through her customers, for Joshua to begin helping in the keelboats that ferried goods up and down the mighty highway flowing past her house. These keelboats ran to seventy feet in length and fifteen feet in beam. A small cabin in the middle was skirted by walkways down each side where the pole men kept the boat pointed upstream. Twelve oarsmen pulled the mighty oaken paddles, which drove the boat against the current upstream. Centered in the craft was a mast which, when winds were favorable, would secure the sail adding further speed to the boat. From this mast a long rope or 'cordelle' was attached. This rope ran to the shore where twelve more men could pull the heavy rope, literally dragging the boat upstream. Loaded with lead from the mines, the trip to St. Louis would often take five days. After a day lay over, the keelboat would be pointed downstream and return to St. Genevieve in a day's travel bringing with it the goods so cherished in the frontier town. The newest in fashions, which graced Justine's body, arrived down the river to be sold in the stores of Bolduc and others flourishing on the muddy street adjacent to the docks.

Joshua's job was to run the water bucket for the thirsty men, toiling to pull the heavy vessel against the currents headed for the gulf. At night during camp upon the shores, the men would share with Joshua stories of their travels north of St. Louis, up the Big Muddy and into the frontier beyond. They spawned pictures in his mind of whirling tornadoes and thunderstorms and huge floating forests of logs riding the rivers currents. Their stories of quicksand scared Joshua the worst. The river men told of cordelle walkers that disappeared within seconds as they walked knee deep in the muddy water. He always took extra care when providing water to the men pulling the heavy rope.

At night the men would pile damp logs onto the fire, sending up thick clouds of smoke burning the eyes of the young boy, but this was far better than being eaten alive by the plagues of mosquitoes that bred in the stagnant channels caused by the constantly changing river. An old keel hauler told Joshua to always make his camps in the thick stands of trees encroaching on the water edge rather than the open sandbars. These trees, he claimed with a smile, would be too close together to allow the mosquitoes to fly into because of the spread of the mosquitoes' wingspans. Bigger than buzzards he would claim, these were the type of bugs that came out at night to carry young boys back to their nests for dinner. The first year

Joshua slept with one eye open waiting for the vicious humming which would signify the attack of the giant, flying mosquitoes.

Sometimes the keelboats passed by streams and small tributaries. Families would come down the creeks to trade with the river men or to pick up supplies either going upstream to St. Louis or back downriver to St. Genevieve or perhaps even further to Cape Girardeau. If the small farms were close enough, the river men might have supper with the families. Joshua liked the opportunity to listen to the stories of farm life on the frontier. During one of the trips to St. Louis, the family of Cuthbert Groffs came down the flowing stream of Labaddie Creek which ran from the Missouri Bottoms. Joshua immediately liked the rough frontier family and Becky Groffs was about his age.

Her red hair and freckles spoke honestly of her fierce temper and open disposition. That night the two played together on the banks of the river, throwing rocks and sticks at the turtles swimming in the shallows. When Joshua left the next day, he promised that he would return on his next trip and bring Becky something special from St. Louis. Only thirty miles upriver, it seemed to be a foreign country to Becky.

The country beside the great rolling river was covered heavily in brush with tall buffalo grass and pea vine. The Groffs raised crops for their own use and when they cleared the land of brush and trees, their field would spout corn, wheat, tobacco, cotton and flax. The family would work through the summer smoking and curing venison and hams. They would also have turkeys and small furs, muskrat, and mink taken from the sloughs to trade. Cut money, or bits, was extremely hard to come by and they preferred trading instead of using their cash. Most of their harnesses and singletrees they made for themselves but the needed iron was only available in St. Louis. Iron was essential for the wheel bands and gouging implements. There were hounds galore at each homestead. The dogs were used for hunting coons and bears. The houses were often small cabins only 14x20 feet with smokehouses that adjoined the structures. The smokehouses doubled as parlors when company came and the children would be shoveled to the fodder pens while the big folk sat, talked, and sipped Mississippi moonshine long into the night. Livestock fattened well on the native grasses, and helped with the heavy work. Oxen and pigs brought good prices in St. Louis, but the narrow trails and the river hills made driving them there almost impossible and it was much easier to send smoked meats by boat upstream. Nearer to St. Louis lived the families on the American Bottoms, which owned thick, deep, rich soil, perfect for planting crops. The dangers of this area were the constant threat of floods and the heavy fogs that blanketed the marshy shores next to the river.

St. Louis itself was a thriving community of over seven hundred people. It consisted of a hodgepodge of humanity drifting downstream by canoe pirogue, raft, maybe even arriving upstream by barge and keelboat. Supplies from the east were ferried across the river from the wharves from Old Cahokia, more commonly called East St. Louis. Several gunsmiths were recently moved to this settlement and this was where Joshua could be found during the layover when the keelboats were loaded for their return trip downriver. Here the men of the frontier gathered to discuss the news of the day and to offer their advice on whether this land would ever become part of the United States. Joshua listened to stories about Old Cahokia, which in 1699 originally was established as a Catholic mission and later became a trading post for the frontier. He also paid close attention to stories about the Chouteau family who, in 1764, established a trading post to meet the needs of the western side of the river. From this, La Clede's Landing was founded. Fur traders returned with stories of the Mandan Indian villages far to the north up the Big Muddy, the Missouri River. It was from among these men that the Company of Explorers of the Upper Missouri came into being.

Justine would sit up late into the night when Joshua returned, marveling at his ability to repeat the stories he heard on the rivers. Business was not a consideration on these evenings and she devoted her time entirely to Joshua. After each trip he seemed to have grown and she watched with pride over the years, marveling at what a fine young man he had become. Strange, thought Joshua, how he could consider two women to be his mother. Each in her way, building and molding what he would become.

With the funeral of Kills-Crowe complete the small party repacked the horses, and slowly, without looking back, left the small meadow continuing on their quest to cross the high plateaus of the blue mountain and reach the high prairies of the buffalo. Kills-Crowe would be mourned again once Night Wind reached home, but now her face was quiet and resolute as she tended to Lone Eagle's finger with salve from the liver of an antelope and soothing wintergreen grasses as a wrap. She was strong and resolute like Joshua's mother and her charges would grow into young warriors of substance and value. When the party gained the next high ridge, Joshua looked back toward the open meadow below him. Someday in a meadow like this he could build a cabin, and with a woman like Night Wind at his side perhaps he would start his life again.

Chapter 5
The Hills

The week ended peacefully for Carrigan, slowly winding down on Friday. The truants were still missing but the office staff didn't try quite as hard to find them, the cheaters still plied their trade, but teachers didn't plan to record the grades and unravel the deceits until next week, and the general mood of the school was not to kick sleeping dogs. Just let the week expire and allow the problems to sleep quietly through the weekend was the unspoken command. Carrigan felt drained--mentally, emotionally, viscerally--as if his life force had taken a vacation from his body. This school year had been a long one, and two weeks remained. Two weeks, only ten school days, forty class periods, sixty hours. The remaining 3600 minutes would be used to assess the knowledge, presented, but perhaps not retained, by the young populace that constituted Lakota Public High School.

Next year's unsigned teaching contract lay before him on his desk. Offered but unsigned, it would remain untouched until the weekend was over. Friday nights were not made for decisions about future roads to travel; rather they were a time for reflection and relaxation. The contract offered a raise of $800 or roughly $60 net per month. It also contained three extra planning days for staff, three extra days that would be spent within the confines of these walls, not on the rivers or in the forests that Carrigan loved.

Relaxation would soon come; reflection was the feeling now upon him. His students next week would present their Wyoming projects. Most groups were making good progress; the shop teacher even commented that Tommy was totally occupied the last two days piecing together whatever items of scrap metal the junk piles would provide. A metal mountain ready to spew out simulated lava was welded and molded by Tommy, and the shop teacher was ecstatic that Tommy was actually using some of the skills taught in shop class throughout the year. The science teachers were grouchy because of the onslaught of questions they had to field from Carrigan's students.

"Why in the hell don't you teach reading instead of trying to teach science?" was the repeated question in various forms that came from them.

"Somebody has to do it," replied Carrigan. Sometimes he just didn't know when to keep his mouth shut, he thought.

Carrigan turned the light out on his week, closed and locked the doors behind him, before walking toward Gertrude isolated and alone in the parking lot. She never complained about being kept waiting, and contrary to the women in Carrigan's life, never seemed to mind which direction he traveled or which road he went down. One woman in his life had changed the direction he traveled, sadly the roads that each of them took were in different directions. As he was driving home, Carrigan thought back to the miles behind him and the woman who hadn't traveled the road with him. I wonder what she is doing now he thought?

During the summers of Carrigan's high school and college years, he earned future college money by working on ranches and in the forest country that rolled through the hills surrounding the community of Rockville. The hard, summer toil helped build his adolescent frame into lean hard muscle and the work ethic passed down to him by his father assured him many job offers in the community. He reflected that he always seemed to take jobs near where the Laramie River rolled, moat-like in protection of the huge piles of granite peaks that rose from the river's banks. His first summer after his freshman year of college he worked for Ranier Ranches, which leased 40,000 acres of national forest in the high mountains west of Rockville. The ranch ran nine-hundred head of mother cows, finishing and fattening the calves by feeding them corn silage in feedlots on Rockville's more temperate flats during the winter months. Carrigan operated haying equipment for the family on their farms, but hated the fact that he was trapped in the small closed confines of tractors and swathers. Riding fence and scattering the bulls amongst the groups of cows and calves in the high mountain pastures seemed a much more engaging pursuit for a young man his age. He paid his dues in the hayfields, and the next summer he was promised by Jackson Ranier that he could work for the ranch atop a horse rather than enslaved in the cab of a tractor.

The managing partner for Ranier Ranches was Jackson Ranier. Jackson sired a daughter with whom Carrigan took classes at the University of Wyoming. Ranier was once married to a socialite from the East Coast but the only remaining sign of her presence was their daughter, Nancy. The Ranier family was really in the oil business, but ranching provided tax exemptions from the mineral royalties and taxes.

Nancy was perhaps the only reason Carrigan passed inorganic chemistry his sophomore year. The sight of her on Tuesdays and Thursdays kept him coming to class and enabled enough of the material to sink into his consciousness, that he received a **B** at the end of the semester. Nancy Ranier truly possessed a beauty comparable to the mountain vistas that appeared everywhere in Wyoming. Her visage glowed with a slow radiance that took the admirer time to appreciate. Slender and hard as a young cottonwood sapling, she moved with a grace that spoke of cat-like quickness, the kind of quickness that allows a bobcat to steal bait from a trap before the iron jaws closed upon the tawny head. Gray clear eyes and long bolts of auburn hair accentuated her perfectly bronzed skin. Sharp cheekbones and thin, tight lips kept her from being classically beautiful. But even at that, she was something far more. Carrigan struggled to keep his eyes from her lean form during class. She liked to wear a Levi jacket, low off her shoulders, under which earth-tone halter-tops accentuated her tan, rounded shoulders, and bare, pierced midriff. From the center of her belly button dangled a small silver horseshoe. Her worst crime was arching her back in a feline-like way when she was tired of class, and smiling sweetly at Carrigan when his gaze locked to her body. They began dating in the late fall of Carrigan's second year of college. One cold, October night when they strolled the frozen walkways ambling beneath the towering pines of the college campus, Carrigan glanced down at Nancy, scarcely daring to believe his good fortune.

"How come I never saw you last summer when I was working on your dad's farm?"

"I graduated high school from a private girls' school in Maine, and attended college at Maine U. last year. I didn't feel comfortable being away from my friends and my mother's family my first year out of high school. But somehow something was missing. I always enjoyed the summers I spent with my father and I finally realized I was just a Wyoming girl at heart, so here I am."

"And I am truly grateful," replied Carrigan. "Are you going to spend any time cowboying with me this summer?"

"Maybe," Nancy said. The cool, gray eyes surveyed him from beneath the long lashes, moist from the snow swirling down from the trees above.

"I have to learn a lot of country this summer, and I may not have time to hang around farmers."

Unsure whether she was teasing him or not, Carrigan stammered that he wasn't going to be driving tractors this summer. "I going to be a cowboy in the Peak country, I can show you the lay of the land."

"My father always told me not to trust cowboys, all they think about is wild horses and wilder women," she answered.

"That's me," he smiled, "a six-pack of beer and a Ford pickup. I have to beat off the wild women."

"Well, I need to get to night lab. You'll have to wait till tomorrow to tell me about what you do to wild horses," she answered laughing. "Do cowboys beat their horses like they do their women?"

"Only if they don't mind the cowboy," Carrigan countered. "See you in the morning."

Carrigan felt good about life when he was in college. Perhaps the closest friends he ever knew were from this time period. The dorm life was his first experience of being away from home. His roommate, John Boggs, from a town in northern Wyoming was a recently converted Latter Day Saint. Aside from this, John was an excellent fit for Carrigan's lack of organization and laid back style. John always explained that he became a Mormon because of the women. Carrigan had to admit there were always young nubiles wanting John to attend this or that church function. Although John didn't drink because of his beliefs, there apparently were no restrictions against sex and Carrigan became used to returning to his room and surprising the tented bed sheets of young, blond flesh.

John's greatest benefit to Carrigan was in keeping him on track. He often accused John of being his second mother.

"Did you remember to type your world civilization paper; it's due next week. Have you done you calculus homework? Remember you promised Nancy that you would take her to the concert on Saturday, you'd better get those tickets today." John was a walking schedule reminder.

"Yes, momma," Carrigan would reply.

In November of his sophomore year, Nancy left for Thanksgiving break on Wednesday morning. Carrigan couldn't follow her home because he was taking a calculus test that evening. A throbbing headache from a fresh hangover caused him to miss calc class the previous Friday, and it took all of his pleading and boyish charm to persuade the young grad assistant to allow him to come in on Wednesday evening. If he didn't take the test at this time, his grade would be awful. Lower than a scorpion's belly in Death Valley was the description that John would say. When

Carrigan displayed an unusual amount of forgetfulness, or disregarded the motherly reminders, Josh would give him the silent treatment, which proclaimed, 'I told you so' with every look.

"If you don't go to class and do your homework, don't whine to me about your grades."

"Yes, mother," Carrigan replied.

The calc test went well. Carrigan never had to study very hard, knowledge just seemed available to him when he needed it. This was a contributing factor to John's henpecking. John would study for hours, and after only reviewing the notes for a short time, Carrigan usually managed a passing grade.

"It just isn't fair," John would complain.

"I'll tell you what isn't fair," said Carrigan. "It isn't fair that you got to roll around with that plump, little thing last night. You must have told her you were Porter Rockwell, and I had to go watch college football in the lobby."

"We weren't rolling around. We were talking about missions."

"Yeah, undercover missions."

The cold north wind was just starting to pick up speed over the Laramie Range when Carrigan entered the math building to start his test. Two hours later he emerged into a blinding snowstorm. Drifts were already up to his knees on the university sidewalks and by the time he made it to the dorm, his teeth were chattering.

"You shouldn't have missed the first test," John said when Carrigan entered the room. "I waited for you and now neither one of us can get home. The roads out of Laramie are closed in all directions."

"Damn, double damn," Carrigan exploded. "I've got better things in Rockville to look at than you. Besides that, a cold turkey sandwich isn't my idea of Thanksgiving dinner."

Carrigan called Nancy back in Rockville and explained that he couldn't get home until the roads opened up.

"That's too bad," she said, "I was going to let you teach me about wild horses tonight."

Damn, triple damn, thought Carrigan.

Boggs left the dorm room to trudge though the snowdrifts for an evening church meeting so Carrigan went in search of Randy Pierz-Nez who roomed down the hall with Gary Ashenfelder, or Ash Man as they all called him.

Ash Man and Nez roomed together because they held similar values, even though Nez was a full-blooded Shoshone, and Ash Man was from

Basque heritage. Both attended the same high school, and Ash Man's parents worked for Nez's parents on a small ranch near the Wind River Reservation in central Wyoming. Although the ranch was small, the Nez families were Elders in the tribe and controlled a large section of grazing land on the reservation. Carrigan didn't know how many sheep they ran, but the yearly wool subsidy that Nez talked about would match the income from several oil companies in the area. Ash Man and his father sheared sheep for a living, and helped with the winter-feeding of the large herds that ran loose on the reservation. Ash Man could make enough money shearing sheep over the course of several months to pay for a whole year of college.

The value common to both was partying. It didn't have to be a large party, and no particular excuse was needed. A party consisted of at least one member of the opposite sex and copious quantities of alcohol. Quarts of beer were the best. Popping the tops on that many beer cans was hard on fingers. Once the party started, a fifth of schnapps was also opened and passed around till it was empty. This, they claimed, settled the stomach so they wouldn't get sick. It didn't always work.

As Carrigan reached the far end of the hallway in his search for the sheepherders, he found them kneeling in front of a dorm door spraying lighter fluid into a plastic baggie that contained paper towels, and from the odor, a large quantity of dog shit.

"Goddamn Indians, never can make a fire right," said Ash Man as Carrigan arrived.

"My people been burning shit longer than White Eyes have been wiping themselves," said Nez in the vernacular he used when he was drunk.

When sober, Nez's English grammar was impeccable and he constantly corrected those around him for their slaying of the language. Any time he resorted to his Indian slang, Carrigan knew the schnapps bottle was empty.

"You're putting too much on," said Ash Man.

"Dog shit need be heap hot. How! Cowboy," said Nez, noticing Carrigan's arrival.

Carrigan knew better than to interrupt the war party and just leaned against the opposite wall to observe the proceedings.

"Death to infidels and the Spanish," said Ash Man.

"Death to White thieves," said Nez.

By this time Nez was trying to light a stick match with his thumbnail. His coordination was suffering from the alcohol in his system but he finally succeeded in lighting the match. The problem arose when he broke the tip of the burning sulfur head off under his thumbnail. Nez watched his thumb sending off smoke signals for several seconds before his mind registered the pain. Quickly he grabbed Ash Man's open quart of beer and poured it over the injured member. The sulfur head continued to burn despite the dousing.

"Damn Redskins, always wasting good beer," said Ash Man, who by this time was trying his luck lighting the sodden, paper towels protruding from the sack of dog shit. The task was made more difficult because the package was soaked with beer.

Ash Man, being not quite as drunk as Nez, was using a Bic lighter, and on the second click, the paper towel caught the small flame, sputtered from the spilled beer, then exploded into flame. Ash Man beat soundly on the nameplate of the door that in block letters spelled the name *Billy Wiley, Resident Assistant*. Resident assistants received free board and room while they attended college. For this financial assistance they were required to supervise the dorms and control the rowdy behavior. No amount of money would be worth watching over Nez and Ash Man, thought Carrigan.

Both conspirators then fled in opposite directions down the hallway leaving Carrigan wondering which one to follow. He decided on Ash Man and then quickly chased after him because Ash Man still held the half-full quart of beer. Carrigan just made the diving leap into Ash Man's room a split second behind the arsonist himself, when he heard Billy Wiley screaming down the hallway.

"ASSHOLES, GODDAMN ASSHOLES, I'll GET YOU FOR THIS."

Carrigan risked peeking back out the doorway to see Wiley standing in the hallway, glaring menacing in both directions, squarely on top of a plastic bag--the same plastic bag that once contained flaming dog shit. In an attempt to put out the fire, Wiley stomped on the sack, exploding its runny, dripping contents in all directions including upward across his pants and outward toward the surrounding walls. The smell of scorched fecal matter was starting to make Carrigan's eyes water even this far down the hall as he watched Wiley attempt to put out his smoldering trousers. It wasn't a good time to get caught in the hallway, so Carrigan pulled his head back in, slammed the door, and surveyed the room.

Carrigan had, indeed, followed the right person as Ash Man's room was filled with quarts of beer, eight to a case. Maybe the snowstorm was a good deal after all. Wiley's ranting soon quieted down in the hallway and the next two days degenerated from there. Carrigan listened to the pair's story a hundred times--how Wiley forced Ash Man and Nez to give him a case of beer when he caught them sneaking the sled full of booze into the dorm. Revenge was a natural occurrence. By the next morning the whole floor was drunk, Wiley was hiding in his room and Nez was threatening to scalp anyone who laughed at his swollen, burned thumb.

The water from the continually erupting water fights helped dampen the smell, but hindered transportation between the rooms. On Friday, Carrigan and Ash Man finally decided they needed to sweep the water down the staircase onto a lower floor so they didn't have to swim to the bathrooms. Grabbing the large push brooms from the janitor's closet, they weaved their way pushing a river of water ahead of them toward the lip on the open stairwell. Unfortunately, Mrs. Sisson, the dorm mother, tired of receiving calls from students on the lower floors complaining about the noise, made the pilgrimage up the flights of stairs. She arrived on the landing of the third flight commensurate with the time Carrigan and Ash Man pushed the tidal wave of water into the open stairway of the top floor. Carrigan was never sure who suffered the worse shock--Mrs. Sisson when the cold dirty water deluged her, drowning her like a wet rat, or himself when he realized what he had done.

Hell hath no fury like a wet dorm mother, he thought, as Mrs. Sisson regained enough breath to begin screaming at him. Her housecoat hung like a wet gunnysack around her bony frame, and her new hairdo would never recapture it pinkish fullness.

This prophecy proved to be truly the case, as that weekend of partying almost resulted in his removal from the halls of higher learning. He was placed on disciplinary probation and his parents were so angry they suspended all monetary support. Cut off from his supply of beer money, Carrigan's headaches improved as did his grades. He was sure that Mrs. Sisson would cut something else off if she ever caught him alone. It was rumored that Billy Wiley suffered an emotional breakdown and returned home to Torrington, helping his father run the family laundry. Carrigan made a mental note never to get any dry cleaning done in Torrington.

By the spring of his sophomore year, Carrigan was busy with his college rodeo schedule, roping every weekend in the far-flung arenas across the western slopes of Wyoming and Montana. When Carrigan spent time with Nancy there was no doubt he was in love. The problem was finding time to be together. She didn't travel with him on the weekends and he didn't blame her for that. The cab of Carrigan's pickup was filled with rope cans, Copenhagen, and other rodeo paraphernalia. Often either Nez or Ash Man, in varying states of sobriety, accompanied him on the long drives. These two weren't exactly her kind of people. Nancy's weekdays were filled with activities at her sorority. Somehow Carrigan never felt comfortable in a sorority house filled with rich girls eating cucumber sandwiches. His style leaned much more toward sleeping in horse trailers and drinking Coors beer. Sometimes when they were together Carrigan felt a deep peace, almost as if they were meant to be joined. Together Carrigan and Nancy often laughed that perhaps they were only fulfilling their roles from past lives and that once they were Romeo and Juliet or Hiawatha and his maiden lover.

With the lengthening of the days, Carrigan felt his spirit being pulled down the long ribbons of highway away from Nancy. Spring was the time for rodeo; he would have all summer to spend with Nancy. Unfortunately Nancy didn't quite see his absences in the same light.

During the last week of school before summer break, Nancy asked him to join her in the student commons after their chemistry class. The day stood bright and still, and only the low hum of insects and the plaintive call of the meadowlark interrupted the silence of their walk from the science building across the green expanse of Prexy's Pasture toward the commons. Carrigan was feeling particularly good this morning, and the admiring glances from other male students in Nancy's direction only served to strengthen his good humor. His grades were excellent this semester and he was no longer on probation from his Thanksgiving activities. His winnings from the team roping last weekend were almost enough to pay for the expenses of gas, entry fees, and beer. Summer was near and Nancy was looking particularly fine this morning. All in all, it was a good day to be alive.

After coffees were purchased in the commons, they found a quiet booth in the back corner. Nancy had taken to drinking some weird type of latte that smelled like the chemistry lab. Carrigan stayed with coffee. He always joked with Nancy that he liked his coffee the same way he liked his women, hot and black.

"James, I don't think I will be spending a lot of time with you this summer," Nancy said, after a long silence. Carrigan knew he was in trouble when she used his given name. "During this spring I've realized that we just aren't headed in the same direction. I have the best time when I'm with you, which isn't often enough because you're never around. You're just like a vacation, you come around once a year and are fun to go on, but too soon it's time to go back to work. All I have to look forward to is the next vacation. I think it's time for me to go back to work. I thought I needed to tell you this now. There is no reason we can't be friends since we might see each other this summer. It's funny, I've been going to tell you for a month now, but ever time I start to, you say something witty and I just can't get it out. It's like I'm screwing up my fate or something. Running away from a relationship that was supposed to be."

Carrigan knew better than to make a joke at this time. He just sat there and watched the tears starting to run in slow rivulets down Nancy's cheeks.

Strange he thought, how he could love her so much when they were together and then almost forget about her at other times. "Maybe I will grow up a little bit and start to realize that you're the best thing in my life," he said.

"I would be if you let me in your life," her voice was throaty and full of expression. I need to be important to somebody, not just another mare in the remuda."

"That's not fair," he said. "I haven't gone out with anyone else but you all year. Hell, I've haven't even looked at anyone else."

"Except for Nez and Ash Man, and every rodeo within a thousand miles," she said.

Carrigan could begin to feel himself drawing inward. It was extremely hard to argue with her when she was right. What did he want? He never felt the desire to hold Nancy close to him and brush away her tears with his cheek more strongly than he did now. He thought he could imagine the fragrance of her hair and how her heart would feel beating close against his chest. Yet here was his chance out. She had given it to him. He could do anything else in the world he wanted, maybe even meet some of John's church devotees and not feel any guilt. He was also feeling stung, rejected. She was telling him they were through. Carrigan felt he was man enough to get her back if he wanted to, but what if he couldn't. Pride is a strange partner. In the end he did nothing. Carrigan brought the back of Nancy's hand to his lips and kissed her fingers slowly.

"Just remember," he said, "I'm not too hard to find if you ever need me."

He looked down at the last vestiges of coffee in his crumpled paper cup, cold and bitter just like his love life. He wasn't feeling quite as good about himself on the long walk back across the grass.

The last week of college ended with a whimper, not a bang. Carrigan never did mention to Boggs that he and Nancy wouldn't be spending as much time together. Boggs was excited about a trip he would be taking this summer to Mexico and Carrigan almost wished he were going with him. Ash Man and Nez finished the year on a sober note and with their bedrolls packed, headed for home. A house, several blocks from campus, was located for all four of them to live in next year on Flint Street. It wasn't much to look at but lacked all of the restrictions of dorm life. Deposits were made and the four parted with promises to get together later in the summer and prepare their new abode for the travails of their junior year. The house reminded Carrigan of a story his father always told about horse-trading.

"I once bought a horse from a horse trader," the senior Carrigan said. "The one and only time I ever did such a thing. This trader shows me this big buckskin with a chest a mile deep and a well-muscled ass end. The trader says he would take $400 for the horse; Keller was the horse's name. The trader says the horse was so cheap cause he didn't look so good. Well, I thought he looked pretty damn good and it isn't often you get to pull one over on a horse trader. So I up and bought Old Keller right out before that slick trader could change his mind. Old Keller jumped in the trailer and off to home we went. When we got home that damn horse walked right through the barb wire fence around momma's garden, got cut up, and it cost me dang near his purchase price to get him sewed up. Got him home again and the damn, stupid horse fell in the creek and almost drowned before we could pull him out with the tractor. The vet had to come out and sew the horse up again so I asked the vet if he had ever seen a horse so stupid. And do you know what that vet says, 'For a blind horse I think he does pretty well.' Just like that horse trader said, Old Keller didn't LOOK so good."

Well, the house didn't LOOK so good either, but all it had to do was keep them warm in the winter and have a floor to sleep on. Carrigan sure hoped they didn't find out about any unpleasant surprises in the house the next year. On the last day of school, Carrigan's dad called and told him the forest service was trying to get reach him. When Carrigan called the number back, he was transferred to Stephen Ridder the section chief for the Laramie Range Forestry Department. Ridder explained that a job opening in the forest service came up for a firewatcher on Laramie Peak during the summer fire season. He wanted Carrigan to take the job. The pay was $600 a month and Carrigan would have to stay on the peak all summer with only a two-way radio and a horse for company. The cabin he would live in was perched on stilts halfway up the mountain to allow the rangers a better view to watch for fires before they got out of hand. Carrigan thought about it for all of thirty seconds and accepted the position. He said he would show up Monday morning and meet Ridder at the bottom of Rainbow Trail. From here they would go up to the cabin together so Carrigan could learn what the job entailed. Carrigan tried for the next several hours to get in contact with Jackson Ranier to tell him he wasn't going to be working for him this summer, but finally settled for leaving a message with Ranier's secretary.

Would have been easier just to tell Nancy, he thought. Not that she would care a hell of a lot what he did this summer, but it would have saved him a long distance call.

When Carrigan and Gertrude The Pickup, rattled out of town that evening he couldn't help but glance at Nancy's sorority house before he turned right on College Drive. Her house, the first in a row of sorority housing, was gaily decorated with paper lights. There appeared to be some sort of party going on as people were milling around on the lawn. Just as the evening shades pushed across the deep rows of trees behind the houses, Carrigan saw the flash off a small horseshoe attached to the bare midriff of young, sorority sister as she flitted across the lawn in the early evening shadows. Ash Man told Carrigan the day before that he saw Nancy in the commons hanging on to one of the rugby players the university imported from New Jersey to play on the college team. Wyoming boys weren't too good at rugby, they didn't like following all the rules. Wyoming boys weren't too good at a lot of things that involved rules, thought Carrigan as he and Gertrude headed for home. Rules, whether they were for games or relationships, just naturally had a way of complicating matters.

The weekend at home with his parents was a nice break from semester tests and his mom's apple pie pushed back Carrigan's gloomy feelings. By early Monday morning his clothes were packed and Joe, his rope horse, was loaded in the small trailer he pulled behind Gertrude. Joe was a little cranky this early in the morning, almost as he if hated leaving home so soon after just getting there. Carrigan's mother, Melissa, worked at a local implement company in town while his father ran a small truck line hauling cattle in the fall and spring to the nearby sale barns. The family lived on a small spread east of Rockville.

"Our place is a 'good year farm'," Carrigan's father always said. "On a 'good year' we can farm some, on most years it's just a good year for cow pasture."

Carrigan hated farming but liked working with the herd of registered Angus cows his parents owned. The problem was the cattle didn't provide enough of a living to support more than just his parents. Outside summer jobs were a necessity as Carrigan's meager scholarships paid for only tuition at the university. Ridder, in last Friday's phone conversation, explained that every three weeks he would give Carrigan five days off. Carrigan made sure to mention this to his mom, just in case she might have another apple pie ready for him when he got back. Waving to his parents standing on the front porch, Carrigan, Gertrude, and Joe headed out for Rainbow Trail.

The sun was just peeking over the eastern foothills when Carrigan saw Ridder bumping up to the bottom of the trailhead in his green government jeep. Behind the jeep, Ridder pulled a small trailer with a four-wheeler attached to the bed. Joe snorted and danced around when the four-wheeler was started.

"I don't like 'em either, boy," said Carrigan, "but he ain't going to be around for long, and beside that, it saves you from packing all of our groceries."

Seeming to consider this, Joe nodded his head up and down and followed Ridder's four-wheeler up the steep trail that wound its way ascending Elk Ridge. At one place Carrigan had to turn his toes inward to keep from scraping the stirrups on the steep rocks that rose on either side of the high pass. Later that evening they passed through a huge meadow bounded on one side by high sabers of granite and the steep ramparts of the Laramie River cliffs on the other. A herd of cow elk watched them start into the meadow but once the sound of the four-wheeler reached the elk, they ghosted like shadows into the dark timber. Just as evening was beginning to fall they arrived at the base of the small forest service cabin. The cabin sat twenty feet off the ground and could only be reached by climbing a ladder and entering through a trap door on the bottom of the structure. The whole building was only eighteen feet square with a deck jutting from the western side of the cabin from which a small telescope perched.

The dark purple of the mountain evening washed over the cabin before Ridder and Carrigan finished packing all of the supplies up the narrow steps and into the small cabin. After a meal of tomato soup and cheese sandwiches, Ridder explained the forest service maps and how to orient them to Carrigan's surroundings. From each wall hung large topographic maps detailing the areas within view of the cabin. Landmarks such as high points and canyon entrances were marked in red. The landmarks would be crucial in helping Carrigan identify the locations of fires that might be started by lightening. Later that night as both men lay in their bunks watching the glow of embers from the wood stove, Ridder related stories the previous occupant told about the strange sights she observed while living in the cabin.

Telling tall tales was ingrained in Carrigan's culture, as it was in much of the West. When he was a small boy, he loved listening to his father talking about past times. The stories of the Indians and trappers were his favorites. Carrigan remembered from a college literature class he had taken, that the folklore of a region was much more than just entertainment. It passed on a sense of tradition, culture, and common sense. Although much of the folklore of Wyoming contained tall tales, there always seemed to be an element of truth in the stories, and if a person thought about them long enough there was usually also a lesson to be learned. Carrigan felt relaxed, almost at home as he lay in his cot and watched the firelight bouncing shapes off the cabin's small walls. Beneath him he could hear Joe occasionally pawing in the dark and snorting heavily at the night's shapes when they disturbed him in the small corral.

"The reason you got this job is because the young woman that worked here last year thought this mountain was haunted," said Ridder. "She got along fine till about August and then she started sending in all sorts of weird radio reports. I told the boss that we needed someone more level headed this year. Women just don't make good fire rangers. I've known you ever since you were a young boy, and I'm counting on your common sense."

"Maybe she just didn't like being alone. The women I've known don't like solitude for long," replied Carrigan.

"Maybe so, but she kept saying that she was being bothered by a bear that hung around the cabin. She didn't have a horse so I wasn't too worried about it. She said this bear would rub up against the stilts of the cabin at night and wake her up. I came up here several times but never did see any bear. She also said that during the day she could sometimes see the eyes of the bear watching her from inside the timber or she felt he was watching her when she went outside."

"Well, bears in this part aren't too weird. August is the time for chokecherries to be out so there probably was a bear. I'll be surprised if I don't see bears every day in August. Besides most black bears are a lot more scared of people than we are of them."

"I know, I know," countered Ridder, "but that was just the start of it. She started to talk about the bear invading her dreams, wanting her to do something. She said that she would dream about going into a cave and it was dark as night and all she could see in the cave was the eyes of the bear. She said she could actually smell him, an odor like wet fur and rotten meat. She would wake up screaming and unable to get her breath. She would calm herself down and lay still listening to the sounds of the night and pretty soon she could hear the bear down below waiting for her."

"Like a 'Were-Bear'," laughed Carrigan. "or maybe she was getting the 'Care-Bear Stare'."

"Well either way, we thought she was going clear over the edge. I came up and got her, hauled her back to Laramie. She doesn't even talk about it now, but she said she wasn't going to come back up here this summer. So if you see any bears trying to lure you into caves this year, let me know."

The next morning Ridder showed Carrigan the ins and outs of the radio and how to work the generator. Carrigan was required to call in to the Medicine Bow dispatch twice each day. If he didn't call in, they would send someone up here to check on him. Ridder took off down the trail on his four-wheeler and Carrigan picketed Joe in a small meadow before checking out his new surroundings.

The summer seemed to fly by for Carrigan. Fortunately there had been a heavy snow pack the year before and snowdrifts lay deep among the tall pine trees until late in July. Carrigan left the mountain retreat twice during the summer. Ridder would have replaced him more often for breaks but there really wasn't anything that Carrigan missed in Rockville. Most of his high school friends were gone now, and the carloads of high school girls driving down the streets seemed somehow immature after being with Nancy the last year. The pies his mother sent with him last time kept his sweet tooth at bay and the cool mountain breezes gave him a peaceful, homey feeling. After radioing in daily, Carrigan and Joe explored every nook and cranny of the mountainside.

Carrigan's favorite spot overlooked the slow meandering of the Laramie River from high, sheer cliffs that fell steeply down to the water's edge. From here he could survey deer and elk coming to drink in the evenings and the smell of lupine and mountain sage hung heavy in the air. Mountain beavers and muskrats co-existed in the ponds, playing loudly during the evenings. The murmuring of a small creek, along with the backdrop of a rough-hewn cabin always gave Carrigan a sense that here he felt the presence of a power greater than himself. A narrow trail ran down the cliffside among the stunted pines as they tried to make a living on the steep cliffs. About halfway down, a wooden ladder hung on the cliff wall bridging the trail between the upper and lower portions. The ladder was old but appeared to be solidly made and Carrigan dared several pilgrimages to the bottom of the canyon, carefully climbing the wooden ladder. Near the bottom of the cliffs, the cedar bushes grew thickly against the granite face of the cliffs and several spots against the walls showed signs where fires had been built. In one place, the granite was layered and a splash of red showed through the dark rock. This place Carrigan named The Devil's Fireplace because of its size and strange coloration.

"How long have men been coming to the river's edge?" Carrigan wondered. "How many people have gathered against these walls for the reflected heat, secure against the darkness of the river night? Trappers, Indians, explorers, maybe even prehistoric man, once stood here on the banks of the Laramie River. Perhaps all were seeking the same things, food to stave off hunger, and beauty to feed the soul."

By mid-August the mountainside could not have been prettier. Yellows and oranges were just touching the aspens and the dark tall pines appeared heavy and full, awaiting their winter solitude. Carrigan reported only four signs of smoke that summer. Two of the blazes were extinguished by the time the crews found their locations. One fire burned a small stand in a beetle kill area and one scorched only several hundred acres before crews hand-trenched a boundary to starve the eager flames.

Early one morning as Carrigan was frying bacon, he heard the unmistakable sound of an engine on the trail below the cabin. The morning arrived with heavy fog and clouds surrounding the cabin, obstructing his view. The air felt wet, almost solid, helping to amplify the sound of the approaching motor. By the time Carrigan reached the ground he could see the form of a person arriving astride a four-wheeler. In the dim light, the person's movements were somehow strangely familiar.

"Hi ya, Cowboy," came a musical voice from beside the machine. "How can we be neighbors if you won't ever come across the river and visit us?"

"Well, hi back, Nancy," replied Carrigan. "You about scared me plumb to death. I thought you were a motorized abominable snowman sneaking up on me. What ya doing way up here?"

"Daddy said we should come up and make sure you were still doing your job after you let that last fire burn up all our fall pasture."

"Your daddy has more grass than ten herds of cows can eat, and besides that, lightning has to make a living somehow," responded Carrigan, just as the words 'we' sank into his consciousness.

With that thought Carrigan heard the sound of another motor coming up the trail. When the second vehicle arrived, Nancy introduced Carrigan to Nigel Kirkdall. Nigel, she explained, was a recently graduated oil engineer from Stanford. He had taken a summer internship with Jackson Ranier to work on reflushing depleted oil wells.

Carrigan shook hands with Nigel, restraining from the urge to try and crush the soft, gloved hand to a mangled pulp.

"Daddy wanted me to show Nigel some of the geologic formations that make up the river canyon. He said if we take Indian Trail down to the river, Nigel could see four different epoch periods. Daddy would have come, but I said that you would be glad to show us how to get to Indian Trail," smiled Nancy as she walked off to pet Joe's nose hanging over the corral.

Damn traitor, thought Carrigan, although he was just as glad to see Nancy as Joe was, except Joe was the one getting petted and loving every minute of it.

"I don't know," Carrigan said, "Indian Trail is awfully steep and it looks like it is about to rain buckets around here."

"Well, if the rains bother you," said Nigel, "just point us in the right direction, my good man. I have climbed in the Alps, and they are a touch bit steeper and wetter than these hills."

The smile froze on Carrigan's face as he pushed the anger back down inside him.

"Are you sure you want to go?" he yelled at Nancy over his shoulder. "I wouldn't advise it today."

"Sure," she answered, "whatever Nigel wants to do."

Joe's eyes took on a much sadder look as Nancy left him to walk back over to Carrigan.

"This ranger thinks we aren't up for a wee climb today, Nancy girl," said Nigel. "Convince him of our bona fides, so we can be on our way. Would be a shame to miss lunch with you in the forests of your beautiful ranch."

"Come on, James," Nancy pleaded. "We'll be real careful and everything. How do we get to Indian Trail?"

"Go back down the way you came up. When you get to the first fork in the trail, take the one that heads west. Follow it until you come to a large meadow. Straight west across the meadow you can see the remains of a cabin. About all that is left are the doorposts and one wall. Leave your four-wheelers there. In front of the cabin runs a stream. Follow that stream until it drops off down into the river canyon. It makes a little falls. Just on the south side of the falls is Indian Trail that leads down to the Laramie River. Watch out for slick rocks and don't both of you climb on the ladder at the same time. It's solid enough, but it wasn't built for two. Be out of the canyon by dark because it gets blacker than hell down in the bottom."

"Thanks James," she said. Somehow his eyes didn't look the same as when he first saw her, she thought. He's still smiling, but his eyes have turned cold like the air. Well, if he still cared about me, he sure didn't show it. The least he could have done was call me this summer. Might do some good to prove to him that someone else was interested in me.

"If I'm not here leave a note on the cabin when you get back, so I don't have to hunt you down," said Carrigan as he turned his back on them to return to the cabin.

"Bit of an asshole," said Nigel to Nancy.

115

"Oh Nigel, you're just not used to Wyoming," she replied. She could call him an asshole, but Nigel saying it made the engineer sound somehow shallow.

Carrigan's prediction came true and by noon the rain was heavy as he and Joe worked their way back down from the north ridge that guarded Laramie Peak. Carrigan wanted to check on a small herd of elk that called that section home. A royal bull still ran with the herd, but the summer of plenty had not been enough to restore his youth, and Carrigan was sure the old elk wouldn't make it through the winter. Several large, younger bulls already fought with the old bull. His strength held, and he won, just barely. His flanks were lean from rutting and the young bulls still hung around the edges of the herd, waiting for their chance.

"Leave the damn cows alone and go eat," said Carrigan when he finally spotted the bull with his field glasses. "They just plain aren't worth it. Though I would like to see you kick shit out of those young bulls just once more before winter."

By five p.m., Carrigan was back at the cabin. Joe was happy with half a bale of alfalfa and the last of the oats from the bin. Joe liked the rain. It kept the flies away. No note was attached to the cabin door and when Carrigan checked the trail cut-off there was no sign of fresh tracks.

Idiots, thought Carrigan.

After several cups of coffee, Carrigan called Ridder and asked him to phone the Ranier Ranch to see if Nancy arrived home safely. When Ridder called him back around seven, he reported that Nancy wasn't home yet and that Jackson was on his way up the mountain. Warming up some stew Carrigan looked down toward the river canyon, hoping that he would hear Nancy's voice calling to him from below. Choking down some of the greasy stew, Carrigan gave up waiting, pulled on his boots and his slicker, and climbed down the ladder into the night storm.

If they're someplace warm and safe, thought Carrigan, I'm going to stomp a hole clear through Nigel. Maybe I'll do it anyway, no matter what. It would be better if he didn't take Joe in the dark, he thought, so Carrigan snatched his rope off of his saddle, and took his flashlight before starting down through the trees angling for the old cabin site.

The rain was really getting with it now and every tree branch that Carrigan bumped dumped volumes of cold rain down his neck. Great flashes of sheet lightening flamed through the clouds above, strangely silent because there were no cracks of thunder.

I'm wetter than a well digger's ass, thought Carrigan as he slipped for the hundredth time in the tangled downfall and boulders.

The flashlight was almost useless, as it wouldn't penetrate the sheets of rain even as far as his boots. At last, he felt rather than saw the meadow as it flattened out onto a wide bench. Patiently he waited until the next flash of lightning to orient him on the meadow. Almost as if in a photograph, the flash came and his mind's eye pictured the cabin wall next to the tall pines a mile across the meadow. Making sure he was walking a straight line through the brittle fescue grass, he started out. Suddenly the ground beneath his feet disappeared and he fell headfirst into the creek.

Well, I can't get any wetter, he thought wryly. Climbing back out of the creek, he pulled the old, gray, felt hat down tighter around his ears and traced the path the creek made toward a waving wall of darkness. He went much slower here, almost counting his steps, extremely conscious of the steep drop-off ahead. Carrigan heard the falls before he saw them. Three other little creeks fed into this one just before it dropped over into the canyon and the falls were shooting water in plumes higher than his head, straight out and then down into the darkness. The beginning of the trail showed wet and slick in front of him. Sitting on his butt with his arms outspread Carrigan began scooting downward. Several times he started to slide out of control until he managed to grasp the limbs of a small tree to break his fall. Calling out would be useless here due to the wind and noise of the water. At last the trail ended on the slick expanse of a huge rounded boulder. Two iron pitons were driven into the rock through which cables were looped. Carrigan could just make out the holes in the top of the wooden ladder that was secured by the cable. The only thing he could see was perhaps a graying ahead of him instead of sheer darkness.

I never was too smart anyways, he thought as he forced himself to turn around backwards and reach for the first rung of the ladder with his feet. Finding the rung, Carrigan made his feet move downward as he pressed his face against the wet granite rock. Almost giddy from the sensation of weightlessness, he at last felt mud beneath his feet. The climb was over. The last 300 yards of the trail weren't as steep and Carrigan managed to stand upright as he focused on the outline of a huge, knotted tree below him. He knew this tree well. He had sat beneath its boughs many times as he watched the Laramie flow sluggishly by thirty feet below the tree. Just as Carrigan was about to the tree he became disoriented again. Water was rushing by the tree; he could see the foam on the waves as it raced by.

My God, he thought, has the river risen that much? If it had, the sandy, brushy shores would be underwater, and there would be no room against the sheer rock cliffs. Frantically he pushed himself onward toward the edge of the racing water. With his back to the tree for guidance, Carrigan looked upstream toward Devil's Fireplace.

117

The next flash of lightning revealed that Carrigan was indeed standing in the river. The water was rolling high and fast and the flat shoreline disappeared beneath the water. He knew that two large boulders the size of houses sat close to the Devil's Fireplace. These were ancient monoliths that, thousands of years ago, rolled down the steep ramparts of the canyon walls finally coming to rest in the middle of the river. Not even the power of the flooding water could move them and the river would be forced to boil around them in its passage. If the water came down the river catching Nancy by surprise, perhaps she and Nigel would have been able to clamber onto one of these boulders. With the feeble beam of the flashlight, Carrigan stared intensely into the darkness of the canyon waiting for the next flash of light to display the boulders. He found himself holding his breath and was surprised when his lungs burned in protest. Just as he drew in a deep gulp of air the lightning cracked again, this time as a jagged bolt that split the air and Carrigan could smell the ozone around him. The boulders stood out in bright relief as they held their ground against the rushing torrent. White spray was splashing over the barren tops, revealing no sign of habitation.

Damn it to hell, Carrigan cursed in his head; where could they be, were they already swept down the river? They couldn't go upstream against the current and downstream the canyon walls were steeper yet. Their only chance was to make it back up Indian Trail. Why didn't they start up the trail before the wall of water came?

Again another thunderbolt caused him to hug low to the ground. Just as the brilliance passed, Carrigan's eyes retained a view of Devil's Fireplace itself. The Fireplace and two bodies were revealed, flattened against the stone cliff on a small, rock shelf five feet above the top of the fireplace and a mere ten feet above the water which rushed by below. The flood swirled against the walls bouncing off in a whirlpool motion and then continued on down the canyon. Carrigan realized there was no way to reach them from his position by the old tree. He would have to return back up the trail and try to come down from above them. Already the water here had risen to above his knees and he could feel the strong pull of the current. If they were sucked off the wall they would be swept along with the flood debris. The return back up the slope was accomplished by hands and toes gripping anything they could because of the slick clay soil. Finally Carrigan made it back to the bottom of the ladder. From here he must cut off the trail and transverse the canyon wall until he was above the inglenook. The driving rain did not feel as strong now, and Carrigan hoped the water below wouldn't continue to rise. Pulling himself hand over hand, from tree to tree, Carrigan moved across the face of the canyon.

It took him perhaps thirty minutes until he reached a small bench above the Fireplace. He was sure of his surroundings because a huge tree, split by lightning from a previous storm, lay with its top hanging above the hearth. He was at the base of the tree that was over five feet thick.

"Please don't be rotten," pleaded Carrigan. He knew that parts of the tree that touched the ground may be soft, but the trunk, suspended by its limbs would be dried and tough as iron. He dulled many a blade by trying to cut this type of tree for firewood.

Holding onto the limbs of the tree for support, Carrigan slid and fell the length of the tree until he was near its tip. His flashlight showed the ground disappearing in front of him. Quickly tying the rope in a climber's hitch around the trunk of the tree, Carrigan pulled, testing the pressure. It seemed secure. The other end he circled around his waist and though his crotch with a spiral hitch. Laying flat on the ground he inched further downward releasing rope with his left hand until his head hung over the lip of the wall into the blackness of empty canyon air.

"Up here," he screamed. The words didn't sound loud to him, but ten feet below two faces turned upward.

Nancy's face was pure white in the flashlight beam, while Nigel looked blank and vacant, almost as if he had been awakened from a deep sleep.

"Help me," drifted up to Carrigan as he watched Nigel's lips moving.

Carrigan inched backwards up the slope until he obtained a firm grip on the rough sides of a branch and then loosened the rope from his waist and let it slide over the canyon wall. He estimated the rope was long enough and that he would not have to tie it lower on the tree. He thought perhaps they couldn't see the rope until he felt it tighten and slap hard against his hands as someone grabbed from below. Within several minutes, Nigel's face appeared from the blackness and he scrambled over the edge quickly grasping onto the branches of the dead tree.

"Why didn't you send Nancy first so you could help her up?" shouted Carrigan at the vacant, gasping face.

"She hurt her leg climbing up the wall earlier; we'll have to go get help to carry her up," shouted Nigel in return.

"Get help?" exclaimed Carrigan in disbelief. "Help is four hours away, the water will take her by then. Give me the damn rope. Help pull us up when I jerk on the rope."

"You can't make it up the wall with two of you; it's too slick. Help me to the top and I will make a run for assistance on the four-wheeler," screamed Nigel.

Carrigan didn't waste his breath on an answer, but instead quickly took the rope and began tying knots in the rope every two feet before throwing it back over the cliff. He could only hope the knots wouldn't shorten the rope too much. Again his stomach lurched as Carrigan swung his feet over the drop off lowering himself hand over hand down to the ledge below. He felt Nancy grab his leg to steady him as he reached the granite shelf.

"What the hell took you so long?" she shouted smiling.

"I thought about waiting until we could swim out," he shouted back. "How bad is the leg?"

"I don't know, I felt my knee give when we climbed up here from below. I can't put any weight on it and it hurts like hell."

"Put your legs around my waist and hold on to my neck. I'll try not to scrape your back against the wall on the way up."

"Only if you don't try to cop a cheap feel, and oh by the way, thank you."

"You're welcome," he said, "and by the way, I get it any way I can these days."

With Nancy clinging tightly to his chest and waist, Carrigan tested the rope once more and jumped, placing both feet against the steep slope. His shoulders creaked and he looked upward into the dark thinking how far ten feet really was. He commanded his mind to think about the rope he was forced to climb thousands of times in high school wrestling, left foot, right hand, right foot, left hand, knot to knot, Carrigan pulled them up and over the edge of the lip and onto the top. When his hand felt the tree limb he allowed the pain in his arms and shoulders to wash over his body.

Nigel was gone, and Carrigan sincerely hoped he had fallen back over the edge. Together they crossed back over the traverse of the slope to the ladder. With Nancy on the downhill side and Carrigan holding tightly around her waist, they would hop from tree to tree. The ladder presented another problem and Carrigan hoped the ladder would hold their combined weight. He faced Nancy into the ladder and then close behind her he grabbed the ladder under her arms with both hands, allowing her to hop a rung and then he would step up to the next rung and she would start again. Even if they had to spend the night on the hillside, at least they were well above the flood below. He just hoped Nancy wouldn't get shocky on him and pass out. Her face was pale and she had bitten her lips until blood oozed from one corner, but she never cried out going up the ladder.

Suddenly as they started up the steep part of the trail a huge form loomed out of the darkness and Carrigan recognized the voice of Jackson Ranier.

"I'll take her from here, son; can you make it the rest of the way?"

The rain had quit completely and the wind could only be heard further down in the canyon. The coarse soil regained some of its properties and the climb to the top wasn't as bad as Carrigan expected. Jackson carried Nancy on his back and Carrigan pushed when they started to slip. Nigel was waiting at the top near the four-wheelers.

"Good thing I went for help," he said, "I knew you could never make it."

"Shut up, Nigel," said Nancy. "You couldn't find help in a hospital."

Jackson, Nancy and Carrigan rode back to the cabin in Jackson's six-wheeler and Nigel brought up the rear. Carrigan remembered climbing up the ladder into the cabin, stoking the firebox, and then falling to sleep on the floor. He first gave Nancy the cot with both pillows to prop her leg while Jackson and Nigel settled down in the corners of the small cabin to wait for morning light in three hours.

Early in the next morning Nancy's leg was feverish and swollen. Carrigan helped Jackson tuck Nancy into the ATV and just smiled when Nancy thanked him again.

Jackson shook his hand and said, "Good job, son; couldn't have done it better myself. Because of you I still have a daughter."

Nigel continued to chatter but no one paid much attention to him. After they left, Carrigan spent the day near the cabin watching for smoke from the storm, but the rain was heavy enough he saw no evidence of fires.

The next day broke clear and bright and Carrigan rode Joe back down to Indian Trail to retrieve his rope from the log. He would play hell getting the knots out of a wet hemp rope, but his saddle would feel naked without it. As Carrigan approached the fallen tree he peered over the edge below. In the morning sun, the ledge below looked like a short step and the river seemed mild and slow, though still somewhat muddy. The air remained heavy with moisture on the mountain slope and Carrigan thought he could detect a strange smell in the air, almost like a wet dog, a dead, wet dog he thought. Bending to retrieve his rope from the tree, he was startled to see the hondo of the rope pressed into the gooey earth, surrounded by a huge bear track deep in the mud. It was if a bear had anchored the rope with its immense weight, making sure the tree did not give way. Quickly looking around, Carrigan saw nothing but couldn't escape the feeling that he was being watched as he climbed back up the ladder and up the trail to Joe waiting above.

His term as ranger ended without further incident and Carrigan, Gertrude, and Joe returned from the mountains to enroll in the fall semester at the university. Carrigan was somewhat stunned to find that the university received a scholarship in his name for tuition and costs for the next two years. Jackson Ranier was just showing his appreciation on his daughter's behalf. After discussing it with his parents, Carrigan accepted the scholarship. When he called Jackson to thank him, he learned that Nancy was being flown to the East Coast to have an operation on her knee. Jackson said Nancy would contact Carrigan in a week or two. Boggs, Nez, and Ash Man gave Carrigan rafts of shit about being a hero and the forest service gave Carrigan a nice certificate for valor. After several weeks of school, Nancy called Carrigan one night to explain that she was staying in the East for the fall to rehab her knee and that she would see him for Christmas. She told him that anytime he wanted to come see her he was welcome, just let her know when.

"Thanks again, cowboy," she said and then the line clicked and she was gone.

There are just too many rules, thought Carrigan; he never quite knew how to play the game. And just like the old bull elk, he hoped he would make it through the winter. His college days were a long time ago now. He wondered why recently he kept thinking back to the people and events in his life. Maybe it was just springtime, and he needed time for reflection.

Oh well, he thought, it's Friday night, maybe there will be something interesting happening tonight. Supper at Ben's and some cold beers sounded quite good, besides his house would just be cold and empty and might start him daydreaming again about what might have been.

Chapter 6
THE POND

The small party of La Ramie, Joshua, Night Wind, Spotted Owl, Lone Eagle, and Little Dog camped that night at the base of a high mountain pass near the bottom of the Big Blue Mountain. Tomorrow they would pass to the north of its summit and travel down the gentle slope of a beaver-filled creek. From here they could ride to the south of their next big barrier, Bull Elk Mountain, and enter the grass plains, which La Ramie claimed were blackened with buffalo.

Camp was subdued and the boys quickly ate and left the campfire to sleep with the horses. Even Spotted Owl went with them for a while before returning to the protection of his mother's side. La Ramie and Joshua missed the company of the old Indian and Joshua felt himself studying the stars that evening, attempting to see the path that Kills-Crowe would take as he walked among the hanging stars that shown so brightly above him. Night Wind pulled her robes adjacent to Joshua's around the dying embers of the campfire, causing La Ramie to look at the trader with upraised eyebrows.

"What are you looking at?" growled Joshua. "I reckon she can sleep anywhere she wants to."

"Yep," said La Ramie, "and it looks like she's chosen you to sleep next to. Poor Devil; well, all of us have our burdens to bear, and it looks like you've got yours. Once a Vision Woman chooses a man, there ain't no getting out of it. It's just a shame that a woman so beautiful had to choose an ugly dog like you. There's no accounting for Indian tastes. I just hope you're not otherwise engaged or she's liable to cut your eyes out when you're sleeping. Ain't nothing more jealous in the world than a Vision Woman."

123

"Goodnight, Jacque."

With Spotted Owl between them, Joshua drifted into a restless sleep. His last thought was of a huge owl, talons extended, striking downward toward his eyes. He was extremely glad when morning came and he could escape from his dreams.

The morning arrived sharp, clear, and cold. The party allowed the horses to break the ice on the small stream they were camped beside before riding out. Beside them, higher in the timber, deep snowdrifts still lay among the pines, dirt encrusted and brown from the previous winter. When the morning sun reached the snow pack, places in the drifts would suddenly explode with reflected light, almost as if diamonds were secluded in their frozen barriers. By noon the pass was reached and the party stopped long enough to wash down several handfuls of pemmican and then they began the descent into a large creek that was thickly choked with willows. A game trail ran beside the water. It was only wide enough for the horses to proceed single file and Joshua fell in behind Night Wind. As they moved downward, Big Blue Mountain grew taller behind them. Joshua found his gaze constantly shifting to Night Wind's slender form as she rode ahead of him, weaving through the evergreens that grew in the trail.

He was brought back to attention when he heard Night Wind's musical voice addressing Spotted Owl who rode just behind her and in front of Joshua.

"Always beware, my son, when riding near the lair of the mountain panther. His reflexes are quicker than the eye, and his strength is equal to the bear but the panther's eyes are cold, unfeeling. He will watch his prey for hours, toying with them until the cat decides he is ready to destroy. Sometimes he will stalk game only for the thrill of the hunt and then after the kill he will move on to other victims. The lowly coyote only kills to feed his hunger. But you can never tell when the panther is ready to strike. Of the two, perhaps the coyote is the nobler animal."

Joshua could not but help grinning to himself, the double-entendre; Rodde had been the master of this. There were times, years ago, when she could tongue-tie him with only a few words. She always was able to tell when she hurt his feelings, and she would then tease him until he stopped sulking. Was it possible, after all these years that Joshua was beginning to feel the same stirring again deep within his chest. Only a boy when Rodde came into his life, and now that he was a man, Night Wind made him feel young again. Was it possible to love two women in one lifetime, or did Night Wind just remind him of Rodde with her spirited, flashing eyes and sharp-witted words. He glanced again at her firm, straight form as she rode ahead of him. The narrow waist flaring into the lean muscled hips, seemingly a part of the horse she rode. Perhaps it was possible to allow himself to feel again. Rodde would be pleased that Joshua could look upon someone else the way he once looked upon her. Joshua smiled to himself again and with the slow gait of the horse allowed himself to flow back, downstream of the mighty Platte, the Missouri, and further down the Mississippi to his boyhood home and his past.

During the Fall of 1788, Joshua enjoyed a special trip up the big river because his closest friend, Jacques Bolduc, accompanied him. Jacques' father arranged with the boy's maiden aunt, who lived in St. Louis, for Jacques to move into her household, thus offering him a chance to attend school and receive training in accounting and the arts. Both boys received schooling that included reading and numbers in St. Genevieve, but little study of literature or music was included. School was easy for Joshua and he especially enjoyed working with numbers and arithmetic. Jacques also did well, but it took him much longer, and he spent many winter hours working and reworking problems that Joshua understood instinctively in seconds. It was in the social graces that Jacques far outpaced Joshua. He could coax a smile from any young girl, and compliments seemed to roll off his lips. He danced well and had an easy way of conversing with anyone. A natural trader, 'with words of honey', was the way Joshua described him.

The journey was bittersweet for the two boys as each realized that this marked a turning point in their lives. Impending manhood and social class would begin to separate them. Jacques would move in circles far less rough than those Joshua was now a part. The trip was completed and both boys hugged each other in St. Louis before Joshua left the next morning to return southward to St. Genevieve, promising to contact Jacques on his next trip.

Jacques' friendship had been constant, even after Joshua lost his mother and father. Neither Jacques nor his family looked down on Joshua for living with Justine and he continued to be included in their family activities, spending long hours in the Bolduc home for his schooling, especially while Justine and her young ladies were otherwise engaged. The relationship between Joshua and Justine slowly changed as he became older. She still listened intently to his stories of the river trips and beamed for days when he brought her something from St. Louis. But instead of expecting Joshua to depend on her, she began to treat him more as an

Greg A. Garton

equal, asking him questions about money, investments, and properties that he thought might be worth buying in St. Genevieve.

The next several years passed swiftly and Joshua grew into his manhood. He no longer ran the water bucket for the men. He now helped pull the cordelle, poled the long staffs, and walked the riverbank, earning a man's pay for these grueling tasks. These positions he soon mastered and was moved to rear oarsman because of his excellent memory and understanding of the river. From here Joshua could help steer the vessel to avoid snags on underwater logs and sandbars. The rough men of the river began to treat him as an equal and by age fifteen he was stronger than most men with whom he worked. The rough and tumble life on the Mississippi and in the docks of St. Louis sharpened his fighting skills, and Joshua became adept with the use of short knives, iron knuckles and the 'boat billy', a short baton of hardened maple.

During an early spring run in 1790, as Joshua was off ramping wooden sledges of smeltered galena onto the docks of La Clede's landing, he noticed several rough looking dock hands surrounding a man in broadcloth suit, taunting and laughing at him. Pushing the sledge into a line with the others, Joshua ambled over to discover what the argument was about. One of the dockhands he recognized as a nere-do-well named Catfish, because of the man's bulging eyes and loose drooling lips. Joshua caught the context of the argument as he neared the men.

"I paid you men to load these boxes and bales, and now I find that half the crates are empty and the others still aren't on the barge. I demand to know the reason for this," said the man in the suit.

"My boys and I decided that the rates need to go up before we do any more work," said Catfish, his bulging eyes intent on the businessman in front of him.

"I will immediately contact the authorities. My name is Renquin Shaw and it pulls some weight on these docks," replied the businessman. "Immediately return my goods, and I will pay a bonus when everything is loaded."

"How about you walk away and we will take our own bonus," leered Catfish.

"You men are fired; now disband into the gutters from whence you came," answered Renquin sternly, not giving an inch of ground.

"Your choice, although a poor choice," replied Catfish, and his hand flashed from his left leg across Renquin's body in a low sweeping motion.

Joshua's eye followed Renquin's quick jump backward, swift but not fast enough to avoid the tip of Catfish's serrated knife blade as it cut a thin

126

ribbon of flesh from Renquin's chest. Knowing the return stroke would cut deeper, Joshua took a quick step forward, bringing his wooden billy down sharply on Catfish's elbow before the ruffian's arm could move forward again. The wood meeting flesh and bone sent a sharp cracking sound floating through the foggy morning air. Catfish's knife dropped from his nerveless fingers as his elbow flopped backwards against the joint, being held in place only by skin and tendon; the joint completely shattered. One of Catfish's men vomited as he watched the elbow flop loosely and the other man, Black and scarred, shifted his eyes quickly between Joshua and Renquin.

"There's a dentist up on Rue de la Granges Street that can set that arm," said Joshua, "although I reckon it's going to be a little stiff from now on. Now get him out of here before I whistle for my crew and finish this job. Scram!" said Joshua, pointing the billy at the Black man.

Together the Black man and the young ruffian, who still looked rather green and had vomit remaining in his scraggy beard, helped Catfish from his knees, half dragging the injured man off the wharf and up the cobblestone street toward town. The high piercing scream coming from Catfish's throat could still be heard a block away as Joshua watched them with cat eyes until the bandits turned the corner vanishing from his sight.

"Thank you," said Renquin, to Joshua. He tightly held his waistcoat against his chest, staunching the flow of blood from his wound.

"I'd get that cleaned and sewed right away," said Joshua, no telling what Old Catfish had that toothpick in.

"I will," replied Renquin, "but first do you know anyone going downriver to St. Genevieve? I must get this cargo downstream and off these docks before they come back."

"We'll be going back down this afternoon," Joshua answered, "and I think we'll have room. For twelve cut bits, we will load it and unload it in Genevieve."

"Agreed," answered Renquin, "now excuse me; I shall return and meet you here at 1:00 this afternoon, and thank you again. Whom do I owe my debt of gratitude?"

"Joshua Timenaux Coural, at your service. We run a keelboat, which is owned by the Bolducs, from St. Genevieve."

Joshua finished unloading his sledges of galena and took the ribbing from his keel-mates about picking on poor old Catfish. By noon the ore was unloaded, and a variety of bales, boxes, metal implements and a whole wagon were loaded on the barge for the return trip. Joshua ate his lunch on the dock and watched the Mississippi roll by, slowly but steadily toward its journey for the ocean. Maybe it's time I started on a different journey, he said to himself. If I don't start doing something different my back isn't going to last; then Jacques will get a head start on rounding up all the money and pretty girls in Missouri.

Renquin returned promptly at 1:00 p.m. looking pale from his recent loss of blood, but in good spirits. The tie lines were released and the return journey to St. Genevieve began. Joshua felt the sluggish current catch hold of the boat swinging her nose downstream on a new journey. The voyage passed swiftly and Renquin explained to Joshua that he planned on opening a trading post in St. Genevieve. He realized that finding any of the missing supplies liberated by Catfish would be hopeless in the myriad of warehouses on the landing and felt that Catfish probably already paid a large price for his thievery. He wanted to talk about his future plans.

"I believe that there is a market for those trappers working the slews and creeks further down the river, I can bundle, grade and bale the furs in St. Genevieve, sell fresh supplies and then market the furs in St. Louis. Bolduc handles mainly trade goods, so there should be room for another merchant dealing mainly in furs. The furs returning from the Big Muddy come in usually only once a year, but my turnover can be much more rapid. I would like to arrange my own transportation, and not be dependent on others. I am also looking for someone who can manage the post in St. Genevieve and oversee the transportation to St. Louis, someone who can deal fairly with the country folk and still make me a return. You wouldn't happen to be interested, would you Joshua?"

The thought of being a merchant just like Jacques appealed to Joshua, maybe this was the change he was looking for in his life. "It sounds like something I would like to do, but you don't know much about me, Mr. Shaw," replied Joshua.

"You're almost 16, an honest man, and good in a fight. Your father and mother are dead, and you are thought of very highly in the waterfront community in St. Louis. I checked with Liquest and Chouteau and they vouched for you. You have some very important friends, young man, so I think I know enough about you. Do we have a deal?"

Joshua merely nodded his head, amazed at how fast his life was changing before his eyes. Joshua could hardly wait to tell Justine when he burst into the house early the next morning, sending men scattering into the early morning fog. As she listened to his retelling of the recent events and Joshua's offer for a new position, Justine could not help but feel the pride of a mother for a son. Also there was a feeling of loss now that Joshua would be leaving her fold and starting a new life of his own. Justine helped him arrange for a house nearer the buildings being constructed by Shaw for his trading post on the northern edge of St. Genevieve and even donated some of the plainer furniture from her home, continually teasing Joshua that it was for her good that she was moving him out because he was always frightening her customers. Justine also was glad to remove Joshua from the clutches of her girls who were starting to look upon Joshua as a man and not as a little boy.

Joshua took to trading like a duck to water, and was soon traveling the thick-brushed backcountry to meet with the trappers and small farmers of the area. He often was gone for several days traveling eastward clear to Potosi and the smelting areas there. When Joshua was in St. Genevieve he worked the post, organizing and inventorying the incoming furs, readying them for shipment to St. Louis. Shaw monthly visited St. Genevieve, but could find little fault with the way Joshua was running the post. Shipwrights were commissioned and two new keelboats were built to ferry the newly bundled furs to St. Louis for sale to the larger fur houses. Shaw took care of the ordering of goods for sale in St. Genevieve and Joshua merely needed to make sure of their safe provision and dispensation for incoming pelts. Joshua still made the trips to St. Louis, but more infrequently now, as the Genevieve post grew and prospered, keeping his attention there. Upon his trips to St. Louis, he was amazed at how quickly the city was growing and the changes that appeared there almost overnight.

The city grew from three east-west streets to nineteen, and its population from 200 to over 1000. Although most of St. Louis was set aside for housing and business, large tracts were used for agriculture also. Some of these such as St. Louis Commons, Grande Prairie, and St. Louis Prairie flourished and beautiful country homes sprung up there. Following European tradition, the land in these fields was divided into long narrow strips and assigned to individuals based on the amount of property they held in the village. These homes varied between poteaux en terre (posts-in-ground) construction with their pavilion roofs and long, rambling porches to different styles of European construction made from mortar and stone. Joshua vowed one day to build a fine, country house like those. With the business thriving, Joshua saved his money from his wages and bonus payments from Shaw during the next several years.

In the spring of 1793, Comandante Felix Valle held an auction from the old church steps for a house that had belonged to Nicolas Caillot. Caillot owned several billiard parlors near Market Street and had recently sold them to Francois Lalumandiere. Caillot was returning to St. Louis to set up new parlors there. The home was north of The Grand Field in New Town or Petites Cotes, along Gabouri Creek, away from the constant danger of the flooding lowlands. With his own savings Joshua purchased the property for 1000 livres and 2000 pounds of wheat that was his share of the last trading run to St. Louis. The house, a veritable mansion to Joshua, sat on over an acre of land that also contained a cow barn, stables, a henhouse with corncrib, an orchard, a vegetable garden, a bake oven and a small slave quarters. Justine simply burst with pride when Joshua showed her around. He immediately went to work planting the garden, pruning the apple trees, and constructing a picket fence around his new home. Happy at last with his station in life at St. Genevieve, Joshua traded all future bonus money from Shaw for stock in the company and began to rise in the society of St. Genevieve.

People took notice of his success and invited him to their homes on Sundays after church service. Even the Parrish Priest, Abbe de St. Pierre, would nod sagely to him when they met on the streets of New Town. That New Year's Eve, he and other young men went from house to house singing "La Guignolee", a traditional song of young bachelors. The danger in this lay that many families in town would welcome Joshua to be a suitor for their daughters and he was careful not to tarry at any one house too long. When he arrived at Justine's house near midnight, her girls laughed and tried to entice him inside with sprigs of mistletoe placed in their hair. Justine quickly shooed them upstairs and made Joshua and the other young men sing to her from the front porch. With added embellishment from the bottles of wild cherry liquor they had been drinking all night, they sang loudly and were in gay spirits.

Good evening master and mistress,
And to everyone else who lives with you.
For the first day of the year,
You owe us La Guignolee.
If you have nothing at all to give,
Tell us of it right away.
We're not asking for much,
A chine of meat or so will do.
A chine of meat is not a big thing,
Only ninety feet long.
Again, we're not asking for very much,
Only the oldest daughter of the house.
We will give her lots of good cheer,
And we will surely warm her feet.
Now, we greet your company,
And beg you to forgive us, please.
If we have acted a little crazy
We only meant it in good fun.
Another time we'll surely be careful
To know when we must come back here again.
Let us dance la Guenille, la Guenille, la Guenille
Bonsoir le maitre et la maitresse
Et tout le monde du logis.

The next spring furs flooded into the trading post in rapid numbers and Joshua kept both keelboats busy ferrying bales to St. Louis. When he made the trip to the city, Joshua sometimes spent the night with Jacques and filled his friend in on the happenings at St. Genevieve. Jacques prospered also and was now a junior partner in the firm of Merdoix and Perault, an established fur company in St. Louis.

That June, Jacques accompanied Joshua back to St. Genevieve to visit his family and to participate in the Du jour de ma fete, or St. Peter's Day Festival annually held on the 24th of June. All of St. Genevieve would turn out and the party lasted the whole day and well into the night. Music would play in the streets and people would visit, drink, and dance the night away to reels and cotillions. It was a festival both of the young men looked forward to. This year it was an especially fine celebration, and both of them were intoxicated by midnight. With this false sense of bravado, they swaggered their way down Market Street to challenge all comers in a game of billiards and to enjoy each other's company. As the pair entered through the blue doors of the Shady Rest Tavern, Joshua's attention was drawn to the center of the room where, seated at a table, two men were playing a card game, Vingt-un, a popular gambling game. Retrieving spirits from the bartender, the two gathered with the crowd to watch the game and the flow and ebb of stakes being gambled. With a muffled curse, the smaller of the two players threw his cards upon the table and glared at the other man's good fortune. On the companions' last New Year's celebration, Joshua was introduced to many young men in the community and knew the lucky gambler to be Hubardeau, a local hell-raiser, and one of his "La Guignolee" companions.

The little gambler arose from the table, looking like an angry weasel, and with the words, "sacre, foutu Berdache" (damned fucking faggot, curse your luck) took two steps to the edge of the tavern wall and clutched the arm of a young Black woman standing there. He dragged her to the table, the weasel's grip on her arm made the young women wince in pain. "The winnings in front of you for this Black bitch," he said, addressing Hubardeau.

Reaching inside his coat pocket, Weasel threw a Bill of Sale on the table and signed it with a flourish. Slaves, although common in St. Genevieve were not gambled as trade goods here, and most of the residents, White, Black or Mulatto, slave or free respected the Code Noir. To do otherwise were very poor manners. Slaves could be bought or sold as chattel, but were recognized as human beings and could not be mistreated. The room grew quiet with this show of disrespect. Hubardeau regarded the pile of notes in front of him, inspected the Bill of Sale, and shuffled the cards.

"Ah, monsieur," Hubardeau smiled, "you have mistaken me for a Spaniard. If I were of this race, you would now be dead for your insult, but being Creole instead, I accept your wager. When you lose, be careful of your tongue, or else you shall lose it along with this mulatto wench."

The cards were dealt and the small man smiled and turned over two face cards, indicating a count of twenty--almost perfect. The smile froze on the weasel's face when Hubardeau, with a yawn, revealed his hand--a perfect count of Vingt-un.

Glancing at Hubardeau as he rose from the table, Weasel, with a snarl on his face, viciously backhanded the face of the Black girl standing beside him, knocking her to the floor, breaking her nose, and sending blood spraying across the white cloth of the table. Daring anyone with his look, he straightened his suit and pushed through the onlookers, out the door and into the summer night.

Joshua quickly knelt beside the young slave pressing his handkerchief to her face to staunch the flow of blood. Her eyes were wide with pain and fright.

"Hold still," he said, "no one will hurt you again."

"Good job, Hubardeau," said Jacques, "you sent that braggart packing. A toast to all, and to your new lady. My, but Mrs. Hubardeau will be happy when you bring your winnings home. Quick, my good fellow, how much will you have for her? My brother, Joshua, is lonely tonight and for his St. Peter's Day present I will buy her for him."

"Five hundred piastres and not one less, you thief, Bolduc," said Hubardeau and laughed as Jacques threw the money on the table.

"A deal it is, but surely you will buy the drinks with my money," laughed Jacques. Hubardeau laughed loudly and the crowd surged toward the bar, the recent unpleasantness behind them.

Joshua helped the young woman rise to her feet, just now realizing that he owned someone. Joshua knew in the morning he would regret this trip to the billiard hall and would have to take the kidding of these fellows for many days to come. For now though, he needed a drink, and followed Jacques to the bar, after all it was the 24th.

Joshua awoke the next morning with a throbbing head and eyes that could barely focus on the nauseating world spinning before him. With trouble Joshua tried to concentrate on the events of the evening before, and slowly through the pain, the previous night's events were reconstructed. He remembered the dancing, the drinking, and Jacques' free spirited dealings. Joshua also began to recall the happenings at The Shady Rest and, last but not least, his St. Peter's Day present. Looking around the room Joshua appeared to be alone. After several wobbly attempts, he arose and made slow progress to the doorway of the main room, finding this empty also, vacant and rather barren except for the papers laying on the dining table. Forcing himself to focus on the papers, Joshua recognized Jacques' writing, a short note scribbled hastily.

Joshua my friend,

   Your snores and drunken behavior have driven me away. I caught a ride with Father's boat early this morning for my return; duty calls. You understand. I pray to see you before the summer nights of July, please write when time allows. I dearly hope that Rodde can be of service to you, perhaps in the post or the homestead.

   Yours in faith,
   J.

Lying beside Jacques' handwritten note was a Bill of Sale for "1 piece d'Inde Slave", dated today, with the inscription *Sold this date to Joshua Timenaux Coural, for the value of past services rendered and in friendship, signed Jacques Bolduc, St. Genevieve*. The bill was labeled Rodde Krispin and gave a physical description of a young Black girl, aged twenty-one years.

The events of the last evening then were true, thought Joshua. He walked across the room and into the garden located behind the house where he saw Rodde, carefully hoeing the weeds from between the rows of his cabbages. Her dress was the same as the previous evening, the crimson splashes now dark on the white fabric. She looked quickly up at him, and then cast her eyes downward again, continuing to hoe. Joshua took a few minutes to reflect upon her appearance before speaking.

Rodde was light skinned, perhaps of Mulatto descent, and of average height, though she appeared to be slightly built, with broad shoulders, a narrow waist and flaring hips. Her dark mane of hair was pulled into a single, flowing wave behind her neck and tied with a red ribbon. From this constriction it then exploded across Rodde's back almost as if it was a capote guarding her shoulders. Rodde's eyes were dark, and her thin nose and facial structure still looked bruised and swollen. Long legs fell beneath the hem of her white linen dress and her calves, strongly muscled, were joined to impossibly slender ankles and tiny feet.

"Good morning, Rodde," said Joshua somewhat shyly, "I apologize for my infirmity last night. Hopefully, my friend Jacques observed better manners."

"Yes, Master Joshua," she replied, "he bade me follow the both of you home last night and instructed me to place my belongings in the smaller house. He said you would need tending in the morning and I was to make use of myself until then. Is this correct?"

"Rodde, before this goes further, let me explain. Although many families own slaves, here in St. Genevieve, my mother would never allow it while she lived, nor do I feel this is proper. Upon the morn, we will go to the Comandante, and I will sign for your emancipation so you may return to your family. Please call me Joshua, as the only Master is our Maker."

Rodde dropped her hoe, and anger bristled in her eyes as she spoke, "And wouldn't that be easy; free just like that, to make my way into the countryside and live the life of a Marrons, without shelter and food, begging from the savages, just to appease your conscience. Even that though, would be better than before," she said. "Garcia lives only because he lost the wager; if he had won, I would have killed him and then been forced to be a Marron in the wilderness. Not once more would I have allowed him to touch me. He was sure his fortune was awaiting him in St. Louis, may the great river swallow him whole before he arrives to search for it. And now you wish to turn me out. Master Bolduc warned me of this."

Joshua's headache got progressively worse when he tried to reason this out. "All right," he said, "of this we will hold further discussion; for now I must retire. Tomorrow you may accompany me to the post where you can begin to learn of the duties there. Do you read and do figures?"

"I'm acquainted with writing in French, Spanish, and English," she said, "most nominal addition, subtraction, their multipliers and rations are not difficult. Now please retire Mas-er-Joshua, and let me continue in this unkempt weed bed."

The summer proved extremely interesting and productive for Joshua. The cleanliness in Joshua's house improved dramatically, and with Rodde in the post, Joshua was freed to travel and advertise for trade, especially with the Osage and Chickasaw bands to the south of St. Genevieve. He found Rodde to be an excellent cook and her food reminded him of his mother's, although Rodde's gumbo or quingombo as she called it, was much spicier to the taste. She used the bake oven daily and insisted that Joshua make a huche for kneading bread. The large, coarse loaves, or miches, when she pulled them from the oven on the long pelle, were the best he ever ate.

Rodde explained to him that her mother died from influenza in New Orleans five winters previous. Her mother was a concubine to a learned Spanish gentleman there, and she supposed this man was her father although he was cold and distant and she never knew him well. He was recalled to Spain when she was still young. When her mother died, she was sold to an Abbe in New Orleans and maintained the church and had taken care of the priests. It was here that she learned her studies from the priests. As she grew into a young woman, the Abbe sold her to the Weasel, or Garcia, as she called him.

One day as Joshua returned from a two-day trip in late August from the Riviere a la Barbue or Meramec River, he found Rodde setting the table in the house for the evening meal. "I've been expecting you," she said. "You smell of skunk and stinking hides. Do not enter this house with those clothes on," she said firmly, shaking her finger at him. "Disrobe outside, before you enter. I have water heating to scrub that smell from your hide. If you are ashamed of your manhood, I will close my eyes."

Not quite expecting this reception in his house, Joshua could do little but comply. Checking to see that she was honoring her promise, he let his clothing fall to the floor and scurried across the cold flagstones into the large iron tub setting near the central fireplace.

"Rodde," he said, "I can take a bath without help."

"No one can remove such stench from the skin," she said. "Today I made soap with plenty of lye. Since you make me eat at your table, the least you can do is not ruin my appetite with your reek."

Feeling extremely uncomfortable from the hot water and his bareness, Joshua sensed Rodde approaching from behind him. He then felt the rough soap bite the top of his shoulders and as she rubbed deep into the thick muscles, the miles of trails washed away. He was quickly alert again when her strong hands pushed beneath the surface of the water to wash his flat stomach, tracing the ropes of muscle there. He felt her breasts through the thin, linen blouse, now wet from the water on his back. He imagined their russet fullness, feeling her nipples harden as she scrubbed, inscribing their firmness into his skin. Feeling his change in alertness, she stepped quickly back from the tub.

"Perhaps you are clean enough," she said. "Step into this blanket and I will finish with supper." She turned her head as Joshua rose from the tub and wrapped the woolen blanket around him to hide his arousal.

The rest of supper quietly passed, with both of them reflecting on what transpired earlier. Rodde quickly cleared the table, left one set of candles burning and bade Joshua goodnight as she returned to her quarters.

A month later in September, Joshua once again broached the subject of Rodde's emancipation. "If you think that little of me" she said, "then pay me wages for what I do and I will buy my freedom and a passage back to New Orleans where I can set up a school for young Mulatto girls to prepare them for their lot in life."

"Rodde," said Joshua, "during the summer I have come to value you greatly. This is the first I have traveled this much, and have complete trust in the post running smoothly. Never have I eaten so well, nor have the grounds and estate been so well maintained. For this I am thankful. If wages are your desire then you shall have them if they are within my means."

"Excuse my sharpness," replied Rodde, "it's just that even around the Abbe I had to be very careful, although his taste ran to young boys. You have treated me with kindness and respect; you allow me to eat at your table and have not forced me into your bed. Thank you for your trust. I'm sorry you do not find me attractive as a woman and wish me to go."

Joshua struggled to find an appropriate answer to this. If he told her how badly he wanted her, he would confirm her suspicions. If he said nothing, then he would insult her sex. Figuring a safe channel down a flooding river was easier than dealing with women, he decided.

The fall cold snap came early and both Joshua and Rodde stayed away from further conversation about emancipation or hot baths. Joshua found that he could not keep his eyes from Rodde as she worked around the post, always seeming to find the tallest shelf to stretch and put items on, accentuating her form against the thin material of her dress. At other times she would crowd behind the counter when he was there, leaving a lingering remembrance of her suppleness as she rubbed against him.

In December, prior to Christmas Mass which would be followed by Le Reveillon, the wake-up, Rodde prepared a special meal of patates anglaises, vegetable soup with peas, cabbage and onions, catfish fried in bear's oil, Boudin (a rich blood sausage) and a dessert of custard and cheese. Joshua washed this down with cups of thick, dark coffee.

"Truly a feast for the Saints," said Joshua as he moved to the fireplace and lit his French clay pipe. The room filled with the strong fragrance of the homegrown tobacco. Rodde also moved to the fireplace, drawing her knees under her as she stared pensively toward the flickering flames.

"Of what do you think so deeply?" asked Joshua.

Turning toward him, Joshua was surprised to see her eyes glistening with tears.

"Never in my life have I been so happy," she said, "nor more contented, and yet the one thing I want more than anything else seems beyond my reach."

"If it is possible, I will try to help to you get that one thing," said Joshua. "What is it you wish for?"

Without a word, Rodde arose and knelt before Joshua. Slowly she undid the loops from around the small bone fasteners on her dress, letting it fall in a cascade from her shoulders and down her slender waist before it wisped over her hips to the stone floor.

"Oh Joshua," she said, as Rodde pulled the red ribbon from her hair, letting it wash across the hollows of her shoulders framing her auburn colored breasts, "what I want is you."

Le Reveillon continued outside in the streets of New Town, but here inside the house the fire burned, unrestrained, long into the night, thrusting and unbridled until it consumed the passion that existed within its walls.

The shrill neigh of a frightened horse roused Joshua from his reverie and he quickly looked forward to see Night Wind's horse sliding down the embankment in front of him. The heavy winter snows that were now melting penetrated deep into the mountainside until the ground on the steep slope became so saturated that it could hold no more moisture. Almost as if the soil were liquid, the trail and ten square yards of the mountainside loosened and began sliding, picking up speed toward the icy creek bed below.

Horrified, Joshua jumped his horse quickly ahead, sweeping Spotted Owl from the boy's mount lest this pony also slid over the edge. Spotted Owl's horse staggered and fell to both knees as the earth buckled beneath his hooves. Finally regaining his footing, the horse spun on the narrow trail and raced out of control past Joshua and Spotted Owl, back up the trail. Within seconds Night Wind's horse reached the bottom of the creek bed, slamming into the ice and rocks of the narrow channel. Her horse, unable to maintain his balance on the shifting terrain, rolled completely over before coming to rest in the shallow water. Night Wind, tiger-like, jumped as the horse began to roll, but the pony's momentum was too fast and she was crushed beneath him. His weight pushed her deep into the soft hillside. The mud flowed over her, trapping her in its folds before she reached the bottom. A jagged rock sitting upright served as a disruption in the slide twenty feet down the hill. This was the only sign, almost like a headstone, that marked where Night Wind was obscured beneath the earth.

Leaping from his horse and throwing the reins to Spotted Owl, Joshua raced over the edge slogging in the deep, cold mud. Sinking almost to his waist, he cried Night Wind's name as he half swam, half ran toward the depression where she disappeared. Her horse, below in the creek, staggered to his feet, blowing disapproval of the cold water and lurched out onto the bank, still shaken by the fall. From the corner of his eye Joshua could see La Ramie and the boys struggling through the mud on the other side of the slide. Reaching the large headstone, Joshua began to tunnel frantically with his hands, slinging mud behind him like a badger digging a hole. La Ramie was soon with him and without spoken words, both men burrowed as if life depended on their efforts. It did-- Night Wind's life--for if they failed to reach her quickly she would suffocate in the rich, brown ooze.

Finally reaching the base of the large boulder, both men turned their shoulders to the uphill side and pushed, straining to gain traction on the slick slope. Unable to resist their combined strength, the granite slab began to topple with a sucking sound and at last gave up its perch in the ground, rolling slowly on down the hill. Within the depression Joshua saw a dirtied foot, scraped and raw from the crushing weight and sharp edges of the stone.

"Dig for all your worth Joshua," said La Ramie, "she hasn't much time."

"Please not again," cried Joshua, "please don't take her again," and he renewed his efforts forcing his numb hands further into the mud.

Joshua stopped momentarily, unable to find Night Wind's leg that should have been attached above the small buckskin-clad foot.

"Here," shouted La Ramie, "dig to the left; she's lying on this side."

With both men scooping mud, Night Wind's leg and torso were soon uncovered. Grasping her by the waist Joshua pulled with all his strength, and was startled when the grave released its prisoner, expelling her, doll-like and limp into his grasp. Gripping her roughly by her hair, Joshua turned her face-up and wiped away the mud from Night Wind's mouth, nose, and eyes. Still and white, her bronze skin appeared ivory and cold to the touch. Without hesitation, Joshua forced a thick finger into her mouth removing the dirt, and then pressed his lips to her mouth. La Ramie watched as Night Wind's chest expanded from Joshua's breath. Three times Joshua forced air into her small frame and then paused to raise her head.

"Nothing," La Ramie exclaimed. "Nothing! She ain't breathing."

Joshua lowered his face to her mouth again when he realized that both of her eyes were open now, unfocused, but open. With a gagging sound Night Wind gasped and then began to breathe, sucking in huge draughts as if she could not fill her lungs. Within seconds her back arched and she bit her lower lip. Concerned, Joshua pulled her closer to hear her hoarse whisper.

"My leg, my leg," she said.

Both Joshua and La Ramie looked down to discover that Night Wind's left leg was lying unnaturally. Her toe was pointed upward, but from the knee it was bent sharply at a left angle.

"Little Dog and Lone Eagle, be quick. Down in the bottom, cut two willows the thickness of your wrist and the length of your arm. Hurry! Your sister's leg is plum out of wack. We're going to have to straighten it, and she's not going to like it much. We will need the splints when we get it right."

"GO!" La Ramie shouted, pushing the two boys down the slope.

"What can I do?" asked Joshua.

"Raise her hips over top of your thighs," said La Ramie, "I'm gonna have ta pull real hard to put that knee straight, and I need to pull down. If I don't pull hard enough, I might break her leg worse."

Joshua grasped Night Wind by the waist and gently raised her, sliding her slender hips over his legs as he knelt in the cold mud. He could see the blood running down Night Winds chin from where she had bitten through her lower lip. Her eyes, clear now, were focused on his, trusting and unmoving.

139

"Sorry Night Wind," said La Ramie, "this won't feel none too good but we have to do it now before we move you."

Her head nodded, but her lips remained tightly clenched.

"Hold tight, Joshua," La Ramie said sternly, "don't let her move."

Turning slightly, Joshua wrapped his arms around her and clutched her to his chest, letting her legs dangle over his lap.

"Do it now, La Ramie," said Joshua, "before I crush her plumb to death."

The trapper put one bear-like hand just above Night Wind's knee pinning it tight to Joshua's leg and then grasp her ankle with his other hand. Joshua felt a tremendous jerk as La Ramie pulled down hard on the leg, twisting it straight at the same time. Night Wind's spasm smashed hard into Joshua before she passed out. Joshua turned his head to look at La Ramie and saw him smiling. Night Wind's leg was straight.

"Done that one time to my own elbow," La Ramie chuckled, "still gives me shivers to think about it. Now quit hugging her and pack her on down the slope. Them boys oughta have some sticks cut by now. I don't think it was much broke, just kinda outa joint."

Joshua rose to his feet gently cradling Night Wind in his arms. He plowed slowly through the mud to the creek bottom wading through the water to lay Night Wind on the grassy bank. La Ramie helped the boys finish cutting the sticks. Using his sharpened knife, he whittled them to his liking and then flattened one side of each one before placing them on Night Wind's leg. Taking a long piece of banded rawhide from his medicine kit, he then wound it tightly around Night Wind's leg, securing the flattened sticks snuggly.

"Kain't make them too tight till her knee stops swelling," La Ramie said, "or her foot might fall off. We'll tighten them down more tomorrow. You boys, fetch them horses down the slope, we're gonna hafta stay here a couple of days until Night Wind gets to feeling better."

Within several hours, camp was established and the horses were unsaddled and strung on the picket line in a small stand of quakies close to the creek. Night Wind's horse, recovered from his fall, was now nipping at the others as if it had been an average day. Night Wind herself came to, and other than wincing when she tried to move, said little as she watched the men in her life setting up camp and starting to prepare the evening meal. Spotted Owl stayed close by his mother's side, pretending he wasn't worried, but he kept looking at her out of the corner of his eye.

Joshua brought Night Wind a cloth, wet with creek water so she could bathe the mud from her face and arms. She finished splitting the rawhide moccasin for her injured leg, which was now badly swollen and blackening.

"Thank you," she said. "My time to become one with Mother Earth is not yet, thanks to a bear that digs like a badger."

"Sometimes I can be good for something," he replied. "What can I do to help you?"

"After supper have Spotted Owl gather some of the low, blue sage. He knows which kind. From this I will make a tea. Now, would you bring me some ice from the creek? It will help with the pain."

She touched her lip that still oozed blood from her bite marks. "I am not sure which you crushed worse," she said, "my ribs which are broken, or my mouth which is smashed from your attempts to blow the breath of life back into me, cheating the earth."

"I'm sorry," stammered Joshua, "you almost scared the life out of me."

Smiling, she caught hold of his hand and brought it to her cheek. "Thank you especially for protecting Spotted Owl. He worships you, and therefore will not revenge me against you for ravaging his mother."

Joshua rose to help La Ramie with the final preparations and chased down Spotted Owl to tell him of his mother's request for the sage. With Night Wind's sharp tongue returning, he felt confident that she would be mending soon. With the passing of the evening meal, Joshua spread his groundsheet over Night Wind and listened to her tales of her home village near the Water That Boils, one week's journey to the west. She told of the games that she played when she was a little girl and of how her mother would hold her when she hurt herself, rocking and crooning songs in her soft voice. Morning Ray, her mother, was a Vision Woman like herself, and she tried to prepare Night Wind for the omens that would stalk her evening sleeps. By the time Night Wind saw thirteen winters, her visions were stronger, and more frequent than her mother's. Morning Ray died when Night Wind was sixteen, and Morning Ray predicted her own death a week before her passing. She was buried with great honor. Kills-Crowe took a new wife, and from this squaw Painted Flower, Little Dog and Lone Wolf were born. Night Wind became the Vision Woman for her people.

"If you see things," said Joshua, "why didn't you see the trail disappearing, and not ride across it."

"My own death is all that I will see of events that happen to me," she said. "It is visions of what might pose danger to my people, my family, and those I love, which come the strongest to me. I saw myself returning to the Water That Boils camp, but I was alone, and not with my brothers or Kills-Crowe. It was for them I worried. Kills-Crowe died as he would have wished, and now I know that my brothers will return without me, for it will be weeks before I can travel that far. I am happy, for now I understand my dreams."

"And of me," asked Joshua, "what do you see?"

"Of bears that crush me," she answered, "I see nothing." Disturbed though, she remembered her vision of Joshua's face and blue hat, trapped beneath layers of ice. About this vision she said nothing. "Besides, my duty is to my family and those I love. Are you one of those?"

"I don't know," said Joshua. "I found myself wondering the same thing earlier in the day."

Night Wind never answered this but fell to rearranging the tarp across her legs.

The next two days the party stayed close to the creek and by the end of the second day the swelling slowly left Night Wind's leg, although she could not stand nor bear any weight upon the leg. Joshua fashioned a cross of willows and padded it with pieces of a blanket. Together with a leather cinch it could be attached to her horse allowing her to ride, keeping her leg straight along her pony's neck. La Ramie suggested a travois behind one of the pack animals but Night Wind refused to even listen to this suggestion.

"Like dragging bait for the Blackfoot fish to swallow," was all she said.

Night Wind was skeptical of Joshua's invention at first but when she saw it fitted to her horse she nodded, grudgingly, that it might work. "It is like the saddle of La Ramie's," she said, "but instead I ride to the side."

She did insist on braiding leather around the cinch ring so her horse would not be galled. Joshua watched her quick fingers spin the leather thongs into a pattern around the circular ring. It appeared very similar to the way his father braided with three long bights, the final knot resembling a turkey head. Seeing that Joshua was interested, she helped him braid another ring from an extra circingle in his packs. She wrapped the thong around the mandrel twice, then brought it back over its own loop and returned it under the standing end. The knot was intricate and she laughed when Joshua's big hands had trouble feeding the leather.

"Our lives," she said, "are like this ring and braid. From it life has no beginnings and endings, each is joined, one into the other. Men and women, too, are like the leather that covers it. Alone, they cannot protect themselves, but when they intertwine, a bond is formed and although they become part of the ring of life, they are never quite joined to it, only to one another. It is this joining which gives meaning to life and enables them to become part of it."

Leaning across Joshua, Night Wind grasped his fingers, helping him count the layers of rawhide before crossing them and turning them under. Joshua relaxed with her touch, enjoying the feeling of strength in her small hands, although both of hers would have fit easily into one of his. When the second ring was finished, Joshua turned the work slowly and admired the way the leather fit the cold metal, thinking of Night Wind's words, delving for the meaning beneath. He could feel Night Wind's breath on his cheek, softly ruffling his coarse beard. He savored the feeling a moment before arising, not wanting to break the spell. Once on his feet he turned to Spotted Owl and tossed him the ring.

"Here, Spotted Owl, we had better keep this in case the other one wears out. I'll just lose it, so from now on, you're in charge of the equipment. Keep it safe."

Spotted Owl took the object and, removing a thong from around his neck, he quickly threaded the cord through the small ring and placed it back around his neck, dropping it inside of his jerkin. Looking at his mother for her assurance, he received her nod, then jumped to his feet to run and brag to the older boys about his importance.

"You will make his head too big," said Night Wind. "He respects you very much."

"He will be a great warrior; one day I'll like being with him," was all Joshua said. "I better go help La Ramie or he will be grumpy all day."

Early the next morning they left their camp by the quakie creek and rode on through a large valley. On their left, the Blue Mountain rose beside them, massive and dark, flowing southward into a long ridge of mountains almost as large as it was. To their right were ranges of hills, much smaller than the Blue Mountain, but rough and rugged with huge boulders and thick, tangled timber. The valley they rode in was perhaps a mile wide and the creek they followed flowed west, continually sloping downward toward a vast plain that ended with a distant mountain chain far into the horizon. They stopped often to allow Night Wind to rest, and Joshua lifted her on and off her horse, balancing her while she settled her leg into his invention. By evening of their second day in the valley, the range on their left veered sharply southward and the hills on their right dropped suddenly into the earth as if it had been swallowed whole. Before them, as far as they could see, was a vast expanse of low, rolling hills. These were La Ramie's plains. Several miles further they arrived suddenly at the banks of another creek flowing from the northwest. The quakie creek emptied her snow-filled waters into this stream and together they turned southward disappearing through a large cleft of blood-red rocks. High and broken, this pass appeared to be a giant's box of earthen china that was broken and shattered before being dumped here. From these fissures in the broken-china wall, stunted evergreens clung precariously to the vertical sides. They camped there at the joining of the streams that night.

"Too damn much quicksand in these parts to go wandering around in the dark," said La Ramie. "It will be chilly tonight, and I don't want to dig anyone else out of the mud."

They feasted well on antelope that La Ramie killed as it came for its evening drink at the river. The men laughed at the boys as they pretended they were young antelope bucks ramming each other with their heads in proof of their virility. The older boys would always jump aside sending Spotted Owl sprawling when he tried to hook them. In the glow of the campfire, Night Wind told Joshua and La Ramie the story of these plains.

Long ago the father of the Plains people lived upon these grasslands. He had more wives than he could visit in two moons, and the horses in his remuda could not be counted. He grew fat and wise, but still he was never contented, always wanting more and more. Of all the people in his tribe only one she-child did he covet and yet was unable to obtain. Her hair was raven black, and she could run with the breath of the wind, faster than the antelope. She was the daughter of Manitou and appeared one spring onto the earth, not from mortal parents. Skediswasha was the Chief's name, and all day he schemed to trick Walira, the daughter of the Great Manitou, into his robes. Fearing the wrath of Manitou if he took her by force, he announced that in the spring, whoever in his tribe could cover the most ground within the hides of buffalo robes would marry Walira, thus proving to the Great Manitou that this would be a man worthy of his daughter. Within the bounds of these robes a mighty teepee would be built to serve as a wedding bed for Walira. Throughout the winter, Skediswasha traded horses for buffalo robes until his teepee was full to the ceiling. There wasn't even room inside to bed his wives. When winter at last went north, a day was announced for the contest for the hand of Walira. On that day from within his teepees, Skediswasha brought forth and covered the grounds outside his village with robes until they spread beyond sight of the sharpest eyes. No other young brave in the village could match their vastness. No other young brave except one. Tui-it-Tusi loved Walira from the moment she sprang from the stars, not for the offering of her supple loins, as did Skediswasha, but for her clear laughter and glad heart. Since he was young and poor he owned but three buffalo hides to offer for the contest, but during the long winter nights he slowly and painstakingly carved each of the three robes into rawhide strings, joining them together until he made ropes and ropes from the three hides. These ropes Tui-it-Tusi brought from his tent and encircled the great mass of robes Skediswasha laid upon the ground. So long were his ropes of rawhide that it took Tui-it-Tusi three days to spread the coils. The land within the thongs ran from the Blue Mountains to the Water-That-Boils in the west. Realizing that he was beaten, Skediswasha screamed in rage and drove his great war lance through the heart of Walira rather than let another man have her. The Plains people turned then upon their chief and tied him to the ant hills beyond the deep ridge until there was no more remembrance of this evil deed among their people. The Great Manitou, so stricken by the loss of his daughter, has never allowed any people to live upon these plains again, within the bounds of that rawhide thong. Only in the summer may they hunt here, and they must return to their lodges in the far valleys during the winter moons. Tui-it-Tusi still wanders these broken hills, lamenting for the loss of his beloved, and during the summer he visits with Walira as she sits with her father among the hanging stars. This is why no tribes live upon this great grassland; if they tried, Manitou would drive them away with his icy, winter breath.

That night as he watched the glowing embers of the campfire slowly fade and extinguish, Joshua wondered which parts of Night Wind's story contained parts that were based in truth. Why didn't the Indians live on these plains, and how were these lands formed so vast and flat between the guarding mountains? Why did the antelope have the strange white coloration that made them visible from miles away?

The next morning the group began winding its way from the flat headwaters into the steep canyon that opened before them. At first the ascent was gradual and then the wall began to grow steeper. Joshua could see the layering of rock on the canyon wall like written lines in a book. Each mile further down the canyon another chapter was written in the rock, telling of times long ago when even this element was tormented by the great forces that shaped this chain of mountains. The effect of depth increased as the river trail ran downward and the mountains seemed to rise. At last La Ramie paused, and just ahead they could see a mist of vapor arising from a jagged tumble of boulders, which eons ago crashed into the streambed from the high cliffs above.

"There is a steep falls ahead," said La Ramie. " There we have to climb the hills. There ain't no way down these falls." The water ran faster now, hastening towards its plunge just ahead. La Ramie turned his big horse up the hillside, taking the slope at an angle and then switching directions every twenty yards or so, making a z-like pattern through the green grass growing from the rocky soil. Old Bay's feet dug deep into the soil as he bunched his powerful hindquarters before making each jump. Spotted Owl's eyes grew big when he saw the trail he must follow and Joshua took the pack horse's lead rope from the boy's hand, dallying it around his own pommel. He didn't want to lose the supplies this close to the end of their journey.

One by one the riders worked their way up the steep slope pausing at the top to glance downward into the valley below. From here they could see the water rushing over the falls plunging thirty feet before resuming its flow down the river. Below the falls, huge rounded stones from years of erosion lay tumbled haphazardly, as if two giant children left their marbles piled in a heap. Joshua could see now why La Ramie chose this trail around the obstacle. A narrow game trail appeared visible as the group rode the knife-edge of high ridge they just climbed. This continued eastward for a mile before La Ramie kicked the big bay through a high saddle and suddenly disappeared from sight ahead of them. Joshua drug the tired pack horse with him and held his breath as he rode through the saddle, observing the full measure of the vista that spread before him.

With the sun in its zenith, the bright spring sunshine flooded off the canyon walls. Here, high above the river, a broad meadow of native fescue and orchard grass shifted gently in the breeze, waving an invitation to the travelers. Ahead a squat brown structure nestled at the far recesses of the grassy lane. La Ramie stopped the big horse, sitting easy in the saddle to take in the panorama.

"I never get tired of this," he said. "No matter where I travel, it is to this place that I wish to return. Promise me Joshua, if it be within your power, it is to this corner of the land I wish to rest in eternity."

Taken aback by the blunt honesty in the trapper's voice, Joshua could merely answer, "I will promise you that."

Even the boys were subdued as they rode across the lush grasses of the meadow into the hollow valley. This quiet lasted momentarily, and then they raced toward the cabin, taunting Spotted Owl who was vainly trying to keep up with them.

The cabin itself was plain, but here in the corner of the world, touched by God's hand, it seemed an oasis from the travails from the rest of the Earth. Just as the small meadow threatened to turn into the rock wall bordering its green flanks, the cabin guarded each work of nature from the other. The rear wall of the cabin with the mountain behind, dug deep into the red earth. Each sidewall was part rock, part timber. It blended the two forms of scenery seamlessly. Small, measuring only twenty feet per side, the roof was laid with large pine trunks, and then sodded to prevent the intrusion of the elements. A small corral was also notched into the hillside, with a pole gate being the only opening.

La Ramie directed the boys to place the horses in the corral after they were rubbed down and watered in the small stream snaking its way through the meadow. The stream flowed past the cabin and down through a crevice just below the saddle they rode through before falling in sheets of vapor down into the river below. Joshua lifted Night Wind to the ground and then helped La Ramie carry the canvas bags into the cabin's darkened interior. The light swept into the cabin as the door was opened, revealing a simple interior of two handmade bureaus, a dark knurled table, and a bed made from the antlers of several large elk. One window on the west side of the cabin was covered with deer hide.

Joshua turned to gaze back out the door, watching the boys rubbing the horses with thick handfuls of grass. The horses enjoyed this game, and tried to nibble the grass from the boys' hands by craning their necks back over their shoulders as the boys made mock threats at them to stand still. Stolen fruit was always sweeter than the lush green they were standing in. As Joshua's eyes swept the view in front of him, they traced the path of the stream as it wandered through the small meadow, pooling into a pond the size of the cabin, before breaking over its rock dam and spilling on into the crevice.

"Are there any fish in that pond?" he asked La Ramie.

"Only those that I brung up from the river below," La Ramie answered. "Them fish haven't figured out how to climb rocks yet."

"Then I'm going to the river and catch some," laughed Joshua. "This here Mississippi boy has gone too long without fishing. I'm tired of riding, tired of eating antelope, and ready for some fresh fish. Night Wind, if you weren't such a burden, I'd drag you with me to clean 'em after I catch 'em, but I reckon you and your bum leg had better stay here."

"I will stay here and wait for the mighty warrior to bring the fish, and then if any appear I will clean them. Perhaps I had better prepare a stew with the rest of this meat before your return," answered Night Wind.

"Just give me some of the meat for bait, or cheese if you have any, and this river boy won't have to eat antelope anymore."

Leaving La Ramie and Night Wind to finish unpacking, Joshua beckoned for Spotted Owl to follow him. Together they walked in the warm spring sunshine, following the course of the little stream as it meandered its way into the pond. The pond itself seemed somehow less inviting than the stream. Formed thousands of years ago by a rockslide; the water was dark and murky. Joshua was unable to see down into the depths, and just as he turned to walk through the crevice and down into the canyon, he thought he caught a stirring or reflection in the shadowy waters that somehow looked like him, but older much older and very pale. Shrugging off the feeling of darkness that came over him, he swung Spotted Owl high into the air, settling him on his shoulders.

"Look sharp little one; the perfect fishing pole is close. I can tell. We have to find it before we reach the river. Fresh fish will cheer your mother up and make that leg heal faster." With one more glance over his shoulder at the pond, Joshua felt relieved to see the water springing down the rocks, bright and clear again, almost as if the water was also happy to escape the confines of the darker pool behind it. The roar of the falls echoed ahead and Joshua could see the mist rising into the air creating a rainbow for them to follow, perhaps even with a pot of gold at its source for the two fishermen to find.

Chapter 7
The Weekend

Saturday broke bright and clear through the un-curtained window of Carrigan's bedroom. He lay still for a short while absorbing the rays of light flooding his eyes, slowly watching the dust particles as they swirled, reflecting in the light. It was as if the dust was a flowing stream, some part of a cosmic torrent coursing through a parallel world momentarily allowing him to witness this alternate universe.

He double-checked his memory before rolling over. No, he didn't have school today; yes, he could sleep in if he wanted to; yes, the starting stages of arthritis in his shoulders and hips would make him arise in a short period of time; no, he wasn't going to hang around here today. Today he would take a trip to the hills, maybe fish a little while in the cold, rushing torrents of liquid snow streaming down from every ravine of Laramie Peak. Maybe he would even lay out a foundation for the cabin he had already built in his mind. This was to be his retreat from the school, the town, and all of its hypocrisy he hated daily throughout the week. Rising quickly from beneath the warm, down comforter, he slid into the faded Levis, roper boots, and wool shirt lying across the saddle stand near his bed.

He felt a particular affection for the saddle on that stand. It had been his grandfather's, and while in use logged many miles crisscrossing the Laramie Plains. His grandfather worked for the Two Bar Land and Cattle Company in the early 1900s. Carrigan replaced the sheepskin and recovered the rawhide pommel on the saddle, but other than these repairs, the saddle and the stand remained unchanged and a perfect clotheshorse. Closets were a little too orderly and confining for Carrigan's taste.

Rich, Arabian coffee was quickly started in the unwashed percolator on the stove. Too much washing could ruin young boys, good dogs, and old coffeepots. Somehow the automatic coffee makers left a metallic taste in his mouth. He much preferred the dark elixir when it was boiled on the stove.

Hot and black, he thought to himself, causing a chuckle to escape his lips.

Suddenly a memory from last night flooded through him like a wave. He glanced down to his forearm, still feeling the fingers that touched him there the previous evening. Breathing in deeply, he checked to see if the faint aroma of perfume was detectable. As an ending to the week, he had stopped by Ben's to check out the Friday night fare, avoiding the can of soup sitting in his pantry at home. The Fat Tire beer and mini-burritos served their purpose and two pleasant hours were spent watching the milling Friday evening crowd surging past his observation post from the end bar stool.

How come the same people were always there when he was? Did he come that often, or were they just always there? Perhaps they were wondering the same thing about him.

He spoke to those he couldn't ignore, and watched the needy in their search, hoping to find something to fill their hunger at Ben's Bar and Burgers. The similarity between this Friday night hangout and the hallways at school seemed eerie tonight. Everyone was trying to be noticed, to get a laugh. Why was it that these were the very things he was trying to avoid?

Suddenly between his ninth burrito and his fourth beer (or was it the other way around?) he was shocked to see someone laying their fingers on his wrist preventing the glass from reaching his mouth. Staring at the fingers for a moment, he tried to determine their intent. They were strangely familiar, slender with square nails. Erotic, yet dangerous at the same time, the hand resembled a feline appendage holding its prey while determining whether to play or dismember.

"Hi, Nancy," he heard himself say, "how's the world treating you?"

Carrigan had seen Nancy twice in the last twenty years. For some reason he never made it to New York, nor had she made the trip to Wyoming while he finished the remaining years at the university. Several phone calls were filled with "HIs" and "How are yous", but the voices were cold and distant. The first time he saw her again after their life and death climb from the cold waters of the Laramie River Canyon was during his father's funeral. Like an apparition from his past, he suddenly noticed her sitting in the church on that cold, January afternoon. She hugged him briefly after the graveside services, surprising him with the warmth of her body and her presence. She explained that her father called her, and since she was traveling to the West Coast anyway, she drove north to pay her respects. As quickly as Nancy appeared, she was gone again, leaving him to feel the full bite of loneliness, both for her and his father.

The second time they met was after he purchased the land in the Laramie Mountain Range from the old moon shiner, Otto, who he visited with during the long nights in the hospital. Otto was quiet company when waiting for the inevitable at his father's bedside. The section of land Carrigan bought abutted some of the holdings owned by the Ranier Family. His attorney called a meeting just after Carrigan took possession to swap forties of land with the Raniers. With this trade, the fence lines between the two places would intersect on the section line instead of the haphazard fashion that existed the previous hundred years. This solidified Carrigan's access to the Laramie River and made the fencing much easier after the deep snows of winter melted from the fence lines. Nancy represented her father at the meeting and signed the papers on behalf of Rainer Ranches. With her small, neat script, she signed the quitclaim deeds, *Nancy Rainer Allen*. She smiled her slow, lazy smile Carrigan remembered from their school days and somewhat shyly explained she was the managing partner of the Ranier Ranches now. Her father was spending more time in the corporate headquarters back East, leaving her to run the day-to-day affairs. She talked about her frequent trips to Wyoming and her new responsibilities.

They retired for a drink after the paperwork was signed and caught up on passing years. Carrigan relaxed, enjoying the sound of her voice, predicting her mannerisms, with which, many years ago, he had been intimately familiar. She proudly showed him pictures of her son, Stephen Allen, and bragged of his accomplishments.

"I'm just like Father," she said. "Stephen's Dad and I have drifted apart over the years, but I want Stephen to be appreciative of Wyoming, so I bring him with me sometimes. He usually spends summers with his father's family in upstate New York, but maybe in a few years he will want to come out here. How about you, any kids or wives?"

"Not that I'm aware of," smiled Carrigan. "Those ladies that had kids scared me off, and those that didn't have any yet, scared me worse."

"I'm sorry," Nancy said, leaving Carrigan wondering what she was sorry for.

Allowing his mind to focus on the present, Carrigan glanced again at the slender fingers still resting on his arm. The hands hadn't changed. Somehow they still held him.

"How about a beer, cowboy?" she said.

One beer led to another and Carrigan found himself telling her about his frustration of teaching at a public high school and about the young people he dealt with daily. He also talked about his dreams for his mountain property and how he planned to start laying out the foundation for a new cabin.

"Of course, I might have to get some fishing in also," he said.

Brightening suddenly with his mention of the mountains and fishing in the river, she asked, "Do you remember the Devil's Fireplace?"

"You mean that place down by the river that some people aren't smart enough to stay away from?"

"Sometimes every girl needs to get rescued," she said. "How about I meet you there for lunch tomorrow? The river is still low enough I can wade across from the south. Father finally built a jeep road down that long draw on the south side. I can almost drive to the river now instead of coming clear around on the Cooney Hills Road. Plus, I don't have to climb down that damn ladder. If you are a gentleman you could help me carry the lunch across once I arrive."

"And ruin my good fishing spot?" Carrigan laughed. "Ok, I'll get there early and catch the big ones before you go splashing in the river. I'm not going to climb that ladder any more either; I'm too damn old. I can drop into the river canyon from my place across the school section and follow Wolf Draw down to the water. If I start early I can be to the Fireplace by noon."

The date was made and Nancy returned to the social crowd she was entertaining at the ranch that weekend. Carrigan returned home rather than meet and be pleasant to people he didn't like very well anyway.

That was last night and now, with the new day ahead of him, Carrigan pulled on his brown, duck Carhart, and headed out to meet the sunshine, glad to have a day away from school. Perhaps he was even looking forward to spending some time with Nancy again. Gertrude was waiting for him outside, frost still glistening on her sleeping bosom.

The morning sun was bright in his rear view mirror as he hit the blacktop heading toward the west. Gertrude finally warmed up three miles out, and the big 390 settled into a rumbling purr as she rolled down the highway. Carrigan reviewed what he would need for the day. In his metal toolbox bolted in the back and cached behind the seat was a variety of fishing equipment--poles, flies, nets, waders and other tools of his trade.

The thermos of coffee and a thick sack of cheese, crackers, and salami rode beside him in the seat. Extra coats, gloves, and hats were stowed away, along with binoculars, spotting scopes, and extra ammo for the pre-'64 Winchester 270 rifle. The rifle rode in its custom case above the visor, always close at hand. Tools galore, along with jacks, ropes, axes, and shovels, filled the rear of the pickup box.

You never know when you might need something in the mountains. It was a lot better to have the item you need rather than wish for it. In the hills, the road back to town could be a long way, thought Carrigan.

Ten miles out Carrigan turned onto a smaller oil road that veered off from the main highway. Laramie Peak was bright and clear in the morning sun ahead of him as he gunned Gertrude up to cruising speed. The road floated out before him, looking like a ribbon trailing from the shoestrings of the giant peak the loomed in his windshield. The highway worked its path across the flat plains and on up to the rough, broken hills bordering the Big Blue range. He soon crossed the bridge leading over the Laramie River that flowed cold and clear from the high country. The water rushed on by beneath him, heedless of his opinion or presence.

It's going to be tough fishing today, he thought, and Nancy is bound to get wet when she tries to wade across this much water, even if she sticks to the rocks.

Here on the flats the river ran broad and straight, trying to make up time for its torturous journey through the mountains where narrow granite channels caused it to twist and turn, always following its downward course. Once he crossed the river bridge, the ground began to rise. Low hummocks of dirt and sage folded in on themselves in intricate patterns. Although the area appeared level, many deep draws cut raw channels through the dark, red ground. Finally reaching the edge of the foothills he again turned from the oil road onto a dirt track, rough and bumpy with many hidden potholes. This trail led to the south of the looming mountain and worked onto the top of a high ridge. Now apparent in front of him was the heavy timber of the mountain. Below him he could make out the river snaking through the flatlands and on to its meeting with the Platte. Gertrude was obliged to slow down periodically allowing the mad dash of livestock exercising right-of-way as they bolted across the road in front of her.

From this height it was easy to see that this area once was a glacial moraine. Large boulders and smaller rocks were randomly scattered and each showed signs of rounding. The pervasive ice masses that once covered this area brought these huge monoliths down from higher areas, grinding them together and then stranding them when the ice retreated.

Just like some high school kids, thought Carrigan, they were just swept along with the flow, wanting to be part of something. In the end, their friends abandoned them, the group taking a different direction, and alone they remained, stranded on the great plains of their lives, waiting for the next glacier to move them along.

Below him Carrigan could see the dotted, green oases of old homesteads where trees delineated their location. The early settlers seemed to favor the planting of cottonwoods as if trying to escape from the evergreens looking down on them from the mountains. These trees grew to huge proportions, some being over twenty-three feet in girth. Most of the smaller homesteaders, unlike their trees, were now gone. A sign of the times.

Vast amounts of land were needed if there was to be efficiency in the livestock industry. Large cowherds could absorb the losses of bad winters and low prices. The smaller producers first borrowed on their cattle to get by, and then not wanting to face the facts, borrowed again on the land to try and make it to the good years. Unfortunately, the good years were few and far between. Most of the small ranchers were foreclosed upon, and the banks gobbled up the property and resold it. Land prices soared to the level where livestock production no longer could pay the interest on the cost of the land, let alone pay for the land itself. The doctors and lawyers even found owning ranch land too expensive a proposition and fled from their holdings. Corporations were now the chief owners and the land served as a write off on their amassing profits.

Carrigan never ceased to be amazed by the fact that the early homesteaders filed on the land further down the river where they could grow crops, and only the latecomers came to the hills, homesteading on the only land left. Now the mountain country was bringing higher prices than good farm ground. He still kept his folks' place, renting it on a yearly lease to a young couple that was trying to get established in the registered Angus business. Most years they made the lease payments, and Carrigan looked the other way when they couldn't. His parents paid for that land with blood, sweat, and tears, and he knew how hard a business it could be. In the spring, he sometimes missed being outside on the small ranch, but the school district paid his retirement, insurance, and weekends and summers were his to do as he pleased. On the ranch, the work was 24/7 and the only benefit was being your own boss. During the particularly trying times at school, being your own boss sounded pretty attractive.

Carrigan saved his money, and when this section of land came up, he bought it with cash. No bank would ever have the chance to foreclose on this dream. He sometimes toyed with the idea of returning to ranching, keeping his herd on the small ranch in the flats during the cold winter months and then trailing them to these high pastures for the summer, but that would interfere with his fishing.

Gertrude arrived at last to the bottom of a steep hill and here Carrigan got out and turned in the hubs, locking the pickup into four wheel drive. Shifting down to low range he gave the big vehicle her head and let her begin to idle up the rocky trail in front of him. For over two miles she climbed, sometimes leveling off to cross small meadows where snow still lay in dusted, brown banks, but then always turning her nose upward again to the sharp corners of the trail that lead to the top of Wild Horse Plateau. Reaching the crest, Carrigan glanced at the left fork that led to that fire station where he once spent a summer and saved a girl. He gave brief thought to turning in, but no one was in the post yet and he would have to climb down the rock face to fish the river.

Besides he thought, I have to make a decision on where I'm going to build this damn cabin.

Gertrude slowed, trying to sense his mood and then obligingly took the right hand trail up through Red Hound Canyon and into the state school land, Section 36. Because of his ownership of the adjoining section, the State of Wyoming leased this section to Carrigan on a yearly basis. He did little with the land other than hike it and enjoy its rugged beauty. Although only a mile in width, the actual distance of the trail across the section was closer to three miles with all the twists and turns. Magpies scolded him from their perches as he drove by, and several times he startled deer returning from the river before they bedded down in the high rocks. A large porcupine guarded the road just before the last turn and bristled when Carrigan honked the horn. Satisfied that his honor was defended, the porcupine turned aside, his tail bristling with threat, and ambled off the trail into a stand of quaking aspens, chattering to himself.

Carrigan thought about the old joke. *How do two porcupines make love?* The punch line being, *Veeeery carefully.*

A wire gate stood before the entrance to the next section of land, Carrigan's land. The gate was tightly stretched with an undue amount of tension. A hardened, pine opener hanging by a wire was required before the tension on the gate could be released, opening the latch. Carrigan took pride in having good fences around his property. His father always told him that good fences makes good neighbors. He remembered how angry his father would become when a neighbor's Longhorn bull would crash through the fence and mount the registered Angus heifers in his pasture before they could be artificially inseminated. Carrigan and his father would then rope the bull and drag him, none too gently, from the new found harem. James Senior would call the neighbor and threaten to castrate the animal if he got through again. Usually one dose of being choked and bounced behind the horse across the rough rocks and cactus was enough to make the errant bull lose all taste for the nubile delights through the wire. James and James Senior would round up all the heifers and give them shots of bovine hormones to make them recycle again, but their pregnancies would be delayed by a month. That practice would probably work on philandering husbands also, thought Carrigan. Just rope them and drag them through the city streets. When enough hide was scraped off, they might not be quite so anxious to snort the flanks of the young teenage girls of the neighborhood.

Once through the gate, he glanced down the long draw that began on his property, curved through the school section and then led down to the river. The draw was choked with thick buck brush but an animal trail in the very bottom was well used and offered easy access to the river below without clambering over the steep cliffs. Supposedly many years ago, during the early 1930s, a man returning from the whiskey still further up in the hills followed this draw down to the river where he had left his horse tied to a log. Upon reaching the bottom of the draw he found his horse dead, her throat slashed and her hocks torn and bleeding. He swore that upon his arrival, yellow eyes watched him from the darkness. Wolf eyes. Realizing little could be done for his ride, he ran back up the draw in the dark. With every stride he was sure the pack was close behind him, ready to make him their next victim. During the next several years other people reported seeing gray, slinking forms stealing through the thick brush in the early morning hours and reported hearing the plaintive call at night of the pack on the hunt. The draw therefore, was named Wolf Draw and the title stuck even to this day, although no wolves inhabited the river valley. The gray wolf was part of the past, just as were the homesteaders and other colorful characters of the area.

Carrigan still felt the pride of ownership in this land. This was something he bought, not something he inherited or was given. Circling the head of Wolf Draw, Carrigan and Gertrude passed through a small notch and then carefully wound their way down the long hill on the other side, ending up on a small plateau. The western edge of this plain rose again into rocky, steep-faced cliffs with a heavy dose of stunted evergreens near the top. Their windward sides were crooked and sparse, bearing testimony to the heavy wind that often roared down the canyon. Two steep canyons led from the northern side. One was filled with acres upon acres of chokecherries. In the fall, their lush fruit filled the entire canyon with the dark, red bounty. The little creek coming from this canyon was aptly named Cherry Creek. Bordering both sides of this canyon were high rock faces on top of which high mesas stretched to the end of Carrigan's land. Just before his section ended, Cherry Creek turned into a box canyon from which even the mountain sheep had trouble scrambling up.

The other canyon led more northeasterly and was shallow in comparison. The bottom of this canyon was the home to large groves of quaking aspens, and dense thickets of willows. The canyon led, in a meandering course, across Carrigan's land and through two immense notched peaks before continuing its course up onto the high Laramie Plains. The headwaters for this creek were near Bull Elk Ridge many miles to the north.

Both creeks joined their flow in the middle of this basin, where Carrigan wanted to build his cabin. Joined together, they flowed over the steep, cliff face on the southern side and on down into the Laramie River. This, he knew at last, was the natural place to build a cabin. Although rough, this area could be reached with a four-wheel drive vehicle, it was less than a mile down to the river, and some protection from the harsh winds was offered by the surrounding landscape. It had taken Carrigan a little less than two hours to reach this point from Rockville, and yet it was a different world. The sight of people here was rare, and only the sighing of the wind through the evergreens and the calling of hawks circling the river canyon's air currents could be heard.

Near the joining of Cherry and Grizzly Creeks, as the other drainage was named, Carrigan parked his four-wheeled lady and walked through the tall grass to a rock structure built there. The morning dew laced his boots with moisture, although the sun was rapidly driving it from the grass in clouds of vapor that drifted in low mist across the basin. This structure was the first of Carrigan's building projects. A barbecue pit, built from the moss rocks rolled from the adjacent hillside, had taken Carrigan three weekends to construct. Cemented at the base with an attached spark arrestor, the structure fit nicely with the surrounding landscape.

The warm, evening fires served as company on the dark nights that Carrigan stayed in the hills, sleeping on the grass with only a bedroll and a blanket for cover. When he first walked this basin, he found an old circle of stones here where once, long ago, someone else built a fire for company during the dark night. This circle of stones was fitted together carefully as if each rock was chosen for a purpose. Carrigan merely expanded on the base not wanting to change what was built before him.

Walking back to the pickup, he grabbed a shovel from the truck's bed. It was now clear to him. The front porch of his cabin should be no more than ten steps to the barbecue pit, and close enough to the small creeks so he could hear the murmur of the water as it flowed through the meadow on down to the river. Any other place on the acreage would be lacking something. It was just a feeling, but here he could put down roots.

Stripping the coat from his back, he dug the first hole in the rocky soil, marking the ground for his cornerstone. Pacing the other distances, he dug three more, enclosing an area of some 480 square feet--his home away from home, and perhaps the residence of his future if he quit teaching. When he had more time he would square the area, stringing lines from one corner post to the other, forming a large X. If the distance was equal, his cabin would be square, if not the corners would need to be adjusted. He thought about continuing the work, but then remembered he was to meet Nancy two miles downriver by noon. Sticking the shovel deep into the ground, he walked back to the pickup to gather his fishing gear and start the trek down to the river.

From behind the seat, Carrigan pulled the compact, aluminum tube and his outdoor tools of the trade. The tube protected a nine-foot Sage Five Weight graphite rod nestled ready for assembly. Checking the air, as if testing for a sign from the fish gods, he finally decided on the Able reel and meshed the pair. Finishing, he used an Orvis size 5 shooting tip. The dryfly line with its eleven-foot leader and 5x tippet should work well today, he decided. Next he ran into problems. Decisions of this nature should be thought about long and hard, but with time running out and a noon date approaching, he decided to take all three of the sets of flies. He would start with a size 18 Yellow Humpy, and then switch to a Pheasant Tail if he needed too. As a last resort, he would have the size 16 Hornburg Attractor in reserve. No fish on the Laramie River could resist all three of these. He threw the Gorton felt-soled waders over his shoulders and packed his fishing vest full of odds and ends such as magnifying lenses, fly dressing, cleaner, hemistat, forceps and nippers. He was pleased with his choices. If the brush was thick he liked the Sage's ability to rollcast a fly, feeding it down the very center of the ripples, tempting the dark brown trout that fed in this type of water.

Gauging the time to be around 9 a.m., he stuffed the thermos, crackers, cheese, and salami into his rucksack and, outfitted with his fishing gear, headed for Wolf Draw and the trail down to the river. The walk was pleasant and he enjoyed the feeling of his muscles, stretching and flexing as he negotiated the steep trail. Here and there he saw tracks in the trail of other voyagers that also passed this way. Half way down he stepped over some extremely large pugmarks pressed deep into the soft ground. Sometimes animals' footprints looked larger because the soft mud expanded when they pressed into the yielding earth, but these tracks were truly huge. Carrigan placed his palm into the indentations and found that the tracks were several times wider than his hand, even when he spread his fingers. Ahead of the pugmarks, deep holes of a larger diameter than his thumb sank into the mud. This showed the animal's claws matched the size of the tracks. Rather than coming up the trail, the tracks crossed the trail from the opposite hillside and then disappeared up the opposing slope amongst the shale talus. He followed their marks in the loose soil until they disappeared over the ledge above him where a huge, pine tree leaned precariously over the lip of the draw. Over the years Carrigan came across some big black bears in this canyon, but never did he see one that possessed feet of this size. Just as there were no more wolves in Wolf Draw, there were no grizzly bears left on Grizzly Creek. They were killed out by the early 1900s. This must be the track of a large black bear that melted and froze and then melted again, making the impression look much larger than it actually was.

Carrigan shuddered momentarily, what if it wasn't a black bear but a grizzly instead? A big, male grizzly this time of year, would be in a very foul disposition and a female with a young cub would be worse. Either sex could ruin the hell out of a fishing trip in a hurry. The only other time he had seen a track close to this size was when he retrieved his rope after pulling Nancy out of the flooding canyon. Was it possible the same bear had survived in this area for over twenty years?

I'm really starting to lose it, he thought. He looked a little closer into the thick brush covering the bottom of the canyon. He proceeded slowly, just in case something that was big, and brown, and liked to bite was watching, waiting for him in the thickets below.

Reaching the bottom of the canyon, Carrigan geared up and floated the line in a long, rollcast letting it feed down between two large rocks in the river. Here whitewater and foam boiled together swirling the fly in a lazy circle. The big brown ripped the fly from the surface before Carrigan was even ready. The reel buzzed as the fish ran hard upstream, stripping the line through Carrigan's fingers. Applying just enough pressure to turn the run but not pull the hook out, Carrigan began the age-old game of take and give. Ten minutes later, the fish was spent and allowed himself to glide the last few feet into the net. Carrigan knew the big fish was just decoying, gaining his strength for one last run. At over three pounds, this brown was the master of his environment and only his greed slipped him up. Wetting his hands first, Carrigan gently removed the fly from the fish's lip and turned him upstream, allowing the current to wash fresh oxygen through the big gills. With an explosion, the fish left his hand like an arrow, running for deeper water and freedom.

Watching the big, brown trout change gears and burst on up the river, he felt a twinge of accomplishment. This fish fought well, too well, to end up as supper. Besides, Carrigan still had a long ways to walk and a steep hill to climb. A heavy creel of fish would just make his pack heavier and harder to carry. He would keep some of the fish he caught on the way back up the river. Carrigan sat down upon a large rock in the edge of the eddying water and wondered what Nancy would bring for their picnic lunch. As the river rolled by, he also thought about another woman in his life, a woman far different from Nancy. They, too, ate a picnic of sorts on the front porch of a small house. Many dusty miles and long years had passed since Carrigan negotiated that fork in his road. He wasn't sure yet whether he had taken the right turn that day.

Following his graduation from the university while Carrigan was working as a police officer, he teamed numerous cases with a juvenile probation agent working in his district. Carrigan caught the young wanna-bes and she tried to change their way of thinking before they became cold and uncaring, more predators in the forest of living things.

Kevin, Carrigan struggled with her last name for a moment before thinking of it. Richmond. That was it. Funny, how could you forget the name of a woman you lived with? All things, one surrenders with age, he thought.

She was young, short, and possessed long waves of flowing red hair with a temper to match. She left her home and her parents on the West Coast, and moved to southern Wyoming after finishing her degree in criminology. Her first position was working juvenile probation for the State of Wyoming. She was very excited that she was accepted for the job; until as she told Carrigan, she found out later she was the only applicant. Her youth and philosophy of life led to innovation, and she worked well with young offenders, blowing off their bullshit and holding them accountable for their actions.

"Why on earth come to Wyoming?" Carrigan asked her. "Was the warm sunshine and gentle, sandy beach too boring?"

"Na," she said, "it's just that it's a long ways from my parents, and my friends. Even the Golden State gets boring after a while. Besides, all they bust kids for in California is skipping school to surf and smoking dope. Out here, there are some real bad dudes, rustlers and horse thieves. It makes life more interesting."

After several months of working together, Kevin offered to fix Carrigan breakfast when he finished his night shift. This was her day off but she met Carrigan at the courthouse where they attended the afternoon probation hearing together. They strode down the steep steps of the local courthouse and Carrigan stopped at the bottom thinking about her invitation. He had been working up his courage to ask her out, but kept getting stalled by her beauty and their work relationship.

"What kinds of foods do California Girls cook?" asked Carrigan.

"Oh, I don't know," she said, "something like eggs sunny side up, with hippie fries, tofu sausage and cappuccino."

"Sounds terrible, but I will try it anyway. I'll see you bright and early tomorrow morning."

Several times during the night shift Carrigan found himself wondering if Kevin was interested in him or just looking for some company? Either way she was cuter than hell. She liked to wear her long hair up in a bun and always wore wire-framed glasses, pulled low down upon a pert and freckled nose. Her business suit skirts were short enough to make everyone in the courtroom come to attention, and the top button on her silk blouses usually couldn't resist the pressure, working their way open to give pale glimpses of her ivory throat beneath. Besides with free food, he couldn't lose on this proposition.

The shift went peacefully with only one stolen car and several bar fights. The stolen car would appear somewhere on the edge of town tomorrow. Sometimes the kids in the town would grow bored and hijack the cleanest car they could find. Two hours of mud bogging and beer drinking would follow. The car would turn up the next day, covered in dry, gumbo mud and filled with empty beer cans. Usually a wash job was all that was needed to set things right. Both bar fights were over by the time Carrigan rolled on the scene, and when the participants were questioned in the bar, they were best friends again. Explanations of the black eyes and split lips were blamed on bars of soap or open doors. The bartenders kept quiet and served the drinks because the combatants were back in the bar spending money. Somewhere in the city there was a big, mean bar of soap on the loose.

Carrigan knocked lightly on Kevin's door just as daylight was breaking in the east. The light flooded the archway to the door chasing away the shadows and revealing a portal for him to enter. He originally planned on returning home to change clothes before coming over, but was afraid he would fall asleep and miss breakfast and Kevin's company altogether. Just as he started to knock again, she opened the door. Two claret ponytails hung loosely braided across her shoulders doing little to obscure the sheer pajama tank top and the ivory shoulders beneath. Long, freckled legs rushed from the short pj bottoms of the same slight material. Carrigan looked longer than perhaps he should have, and then ducked his head. The business suits only hinted at what the filmy material revealed.

"It will be hard for me to concentrate on breakfast if that's all you're going to wear," he said.

"I was hoping it would be," she said, looking at him with sea green eyes over the top of the glasses riding low on her nose. "Come on in and maybe we can do something else until you get your attention back."

Carrigan remembered being fascinated by the gold toe rings she wore, circling three toes on each foot, nearly aboriginal, as she led him by the hand into the house.

They never got around to breakfast and Carrigan called in sick for the next night shift. Later, much later, by moonlight, they both feasted, regaining their strength, on cold milk from the refrigerator and peanut butter licked from each other's fingers, finishing their hunger with thick slices of bread torn from the loaf…and more of each other. Finally by early the next morning, breakfast was over. Carrigan returned home, spent and shaken by the hours of raw emotion. Within a week they were living together, each taking from the other the needs that were unfilled for so long.

For the next year Carrigan worked nights and Kevin worked days. She would return home in the evenings to wake him for his night shift, always stripping the business suits from her body in a trail across the bedroom floor, before sliding into the sheets beside him. Her passion seemed unending and Carrigan found his desire for her grow stronger as the months went by. As he left for work each night, she would lay sleepily in the bed, languid from their lovemaking and watch his lean muscled frame as he dressed. She often tried to tempt him back under the covers by exposing enticing flashes of ivory freckles that lay beneath the slick sheets. Forcing himself not to look, he would flee from the house to the waiting patrol car. The endless hours of his shift passed slowly until he returned to her sleepy embrace and tangled waves of scarlet tresses.

One spring morning, Carrigan avoided her as she tried to rub up against him. She stopped; arms raised to the pin holding her controlled red mane, she fixed him with her emerald stare. Carrigan watched her pulse beating slowly, measured in the hollow of her throat above the small rigid breasts pointed accusingly at him. Propping herself on her elbow she waited for him to speak.

"Where do we go from here," he said? "I didn't know people could make love this often or this well, but sometimes I think that is all we do. Let's take some time off and get out of this place--time just to relax and think about our future. I feel trapped in a time warp, a routine, not that I'm complaining, nothing about what we do together is routine or boring. I want to meet your family, see where you came from, and make sure you're real."

Kevin rolled away from him drawing her slender legs into a ball. "I don't know, James. I love you more strongly than anything I've ever felt before in my life. Some days I don't think I can live until I get back here to you. But as much as I want you, I don't want to be stuck here the rest of my life. There are places I want to see and things I want to do. I would have been gone long ago if you weren't here. You're like a drug. I just keep craving you. The more I get the more I want."

Carrigan traced the pale skin along her spine with his knuckle, marveling at the interplay of muscles rippling beneath his finger. A small moan escaped her lips and he could feel her back beginning to arch, absorbing his touch as he stroked down to the hollow above her full hips.

"Just touch me James, make love to me, I promise we'll talk more later."

That night Carrigan was off duty and they ate pizza and drank beer on the porch of the small house, watching the neighborhood kids playing in the evening twilight. The sound of laughter and bouncing balls echoed among the trees. Even they way she ate, slowly savoring each bite, aroused him.

"Kevin, let's have a child," he said feeling this was the time to broach the subject again before she distracted him. "Everyday I see my life passing before me. I want to show my parents their grandchildren before it's too late. I want to have someone to share our lives with, to teach, to carry on our names. With the ranch and my job, money is no problem; you can be a stay-at-home mom if you want to. Marry me, have my children."

Kevin finished the last of her pizza, licking each finger clean, before draining the last half of her beer in one gulp. The long line of her throat beading with moisture as she held the cool bottle against it; she frowned before she answered.

"I knew it was coming to this," she said. "Carrigan, what am I going to do with you? You're the best lay I've ever found. You're caring, gentle but strong when you need to be, and with me you need to be a lot. I love you; especially I love what you can do to me. I need you so badly sometimes I shake. But I knew the day would come when my loving you and needing you wouldn't be enough. You are the type of person who wants more, and this is all that I'm willing to give, my love and my body, but nothing else. A child has wants of its own. Mine come first. Why isn't that enough for you? Why do you have to make it so complicated? We live, we work, we fuck, and we eat. There is no grand plan.

Finally hearing what he had known for a long time, he felt the cold spreading deep within his chest, driving his love for her locked into confinement.

"It is enough," he said, "most of the time it is enough."

Even after hours of making love that night, somehow he wasn't satisfied. Kevin was right; their bodies were almost a perfect match. Drug-like they used each other, always needing more, but never quite finding satisfaction from the high. He knew there was something more waiting for him and perhaps so did she. For him, he felt it was a family to come home to, a reason for his presence on this earth. For her it was the next horizon and her immediate gratification. He would never be enough for her; the sameness of their routine would push her to look for something new. Carrigan felt a deep sense of loss as she bit viciously into his shoulder, pulling him deeper into her. In her way, perhaps she had tried, but something in him wasn't able to break through her reserve, and when he was honest with himself, what they had wasn't enough for him.

The next month they slowly grew apart, their lovemaking became exercise instead of passion. Carrigan wasn't surprised when she told him she was leaving on vacation to take a trip to Mexico with some friends. She said she would call him from Mexico to let him know how long she would be gone. The day she left, Carrigan turned in his resignation notice on the police force and disconnected the phone just in case the call came. 1,041 night shifts and he wasn't able to change the city; 365 day shifts and he couldn't change the woman. Actually he was thankful to her for forcing the decision. It wasn't just her. Like their relationship, the job, the badge, and people's perception of his authority had worn thin. The constant vision of humanity at their worst had made him callous and cynical--things he didn't want to be. It was time to travel another road, perhaps get back to his roots. Going home sounded good.

I was looking for a job when I found this one he thought, and although I wasn't looking for a woman, I certainly found one. I had better be careful he thought, the next one I find might kill me.

Gertrude wasn't sure if Carrigan was talking about the job or Kevin, as they drove off into the night, but either way the road was calling them onward and she was happy to have her head and a free rein. The music on the radio played loudly in the cool night air, a song by Meatloaf, *Two out of Three Ain't Bad*.

A large splash in the water beside him caused Carrigan to jump, almost dropping his pole in the river. It took him a minute to refocus before he remembered where he was. The muskrat that made the splash was doing his best to vacate the area, swimming hard upstream. He was more startled than Carrigan when he suddenly realized the big rock was occupied.

Wow, Carrigan thought to himself. I'm getting just like my old man used to be. All of his stories started with *When I was young*, and now I'm doing the same thing. What in the hell caused me to start thinking about Kevin? I bet I scared the bejesus out of Ol Mr. Muskrat. Nothing worse than doodling along and suddenly finding out that you should have been doing more paying attention and less doodling.

Quickly glancing up at the sun, he realized that he better hump it on down the river his own self or Nancy would be eating lunch alone. Even if his weekend fell to hell from here, it had already been a good one. Sometimes he wished he could just stay in the hills and never return to civilization. After lunch with Nancy, he would fish a little more and then go back to work on the foundation for his cabin. It would be good to spend the night in the hills. He could leave by noon tomorrow and make it back to town in plenty of time to catch up on his chores back at the house. He would make a list of all the building materials he would need and next time he came up, begin in earnest on building the cabin. If he kept at it, by the end of summer most of it would be done.

Yep, he thought to himself, this is a good weekend. It might even get better if Nancy brought some apple pie.

Skirting the edge of the river, he walked on downstream toward the Devil's Fireplace. He wanted one chance at fishing the deep hole there before Nancy went wading in the water messing up all chances of catching any fish. Years before he spent every weekend he could away from her, traveling the long road from rodeo to rodeo, and now he was planning his weekend around her.

The more things change the more they stay the same, he thought.

Tommy's weekend went well also. By eight Friday night he grew bored with the bare walls of his home. Even his drawings and pictures concealed within his room failed to hold his attention. The night air was growing cooler as he banged out the back door of his house leaving it open and flopping in the chilling night air.

Nothin' in the damn place to steal anyway he thought. Maybe the ol' man will get home and think somebody robbed the place. Kinda like Huck Finn. Nobody gave a damn about him either, and he fixed his ol' man good, faking his own death and everything. Maybe that English teacher ain't so bad, making us read that book out loud. Old Huck had some pretty good ideas, he just talked awful weird, that shit was hard to read too, but Huck was a cool dude.

Tommy thought about walking downtown, but if somebody saw him they might look down on him for walking instead of riding in a car like the rest of the kids. A new thought struck him. Maybe Old Maid Libly had fixed the window in her garage by now. She lived two blocks down and her garage was in a dark alley. Tommy broke the garage window twice before and she fixed it right away the first time, but the last few times he checked she left it broken, just like the night when he first threw the rock through it.

Old Bitch better get it repaired, or she'll have more to fix than just her window he thought. Then a better idea came to him. Billy Lenz. "Billy Lenz," he said to himself. Last week that crack head said his old man was going to let him drive the painting truck to school. Billy will let me ride around, hell; Billy would let me drive if I told him to. Goddamn glue head anyway. All he does is huff and jack his mule.

Pleased with his idea, Tommy switched directions and picked up the speed of his walk, heading back to Northtown were Billy lived. Northtown was were all the migrant beet workers lived because the housing was cheap. The structures were small, rundown and the yards long ago were left to go to weeds and dirt. Billy's dad did a little bit of handyman work on the side, sometimes some roofing and he claimed to be a housepainter. Mr. Lenz recently deserted his construction profession and went to work at the Northside Liquor Store, manning the night shift. Since he was working nights, he supposedly told Billy that he could drive the painting truck when he didn't need it.

Little shit better not be lying to me, thought Tommy.

By the time Tommy got to Billy's house the night air seemed a lot colder and Tommy thumped his sides with his arms trying to warm up. Tommy walked around to the back door careful not to trip on the engine parts strewn across the back yard. He almost made it to the door when his toe caught some plastic drop cloths hiding in the weeds. He managed to stay upright and kicked the tattered end of the paint stained plastic out of the way before pounding on the door of the house. The frame of the screen door was intact though the screening long ago had fled these surroundings. Tommy reached through the frame to beat on the interior door beneath. The door opened a crack and Tommy could see Billy's eye peering out at him from inside.

"Let me in you crack head," Tommy said, "it's colder than a witch's tit in a brass bra out here."

The eyes continued to look at him for a while before the door opened and Billy stepped back to let Tommy come in. Tommy looked around the kitchen at the trash overflowing from the garbage can and the table with a big crack running through its Formica center. Billy just ducked his head waiting for Tommy to speak. His eyes stared at Tommy from beneath wet, encrusted lids. The pupils were glazed and fixed, indicating a few rounds were already huffed from an open can of mineral spirits sitting on the scarred counter. A long green trail of snot drooled from his left nostril threatening to launch an attack on the loose lips and dirty teeth below.

"Come on, Billy, let's go up town," said Tommy, putting on an attempt at being friendly. "You said you could take your old man's truck, and for Christ sake, wipe your nose."

Seeing there was no use to resist, Billy backhanded the attacking stream of mucus, and followed Tommy outside. One place was as good as another to Billy. He just shrugged when Tommy pushed him over into the passenger side of the truck, wincing a little as the starter stuck making a high grinding sound that penetrated even Billy's clogged senses. The engine finally roared to life kicking off the starter as Tommy dropped the trany in low, peeling pistons, plastic and paint out from behind the tires as they bit into the dirt. Cranking it hard out of the alley, Tommy gunned the old truck onto the street and headed uptown. After all, it was Friday night.

Friday night downtown Rockville was filled with young people. No mall was available for them to cruise checking each other out, so any parking place large enough to hold two cars was used for the mobile mall. Kids would pull up and park, visiting and trading insults, and then drive on again, scoping out all the other groups of cars doing the same thing. The streets resembled the school hallways. Some groups of cars were exclusively preppies and jocks, with BMW's and other high dollar foreign cars. Some groups were the cowboys with their jacked up trucks, and some were simply metal and wheels. These kids just drove whatever they could get their hands on or beg away from their parents. The out-back group of kids usually didn't have access to wheels, but they owned the dark places in the schoolyards and parks.

Tommy and Billy cruised the main street twice, flipping off the herds of cars, even shouting obscenities out the windows when the cars' owners didn't look too aggressive. This game soon grew old and some of the cowboys were starting to get in their trucks so Tommy decided to check out other parts of town. Driving down by the park, Tommy and Billy found a crowd more to their liking. Small groups of the outbacks stood in huddles, some of them listening to rap music on boom boxes, passing cigarettes and swaying to the heavy bass beat. Tommy swung in the pickup next to one of the larger groups and starting bobbing his head to the beat of the music.

> *Poke them in the guts,*
> *Stab them in the ass,*
> *Kill all the old Grandmas,*
> *Make me free at last.*

The fresh, night air must have even refreshed Billy because he was nodding his head to the dull thumping. Unspoken, one of the younger members of the group walked up to the pickup and passed in a cigarette for Tommy to take a drag. Tommy started to pass the butt to Billy but the green menace had reappeared and Tommy thought better of it and finished the last drag himself.

"What's up, Dude?" said the youngster. "You guys scoring any shit tonight?"

"Na," said Tommy, "just doing the main, messing with the preps, what's up wich you ese?"

"Nada, man it slow, slow tonight man, no bitches, no nuthin'."

"Check it out awhile man, friz here man, sommin' will drag by, Herbi's got some tacts and we're splitting the colors, man you want to help, Herbi don't care."

"Cool man," said Tommy, "yah, me and Billy will stick awhile, I'll help you with the colors, but Billy, he ain't feeling too good," as he mimed sticking his head in a paper sack.

The younger kid grinned, and said, "Ya man, Billy, he huffs too much man; he's freaking brain dead."

Tommy got out of the pick up and wandered over to the group kneeling around a white dish towel spread on the grass under the only feeble light in the park. Split open on the stained dishtowel were several packages of

Contact Cold Pills. One group was pulling the capsules apart and dumping the contents in a mounding pile in the middle. Several other youngsters with toothpicks were rolling all the blue particulates into one pile, while others were separating the red and white groups. Once separated, the kids would re-capsule the pills. Ten of the blue taps could give a person a reasonable high. During the night the kids would do 'the pepper'. First they would start with ten blue tabs, and then follow that with two white ones, which were the weakest, and around midnight they would take four of the red ones. Tommy didn't like the other colors, and preferred just to take blues all night. Several of the smaller kids were already worrying about how they were going to get their share of the blues if Tommy stayed around. The rhythm of the rap served as the group's chain gang song as they bobbed with the music, mouthing the words of rape and sodomy while they separated their evening's entertainment. With Tommy helping, the stash was split within the hour. Tommy claimed his share and returned to the truck. Billy was still in the seat looking at his hands.

"Hey man," said Tommy, "got you some blue, how many you want?"

Bill just kept bobbing, occasionally turning one hand upside down. With this he would grin as if he was pleased with the trick of magic.

"Screw you then dude," said Tommy, and pushed the pills into his own pocket. The starter worked better this time and Tommy caused the poor old truck to shudder as he slammed it into reverse gassing and braking at the same time.

"Piece of shit truck," he said, "ain't got no guts."

The smell of burning brakes floated across the park as Tommy and Billy headed on down the trail in search of the next item of interest they could find.

Soon Tommy found himself in Becky's neighborhood. After driving by the cul de sac several times, he pulled the truck several blocks away and parked it where several construction trucks were parked on an empty lot where contractors were putting in a basement for a new house. The old truck's frame pipe rack mixed well with the cement mixers, trailers, and dump trucks surrounding it.

Even the pigs in this town won't think this truck is out of place, thought Tommy.

Billy was really starting to come around now, and had managed to turn his left hand over to match his right one, but was becoming frustrated because he couldn't remember how to fix his right one.

"Come on Billy; let's check this out," said Tommy, dragging Billy with him.

The night air was still icy but the blues were kicking in, and with the thought of Becky, Tommy didn't even notice the cold. The boys walked across the empty lot skirting the basement pit dug into the earth, and headed for the wire fence separating the housing area from the golf course. Billy got stuck half way through the fence and Tommy pulled hard on his arm dragging him through the wire. Billy grunted as the rusty barbs bit into his flesh, but followed Tommy on down the fairway toward Becky's house. The first two houses they passed were guarded with tall, woven, board fences but Tommy stayed in the middle of the fairway in case dogs were in the backyard. When he was even with Becky's house, he pushed Tommy down on his belly and they crawled Indian style toward the river rock fence that loomed in front of them. Tommy could hear voices coming from the backyard.

Tommy raised his eyes just above the level of the rocks and saw four girls huddled together with a blanket over their shoulders collecting them together into a small circle. Tommy caught the red glow of a cigarette burn brightly and then diminish as the girl quit inhaling. This girl Tommy recognized as one of the school's cheerleaders. She then passed it to another girl, the captain of the cheerleading squad. The bright, red glow burned fiercely again as she, too, took a deep drag.

"Yo, bitch," said the first one, "I know you're a ho, you told me yourself you banged David last weekend, and all week you've been giving Ritchie hand jobs. You got no respect girl."

The second girl just laughed, "I had to ball him," she said, "he didn't have enough to get my hand on."

This caused the other two girls to burst out giggling. Their high voices were loud in the night air, and the group's blanket flapped loose as the girls wrestled and poked each other, continuing their teasing. The breeze shifted slightly wafting the smell of burning *grass* to Tommy's senses. Billy even poked his head over the wall when he caught the strong smell of marijuana. Tommy checked out the rest of the backyard but didn't see Becky anywhere until he started to duck his head down, and then realized there was another girl almost directly in front of him with her back to him. Her dark hair and dark blanket blended perfectly into the yard and Tommy had been overlooking this one. Except this wasn't Becky either, the girl in front of him didn't have blond hair. Squinting, Tommy realized this was Bertie Eliza, the school's only Black student. She was the star basketball and volleyball player. She could run and jump like a boy, and most of the boys were scared to death of her. Rumor was she could bench-press over 200 pounds. Looking closer though, sticking from under the blanket two legs poked out in Tommy's direction but Eliza's head was pointed toward the house.

What is this, he thought, she's doing some sort of Exorcist movie trick turning her head around. Suddenly one of the other girls got up from the first group and started toward Berti, "Are you two having fun over there," she said.

Bertie turned her head to answer and Tommy finally saw Becky. Bertie and Becky had been sitting face to face, each of their legs wrapped around each other's waist, and the dark blanket covered this joining. It was Becky's legs that Tommy had seen. Because the two bodies were so close together Tommy could only see Bertie's head.

"Come on Bertie, we're getting cold, let's go in, bring Becky and we can go watch some flicks inside. Is that Ok with you Becky?" said the interloper.

"Sure, Ok," answered Becky. "Mommy said we could stay up as long as we want to." Tommy couldn't take his eyes off of Becky as Bertie kissed her once more on the neck, and then wrapped the blanket back around both of them as they got up and walked toward the house.

The porch light winked off as the girls entered the house and Tommy saw spots before his eyes as he tried to adjust them to the darkness.

"Lesbos, freaking Lesbos, did you see that Billy, the whole bunch, nothing but a bunch of freaking Lesbos," Tommy whispered. "How come they do that shit?"

Billy gave his usual answer and just kept looking into the back yard. Feeling tired from all the exertion, he was resting his head on the top of the rock wall by now. Billy could see the long, bloody scratch on his check where the barbwire cut him. The blood had dried, but not before mingling with the green menace, giving the wound a bluish tinge.

"Ah Jesus," said Tommy, "wipe your damn nose."

Tommy stood up, dragging Billy with him. The need for secrecy gone now, they walked back up the fairway and scampered back through the barbwire. Billy was really quite "with it" now and made it through without hanging up once.

Walking by the basement under construction, Tommy paused for a moment beside the big trailer parked there. A big sign on the door stated "DANGER, EXPLOSIVE GASES INSIDE, NO SMOKING WITHIN 1OO YARDS". He tried to jump up and look through the small window on the door but all he could see were piles of boxes inside.

"I bet there is some neat shit in there," he told Billy. "I bet there is some real neat shit in there."

171

Realizing that Billy wasn't behind him, he was just able to catch him before Billy walked into the gaping hole of the basement. Tommy pulled hard and both boys teetered on the edge for a minute before falling back from the edge.

"Come on crack head," said Tommy, "let's get outta' here. Is it Ok if I stay with you tonight? My Old Man doesn't like it when I have to stay alone. He's afraid somebody's going to break in and kidnap me or something. He said it was all right if I spend the night at your house. And no more of that huffing shit, that stuff will kill you. Let me know if you want something. I still got some blues left. Say Billy, does your Old Man have any tools around? You know like bolt cutters or big crowbars, him being a carpenter and all, I figured he's got a lot of that stuff around that he doesn't ever use. Let's check it out tomorrow."

The old truck started one more time and the boys headed back to Northtown.

Maybe there were some dogs they could run over, thought Tommy. All them Mexicans down there, there just had to be lots of dogs.

With a new plan of action, the old truck banged and rattled its way on the outskirts road that headed north but bypassed the downtown area. The streets were a little quieter now but a few cars were still out. Tommy was glad they didn't pass any cops. He didn't know if this old truck even had license plates, let alone all of its headlights and taillights. Reaching in his pocket, he pulled out the last of the blues, popping them in his mouth. He bit down hard on the gelatin tabs liking the acrid bite of the medicine in his mouth as it invaded his taste buds. Turning on the radio he jiggled the knobs on the old tube radio until he picked up a late night station out of Denver. The reception came in clear even if the speaker did sound a little tinny. It wasn't designed for the heavy dose of bass imbedded in the music. The dull thumping started Billy's head bobbing again. Words and music of a generation of lost values floated out into the night air as Tommy pushed the old pickup hard down the road.

BITCHIN' HO'S ALL NEED TO DIE,
THEY SPENT MY MONEY AND ALL THEY DO IS LIE.
SHOOT THEM, BURN THEM, CUT THEM DEEP,
PULL OUT THEIR GUTS AND PILE EM IN A HEAP.

Chapter 8
The Dilemma

Everyone was soon settled in the small cabin. La Ramie insisted that Night Wind with her knee, take the bed and sleep inside the cabin. La Ramie, Joshua and the boys slept out near the horse corral where they kept a small fire banked at night to ward off any chills. Night Wind protested about being isolated, but La Ramie finally won the argument by convincing her the leg would heal faster if she didn't sleep on the ground every night. Upon the bed were layered many soft elk hides and after the first night, even she admitted to resting better.

Night Wind cleaned and freshened the inside of the cabin while Joshua and La Ramie threw fresh sod on the roof to patch the holes. La Ramie set the boys to mixing fresh mud from the creek with dry grass together in a brick like compound. With this he instructed the boys to re-chink places between the rocks and logs of the cabin that worked loose during the last year. Mixing the mud was hard work and soon the boys found better things to do with their time--such as teasing Spotted Owl and throwing mud. Before long all three were mad at each other and they came racing into the cabin bitterly complaining about the injustices that were being heaped upon them.

"Whoa there," said La Ramie, "what's all this darn commotion about. You three are bickering worse than a flock of magpies over a dead fish. Let me tell you a story about what the Great Manitou said to his children that argued with each other." The three boys stopped pushing each other and waited for La Ramie to continue. He settled himself down crossing his long legs over each other and began his story:

Long ago when the Great Manitou made this world, it didn't take long before he knew he was lonely. So, instead of bein' the only one around, he made Great Bear, River, and Lightening as his children to keep him company. When these three were young they played together, racin' across the hanging road of the stars, and all amongst the vast lands of Manitou's world. As they grew older they began to fight, whippin' up on each other, striving to be the best in the eyes of their father. Now purty soon the Great Manitou grew plum tired of listening to the bickering that came from the world and the beings he'd created so he gave each one a chance to explain why he couldn't get along with his brothers.

Lightning went first and said that he was the most important causin' he could light the night sky with his mighty bolts, and if he was of a mind, he could strike the Earth a blow, burning it with his breath. 'I am the strongest and should be in charge. If my brothers don't do as I say, I will likely strike them dead.'

Next was the Great Bear's chance to convince his father of his importance. 'Although Brother Lightning may burn me and kill me, you molded me from the earth and clay and from this I will be reborn again. Because of my great strength, I can run all day and even Brother River kain't keep up with me. I kin bury him by pushing the mighty mountains on him so he cannot move and run free.'

The last to speak was River. 'What my two brothers say is true mostly, but I alone am the most powerful. When brother Lightning strikes me, it is as if I am struck by a feather, he kain't harm me. If he comes from the sky to burn the Earth I flood across him, drownin' his power as ifen he were nuthin'.'

Then all three turned to their father and asked him to choose who amongst them was most powerful.

'I can see that it is time. I explained why I made

all three of you. Lightning, although you are strong and can hurt your brother, Bear, you kain't kill him for he will be reborn again. Bear, you may be able to outrun River and control where he goes, but not even your strength can match his'n when he gathers all the rain and flows together. River, although you cannot run where Bear goes, or hold him when he swims in your waters, you can stop the power of Lightning when he flashes from the sky. This is the way of all things; each has special strengths within the family, and the family can reprimand each member. To be a proper family everyone must work together to helpin' one another.

'To my son Lightning, I give the heavens to rule with your flashing brightness. When you try to use your power on Earth, River will wash away your strength. To Bear I give all things on the land, to rule over. When Bear grows too powerful, Lightning will strike him to remind him of his place. To River I give all water in the sky and the land. He alone may bring them together and he may run where he will. Should he grow swollen with pride, Bear will knock some sense into him with mountains and rock. Each will have his place and each brother will watch over the other.'

With this Lightning, River, and Bear came into their inheritance and was plum satisfied with their roles in the circle of life.'

Lone Eagle and Little Dog looked at each other and turned to go back outside. They even allowed Spotted Eagle to follow them without pushing him away.

"You tell that story better that Kills-Crowe," said Night Wind. "Next time the boys are fighting I will call upon you."

"Ah, shucks," La Ramie answered, "they're good boys, they just need some excitement. Tomorrow we'll go get us some buffalo. That'll keep 'em occupied."

"My knives will be sharp for your return," she answered. "May the Great Spirit grant you luck in your hunt."

Joshua was ready also, although he had shot many buffalo before, they were usually in small herds or singles that he found along the Platte. This would be his first time of taking on a whole herd.

The next morning La Ramie, Joshua, and the three boys left the green basin and worked their way back up river to the plains. They planned to be gone two days and Night Wind was glad to see them go. A little time by herself filled her with relief after the long days on the trail. By noon, the hunters arrived at the site of their last campsite while on the trail. From here they crossed the river, carefully watching for quicksand. The group followed the waning afternoon sun westward toward a snowy range of mountains they glimpsed far in the distance. Several antelope herds were startled by their passage, exploding out of the hollows to run pell mell for several hundred yards before turning to see the reason for their flight. Twice coyotes flashed out of the deep sagebrush causing the horses to snort at the sleek, gray shadows. Just before cresting a large upslope late in the afternoon, La Ramie, raising his hand, halted.

"Smell sumthin'," he said.

The boys all began testing the air with their noses but soon started looking at each other, hoping they weren't the only ones unable to detect an aroma. Joshua found himself trying to sniff any strange smells other than the pungent sage and resin weeds that covered the plains.

"Right over the hill," La Ramie pointed. "We got fresh meat boys if my nose don't lead me wrong. We'll ground hitch them horses here and shinny up Injun fashion to take a peek."

Joshua laughed as he watched the boys following La Ramie up the hills wiggling like snakes. Spotted Owl did his best to avoid the cactus, but halfway up he drug his elbow through a large patch. The first whimper barely escaped his lips when Lone Eagle turned to scowl at him sharply. Spotted Owl continued his crawl after biting the protruding cactus thorns from his elbow, his small lips white and tightly clenched. When Joshua reached the top, the others were spread a short distance apart peering through the stubby limbs of a large clump of sagebrush on the crest. Below them the ground sloped sharply downward into a deep, washed draw and then swelled again to the next ridge. Across the entire expanse of the opposite hillside were buffalo. Some were standing idly, switching their tails at the early flies, while others lay curled, their shaggy heads resting on the ground. Whispering quietly to the others, La Ramie pulled two small shooting sticks from his belt. These he unfolded into a cross joined in the middle by a piece of rawhide. He then laid out four paper cartridges from his belt pouch and thrust the long Hall Rifle through the sagebrush, resting the barrel in the notch made by the shooting sticks. La Ramie licked his thumb and then wiped the rear sight clean before settling his cheek tight against the stock. Joshua glanced through the brush wondering which animal would feel the bite of the .69 caliber ball.

The rifle exploded and their eyes felt the stinging wash of powder smoke. Ten feet up from the deep washout below, a large bull suddenly sat on his haunches. His shaggy head cast about for a minute searching the cause of his demise and then he slowly rolled to his side. Buffalo within several feet of him snorted as the big bull toppled over into the dirt but did not move. La Ramie quickly reloaded and after returning the frizzen and locking the plate, rolled on his side offering the shot to Lone Eagle. The boy's eyes were wide and excited as he settled his thin, brown check against the heavy rifle. Again the big gun exploded and Lone Eagle slid backwards as the firearm crashed into his shoulder. The ball tore a massive wound in a cow just a few feet from the dead bull. Spurting blood from her nose, she dropped to the ground.

Rolling back, La Ramie reloaded and with his eyes, asked Little Dog if he wanted a chance. Not wanting to fall behind his brother, he slid onto the gunstock. Seconds passed before at last the rifle bellowed again and another bull in the herd humped and then began kicking at his belly. Knowing from the hollow sound the animal was gut shot, Joshua sighted down his Hawken at the point where the massive neck of the buffalo joined its shoulders and, after setting the trigger, squeezed off the round. The big bull dropped as if his legs disappeared from beneath him. By this time the herd was growing agitated and were on their feet, pushing each other over the top of the next hill away from the booming thunder. As Joshua reloaded the Hawken, once more did the Hall speak felling one more large bull as the herd in an ever-growing dust cloud disappeared over the horizon. Although Joshua was sure Spotted Owl wanted to shoot, he saw the tears in Little Dog's eyes from the massive recoil of the big rifle and knew Spotted Owl had seen them also. The hunters got to their feet and descended the slope. Now the work would start.

Until darkness fell around them, all four worked dressing the huge animals, and striping meat in large chunks from the still warm carcasses. The chunks they laid across the tops of sagebrush to protect the meat from the dirt. Later that night they feasted around a small fire eating fresh hump and tongues. As the boys slept, La Ramie and Joshua took turns on watch, ever wary for both two and four legged predators attracted to the kills. The next morning all was peaceful and the hunters finished their chores and packed the load of meat onto the horses before heading back to the river canyon. By late afternoon they were back at the cabin, their only remaining obstacle getting the loaded packhorses up the steep slope from the river. Finally they were forced to unload half and make two trips up the steep hill.

The two older boys bragged to Night Wind about their kills, and Joshua made sure he told her how Spotted Owl had helped him aim and bring one down.

"My but you are mighty warriors," said Night Wind, "but now since I am lame you will become mighty squaws also. Everyone must help cut this meat in strips to dry or it will spoil. La Ramie, you and Joshua need to build me a willow frame outside to hang this from while the boys and I cut it into strips. There will be no supper for any of you until this job is done."

Joshua and La Ramie rolled their eyes at each other but did as she ordered. The boys made several attempts to flee but Night Wind's discipline was harsh. Late that night the chore was done. So tired were the boys from their adventures they fell asleep before eating supper. Night Wind's face was pale and drawn also, and she struggled to the bed before lying down, exhausted from her labors. Joshua checked the tightness of the rawhide binding her knee, tying and retying the laces on the firm brown thigh until he was satisfied. The old knife wound from Lame Wolf's blade was healed now, merely a pink gash against the smooth, copper skin. Night Wind wondered at the bear-like paws that could so gently touch her leg, a touch she was beginning to like very much.

"When the meat is dry," she said, "Lone Eagle and Little Dog will return to the Water that Boils. Our family will be expecting us. With your leave, Spotted Owl and I will stay here until I am stronger, if we aren't in your way?"

Joshua didn't raise his head as she spoke, until he realized that he still was holding her thigh. He quickly released his grip causing her to wince, and then stammered an apology, before acknowledging her question.

"Yes, I'm sure La Ramie will be glad to have you; there is plenty for everyone to do. With this extra meat, our supplies will last for a long time." Looking at her now he said, "I'm glad you and Spotted Owl are staying for a while. I've grown very attached to the boy." With Night Wind's inquisitive look, he lowered his head again, and mumbled, "and you, too, of course," before quickly turning away to stoke the flames in the fireplace.

By the end of several days, the thin strips of meat on the rack were air-dried and cured, some other meat Night Wind smoked over a slow fire. These larger roasts too became cured and could be stored for the winter. With the tougher strips from the shoulders she used a different method. Sending the boys on excursions downriver to gather tubers and mint, she pounded these into the meat and then dried the mixture making pemmican. Joshua and La Ramie dug a tunnel into the hillside behind the cabin and lined it with flat flagstones from the hillside to serve as meat storage. They covered the entrance with a large boulder to prevent unwanted dinner guests.

Lone Eagle and Little Dog started making preparations to return home and even though Lone Eagle traveled the way several times before, he seemed glad that La Ramie offered to go with them across the plains, through the Snowy Mountains and on down into the valley of the Water that Boils. Traveling light and fast, La Ramie figured they could make the trip in three days.

"I should be back within a week, ten days at the most," he said. "Do you suppose you three can make it without me? Oh, well Joshua, at least you've got Night Wind to keep you out of trouble and Spotted Owl can fish, so you should be all right," he finished, laughing as Joshua reddened with the teasing.

Two days later, early before the sun could peek into the isolated glade, Night Wind hugged her two brothers and waved good-bye to La Ramie as the three riders trailed out of the camp heading north and west to the ancestral Shoshone home past the Snowy Mountains. She instructed Lone Eagle to tell Painted Flower of her injury and that she would be home by the fall. That was when a new elder would be chosen to fill Kills-Crowe's leadership. Night Wind was aware that her position of Vision Woman was important to her people, and they would need her to help give wisdom to her tribe. That night in the cabin, the inhabitants were quiet, thinking of their friends and family now far away on the plains. Joshua and Spotted Owl were playing tic-tac with a burned stick in the ashes of the fireplace. Night Wind was scraping the hides of the buffalo, working the inner hide paper-thin. This took many hours but she enjoyed making the skin soft and supple. From the largest one she planned to make Joshua a coat to protect him from Manitou's icy breath when winter came to the mountain country.

As the fire burned lower, Spotted Owl drifted to sleep and Joshua turned to find Night Wind's eyes watching him. They appeared as deep pools, absorbing the flickering firelight rather than reflecting it and Joshua felt himself falling into their limpid depths. Shaking his head he realized she was speaking to him.

"And what of the women behind you on the trail, Larapihu?" she said. "Tell me of your children and your wives."

Seeing the quick stab of pain flicker across his face, she continued, "I am sorry. I have no right to ask about your life. I can tell you have done many things and are both a brave warrior and a natural teacher. I did not mean to cause you pain. All lives under the heavens are for a reason, even yours trader. I do not know the reason you come to these sacred hills, or what it is that you search for. In my visions, I can see that you have a purpose and in time you will know this also, perhaps in this life or maybe in your next one. Do not lose your way, as you still have much to do. Kills-Crowe died but I live on to help my people, as does Spotted Owl who came from my loins. Do not blame Manitou for your life, but search to find his purpose for you."

"You see far more than perhaps others would want you to," Joshua replied wryly. "Yes, everyone I have ever cared for has been taken from me. My mother died so I might live, my father followed close behind. All my life I too, have dreamed of these mountains and wanted to follow the mighty flowing rivers that ran from them. My God has deserted me, so perhaps yours can show me the way."

"No Joshua," she said, "your God and mine are the same, no matter what you call Him. He did not leave you, or take your loved ones from you because of your dreams, but rather He shared them with you to help you dream. He still shares them in your memory."

Night Winds words stayed with Joshua long into the night as he watched over her offspring and guarded her sleeping form. That night as she drifted on the currents of her dreams, she was restless, moaning several times in her sleep.

Of what does she see, he wondered, does she fly above my death, or view the path to my future? That she witnessed his past he had no doubt. She knew too closely the pain in his life. What Night Wind said was true. Rodde was still with him and he only had to think back to remember his love for her.

Never in his life had Joshua been happier. During the long winter months in St. Genevieve, he fought with his desire to stay with Rodde, rather than to trek the backcountry. Each day out seemed an eternity until he was home with her, tight against the ebony texture of her skin so that he could breathe her vulnerability and reassure himself that she was real. Rodde acted as if she expected to have this effect on him; after all, she had loved him since he first helped her in the tavern. Justine was ecstatic when Joshua confessed that Rodde no longer occupied the servant's quarters and was indeed sharing his bed. They were married on March 21st of that year and St. Genevieve celebrated their joining with them. Even Jacques returned to celebrate the marriage and teased Joshua about the coming wedding night. Mixed marriages, although not common, were accepted and recognized by the church. Joshua, without ceremony, filed and recorded Rodde's emancipation the day prior to the wedding.

During the next few years Joshua and Rodde prospered and with assistance from Shaw, they expanded the post, making more counter space and adding storage. A ferry was started just upriver from the post and Americans came crowding through St. Genevieve and into the woodlands further east. In 1797, Jacques returned to help his father and was soon married into the Bauvias family, long established in the area. Although they remained close friends, Rodde somehow separated Joshua from the elite society. The one longing both Rodde and Joshua found unfulfilled was that no children were born to their union. Twice Rodde miscarried early in her pregnancy. This emptiness seemed to draw them further together instead of apart, and their passion for each other continued unabated and strong.

One of their favorite activities was to pack a basket full of bread and cheese for an evening meal and hike the path downriver to a monolith long ago fallen from the sheer escarpment above. By climbing the boulder, they could view the mighty river as she rolled by. Often they fished the deep waters, tempting the large catfish beneath the rock. Rodde always used cheese for bait, but Joshua used sausage.

"I couldn't eat a fish that liked bloodmeat," she said. "Their nature would be too vicious and their flesh too tough."

"Ah, my love," said Joshua, "the bait is merely part of nature. There are only those who eat meat, and those who wish they could. The big fish eat the meat, little ones each cheese."

Rodde laughed with delight when she caught the first fish, flopping and wet she pulled it upon the rock, squealing with delight that she caught one before Joshua.

"All right, all right," Joshua scowled; "give me some of your cheese. Maybe there is more than one way to catch a fish."

They spent the evening hours fishing and watching the river until they caught more fish than Rodde could smoke the next day.

"Enough," cried Rodde, "while you're out chasing animals, I will be home all day, my eyes burning from Hickory smoke."

Turning suddenly serious she grasped his hand folding it tightly to her breast. "Joshua, do you still love me? More than anything in this world I want to bear your son, so that you can take him hunting and fishing, to teach them the wiles of the big river. Each night I pray to God that he will allow me to bear your children."

Joshua, realizing the depth of her feeling, wrapped her in his arms, fishing now forgotten. How could he tell her that more than anything he wanted the same thing. Taken from him were his mother and father. Happiness flowed back into his life with the coming of Rodde, but here, too, God took this happiness from him with the death of his children before they were born.

"Rodde," he said, "more than life itself do I love you. Without you, all enjoyment of this life, this river, and our home would be gone. We will have children soon, I promise. Trust me, my sons will fish with me from this very rock, I swear."

Nodding, she nestled deeper within her arms, wondering at his feelings he kept so deep inside. That he loved her she had no doubt. Merely acting angry with him would cause him to despair for weeks. She knew the power that her body held over him, but she also knew of his desire to see the far Blue Mountains about which he dreamed. Her greatest fear was that if she were barren, he would leave her, searching for something she couldn't provide for him here, something to fill the losses in his life. She would become pregnant, tonight she thought and she pressed hard against him making him feel her desire.

Later that night as both lay tangled in the patchwork quilt covering the bed, she held him, rocking and crooning to him as he slept, spent and tired from her fierce demands. Somehow she knew that because of this depth of love she felt for him, she would have to repay God for her happiness.

She remembered her mothers words, 'Anytime you wants somethin' so bad and gets it, there's going be a price to pay, little missy, don't you ever go fogettin' that.'

"Joshua," she said softly, "promise this unto me. Promise me that if I should die you will not stop your search. I will always be part of you, always with you even to your mountains and beyond."

Shaking him until he murmured, she took this as assent and allowed his head to again seek the warmth of her heart that beat so strongly for him. She lay awake till the morning, careful not to move, savoring the feeling of his warm breath filling her soul.

The years passed slowly but steadily and in 1803, Joshua received a new contract from a man named William Ashley; the job was to haul supplies downriver. Joshua and Ashley had met the previous year in St. Louis. Joshua was very impressed as Ashley talked about his plans to obtain a foothold on the fur market in the frontier areas further up the

Missouri River. Ashley's description of this country filled Joshua with wonder and made him long to see the area for himself.

Ashley introduced Joshua to Manuel Lisa and Andrew Henry who sometimes joined with Ashley in various enterprises in the fur trade. Ashley, himself, was born in Powhatan County, Virginia, in 1778, and attended the common schools there. He was now planning a move to St. Genevieve and hoped to become engaged in the manufacture of saltpeter. His interests were in surveying and because of Joshua's knowledge of the frontier; Ashley sought him out for references and questions about large caves in the area. Ashley said both Lisa and Henry would be joining him later. If saltpeter could be found in large enough quantities, they would start a business in St. Genevieve. Ashley also intimated that this entire area might soon become part of America and the French and Spanish control would be ended. St. Genevieve, being so far west of American influence, took little interest in which sovereignty they owed allegiance. Joshua could see the potential for tremendous growth if the frontier became part of America. With protection from American troops, and licenses to trade from American authorities, the wild rivers further to the west would open quickly.

Ashley's prophecies proved true when on March 10, 1804, the transfer of the northern part of the Louisiana Purchase from France to the United States took place in St. Louis. The St. Louis settlement became a key in the United States western expansion. Newspaper accounts of how President Jefferson organized the Lewis and Clark Expedition reached St. Genevieve. This was to be the first extensive exploration of the new territory. Lewis and Clark left St. Louis for their westward exploration. The news of the expedition filled Joshua with wanderlust, and he wished he could go to see the heights of the far Blue Mountains he long dreamed about.

One day in early June, as Joshua entered the trading post late in the afternoon, Rodde informed him that a man was waiting for him outside of the backdoor of the post. Rodde said the stranger arrived about noon and stated he would only speak to Joshua.

"I sent him out back because he smelled so bad, worse than you when you have been skinning for three days," said Rodde. "He makes me nervous Joshua; if you hadn't gotten back soon I would have shut the doors and gone home. I don't like his eyes; he talks but doesn't look at you. He reminds me of those polecats you bring in. I still have that pistol under the counter. You tell him not to come in here any more or I might just use it."

"Relax my dear, he's only one man, and everyone in St. Genevieve knows better than to annoy you and your pistol. Now hurry home, I will lock up."

"I'll leave when he leaves," answered Rodde, crossing her arms over her chest, daring Joshua to argue with her. "Then we will walk home together."

Joshua went through the back door of the store and paused before speaking to the little disheveled man standing there. The stranger wore what once might have been a military coat but the garment was so covered in filth, Joshua could not make out even the country from which it originated. Long, grayish-blond hair overhung the collar down the man's back and this too was matted and held small sticks and leaves imprisoned in its knarled tresses. The absurd outfit was completed with blackened, greasy leggings and leather moccasins. The smell reached Joshua even though the man was several feet away. Joshua jumped as the little man spun around, sensing something behind him. A scraggly beard matched the long hair. The man's skin was scabbed and Joshua realized his visitor was an albino. What held Joshua's attention was the eyes with their white mucus appearance interrupted only by pale blue catlike pupils. The ghastly, white face was lined and wrinkled but the man's age could have been anywhere between thirty and fifty.

"My wife told me you wished to speak to me," stated Joshua. He began to realize why Rodde did not welcome this apparition into the post.

The man seemed to unwind slowly and withdrew his hand from beneath his tunic. Joshua noticed his fingernails that were abnormally long and dirty. They almost seemed to be filed to points. The backs of his hands were scabbed like his face.

"Whitey is the name folks call me," said the albino. "I traveled two days to get here. Folks say you buys hides and pays cut bits, is'n that the truth?"

"I do," said Joshua, "if they are prime and well cared for. What do you have?"

"One day's slow walk south of Saline Springs, there's a creek that runs itself into the river through two high rock walls. Half a day's walk upen' that creek, me an' my sons have a campsite. We'z been trapping all winter and have two tents plum full of varmint hides. My boys is young but they done those hides right. We don't have no boat to bring them ups, so I done walked here to gets ya, if what they say about you havin' cut bits is true?"

"I know the creek well, the locals call it Bilge Creek," said Joshua. "I have traveled it many times, but never came across your camp."

184

"We has been trappin' way inland, and just came there. Took us nigh on two weeks to pack 'em that far, and my boys is plum played out. I thought you could bring a boat and the money down and we could do some swapping."

"I can make a trip downriver two days from now," said Joshua. "I have appointments all day tomorrow, but the next day we can bring a boat downriver to Bilge Creek. There we can tie up a mile of so up creek and load the fur."

"After we gets our cut bits, and I don't want a whole bunch of people messing around my camp," Whitey said, "you bring one man and that's all. I see any more comin', I will know funny bisnes' is going on and you won't get no hides."

"Mid day, two days from now," said Joshua, "I will be there, Mr. Whitey."

Joshua didn't offer to shake hands, and Whitey didn't extend his grizzled claw either. Turning, the strange little man just jumped off the porch and walked on down to the river, looking back only once before he reached the water's border, and then followed the shore out until he was hidden by the thick brush on the river's edge.

Joshua returned to Rodde, and as they walked home, Joshua told Rodde of the strange meeting. She was dead set against Joshua going, and stopped talking to Joshua after she realized he was set on keeping the meeting.

"You come back smelling like him, and you will be sleeping alone," was her last comment.

Joshua trusted Rodde's instincts even if he did not acknowledge her concerns, and the next day he spoke to Jacques about his meeting. Together they talked to Henry Dodge who was the sheriff of St. Genevieve county. Dodge was a good man to have on one's side if any short of trouble was brewing. Joshua witnessed him in action several times in the last few years and 'Hell on Wheels' was the only way to describe him. Joshua didn't believe there was a man alive that could whip Dodge in a fight. The sheriff agreed that Joshua should not go downriver without some protection. Together they worked out a plan where the four of them would take a keelboat downriver almost to the entrance to the creek and then Dodge and his deputy Trenton Hunter, would go ashore. Here Dodge and Trenton would cut inland while Joshua and Jacques took the boat up the tributary as far as possible until shallow water stopped them.

If everything was on the level, Joshua and Jacques could load the furs and return back down the creek and tack upriver where they could pick up Dodge and Trenton, returning to St. Genevieve. If anything were amiss, the officers would be in the hills above them to offer some protection.

Jacques and Joshua each put up half the money to buy the furs and agreed to share equally in the profits. Both men carried a small sack of coins so that all the funds wouldn't be with one person should trouble arise. Shortly after midnight on the second day, Joshua met the others on the landing by his post, and silently they started the boat downstream, drifting slowly with the current. By early morning they should arrive at Bilge Creek and have time to size up the situation before proceeding further. Rodde threw her arms around Joshua's neck before he left and begged him with her eyes to be careful. The men took turns steering the low, drafting boat close to the river's edge as they floated downriver, while the others dozed fitfully, huddled in blankets, warding off the chill air of the early summer night. The full moon provided a cloaked view of the river and Joshua had a strange feeling overcome him as he looked at the reddish tinge of their light source.

Just as dawn was breaking over the forested hills to the west, Joshua dropped Dodge and Trenton ashore, where they began climbing the trail leading to the ridges above Bilge Creek. Joshua and Jacques floated on downriver to the opening in the granite cliffs through which Bilge Creek joined the Mississippi. Both men were forced to pole the boat through the sandy creek and it took them several hours to make it two miles inland before the shallow water stopped them. Here they built a small fire and made morning coffee. Looking casually in the hills to the north of them, they were unable to catch a glimpse of Dodge or Trenton.

"This feels good," Jacques said, "like when we were younger. Our blood is racing and adventure awaits us, but I hope Dodge didn't get hung up on the trail."

"He will be there if we need him," replied Joshua, "but check your loads just in case. Rodde is starting to rub off on me, even I'm getting nervous. We'll just sit here easy for a while in case anybody's watching. I don't want any trouble if we can avoid it."

"For a man not wanting trouble, you're certainly ready for it," Jacques said, "I know you're carrying at least one brace of pistols, and you've checked the priming in those muskets three times already."

"Nothing worse than wet powder," Joshua returned. "It's better to be ready, than wish you had taken more time earlier. I want to make it home to Rodde's custard pie tonight."

After they were rested, the two men began the walk up the shallow creek. Low shrubbery on both sides of them grew denser as they climbed the trail up the sandy draw. Rounding a sharp turn in the creek, the draw opened up, flatter and wider, giving the two men a view of the ridge of hills ahead of them. Here the creek was dammed from last winter's debris and Whitey sat on the edge of a large driftwood log, his pale eyes fixed on them.

"You boys took you owns' time," said Whitey. "I been waitin' fer hours."

With that Whitey arose and without another word turned his back to them and started back up the trail that ran beside the creek disappearing around the next bend. Joshua and Jacques looked at each other, shrugged and then followed Whitey up the trail. As they were walking Joshua placed his hand beneath his capote, half cocking the pistol he carried on a thong around his neck. He secured the firearm tight to his body with a broad sash around his waist. Another pistol rode snuggling against the small of his back. Each man carried a musket and two more rifles were secured beneath a tarp in the boat down creek.

Joshua smelled the smoke from the campfire before he saw it, and rounding the bend, Jacques and Joshua paused to take in the view in front of them. Here beside the creek, a grassy flatland spread against the hillside. On it sat two small hide tents surrounding a fire burning brightly in the mid-morning air. The wood must have been a little wet because Joshua could hear it popping and dusty, gray smoke drifted out low over the water, hanging in the small glade. Seated around the fire, two men arose as Joshua and Jacques came into sight.

"You boys minds yer manners now, we got company," said Whitey addressing the two men near the campfire as he strode up to them. "This un's Rafe and this is Ramon," said Whitey by way of introduction. "They ain't too bright, but they's good boys, just the same."

Both of the boys appeared to be in their twenties and were carbon copies of Whitey except that neither were albino. Strong Indian features peered out from the greasy hair and they appeared to have the same tailor as their father. Joshua paid closer attention to the huge Spanish musket lying on the log between them. Beside the musket, a shorter- barreled shotgun with wire wrapped around its clubby stock also was part of the arsenal.

"Welcome to our camp gentleman," Whitey fawned, waving his hand to the logs beside the fire. "Have some coffee whilst we palaver some turkey."

"No, Th---," Jacques started to say before Joshua slapped him hard on the back.

"Don't mind if we do," Joshua said finishing Jacques answer, sitting down on the nearest log directly across from Rafe and Ramon and the weapons. Whitey picked up several tin cups from the trash piled around the campfire, and filled them with a steaming brew he poured from the blackened pot hanging over the fire. The coffee melted the grease in the cups causing the mixture to froth and foam as Whitey handed the cups to them. The cup felt slick in Joshua's hand, and he avoided Jacques stare as he wrapped both hands around it.

"Now you fellers show me the cut bits, and I'll have my boys start packing them hides on down to your boat," Whitey said, smiling broadly exposing his mouth of broken stained snags.

Joshua reached his hand beneath his coat and jingled a leather pouch full of coins.

"We brought the money," Joshua said, "but being businessmen, we would like to see the furs before we talk about price."

"Well sure," Whitey answered, "we'll give you an eyeful. Right there over in that tent, just you help yourself."

Joshua rose from the log and walked to the flap of the nearest tent. Smiling Whitey motioned from him to enter. Throwing the deer hide flap back, Joshua stooped to peer inside the dark interior. A powerful odor assailed his senses, and as his eyes adjusted to the gloom, Joshua felt bile rising in his throat. Inside the tent was a single pole set in the middle. The soil was covered with gnawed bones and pieces of food. Everywhere in a circle around the pole were clumps of feces; outlining the length of the tether the small naked form of a female creature was tied to. A fur gag cruelly forced apart her small, cracked lips and leather thongs bound her feet and ankles cutting deep wounds into the flesh, making it puffy and raw. Every inch of her body was covered in dirt, from her small pubescent breasts to the frail hips and legs. Shorn, blond hair accenting dead blue eyes looked toward Joshua. Behind him, Joshua heard the distinct sound a hammer being drawn to full cock.

"Now, Mr. Coural, very slowly stand up and tell your friend to hand his rifle to Rafe, you done seen our hides, now you're gonna show us the money. Be very careful, I can always take your money off'n your dead carcass."

Joshua slowly rose to his feet, cursing himself for his stupidity. He was sure that if Whitey planned to steal the money, the attempt would be made later when the furs were loaded in the boat; it never occurred to him that the furs didn't exist. The sight within the tent slowed his reactions and he now knew he should never have taken his eyes from Whitey. Once on his feet, Joshua turned slowly to face Whitey, looking closely at the pistol pointed in his direction. The handgun, although small, had a large bore. Joshua witnessed wounds from this type weapon before. Its accuracy wasn't good, but at short range they could be loaded with several balls, or iron nails, and were extremely deadly.

"Jacques," Joshua called, repeating his friends name as he found his mouth was very dry. "Jacques, please hand you rifle to the boys. Mr. Whitey has rather an evil looking pistol pointed directly at me, and I think it best we do as he says."

Whitey's back was turned to Jacques, and it took Jacques a minute to comprehend Joshua's request. Making eye contact, Joshua smiled and nodded his head.

"Get his gun, Rafe," hollered Whitey, "and cover him with that shotgun. We don't want these two river rats trying to be brave. Our hides in there is just about used up," said Whitey speaking again to Joshua. "She's getting so she's not much fun no more, and the boys thinks we should find us a new one. With all that money we kin buy somethin' real purty up in St. Loui. Now gives me that moneybag."

Joshua reached inside his coat and jingled the leather bag to cover the sound of the hammer on his pistol coming to full cock. Breaking a vow made to his mother long ago, he said simply, "Jacques, Baisser la tete" and squeezed the trigger. His coat jumped with the explosion as the ball cut through the fabric of his capote and into Whitey chest exploding a button from the dirty jacket before penetrating through the albino's body spraying, the tent wall with a foamy red. Jacques needed no further warning and he threw the rifle toward Rafe as he dived for his legs to make sure Rafe could not reach the shotgun. Ramon appeared frozen in time. First he looked toward his father who was now slumped to both knees looking down toward the unfired pistol in his lifeless hands, and then Ramon cast his eyes toward his brother, wrestling on the ground with the trader. As if in slow motion he moved toward the log and the shotgun propped there. From the edge of the glade a puff of white smoke appeared from the trees and Ramon felt a burning sensation rip through his stomach. Startled, the half-breed took one step before the sound of Dodge's shot reached him. It was the last thing he heard as he fell headlong into the fire causing the coffeepot to overturn and scald his now lifeless form as it lay smoking in the fire. Beating the front of his burning jacket, Joshua ran toward Jacques and together they quickly subdued Rafe, pinning him face down into the damp earth.

"Kind of like wrestling a lynx," said Jacques. "Thanks. Are you all right?"

"Better than Mr. Whitey and his kin," replied Joshua, "but Rodde is going to give me hell for scorching this coat. Sorry about the short warning, I didn't want Rafe to get his hands on that shotgun."

Dodge and Trenton walked slowly across, the glade, searching the surrounding tree line for any other movement.

"There's a young girl in that first tent," said Joshua. "Brace yourself, it's bad. She's still alive, but not by much."

Removing the young girl from the tent, the men set both of the tents on fire. The second tent held only tattered possessions of the renegade trappers and smelled as badly if not worse. Joshua gathered the Spanish Musket, old shotgun, and the small pistol and, after discharging them, threw them on the fire. He never wanted to face these weapons again. The girl was wrapped in a blanket and Dodge carried her in his arms back down the creek to the small boat while the other three kicked and pushed Rafe down the streambed, hoping the muddy water would improve his smell. Rafe said little and showed no emotion about the loss of his family. Whitey and Ramon were quickly buried in shallow graves along the edge of the glade, with no markers or stones. Unfortunately their memory would always be etched in the mind of the young girl they tormented. The frontier was a much better place without them.

The afternoon wind was in their favor and before dawn the next morning the party arrived back in St. Genevieve. Dodge and Trenton took charge of the prisoner and the girl.

"Thank you my friend," said Joshua, grasping Jacques hand firmly. "If ever you have need, just ask."

"I will," replied Jacques, "besides, what are friends for?"

Neither spoke of what they witnessed back in the glade. As the morning light was just entering his bedroom, Joshua scrubbed his skin raw before falling asleep, exhausted, while Rodde held and rocked him. Although his body was clean, he could not wash away the horror from his mind, and nightmares would plague his sleep for months to come. Within the next week the young girl was identified and returned to her parents in Cahokia where she had been missing for several months. Rafe was tried and hung. Little mercy was provided him when the story reached the citizens of St. Genevieve, and like his family, was buried in an unmarked grave. No one wished to be reminded of the events that transpired. June was to be a time of rebirth, not death and depravity.

Joshua again met Ashley late in 1805, along with Ashley's friends, Manuel Lisa and Andrew Henry. Henry was to be married to a girl from a local family in St. Genevieve, Marie Villars. The wedding was spectacular and Joshua and Rodde attended. The gala lasted all day, December 16, 1805, and the streets of St. Genevieve echoed merriment long into the night. Ashley was one of the witnesses to this marriage.

Ashley was doing some courting of his own, another young woman from St. Genevieve, Mary Able. Her father owned a large Spanish land grant along the sprawling Mississippi, and was part of the elite society in this new and growing community, but as yet no plans for their marriage had been announced. It was after Henry's wedding that Joshua took Lisa and Ashley inland to explore the thickly wooded hills that rolled up and away from the Mississippi River banks.

They explored the sites of the ancient burial mounds close to St. Genevieve and the roaring caves further back in the rock escarpments bordering the twisting river. In these caves, the rock crevices led far into the earth and the wind blowing down the sinkholes on top of the hills exited the entrances to these caves with moans and wails, sounding like catamounts after a kill. Some of the locals believed this area to be haunted because of the bones found in the burial mounds and because of the sounds issuing deep from underground.

"What happened to the Indians that lived here?" Lisa asked Joshua. "Are they still in this area?"

"I don't rightly know. People here say that the Indians that built these huge mounds were here hundreds, maybe thousands of years before we came, and then they just disappeared. Whether the floods took them or they were all killed out, no one seems to know. Most folks around here tend to stay away from that area. People believe if they go messing around in those mounds, spirits and haunts will be released. Better just to let them be."

"That sounds like good advise to me," replied Ashley. "I don't think what we're looking for is down that low anyway."

"I've spent some time down by Cahokia," said Joshua. "There is one great big mound with a bunch of smaller hills built around it. In places it looks like there was once a big stockade that went all the way around it. There are still a few pitch logs set in the ground. Them pitch logs don't ever rot. My mother told me that in St. Genevieve there are some records from Father Marquette. He wrote down stories telling about what the Illinois Tribes said concerning the mound builders. Marquette said they were great traders and that all kinds of shells, copper items, and flint tools were found there. Many of the tools weren't made around here. The records talked about those people building calendars, big ones made from rings of trees that told them when to plant and when to harvest. They knew all about corn and grew huge fields of it down on the river islands."

"Well," Lisa said, "all things change over time, that's one lesson I've found out. I've been trying to get along with the French, then the Spanish, and now the Americans. A person has to stay one step ahead all the time or else they are liable to end up like the mound builders. All people will find of us two-hundred years from now are our graves, and not know a thing about us, what we did, how we felt, whom we hated, or even whom we loved. Never quit learning, Joshua, maybe something you found out about the past, might just save you in the future."

"That's one thing my mother set store by," answered Joshua, "passing down history. She thought it was important also."

"I've held a license to trade with the Osage Indians while the Spanish controlled the Louisiana territory but lost all my influence and control to the Chouteau family while France held the land. In 1804, all of their licenses were cancelled because of the American control. What I learned was you have to stay one step ahead. The next few years I'm going to build several permanent trading posts up north on the Missouri where trappers can bring in furs from the West. The West, Joshua, that's where the future is going to be."

After several days travel, Joshua led them to a river that ran northward, slow and shallow, the waterway was overhung by thick stands of trees. Joshua related how during the summer months hundreds of turtles basked in the sunshine and huge fish swam lazily in the shallow waters. Here on the sandy banks of the slow moving tributary to the Mississippi, Joshua pointed out the entrance to a mammoth cave that he found many years earlier while exploring the area. Joshua liked to come hunting in these remote parts and found the settlers further inland near Potosi to be a hardy and friendly people. He met them when he traveled with his father in search of locations for lead smelting westward from the river.

Joshua showed Lisa and Ashley the deposits of saltpeter in the cave. This saltpeter was of great interest to the two men, because from this substance gunpowder could be made. Both men were very excited about the find and immediately began making plans to obtain licenses to mine this location.

Lisa believed he could hire away miners from the Hart Brown Mines in Kentucky and bring them here to mine saltpeter. This sediment could be removed from the caves and leached with water in huge vats generating the 'mother liquor' from which saltpeter was made. This could then be mixed with wood ash, burned hot and quickly leached again which in turn yielded potash. The liquid from these two leachings were mixed together and boiled until all remaining water was gone. The result was the crystalline powder. It took over two-hundred pounds of sediment to make one pound of saltpeter. The crystals, lustrous in appearance, tasted slightly salty. Lisa explained to Joshua, that water running in the caves down through the holes on top was continually making more of the sediment and even constant mining would fail to deplete the supplies.

"If we can get the licenses and bring in the miners, I believe we can set up operations on Ashley's land. With plenty of charcoal around and this saltpeter, there is some money to be made from gunpowder. I wonder how come no one else started doing this before? What do you know of the early miners in this area, Joshua?"

"Well," said Joshua, "people have been traveling over this country for a long time. Most of them were looking for gold and silver instead of having to work to make a fortune. When I was in school we learned about De Soto who traveled through here as early as 1542. He had all sorts of fights with the Casquins. Some of these burial mounds might even be from those people. Two of his soldiers, Hernando de Silvias and Pedro Moreno, spent some time right in this area. They brought back copper and salt. The only place there is salt that is easy to come by is over on Saline Creek. They were probably looking for gold but never found any. Other Spaniards came through here, too. There are old records that men name Coronado, Onate, and Penalosa traveled this far north. In the late 1600s, the priests came through here thinking that they could convert the Indians, some of them died trying. Father Marquette was probably the most successful with the Illinois Tribe. During the early 1700s, a lot of Frenchmen came here trading with the Indians and Father Gravier set up a mission at Kaskaskia.

"A man named Le Sueur probably was the first to start lead mining. He went up the Meramec and found the big cave there. After him came D'iberville and Crozat. Crozat sent Cadillac into this area to look for mining possibilities. Dustine came down from Canada for the French but he tended to tell a lot of tall stories about Missouri and the people. When he went back home, they didn't believe all that he said. Big trading companies from Spain and France began to set up operations in this country then, but Phillippe Francois Renault was the smartest of the bunch. He improved the smelting process so more lead could be taken from the galena. The Indian wars made mining a risky proposition though and a lot of these big companies went broke. People first settled St. Genevieve in 1732. Some of the first settlers were La Rose, Valle, Joyane, Bauvis, and Baugy families. Most of them still have relatives here."

"Were they miners, river men or farmers?" asked Ashley.

"Some of these families got into mining. All they needed were some good pickaxes, shovels, and sometimes drills and blasting equipment. They just looked until they found a good spot and dug a shaft by hand down ten or twelve feet. When they found an ore vein they used a pick to get it loose and hauled it to the surface. Smelters were built close by. My father was in charge of running the smelters for years; sometimes they even found silver and other minerals with the lead. The early smelters were just like a big oven, with three walls and room for air to get in the bottom. They filled it full of wood, poured in the pieces of lead, and then put more wood on top. After this pile burned for a day or so, most of the sulfur was burned off and they hauled the lead down to St. Genevieve for the trip up river. Mr. Austin over in Potosi is using a lot better furnace now and can smelt the lead down further. That's why I was thinking that if you catch the sulfur from the lead and mix it with good charcoal and saltpeter from the caves, a person doesn't need anything else to make gunpowder. Gunpowder and lead, right here."

"Ashley was right when he said we needed to come to you," said Lisa. "You know more about this country than even the savages."

"A person has to be careful where you start mining though," Joshua continued. "John Alley got kicked off his Mine-a-Joe because the Baugys mined there forty years earlier. Once they saw he was making a go of it they took it back and their old claims held up. Make sure all of your licenses are in order, and double check to see that no one else has any claims to this cave."

"Thank you for the advice, Joshua," said Lisa, "your help has been invaluable. Should you choose to be part of this concern, William and I would be glad to have you. Young men with vision, such as yourself, are few and far between."

Joshua, along with Lisa and Ashley, returned to St. Genevieve the next day and Lisa immediately went to find the proper place to register his claims and to petition for the rights to the saltpeter. Joshua returned to Rodde and the business of running the post. He found that he thought of her constantly when he was away, almost to the point of experiencing guilt when he roamed the wild backcountry. Few things in this world would keep him from following his dreams of seeing the great mountains far to the west. Rodde and her love were among those things.

How could he reconcile the two, he wondered? If he couldn't stand to be away from her on a three-day trip, how could he leave her for several years to follow the rivers west? Perhaps it was for his children to carry on his dreams, his visions. Maybe it was his purpose to dream only, his life was here with her and the trading post. This was where his father was buried; here he was close to the memory of his mother. Just as his father dreamed of plans that never came to be, he inspired Joshua with his stories. Joshua would do the same for his children. They would be the ones to see what lay upstream. Joshua thought back to his trip to the caves with Lisa and Ashley; Lisa's plans made sense to him.

It was a natural jump for Lisa to begin plans to also manufacture gunpowder rather than shipping the crystals to St. Louis and points east. After filing for his claims and permits, he checked with the blacksmith shops in St. Genevieve to see if they could build to his specifications two huge drums secured on wooden frames. These drums contained round, wooden balls and with several men turning the cranks, could be constantly rotated. Into the drums he could place the charcoal and the sulfur. The saltpeter would be run through heavy metal rollers pulverizing the contents and mixed with the sulfur and charcoal. In a second drum the contents would be mixed further with heavy iron wheels. Water could then be added to keep the mixture moist. Two huge wooden rollers would feed this coarse ground powder in sheets of gunpowder cake. The last step would break this highly compressed mixture in grains that were stored in wooden casks ready for shipment.

With the use of the plank road from Potosi, movement of supplies and finished products would be made easier. The plank road came about because those who lived a distance from the rivers remained relatively isolated. Dirt roads in good weather were dusty and rough; heavy rains made them impassable, muddy quagmires. In a few places, sawed wooden planks or unsawed logs covered the surface of dirt roads providing all-weather roads. But these roads were expensive, their builders charged high tolls to cover building costs and they quickly deteriorated, still it offered a viable route to move the gunpowder to the riverbanks for shipping.

Both Lisa and Ashley were excited by the finds that Joshua showed them and talked constantly about their plans for this venture. Gunpowder and Lead. These two elements would be vital to a new nation as it expanded the frontier boundaries.

Two weeks later as Ashley and Lisa were getting ready to leave St. Genevieve, Rodde told Joshua that Andrew Henry and his new wife, Marie, were separating and Henry was returning to St. Louis with Lisa and Ashley. Marie planned to stay in St. Genevieve. Henry said little to Joshua or his other friends when they left that cold morning just before Christmas to return to St. Louis.

195

"That's just like a man," Rodde said. "Poor Marie. Don't you go doing any business with that Andrew Henry. Shame on him for leaving Marie like that. He got what he wanted, and now he's leaving."

"Rodde, Andrew is an important man. He has lots of business concerns in St. Louis. He needs to think about their future. How is he to make his fortune if he just stays here in St. Genevieve?"

Suddenly seeing that his own thoughts crept into the conversation, he dropped the subject saying only, "Rodde, St. Genevieve is the end of the road for some people; perhaps others still have a ways to travel."

In September, 1806, Lewis and Clark returned to St. Louis and their descriptions of the country, reunited interest in the fur trade. Joshua was extremely envious when he heard the description of the vast journey. He loved hearing the tales of exploration and listened again and again to the famous accounts of Lewis and Clark and their journeys across the Louisiana Purchase and their travels to the Pacific Ocean. He was especially interested in the stories of how a Shoshone woman, Sacajawea, helped the explorers across the high rocky mountains far to the west. Their stories of the Clearwater, Snake, and Columbia Rivers, made his day to day duties along the Mississippi feel almost tame, and his desire to see the new country washed over him again.

Several more years passed before Joshua and Rodde bought all of Shaw's interests in the trading post. Rodde even convinced Joshua to start carrying some household items such as clothing and furniture in the store. By this time Lisa and Ashley received permission to start the saltpeter operation. They established warehouses in St. Genevieve and shipped some of the product to St. Louis to pay for wages and mining operations, but stored much of it in the warehouses. They still planned to open a plant to produce gunpowder but Lisa was detained on the upper reaches of the Missouri with his plans to establish trading posts there, and all of Ashley's time was taken up by his business dealings in St. Louis and the supervision of the saltpeter production.

By 1809, Joshua and Rodde celebrated thirteen years of marriage. No children had yet arrived to bless the marriage although it wasn't from lack of effort. Since Rodde's early miscarriages she had not become pregnant again. The loss of her second baby was accompanied by heavy bleeding and Joshua was afraid for her life for several days before she recovered. Perhaps it was best no children came; Joshua could not have stood to lose her. Sometimes he wondered if he were cursed, perhaps he should never have explored the caves and burial mounds.

He and Jacques still visited weekly. Jacques' father passed away the previous winter and he now ran all the business concerns in St. Genevieve. Jacques was a natural businessman and the family's finances did well under his leadership. Three children graced his life, two boys and a girl. The boys, Renard and Jean, called Joshua 'Uncle' and badgered him to take them with him when he went on his trips to obtain furs from the backwater areas. Sometimes Joshua relented and took them if the trips were to be short.

"You spoil them too much," said Jacques. "They would rather be out with you than doing their chores. How will they ever learn this business if they are out all day playing Indian?"

"How quickly you forget, Jacques, how many times did we sneak away to attack any poor innocent we could find? The river and the forest were our homes. We learned. Work is always there; perhaps we should all play a bit more."

"As always, you are right my friend, just wait until you have children. I will make it my personal mission to spoil them rotten; you will have to hire someone to do the chores, as they will never be home," he said laughing.

Renard and Jean filled some of the void in Joshua's life and Jacques' daughter, Antoinette, would often spend time with Rodde when he was out with the boys. Like Rodde, her hair was wild and untamed and Rodde would braid it in different ways, always tying the ends with bright ribbon. Antoinette loved playing with the bolts of fabric in the trading post and sometimes Rodde would cut clothes for Antoinette's dolls, dressing them in the latest fashions she found from the newspapers sent from St. Louis. Joshua and Rodde rarely spoke of the lack of their own children. This sorrow bound them even tighter and both valued their time together when they would wander the riverbanks telling each other of their dreams.

"Next year," Rodde would say, "you are taking me to Paris for the summer. We will return to New Orleans and from there, berth a sailing ship, first class to Paris. Think of the things we will see! With the items we could buy and resell, we would become fabulously rich. Perhaps even stay in France, buying a castle and living the rest of our lives among the aristocracy."

"Ah yes, my queen," Joshua would laugh. "Possibly we should first earn our fortune before you spend it. And would this castle have a bed for the king to ravish his wife?"

"Oui, Mon Cheri," she whispered pulling him close, "the castle would have many beds for their pleasure."

That night they made love slowly and gently, cherishing each minute, assuring each other that they alone were enough. Rodde slept restlessly and every time Joshua tried to move she clung tighter to his body as if to assure her of his presence. Joshua at last drifted off to sleep. In his dreams he soared high above the Mississippi. He looked westward across the vast plains and saw the high Blue Mountains full of dark timber and rushing cold water filled with beaver. Snow glinted off the high mountains guarding their secret entrances. He awoke suddenly; something else had been part of this dream--something that stalked him, waiting for him. He couldn't recall what it was, but he arose from his bed and checked the loads in his rifles by the door. Whatever was waiting would have a fight on their hands should it find him.

Ashley returned to St. Genevieve early that spring and hunted Joshua down to tell him the latest news. Joshua learned that Manuel Lisa, with forty men, established Fort Manuel far up the Missouri in 1807, and returned in 1808, loaded down with furs. Lisa and Ashley formed a partnership with William Morrison and Pierre Menard of Kaskaskia. Morrison and Menard sent as their representative on the expedition, George Drouillard of Lewis and Clark fame. John Potts and Peter Wiser, two more Lewis and Clark men, were also on the trip.

Ashley also told Joshua about the party of Andrew Henry and Pierre Menard guided by Drouillard and John Coulter. They left Fort Manuel to strike deeper in the heart of Indian country and found the Blackfeet to be fierce warriors.

Joshua listened intently to the stories, especially when Ashley told him about John Colter's accounts of his travels from Fort Manuel. Colter's task was to travel alone, in winter, through the region and inform the natives of the party's desire to trade for furs. During his travels, Colter headed south to a place the Indians called Wind River and then to a wonderland that people in St. Louis were calling Coulter's Hell because of what he described seeing there.

He tells of fountains of hot water shooting from the Earth in tall geysers. He speaks of mud pots boiling with no fire and of great waterfalls and vast lakes guarded by tall, sharp mountains. "Some people don't even believe him," said Ashley, "but I do."

"And what of Lisa?" asked Joshua.

"In the spring of 1808, he built a fort at the mouth of the Big Horn River, naming it Fort Raymond. Last summer he traveled back down river to St. Louis and I spoke to him in July. Andrew Henry was left in command of the Fort. Lisa told me many fabulous stories of the Indians and the country."

"Is Colter still in St. Louis? I would dearly love to visit with him."

"He was, but has just returned to the Three Forks area where a year earlier he and John Potts had been trapping in the that region. A large party of Blackfeet warriors surprised them and killed Potts. They made Colter race for his life, giving him a short head start. He killed one of the braves and took his clothing and weapons. He was able to escape the rest of the Indians by hiding in a beaver pond. Eleven days later he made it back to Fort Raymond. He survived by eating only roots he remembered from Sacajawea's training while she was with Lewis and Clark. Andrew Henry did not even recognize him as he arrived at the fort, emancipated with raw, swollen feet. He traveled across vast sections of the country, and tall mountains with only his senses for his guide. He is very lucky to be alive."

"Yes," agreed Joshua, "but think of all that he has seen. Perhaps he is the first white man to witness these wonders."

"Lisa is organizing a new trip. He is getting together more investors to finance a party to return to Three Forks. He asked me to implore you to come with us."

Joshua thought for several days how to approach Rodde with this news. More than anything, he felt the desire to travel with Lisa into new country few men had seen. This was his chance to mesh his dreams with reality. Several times he tried, but then thought, how could he leave her? Who would bring the furs to the post, who would arrange the shipping north to St. Louis and how could she handle the men? These were things she could not do. Rodde sensed his mood and at last confronted him.

"Joshua, go if you must, I know the far wilds draw you. We can hire someone to help here. I will miss you terribly, but if you promise me to return within the year I can wait. My prayers and my love will be with you."

With her permission to fulfill his unspoken desire, the realization that what he built here with her meant far more to him than what might be waiting upriver. Surprised that these feelings came so clearly to him, he grasped her, swinging her high in the air.

"But Madame," he replied, "and then who would be taking my pretty queen to Paris, and who would be sleeping in the king's bed on those cold winter nights. Me thinks the queen is trying to get rid of me, to push me into the wilderness so that she can run off with one of his knights."

Rodde buckled with relief, and she fell to her knees hiding her face in her hands weeping uncontrollable. She faced her worse fear, her heart shrinking inside and Joshua chose her. She would never let him regret this decision. No matter what happened, she would dedicate her life to him. Into this world she would bear his sons, regardless of the price. The merciful God had answered the question she dreaded for so long.

Ashley returned to St. Louis where, with Lisa, they organized the St. Louis Missouri Fur Company. Lisa began planning a new trip to the rich fur grounds. Many of the trappers were Americans who disliked the French Canadians and Creoles from Kaskaskia. They also did not trust the leadership of Lisa and Chouteau. Unfortunately, fights soon broke out between the two groups of men and almost led to bloodshed. The trip did not go well from the start. With the party splitting into different factions, Lisa left Henry in charge of trapping and he and Chouteau turned down the river back to St. Louis. The Blackfeet continually raided Henry's trappers and killed many of the men.

Joshua kept in touch with Ashley but learned little news of the trip he missed until Ashley related the troubles of Lisa's journey on a bright spring April day in 1811. Joshua felt more strongly than ever he made the right choice. His death by the hand of the Blackfeet would have crushed Rodde.

Joshua laughed when Ashley told him Lisa's story of Andrew Pelton, one of Henry's trappers. Pelton had very narrow eyes and a strange, inhuman face. One day he was attacked by a grizzly bear that, after biting him once, ran off.

"Lisa swore," said Ashley straight-faced, "that Pelton scared the bear away with his strange appearance."

"That proves it," laughed Joshua. "It's better to be ugly than rich; if Pelton were rich he would have provided a meal to the bear."

"Henry has just returned to St. Louis and is asking about you," continued Ashley. "He should be downriver in several weeks and wants to begin plans to build the gunpowder plant. The furs he brought back saved the company but he is ready for a little less adventure. Last winter he almost lost his life to starvation and many men did die. Until the army drives the Blackfeet out, more expeditions are not being planned."

Perhaps the best news that Joshua learned later that warm day in April was when Rodde smiled and held his hands to her stomach. With tears glistening in her eyes, she told him that she was pregnant again. She carried this child three months before letting him know she was with child. The other pregnancies ended before this, and she kept this pregnancy to herself, fearful that this one also might end in miscarriage. Although something inside her told her this would be the last child she bore, her heart soared that finally she could give Joshua what he most wanted. Joshua was elated, although he was careful not to allow himself to become excited. Maybe, just maybe, God was rewarding him for his decisions. The past taught him though, that everything he lived for could be taken from him in an instant.

Night Wind said little of her dreams to Joshua when he awoke the next morning to find her studying him as she laid on her side atop the mounded piles of elk skins. During the night, Spotted Owl squirmed his way on top of Joshua's chest and now lay there still, arms and legs protruding in all directions.

"Don't just stay there," said Joshua, "help me remove this weight. I feel like I'm drowning. This child is growing heavier by the minute."

Night Wind rose from the bed and helped Joshua move Spotted Owl, trying to prevent him from waking up. Spotted Owl murmured in his sleep and then curled tighter in a ball and was quiet again.

"How is your leg today?" whispered Joshua.

"It grows stronger, now that I am spoiled. Soon I must remove the willows and walk alone, or it will grow weak and withered."

"My mother loved the willow," Joshua mused. "She believed that the Willow Tree possessed magical qualities. When I was little she would build hoops from willows, weaving them in a circle. These hoops she hung from the porch. I can still remember the evening breeze blowing off the river, spinning them 'round and 'round. Sometimes she would take small cuttings from my hair and creasing the bark of a live willow, insert my hair next to the smooth skin of the inner bark. The next morning the crease would heal over sealing in my hair forever. My mother claimed this protected me from the river spirits and should I ever need help, the willow would treat me as a brother. My father never believed any of her superstitions, but allowed her to follow her customs because of his love."

Drawing the knife from a sheath at her waist, Night Wind cut a small lock from her long braid and handed it to Joshua.

"When you make the trip to the river today to scare the fish, do as your mother did. When I am stronger I will walk to the river with you to meet my new brother and thank him for his guidance and protection. If we do not take time to be one with all that is around us, when we are in need they may not listen to our pleas. Your mother was wise, and this knowledge runs in you also."

Later that day, Joshua did return to the river. Several miles below the falls the canyon widened and here the river slowed, becoming more circumspect as if taking time to think deeply before flowing on. Near the northern edge of this pooling, a thick stand of willows crowded the water's edge, lush with their abundance. Parenting the young saplings, a mighty tree stood guarding them from the encroaching canyon wall. Twelve steps Joshua walked around the base. Pulling a long slender branch down from a low limb, Joshua carefully slit the bark and inserted the dark strand of Night Wind's hair before releasing it to sway in the afternoon breeze. As he wiped his hand across his cheek, he felt moisture. Whether it was shared blood of the willow or a tear for his mother he did not know, but he felt more at peace as he walked back up the river to the cabin and Night Wind waiting for him there.

Chapter 9
The Plains

As the alarm went off jangling him awake to begin the day, Carrigan reflected on the two weeks left for him in the school year. Several cups of coffee later he decided that he didn't mind returning to school, actually he was looking forward to the end of the year. Late last night Carrigan arranged the schedule for his students to begin their presentations. He drew the names randomly, but knew few students would be ready on their appointed times. If the presentations crossed his desk in the time remaining he would give them full credit. A call to the media department teacher made arrangements for her students to videotape the presentations. Watching themselves on tape as he graded their presentations might bring them to concur with his ideas. Probably not, but it was worth a shot.

Carrigan's back and shoulders were still sore from the work he put in on the cabin, but it was a friendly pain born from a personal dream, hard work with an end in sight. A cabin was something that could be started, and completed, unlike teaching where closure was often very nebulous. By the time he returned to Rockville Sunday afternoon, all holes for the cabin's foundation were dug. Carrigan made sure to leave the openings large enough should any adjustment be needed when foundation posts were tamped into the rocky soil. Working steadily over the weekend enabled him to excavate twenty holes that were ready for further work upon his return. The last hole took him the longest because Carrigan was forced to bar through a heavy, fossilized rock formation which clung to the red earth and only grudgingly released its hold on the soil. At first he thought the hard layer was a limestone or shale, but as the heavy bar smashed its way through, Carrigan realized that what he was digging were old bone fragments long since turned to stone.

I'm probably destroying a complete fossil of Tyrannosaurus Rex, he thought. Damn dinosaur shouldn't have died right where I want to dig a hole. Taking extra time he dug around the formation and finally wedged it free from the hole.

Throwing it into the back of the pickup, Carrigan planned to ask the Mr. James if he could tell what type of fossil it was when he arrived at school on Monday. The only time Carrigan took away from his foundation task was when he ate lunch with Nancy. Carrigan couldn't decide which he enjoyed more, her company or his work on the cabin project.

Just like twenty years ago, he thought, I like to be with her, but there always seems to be something else I should be doing.

Carrigan had arrived at the Devil's Fireplace with a little time to spare before she showed up, and caught several small rainbows before seeing her jeep negotiating the steep switchbacks on the road across the river. The word 'road' was really an overstatement as it was merely a track cut by a bulldozer, zigzagging down the steep terrain. Nancy waved to him when she reached the bottom and began struggling with a small, red cooler in the back of the jeep. Sighing and unable to dodge the unavoidable, Carrigan forded the river, barely managing to keep the water out of his waders as he jumped from one rock to another. He left his fishing equipment on the far side under the fireplace, not wanting to risk falling and losing any of it to the fast moving water.

Nancy, having lost the fight with the cooler, feigned defeat and perched herself on the hood of the jeep to watch his balancing act on the slick stones. With sunglasses holding back waves of untamed hair, she laughed and encouraged him on until finally the safety of the far shore was reached.

"That's it," he said, "we're eating on this side of the river. If I try to pack that cooler across, I'll have to go swimming for sure. Sorry to disappoint you and arrive dry."

"What was all that hand waving going on halfway across? You looked like a drunken ballet dancer."

"Ah, I was just scaring off the river snakes before I jumped to the next rock," he said. "If I wave my arms a lot they head for other parts, now out of my way woman, let a man handle that cooler."

They started a small fire to heat the coffee with there in the sand by the river's edge; Nancy spread a red striped Hudson Bay blanket on the ground before opening the cooler. The lunch was more of a feast than a lunch with cold chicken breasts, mounds of potato salad, bags of pickles and carrots with sourdough biscuits and gooseberry jelly. A bottle of wine washed it all down and they stretched out on the blanket to finish off the feast with black boiled coffee steaming in tin cups, as the watched the river rolling by.

"I've kept pretty good track of you through the years," she said. "I know all about you being a cop down South. Father would send me clippings ever so often when you performed some valorous feat or caught a bad guy. I know you worked for the state with abused children and I know you teach school. I just lost track of you after you quit the police force. What did you do, go live in the mountains and become a hermit, or just rodeo every day? I visited with your father several times after you mother passed away, but you know your dad never did have much to say."

"Sometimes a person just needs to run away for a while," Carrigan said. "You were right when you told me in college that I didn't know what I was looking for. Problem is I still don't. You told me you were the best thing in my life and I probably should have believed you. I haven't found anything better yet."

Coloring a little at the emotion in his statements, Nancy looked away, following the flight of a magpie as it circled the canyon's air currents hoping for a chance at some of the leftovers from lunch.

"That was a long time ago," she said. "It's so strange, you're still easy to talk to. Sometimes I think you are the only one who doesn't want something from me. I deal with men every day and most of them either want my body, my money, or my ranch. Hell, twenty years ago, I would have given you all three, and you didn't want them."

Now it was Carrigan's turn to study the magpie before answering. With calculated words he finally replied, "Your body definitely. Your money and your ranch never. I just miscalculated on how much time I had before you gave up on me. I kept looking for what I was supposed to do in this life, but have never quite found it."

"Maybe you found it a long time ago, and just haven't recognized it yet," she said. Then realizing the conversation was getting too serious, she laughed and shook him by the arm. "And just where did you disappear after you quit the police force? I don't like a man that has secrets in his life."

"Well," said Carrigan, enjoying the feel of her hand on his arm, "after I quit bein' a cop, I tried to find a job as far away from people as I could. I was tied up with a woman who didn't have kids, nor did she want any. After a while she didn't want me either. One night Gertrude and I left both the job and the woman behind and headed north. Wow, that was a long time ago."

Carrigan told her how he returned home to Rockville, but the ranch was too small for him and his parents. He applied for and was hired as a manager on a ranch owned by Trabing Tires. Trabing was a large company headquartered in Chicago that dealt mainly in pharmaceuticals and chemicals, but also made tires. "I think every new car a person buys these days comes with Trabing Tires," he said. "Personally, I won't own them." During the course of the afternoon Carrigan found himself telling Nancy about his career as a cowboy, not on the rodeo circuit as when she had known him in college, but as the foreman of this large spread on the far reaches of the Laramie Plains.

Carrigan relaxed and spoke of the partnership he once made with a corporation. Trabing owned close to 50,000 acres, running clear to the edges of the Laramie Mountain Range to the west. Together with national forest land, they controlled enough grass to run 3,000 head of yearlings. Most of the country was not suited to wintering cattle due to the high elevation. Carrigan's job was to manage the ranch and oversee the cowboys working for the company. During the spring he frequented the auction barns buying lightweight cattle that would fatten on the strong, mountain feed. The summer was spent just trying to keep track of that many yearling cattle and the fall was filled with roundups, shipping, and sightseeing tours for the company executives. Winter months were a slower pace, when new horses were broken, equipment repaired, and the board of directors assessed the profits for the past year. These were the kind of boardroom executives who didn't know a steer from a heifer and to whom Carrigan found himself explaining endless, basic, ranching details.

Carrigan was interviewed for the job and hired by phone. He then drove to Denver and met with John Ashton, the Denver Director for Trabing, early in the summer. Ashton was a little man with no understanding of the West, and little or no experience in the livestock business. He was, however, the disperser of the funds that Carrigan would use to buy yearlings. Ashton sat on the Chicago Board of Directors and was in charge of all sales and operations in Colorado and Wyoming. He, therefore, accompanied Carrigan on every trip to the sale barn, questioning his judgment on every purchase, making innumerable asinine statements, and was, in fact, a general pain in the ass. Actually Carrigan couldn't blame him, the office building in Denver were boring and drab. (Carrigan vowed never to stoop low enough to be saddled with a job in any surroundings of this type.) Purchases for the ranch would then be faxed for approval to Denver where, hopefully, the auditors would understand his notes and wire the money to a local bank in Laramie. Ashton always encouraged Carrigan to buy as cheaply as possible rather than paying for healthier, quality livestock.

"You can buy any cattle you want to," said Carrigan, "as long as you're the one that ropes and doctors them once we turn them loose on the plains."

Feeling this threat might be sincere, Ashton finally shut up and let Carrigan do most of the buying. The first year 3,000 head of cattle were bought in less than two weeks. Sixty trucks were arranged and the caravan headed westward to the home base of operations near Elk Mountain, Wyoming. The summer went well except for the monthly fights with Ashton to get all the bills paid. Checking the fences and doctoring of the cattle kept Carrigan, and the young cowboys working for him, busy from daylight to dark. Carrigan finally realized that paying the young men monthly put too many dollars in their pockets. He would have to hunt the bars and taverns of Laramie every Sunday to drag them back to the ranch. By July, he paid them weekly, putting half of their wages away until winter in a savings account he maintained for them. This gave them just enough cash to have a good time each weekend, but without further funds they came dragging back to the ranch before Monday.

The only woman on the isolated ranch was the cook. Carrigan never knew her age. She claimed to be of Sioux extraction and went by the name of Two Hills. She was thickened and bent by age but the food she cooked was decent if plain. Carrigan was pleased she took a motherly interest in the young men--darning socks, blending concoctions to cure their hangovers, and doing laundry for them. She gave them stern but maternal advice as she bandaged and iodined their wounds from the weekend forays.

She spoke little to Carrigan, and he wondered if she associated him with Ashton, who periodically spent time on the ranch ordering her about. She dressed daily in Levi's and sweatshirts. A different sweatshirt was worn each day and she very seldom deviated from her routine. This was how Carrigan kept track of the week. Mondays a University of Wyoming sweatshirt peeked from beneath her apron. Tuesdays were reserved for a gold sweatshirt with the Doobie Brothers on the back. Wednesdays and Thursdays were some favorites she'd apparently picked up from yard sales somewhere. Evidently she just couldn't resist a good bargain but the fit left much to be desired. Saturdays seemed to be anything that was clean.

Sundays the Denver Bronco's displayed their blue and orange proudly from her broad shoulders. She listened to every game on a small transistor radio she carried. God help anyone who spoke when the game was on. A slow, withering glance was her only reply and then she returned her attention to the game, leaving no doubt what would happen if she were interrupted again. If the Broncos won, supper would be excellent and freshly cooked; if they lost--well, the young ranch hands searched for their own vittles while she pouted in her quarters. Unfortunately that year, the Bronco's didn't do well, and Sunday meals were scanty affairs.

That fall the cattle were rounded up into large corrals and trucked out weekly to various sale barns in the area. Carrigan felt the risk for a low market should be spread over several time periods with different sale barns. The cattle gained well, averaging almost two pounds per day while they ranged across the pastures. The thin steers Carrigan bought weighing five-hundred pounds, added half again that much to their frame. This gain translated into a hundred dollars profit per animal. When multiplied by 3000, head the board of directors were pleased with Carrigan's first year. His death loss on the cattle was small and minus wages, the company netted a little over a quarter million dollars.

Ashton was even pleased, undoubtedly because he received a bonus. He agreed to keep Two Hills and one other hand on for the winter to help Carrigan with the winter ranch work. Carrigan chose the youngest cowboy, Jeremy Hanson, as the one to stay. The other hands were ready to leave anyway, anxious to spend their savings Carrigan dispersed to them. Within several months, he was afraid this money too would be gone. Easy come, easy go.

Jeremy didn't have any place to go for the winter, and Carrigan could at least be assured he had a table to pull up to if he stayed on at the ranch. Besides, Jeremy was a good hand, and complained little about his daily chores, unlike the other cowboys. If they couldn't do the job from the back of a horse, they felt the chore didn't need doing. Jeremy actually liked fixing fence and Carrigan didn't have to check the job once Jeremy completed it.

In late November, Carrigan returned home to his parent's place for Thanksgiving. Two Hills, left with several grunts of goodbye and all of her sweatshirts, headed north to meet family on the Pine Ridge Reservation. Carrigan thought she would be gone about a week, judging from the number of sweatshirts that accompanied her. Jeremy looked so forlorn at being left alone that Carrigan loaded him in the pickup and took him along. The Thanksgiving meal was a special treat that year and Carrigan passed up his third helping so he could hold more pie. Jeremy kept eating long after everyone else gave up making Melissa Carrigan beam. She talked about what a nice young man James brought home. Something about Jeremy made everyone want to mother him.

"James," said his father, "I been waiting for you to get home. I need to patch a stock tank out back and I can't hold the damn thing up and weld it at the same time. Come give me a hand and work off some of that dinner that your mom fixed."

The two men left the table, piling on hats and coats before going out to work on one of the many projects the Senior Carrigan was always going to do, but recently never quite got around to.

His father was aging and Carrigan realized that his dad couldn't work as hard anymore. I need to get home more, he thought; pangs of guilt ran through him when he saw the numerous projects in the shop that needed done. Nothing large, just time consuming. It was hard because no matter how Carrigan did something, his dad usually wanted it done a different way. Eventually over the last few years, Carrigan just stopped coming home to help. But today, pleased by his father's request, Carrigan vowed to come home more often. He did miss his mother's company, and to be truthful, also her cooking.

Together the two men lifted the large tank on its side and rolled it near the welder. James Senior began welding the rip in the metal while Carrigan steadied the circle of metal to keep it from falling. Through the shower of sparks Carrigan realized that Jeremy was pulling on his arm dragging him from the shop.

"Your mom. Your mom!" was all Jeremy kept saying.

Seeing the look on Jeremy's face, Carrigan headed for the house on a dead run. Inside the living room, he found her lying on the braided rug near the fireplace. The massive stroke took her just as she was cutting another piece of pie for Jeremy. In falling, she hit her head on the edge of the table and blood still glistened from her temple slowly pulsing down the side of her cheek, too slowly. Carrigan realized she was dead before he knelt beside her. He never felt his father join beside him as he held his mother, rocking her slowly, wishing he had told her he loved one more time before leaving the Thanksgiving table. Long minutes passed before Carrigan released her back to the braided rug. Her rug—the one she was so proud of, the one she badgered James Senior about for a whole year before he relinquished and bought it. Rising, Carrigan left his father's side and went to the make the call. Someone had to make arrangements and James Senior never was very good at those things. Jeremy still stood silently by the kitchen door kicking his toe across the scuffed linoleum as Carrigan picked up the phone.

Carrigan stayed the next week after arranging transportation for Jeremy to leave for the ranch. His father grew even more alone and isolated, letting Carrigan make all the arrangements for his mother's return to the earth. Although not overly religious, she did have ties to a small church in the community. The service and internment went smoothly but limited seating forced many people to stand outside in the chilly air. Carrigan was amazed by the turnout. He never realized how many people respected his mother, and from their kind messages afterwards he began to understand truly how many lives she affected. Family after family told him of the times she brought food when they were experiencing trouble. She helped people with battles against social security and city utilities, donating countless hours to fight injustice. Young adults told of her help with scholarship applications, and older people explained how she took them shopping, cleaned their homes, and provided companionship when they sat alone in their small houses. His mother had always just been his mother. He loved her deeply, but until that day he never thought of her as a community resource, an integral part of the small town near which she lived.

The night after the funeral, he drove far into the hills and walked along the banks of the Laramie River, reliving memories of his mother. Still clutched in his hand was the funeral program with her favorite poem outlining her philosophy of life, the philosophy of life she taught him, not by lecture but rather through example and love. Unseen by anyone but the river, he cried for hours, his shoulders jerking in great sobs.

Oh, Lord, I've never lived where churches grow.
I love creation better as it stood
That day you finished it so long ago,
And looked upon your work and called it good.
I know that others might find you in the light
That's sifted down through tinted windowpanes,
And yet I seem to feel you near tonight.

Let me be easy on the man that's down;
Let me be square and generous with all.
I'm careless sometimes, Lord, when I'm in town,
But never let them say I'm mean or small.
Make me as big and open as the plains,
As honest as the hoss between my knees,
Clean as the wind that blows behind the rains,
Free as the hawk that circles down the breeze.

I thank you, Lord, that I am placed so well,
That you made my freedom so complete;
That I'm no slave to whistle, clock, or bell,
Nor weak-eyed prisoner of wall and street.
Just let me live my life as I've begun
And give me work that is open to the sky;
Make me a partner of the wind and sun,
And I won't ask a life that's soft or high.

Forgive me, Lord, if sometimes I forget.
You know about the reasons that are hid.
You understand the things that gall and fret;
You know me better than my mother did.
Just keep an eye on all that's done and said
And right me, sometimes, when I turn aside,
And guide me on the long, dim, trail ahead
That stretches upward toward the Great Divide.

By Badger Clark

Late that night Carrigan returned home, his emotion spent. He was proud of his mother's life, and proud that he was her son. The finality of her death reached deep inside of him as he entered the house. His father sat in a rocking chair in the living room, eyes focused straight ahead. Carrigan did not speak to him, each needed to grieve in his own way.

He never knew much about his mother's childhood. She was born in Pavilion, Wyoming. Melissa and James Senior were married in 1939 just before James Sr. was sent overseas to fight for his country on the bloody beaches of Normandy. Melissa stayed in Pavilion until her young, soldier husband returned home, weary in body and spirit. Together they traveled to Rockville and made a life together. Several years later James Jr. was born into the family. She sometimes told Carrigan of her early years. The town she was raised in expected a rail line to come through bringing prosperity, to the little community on the edges of the Wind River Indian Reservation. She had laughed when she told him how she loved to walk

211

among the sandstone formations protecting the city, and of Herder's General Store, and Jones' Basketerium, the primary businesses in town.

"All I ever wanted, I could find on the shelves of those two stores," she had said.

Her father died when she was young and her mother raised her--the rail line never came. A small pension and payments from her mother's share of the profits from the Arapahoe Ranch were their only income. The Arapahoe Ranch was part of the Wind River Reservation and all tribal members received a share when there were good years. Carrigan knew that Shoshone blood ran in his veins, but never thought much about it. His grandmother was a half-breed or less, but still entitled to a share of the ranch's revenues. Melissa always teased him that between his Indian blood, and his Irish heritage, he was an Irish Red. Of his great-grandparents on her side, he knew little. Melissa's father was an itinerant laborer and worked as an irrigator before his death.

Carrigan did know that his parents' marriage was a strong one, and growing up he was cognizant of their shared affection and respect. As he reflected back, he was able to understand that although James Sr. was much louder and sterner than Melissa, she was, in fact, probably the stronger of the two. The future would be a lonely one for his father.

Upon Carrigan's return to his ranch job, he found that Jeremy had been busy and several jobs were already completed. Floorboards were replaced in the horse trailer, and shingles were nailed on the roof of the bunkhouse. Instead of tearing off the old shingles, previous owners just added squares when needed. The ranch's inhabitants before Carrigan must have purchased whatever shingles were on sale. The roof looked like a speckled, guinea hen proudly showing colors of green, brown, black and red, giving it a unique appearance. It didn't have to be pretty, just leak-proof. Two Hills also returned and Carrigan realized it was Friday from her choice of clothing, eight days since the death of his mother.

"All things from this earth must pass, Mr. Carrigan, yet still it brings sorrow to our lives," Two Hills said as they ate a quiet supper that evening.

Carrigan acknowledged her condolence. This was perhaps the most she ever spoke to him. He glanced quickly at her dark features but read nothing there, and returned to eating supper. Jeremy, quiet as always, helped himself to seconds, keeping his eyes on the food.

During the next week they replaced old corral poles and re-hung several gates that were knocked down during shipping. Early in December, Carrigan realized that they needed to ride to all of the windmills to make sure the pumps were shut down. If the pumps were still turned on, the hard

January freezes would lock them tight, ruining the rods and breaking the waterlines. Joe, Carrigan's rope horse, made the trip to the ranch although he was getting pretty long in the tooth. Joe didn't seem to mind his new surroundings and some days he still showed the same spunk from his arena days. Letting him rest after the long shipping season, Carrigan turned him out to run with the mares in the bluffs pasture. Two young horses replaced Joe in the corral, and a long ride around windmills would be good for them. As the two men left the ranch house the next day, the gray winter clouds seemed a bit thicker and a strong breeze from the east blew in their faces. By noon they managed to shut down the pumps in the trail pasture and they turned north to attend to the three windmills situated against a low range of bluffs to the north. The wind died down a few knots, but large flakes of snow were beginning to swirl and the temperature fell with each mile. Jeremy said little but Carrigan could see he was turning blue and getting colder. He felt the chill himself and his toes ached, the leather riding boots offering little protection from the wet snow.

By the time the men reached the shelter of the bluffs, Carrigan decided that no more could be accomplished today and motioned for Jeremy to turn his horse homeward.

"Find the north fence line and follow it home," Carrigan said. "I've seen these blizzards before; they can get bad, quick. Keep the dun's tail to the wind once you find the fence line, and you'll be fine. I am going to find Joe and bring him in. He's too damn old to be out in this weather."

Jeremy nodded and pulled his old felt down further to protect his ears. Turning for home he started the long jog to the ranch house, seven miles to the west.

"Now," thought Carrigan, "if I were an old stud, running with a bunch of young mares, where would I be? Tired," he said to himself.

He mentally checked off the protected draws in this pasture and finally decided to ride over the bluffs and look in a rugged arroyo on the far side. With an east wind, the deep cut would offer the best protection. Fighting his way up the steep slope, Carrigan felt the full bite of the wind once he topped out. Here the storm hit him full force and the snow stung his eyes and cheeks, blurring his vision and causing his teeth to chatter. Riding the top of the ridge, he ducked his head low kicking the colt into the face of the storm until he found the slick trail leading down. The wind immediately lessened as he descended and he worked his fingers inside his gloves trying to gain feeling in them again. Carrigan tried whistling for Joe but his lips were too cold to pucker. Leaving the reins loose on his horse's neck he cupped his hands to his mouth attempting to gain feeling in his numb fingers. That's when the world around him exploded.

213

Too late, his father's words flashed through his mind, 'Never trust a colt.' Something on the slick trail caused the young horse to jump and when the horse's feet hit the ground they found little purchase in the slick gumbo. The colt reared again and then righted himself momentarily before cart wheeling head over heels twice down the icy track. Pressing hard in the stirrups, Carrigan jumped up and away from the falling horse and over the edge of the trail, judging the cold rocks below offered better chances for safety than being pinned beneath half a ton of horseflesh. He briefly felt a tearing pain in his right shoulder before a rock smashed against his head sending him into darkness as he slid the remaining distance to the bottom of the draw. Above him the storm continued growing in strength, howling with fury as the icy breath of the Great Spirit descended on the plains.

Hours later as he came to, bits of memories flashed in his thinking. Swirling wet snow, the odor of wet fur and bright flashes of light were all that he could remember. His temples pulsed with throbbing pain and his body was cold and numb. Beside him, Joe stood, the winter storm whipping around him, head down, he patiently waited for Carrigan to take him home where a warm barn and bins of oats waited. Later Carrigan remembered trying several times to pull himself onto the old rope horse before finally climbing a rock and then crawling aboard Joe's patient, thick withers. He buried his face into the deep mane and he felt the rhythmic working of the horse's strong shoulders beneath him as the wind screamed in hatred behind them. By midnight, Joe stood at the barn door nipping at Carrigan's pant leg. Conscious again Carrigan slid from Joe, collapsing to the ground. Jeremy and Two Hills found him, shortly thereafter, his hand on the latch of the barn door, and Joe nuzzling him and pawing the growing snowdrifts. By late morning he felt marginally better, though his shoulder was stiff and inner bleeding swelled and darkened the skin around the bruise. Two Hills told him that Jeremy took the six-wheel drive Tyrol to look for the young horse out in the pasture and at least retrieve the saddle if the pony couldn't be led home. Jeremy woke Carrigan again late in the afternoon and with his quiet manner explained how he found the colt, dead at the bottom of the trail, whether from the shock brought on by injury or from the freezing cold, he didn't know. The look on his face spoke volumes and Carrigan knew that it could have been his stiff and frozen body Jeremy retrieved--if Joe hadn't been in the right place at the right time.

Several weeks were required before Carrigan could stand without feeling nauseous and his shoulder was still sore and bruised. Outside, the snow continued piling in huge drifts between the barn and house. At night wild shrieks emanated from the eaves of the house that bore the full brunt of the attacking storm.

People weren't meant to live on the plains in the winter, Carrigan thought. For a solid month, the storm swept all things from the open plains. Antelope across the prairie died in piles, frozen together as they made their last stands. Other animals that found shelter still died from lack of food. For years the hardy souls that made these wind-swept plains their homes compared this storm with those of long ago. Carrigan, Jeremy, and Two Hills spent Christmas together, fashioning treats and presents from items they found in the well-stocked larder. Carrigan relayed a message to his father by two-way radio, wishing him Merry Christmas, knowing his father was home alone. On Christmas Eve, the trio of Carrigan, Jeremy and Two Hills exchanged their meager presents and toasted with hot chocolate before the large, snapping and crackling fire as it burned the pitch logs. Sipping the rich cocoa before the fire, Two Hills began to talk, her voice raising and lowering in a singsong chant:

> *My mother told a story that many years ago her people came to these plains to hunt the buffalo. By the long days of summer their travois were always full of meat and they would return to the land of the tall rock tower and dark trees. One year the buffalo were scarce and the warriors ranged from the 'Water that Boils' to the great river, north running in flow, but no buffalo could be found. Day after day they hunted, surviving only on the prairie dogs dug from their earthen burrows. The hunters gained only enough strength to hunt another day. Knowing the tribe would starve without meat, the warriors stayed longer than they should have and across the plains came deep snows trapping them on this side of their sacred mountains. One brave, being stronger than the others, went out day after day searching for food and at last his patience was rewarded. He found an old buffalo trapped in the snow. Killing the buffalo, he drew his knife to spill the warm blood. From the snowstorm a great white bear arose and challenged him for the meat. Facing each other across the warm kill, neither backed down until finally they both*

ignored the other and began to take nourishment from the fresh meat, sharing it side by side. After feeding, the great bear disappeared back into the swirling snow and the warrior returned to his hunters brining with him the life-giving sustenance. The next day a warm Chinook wind drove the snows from the prairie and the warriors found the herd of buffalo for which they long searched. Killing only enough to fill their need, the hunting party returned to their black-forested hills. This warrior, the ones the Whites call Crazy Horse, never hunted his brother bear again, and called upon this spirit brother many times before going into battle. Perhaps it was the great white bear that you met, Mr. Carrigan, out in the storm.

With that, Two Hills finished her chocolate and retired for the evening, leaving Carrigan and Jeremy to ponder her story. That night Carrigan dreamed of buffalo covering the snowy plains from horizon to horizon, their great, shaggy humps and thick hair protecting them from the icy storms.

That warm spring, winds did come to the Laramie Plains and the snowdrifts fled, leaving the hills green and lush. With the knowledge gained from the previous year, Carrigan returned to the sale barn to purchase cattle for the ranch's pastures. Events far from the hills of Wyoming drove the eastern markets downward in an ever-increasing spiral throughout the long, dry summer, depressing all sections of the economy. The cattle market followed the trend and that fall Trabing Tires barely recouped the purchase price on the cattle. Interest and operating expenses had to be drawn from other divisions of the corporation to meet the ranch expenses. In October, Ashton made the trip to ranch headquarters displaying gloom in every mannerism as he exited the car and found Carrigan splitting wood near the house.

"The board has decided that they won't keep anyone on the ranch during the winter this year. November 30th will be your last day of the season. The board still has confidence in you and wishes to employ your services next spring, but with declining profits, the concerns of the shareholders must be addressed," said Ashton, looking at everything around him except Carrigan.

"What about Two Hills and Jeremy?" asked Carrigan incredulously.

"They have been good employees and have worked damn hard the last two years. Are you just letting them go, no severance, just thanks and good-bye? And what about you, did they see fit to include a bonus for you, or are you down the road also? Trabing made enough money last year to make ten payments on this ranch."

"Maybe a small one," Ashton stammered. "They understand how hard I have worked to hold this concern together."

"Yeah," Carrigan replied, "it was damn hard work last winter, snug in your warm little office watching the secretaries hustle ass to meet your demands; you wouldn't have lasted a week out here. Tell Trabing they need to find a new 'boy' to run this place, next spring, and if Jeremy and Two Hills don't have at least two months severance pay in the next paycheck, every newspaper in Wyoming will get an exclusive from me about what good neighbors large corporations are. Now why don't you jump in your little foreign car and find the way back to Denver before something big and mean bites you out here? We'll be gone by the end of week."

"But, all the board members are coming out next week to go hunting. Who's going to take them out and show them where to go? Who will cook for them and do their laundry?" Ashton countered, not really expecting the conversation to take this turn.

"Well, Mr. Ashton, it's about time you learned what goes on around here. See ya down the trail."

"What trail?" Ashton replied, the western terminology totally slipping over his head.

Carrigan never answered, he just turned on his heel and walked away to find Two Hills and Jeremy. Where he was going from here he didn't know, and didn't really care, as long as it was a long ways, and in a hurry.

"And that is why I won't use Trabing Tires," said Carrigan, "and that is how I occupied several years of my life. Now the man you looking at has no mysteries. Do you like me better now?"

"Corporations aren't known for their human concerns," Nancy returned, ignoring his question. "It's not personal, Carrigan; it's just business? What happened to Jeremy and Two Hills?"

"Well," Carrigan mused, "they probably are doing better now than they were on the ranch. I got a Christmas card from Two Hills several years ago. She's working in a casino over on the Pine Ridge, running the whole kitchen operations for them. She sent me a clipping from an Elko newspaper talking about Jeremy. He's big into cowboy poetry now, and singing western songs. He's published several books and has recorded three albums. Duded up in a fancy hat, silver conchos and holding a guitar-

-I barely recognized him. I guess he found a commercial venue for his way of life. He always was a good kid."

"And your head, does it still bother you?" Nancy asked.

Releasing his arm that she had been holding during his story of the plains, she stroked a comma of hair back from his forehead, revealing the puckered flesh on the edge of his temple caused by his collision from a rock.

"No," he said vacantly, thinking back to his days in law enforcement, "my head was meant to take a lot of abuse. Other than some nightmares from time to time, I guess everything healed all right."

Nancy noticed that running from his forehead back along the part of his hair, it was a shade lighter than its normal blonde, not really like the other gray she found hiding there, just lighter as if light reflected from it differently.

Checking the sun slipping lower in the afternoon sky above the canyon walls, Carrigan realized that laying here wasn't doing the work waiting for him back on his section. He helped Nancy re-pack the cooler and they laughed together as the magpies were finally rewarded for their patience.

Turning to him, Nancy met his gaze, "This was fun," she said, "next week, same time, same place?"

"I'll go you one better," he answered. "Meet me by the river bridge, say seven in the morning and ride up with me to my homestead. See how common people build cabins; maybe I'll even put you to work."

"Stephen will be with me; is it Ok if he comes too?"

"Sure, does he know how to swing a hammer?"

"Well, no, he's only seven, but that's what you're for, isn't it? You're the teacher."

"We'll find out," he laughed. "Till next week, then, and thanks for lunch; it was great."

Carrigan didn't fish the dark holes on his return back up the river. His mind was reviewing what occurred during his lunch date with Nancy. Did anything happen, or was it just a chance for two friends to catch up on past times? Somehow when she touched him, it didn't feel like just friends. If felt good, comfortable, like an old coat that was broken in just right, as if a piece in a puzzle was just found and fitted into place.

Gertrude and Carrigan negotiated the mini-traffic jam near school. Mondays saw students hurrying to complete projects and assignments that should have been done the previous Friday. Most cars gave him a wide berth as he rolled Gertrude into her usual stall. Remembering the fossilized rock in the back of his pickup, he retrieved it and walked briskly to Mr. James' classroom, hoping for enlightenment. James, as always, was in place early, tinkering among the dead animals and lab projects. The aroma was slightly better than Carrigan's last visit, probably owing to the open door and the fresh air trying to gain admittance to the stuffy classroom.

"Mr. James, how was your weekend?" hollered Carrigan across the classroom.

"Great!" James replied, "My yard is raked, the flowerbed is turned over, and Momma said I have the next few days all to myself. Life is good."

"Well, mine was good also, really good. This warm weather makes my whole attitude a little more positive. Say, I stumbled across this rock or fossil or whatever the hell it is this weekend and brought it in to you. Hopefully you can tell me what I found. The damn thing was right where I was trying to dig a hole. Whatever it is, it's harder than hell. Would you mind checking it out for me?"

"Might be a day or two; I'm trying to get some finals written, and I have to go traipsing off to some reading teacher's classroom to listen to boring science projects, but throw it there on the table, I'll get to it."

"Thanks," Carrigan answered, "you know how I am, something gets me curious and I just have to find out more about it. I'll check with you in a couple of days, see ya' second period." Carrigan smiled to himself; James, preoccupied with whatever he was working on, had tuned him out again and was rummaging through the bottom drawers of a cabinet talking to himself. Papers and equipment were flying out behind him like a badger digging a hole. Carrigan made it to class and settled into his desk searching through the mounds of papers there, in a vain attempt to find his grade book.

Probably hiding from me on purpose, he thought.

Bells signaled the start of the day, and he gave up. He could write the notes from the projects on a piece of paper and then transfer them later when the item showed up. As expected, the chorus of excuses started immediately. He mentally ticked them off as the kids used the same ones he was familiar with from the last nine years:

'My mom lost my disk.'—'The computers in the library don't work.'—'My printer ran out of ink.'—'I already gave it to you.'—'Johnny isn't here today and he has all the work.'—'I didn't know it was due today.'—'It's not fair, the other classes don't have to do a project.'

The irresistible force finally hit the immovable object. Carrigan just smiled and with each excuse handed the complainer a grade slip with a neatly printed *F* on the page.

"Let me know when you're ready and I'll change your grade," was the only acknowledgement he gave them. "Work on it this period if you need some more time."

Actually, two groups were ready to go and after the equipment hassle of setting up projectors and white boards was overcome, the kids gave great presentations, just like he knew they could. The first group spoke about The Laramie Range that originated in the Laramide orogeny. This was the beginning of the Rocky Mountains, which were named for Jacque La Ramie a trapper who frequented this area in the early 1800s. The continental crust was uplifted to form the Rocky Mountain chain. The kids explained Laramie Peak was the highest point at 10,274 feet and could be seen for over 100 miles as travelers arrived from the east. The Laramie range is composed of northern and southern halves.

Carrigan even learned facts that he wasn't aware of, such as the northern half was much older and took in the area between Casper and Wheatland. These rocks were made from Precambrian granites. The southern half was called the Sherman granite, which contains a specialized igneous rock called anorthoside made from the mineral plagioclase feldspar. These mountains were raised up and shoved over the plains during the Laramide orogeny. The students showed pictures of both halves and slides of the minerals found in the chain. Carrigan was impressed! They actually learned some information.

The second presentation was equally interesting, and dealt with the Snowy Range and the Saratoga Valley. These students did a nice job talking about Cretaceous marine shales in the area and how they were overlaid with gravels from the Pleistocene time. The very top of the mountains, they explained, contained Precambrian quartzites that reflected sunlight making it look like snow. Hence the name "Snowy Range". A dry basin led up to this area with no water running through it and was probably caused by wind erosion during the glacial ages. A lot of evidence of glacial moraines near Centennial was evident in their slides. They spoke about Glacial cirques and even showed some slides to prove they weren't just using fancy terms. One student brought in samples of feldspar and quartz from the area and they had pictures of some fossilized algae, which were some of the earliest forms of life on the planet. The team explained how the Saratoga Valley lay between the Medicine Bow Range and the Sierra Madre Mountains. The mountains on this high pass were turned so they stood upright on their ends overtop much older rocks. They finished with photos of the hot springs in Saratoga and talked about how the early Indians in the area called the thermal activity 'the water that boils'.

Carrigan finished the day and was pleased. Being immune to excuses, he finally forced all of the students either to give their presentations, or at least realize escape was impossible. They finally settled down to work on completing the assignment. Tuesday was equally productive till third period. No one was ready and he loudly voiced his displeasure to each and every one. Neither Tommy nor Becky was in class, and he began to feel their paring wasn't such a good one although he knew Tommy had completed some of the work. Where Becky was he didn't know, she rarely missed class, one of her saving graces.

By Wednesday he was positively pleased with himself and was beginning to worry that he might have to think of other projects for the students that were finished. Pondering this, he realized the error in his ways, and showed up at school with chessboards, jigsaw puzzles and other fun games for the students to occupy their last class periods. If any wandering principals passed his classroom, they would think nothing was being accomplished, but the kids worked hard to earn this privilege. Taking state mandated final exams and cleaning out lockers would occupy next week as the kids prepared for their coming summer vacation.

Thursday during lunch Mr. James caught up with Carrigan as he walked to the commons area to spy on who was cooking today. "Well," Mr. James said, "what you brought me was really quite interesting. I thought maybe what you found were the fossils of several different animals that died together. When I first looked at the bones they reminded me of Ol' Urssus Arctos because of their size, but the shape wasn't quite right. I sent them off to the university and they called back all excited, wanting to know where the bones came from. They think what you found was Mr. Hemicyoninae, quite a rare fellow indeed."

"Well, that's just fine," said Carrigan. "Now treat me like I'm five. What is the difference between Ursula Arctic, Ursula Andrews, and Hemi-whatever?"

"Urssus Arctos, not Andrews; you know of the Family Ursidae, bears Carrigan, big brown bears. You know, the kind that bite, stand nine feet tall and weigh a ton?"

"Great," said Carrigan, "now I'm digging up some sort of bear graveyard. But how in the heck did a brown bear turn into a fossil? They haven't been around that long, evolutionarily speaking."

"That's just the point; my, I do need to treat you like your five. Hemicyoninae with the generas Hemicyon and Plithocyon were the brown bear's great, great- granddaddies. In school we used to call them dog bears, other people called them cave bears. The term cave bear really refers to Ursus spelaes of the late Pleistocene, which is the European cousin.

I'm guessing what you found was a Hemicyon ursinus. He was truly a big fellow, much larger than the Alaskan Kodiaks. He had short massive limbs, five toes, huge canine teeth and molars the size of dinner plates. He used to run around in the late Miocene and Pliocene epochs eating anything he could catch. His head was shaped kind of like a dog and partly like a bear, hence the term dogbear. And by the way, do you want me to tell them where you found this item? What you found was the lower part of a very large jaw; the rest of the skeleton is probably buried right in the same spot.

"Hell no," said Carrigan, "I don't want a bunch of people poking around my place. Is it worth anything?"

"Well, they found a dinosaur skeleton up north a few years back and it just brought a million dollars at Christie's Auction, but people aren't as crazy about bears."

"For now just tell them somebody dropped it off to you and you don't know where it came from. I'll think about it. And by the way, thanks for the info; I think I'll go dig up some information on bears."

Carrigan couldn't help but connect the large footprint he found in Wolf Draw with the fossil from his cabin's corner post. He shook his head laughing to himself. Just like Lock Ness. Before long everyone would be invading my river country looking for some prehistoric cave bear. That's it, he thought, that is one bear cemetery that was just going to stay buried. If he had to dig any more holes, he would change the location of the cabin. It usually didn't pay to go digging up things that had been buried long ago.

After lunch, Carrigan returned to his classroom to get ready for the next round of presentations. This was the tough class. He wondered if Becky and Tommy would have their project ready. The volcano was probably ready to blow but the written work was still at home--or the dog may have eaten it.

While he was waiting for class to start he pulled up some information on bears off the Internet. Information concerning the names Mr. James was talking about was scarce and couched in such technical jargon that it was hard to understand. He found the stories on grizzly bears easier to understand. These bears could weigh 2000 pounds! They were extremely strong with tremendous endurance. Capable of killing large animals with one blow of the forepaws, or dragging large elk up steep hills, they could be fierce adversaries. Their sense of smell was excellent although they possessed poor eyesight. In coloration many ranged from whitish blonde to dark brown, and at onetime were spread through the mountainous areas of much of the western United States. Bears had a gestation period of between six and nine months and could live up to fifty years. They sometimes claimed territory as large as 2500 square miles and partially hibernated during the winter months. Most big bears liked water and were adept at catching fish, although they weren't averse to eating most anything they could find. He did find some reference about bears being territorial. Over long periods of time, offspring from the same family would stay in the same locality, generation after generation.

The class bell rang and Carrigan was forced to stop his research, attending to the chorus of whines, complaints, and excuses entering through his door. Becky was in class today but Tommy was still absent.

"I talked to Tommy on Sunday," Becky offered. "He promised that his end would be ready the very first part of next week Mr. C. Mommy helped me do some slides and we can watch those today. Dawn said she would help me with the projector. Daddy wouldn't let me come to school last time, he was mad at me."

"Well, a little bit is better than nothing. All right Becky, show me what you have, and we'll do the rest next Monday if Tommy is ready."

"Goody, goody," was her reply and the class snickered to one another before his menacing glare silenced them.

Fat Dawn was helpful and after moving her considerable bulk from her desk, she helped Becky set up the PowerPoint slides and whispered words when Becky couldn't read some of the long names in the presentation. Mrs. Lansing, indeed, did a fairly good job for Becky as the slides marched across the whiteboard outlining some interesting features of Yellowstone Park and Jackson Hole. Becky showed the Grand Tetons and explained the name was really les Trios Tetons or the Tree Grand Teats. This was the title given to these massive peaks by the French fur trappers.

Here the classroom couldn't contain itself any longer and elbowed each other, the girls giggling about the types of bras that could hold a third breast, and the boys loudly proclaimed they wished their girlfriends had three, giving them one more to play with. Becky didn't really understand what they were talking about but smiled and laughed along with them. Carrigan finally got the kids to pay attention again and told Becky to keep going.

She finished up with explaining the Indians called the mountains, Tee-win-ot. She did know they were a very young range, but anything beyond the number of her fingers and toes was higher math to Becky. The rest of her slides talked about when the Tetons were raised by seismic activity, Jackson Hole dropped, giving it the curious name. Yellowstone received its name from some of the yellow rocks and has areas of boiling mud pots, geysers, and huge waterfalls. Heat was supplied from deep in the earth, Becky proudly read. Due to lots of snow pack from the winter, and cracks in the earth which lets the water sink in, the water then erupts, blowing back up the tunnel. There were lots of volcanoes there she said, and a real cool place called "Old Faithful, which was named after her favorite Christmas Carol."

"Well maybe," Carrigan carefully dodged this statement. "I can see your Mom did a nice job, Becky. What did you learn from this presentation?"

Becky thought for a while before answering, and then smiling she said, "There's lots of bears up there, Mr. C."

When the boys made it back to Billy's house early in the morning after their Friday night visit to Becky's house, they managed to maneuver the big truck back into the proximity of its original parking place. Billy creased a water meter with the fender, but both the meter and the fender were used to this type of abrupt meeting and neither were much the worse for wear. Tommy poured the paint thinner down the sink in case Billy was prone to early morning sniffs, and the boys crashed in Billy's room. Tommy set Billy in the corner atop a pile of laundry, and he commandeered the wrinkled blankets he found on the floor. The old, floor furnace vented into this room through the cracked boards of the hardwood flooring. With his blankets atop the grating, he warmed his chilled frame. Tommy slept dreamless that night, satisfied with his raids through the streets of Rockville.

Tomorrow he said to himself, tomorrow things would start to come together.

Billy's old man made it home a short while later, and collapsed on the couch in the front room. He had stayed to sample the wares of his employer after closing and it was truly providence he didn't drive the old pickup to work that night or the water meter might have suffered far worse damage.

By noon Saturday, Tommy was awake, and he stole in the kitchen hoping to find food. Little was available there but he did salvage a stale loaf of bread and slipped back past Billy's parent, wolfing down the slices when he reached the safety of the bedroom. A few pieces of the bread were in the beginning stages of becoming an antibiotic but Tommy didn't mind. He needed something to settle his stomach from the affects of the *blues*, which still gave him a slightly jangling feeling, as the lingering effects of the drugs worked its way through his system. Finishing the bread, he slipped into the bathroom, drinking huge handfuls of water from the sink, wrinkling his noise at the warm chlorine taste. Having fed and watered, he began to feel better and was ready to rouse Billy as he slept in the corner. During the night Billy pulled the laundry from beneath him as covers to ward off the chill and the soiled underwear still hid his sleeping form.

"Come on, Huff Head," Tommy said as he shook Billy, trying to avoid touching the underwear. "We need to get busy before your old man wakes up. Thanks for letting me borrow some his tools; you're alright, Billy. I'll let you hang out with me more often."

Tommy finally succeeded in getting Billy awake and by pushing and steering him at the same time, got him out the back door of the house, leaving a trail of dirtied shorts behind him. The fresh air had therapeutic effects and Billy watched as Tommy rummaged through the garage, finally deciding on a hacksaw and a pry bar for his armaments of the day. Tommy patted his friend on the shoulder and with the tools headed for home.

Billy stood in the garage for a while till his bare feet got cold and then realizing he was hungry headed back for the house. He remembered there was still some bread there, right beside the mineral spirits. Together he could fill the needs crawling in his belly.

Tommy found his house much as he left it and after rummaging beneath his bed, he came up with an old school duffel bag he had stolen several years before. Pawing through the drawers in his kitchen, he located several screwdrivers and a broken hammer. Together with the items he liberated from Billy, he folded several towels around the tools and thrust them into the bag. Throwing his toolkit by the front door, he left the house again headed for the public library.

Free access online through the library's computers waited there, and if he timed it right, there was usually a bake sale going on in the lobby where he could snitch some lunch. The bread hadn't been quite enough and he was still hungry. By eight that night the library closed and the librarian looked disapprovingly at him over her glasses when he left the cubicle, piles of cookie crumbs covering the carpet beneath his chair. A half eaten mincemeat pie still sat by the mouse; Tommy didn't care a lot for mincemeat.

He made his way back home from the library to retrieve his duffel bag but on the way rummaged through the dumpster behind the little Mexican food restaurant downtown. This was really his weekend, he thought. Sitting right on top was a whole plastic container of green chili. He even managed to find some tortillas clear in the bottom of the dumpster but he wasn't able to catch the small kitten that found this bounty first. Already experienced, the kitten instinctively knew that safety lay far away from this alley, and supper could be found elsewhere in the town.

By ten, Tommy managed to finally hit the street light near the construction site with a large enough rock to shatter the bulb. The vapor hissed angrily as it escaped from the beam. Tommy rolled back under the cement mixer in case the sound of the breaking glass brought any attention. After an hour no one drove by, and he carried his bag to the door of the construction trailer. He tried the hacksaw on the hardened lock but it was too close to the frame of the door and his arm soon grew tired. His next assault wedged the screwdriver behind the hasp of the lock and after covering this with the towel he pounded it deep into the wood frame with the hammer, periodically stopping to work the opening bigger before resuming effort again. In a short while the torn wood was fitted with the pry bar, and on his second pull the metal door swung open. Putting the tools back into his bag he closed the door, tying it shut with a small string and retreated to the safety of the cement mixer to watch his surroundings again. He had all night, and he wanted to be sure no one came to investigate the muffled pounding.

Several cars drove by, their headlights flashing across the side of the metal trailer but none of them stopped, and Tommy recognized them as kids from school prowling through the rich section of town. This street dead-ended against the golf course and no one would drive in here late on a Saturday night. The action was downtown. Tommy pulled out the green chili and the grease covered tortillas, wiping his face with the towel when he finished his meal. Although cold and coagulated now, the chili was spicy hot and he wished he had a beer to wash it down.

Inside the trailer it was dark and dusty. It seemed completely full and boxes were piled high, each with a bill of lading attached to the cardboard cover. It was too dark to make out the labels and he thought about lighting a match, but remembered the sign on the door and quickly put that thought aside. Clear at the end of the trail stood a large metal filing cabinet labeled Welding Gases, in large red letters. This, too, was locked, but the hacksaw worked much better here and the small lock finally yielded to the dull blade. Inside setting neatly on rows of shelves were five yellow metal canisters, five red ones, and three larger, green bottles stacked on the bottom row. The green bottles were too heavy to carry so Tommy took a yellow bottle, surprised by its weight, and packed it back out the door of the trailer. Outside he tied the door shut again and after placing the bottle into his bag, he started his way home. The bag was now very full and heavy. Tommy finally resorted to dragging it, opting for all the dark alleys on the way to his destination.

Tommy found himself unable to sleep in Sunday morning. Several times he got out of bed to check the contents of the duffel bag he stashed there last night. The round yellow bottle, about a foot tall, felt cold to his touch and he liked the heavy, substantial feel of the metal when he held it. Finally tired of getting out of bed, he lugged the bottle with him under the covers, shivering as he held it against his chest, the warning label turned so it pressed tightly against his heart.

Finally forcing himself out of bed, he changed clothes and washed. He took pride in never going to church, dirty and disheveled. Late Mass was always at eleven and afterwards the ladies of the guild served refreshments. The first several times he attended he stole food from the white tables filling his pockets full, until he realized that all he needed to do was sit for an hour and the greeters pleaded with him to come over to the Parrish Hall to partake of the food. The sermon that day dealt with good versus evil, and the young priest talked about the necessity of evil in the world as a motivator for people to turn to good works. Tommy didn't understand a lot of it, but the weird Latin talk was pretty cool and he especially liked the last part of the sermon when the priest said that fire was cleansing and good, preparing the way for the soul. He left the pew quickly during the last song, wanting to be first in line for the food.

After church he used the phone near the door of the Parrish Hall to call Becky. He explained carefully to her what she needed to get from her dad's drug store and made sure she wrote down his words. He finished talking and then had her read back to him the instructions he had given her.

"Five pounds of Lawn Fertilizer, a can of deck wash, (the kind in the red can with the silver lid), one plastic jug of Dandelion Dead, one can of carburetor cleaner (make sure that I get the kind with the name Karb-Klean), a big thermometer and one can of liquid stove fuel," Becky read back.

"And what do you tell the clerk when he asks you any questions?" queried Tommy patiently.

"I tell him that Daddy wants it at home and that I'm am supposed to get it and bring it to him."

"And why can't you tell anybody about this?" asked Tommy.

"Because we don't want Mommy and Daddy to know until after we get our prize for the best presentation in school," said Becky.

"One last thing, Becky, tell Mr. C. that I might not be there this week. I'll get the stuff from you Monday night after school and finish building our volcano. And Becky," Tommy said, making his voice very firm, "remember--don't tell anyone what we need this for; no one, do you understand? Not your friends, not your parents, not Mr. C., nobody." Waiting until she answered in the affirmative, he continued, "If you tell anyone then I won't finish building the volcano and you won't win. Mommy and Daddy wouldn't like that, would they, Becky?"

"I promise I won't tell anybody."

CHAPTER 10
The Danger Within

North of the Blue Mountain, Prairie Dog and his brother Flat Turtle followed the trail of Lame Wolf away from the meadow. Lame Wolf almost led them to their doom in the green field above the rough ridges, but Prairie Dog was cautious, and because of this he was alive. He thought briefly of charging out to count coup on the trader, and then the Vision Woman and her pup came racing toward him. How did she know he and Flat Turtle would be there, licking their lips as the trader drew nearer? Completely unnerved, he fled. Flat Turtle, being the younger brother, did not question his judgment but silently withdrew also. Another day and stronger medicine would be needed. From the trail of Lame Wolf, they knew where once there were nine, eight warriors and their leader Lame Wolf, now there were only three. Five of their band died upon the green field trying to take the life of the white trapper, a trader, an old man and his whelps. One died when he laughed at Lame Wolf. None of them predicted the strong magic of the Vision Woman. They would not make that mistake again.

Down the long pass north of the Blue Mountain, Prairie Dog found Lame Wolf's horse, and near the bottom was Lame Wolf, bathing his face in the cold waters of a stream. Lame Wolf's face was reddened and splotchy from the powder grains that burned his eyes when Dance Walker fired too soon at the big trapper. Prairie Dog told Lame Wolf what he saw of the battle before fleeing from the meadow. All three of the warriors that charged the old man were dead, and only La Ramie returned from the timber. Lame Wolf knew this meant his end of the trap failed also. Slowly the Blackfoot leader's vision returned, and with it the hatred he harbored returned also, deeper, and more malignant. Prairie Dog and Flat Turtle knew better than to say more and quietly sat their mounts while Lame Wolf ranted and raved, tearing willows from the creek and slashing the water and earth around him, until at last he was quiet. Looking at each other, Prairie Dog and his brother did not know which made them more nervous, Lame Wolf's fits of anger or his quiet. Both could be deadly.

Unquestioning, the pair followed Lame Wolf as he led them down the long valley, headed for the rolling plains to the west. The warriors pushed their mounts hard, building distance behind them away from the trapper and the magic woman. All had hoped to be able to return to their home, north of the land of dark trees, the lowland river country, but embarrassment now would not let them. Three could not return when almost two hands of warriors left, hoping to steal horses and garner scalps. So far they killed only one poor trapper and traded his goods for firewater, which was too soon gone. The Crowe whore was pleasurable, but Lame Wolf took that from them also. He promised them the Vision Woman and all the goods of the trapper. Now only three of them were left, and they had no women, supplies, or scalps. At least they had their lives, and if they kept quiet, these they might keep.

Two days they rode, crossing the river of the rendezvous again on the high flats. The urgency for distance was now gone. They could see the signs of approach from long distances, and Lame Wolf allowed them to rest, even sharing the best pieces of meat from the antelope he killed. That night they sat around a small fire and Lame Wolf spoke his thoughts.

"It is my fault we did not gain our share of the bounty," Lame Wolf told them. "I should never have brought Dance Walker with us. La Ramie would have ridden to his death in our trap. Perhaps it was the magic of the vision woman; perhaps La Ramie has luck on his side. We can never return until we have counted coup on his body and regained our honor. But the time is not yet, not until our magic is stronger, and we have purified ourselves, purging the shame from our souls. Far to the west lies the land of the snowy mountains. Just as this river rises to meet the great fields of snow, it turns aside in honor of the mountain's power and runs then south through a high pass. Here at the headwaters lives a small band of Arapaho, our brothers in hate for the Shoshone. In this sacred place a great Shaman stays, with his brother, the man-woman Berdache. Red Willow is the Shaman's name, and he is of the Nawuenea tribe. This is the place we will go to ask for his help and guidance. He will show us the way, testing us. If we are brave, he will allow the Sun God to replenish our souls, filling us with magic more powerful than the Vision Woman. Rest well tonight for tomorrow our test will begin."

The three rode on early the next morning before the sun broke through the mountains behind them. Heading west, they traveled to the mountains of snow, following the course of the Arapohay across the broad flats. They traveled through the land of the round rocks where legends told of great sheets of ice that once covered the earth. Here they carefully let their horses pick and choose a path among the sharp stones, but never did the party stray far from the river. Once, they saw the tracks from many unshod ponies, probably a party of Shoshone traveling to the "water that boils" over the snowy mountains, but the sign was old. With ten more warriors, they might have followed the trail hoping for fresh scalps and horses, but with only three, they stayed close to the protection of the thick brush on the river, avoiding detection. Gently the river turned them away from the rising heights of the west, heading southward although constantly climbing in elevation. By the fourth night, they rested just before the Arapohay fell from a massed jumble of boulders and camped between the small copse of aspens, the smoke from their fire hidden among the budding trees.

Here Lame Wolf warned them that the Shaman knew all that climbed this way. Any who showed weakness were weeded away, allowing only the strong to continue following the course of the river. Prairie Dog and Flat Turtle were fearful to go on, but they were more afraid of Lame Wolf if they didn't. The days of hard travel, gaunted their bellies as the dried antelope fed only their muscles and not their hunger. The horses even began to show signs of weariness and were quiet on their pickets at night, eating sparingly from the patches of green feed beginning to awake to the summer. The next morning they continued upward entering heavy forests of dark trees reaching high into the sky competing with their brothers of the forest. The timbered floor was littered with deadfall, and the obstacles slowed their climb. By nightfall they reached a park, and in the evening twilight, they heard elk bugling across the glade. The river slackened its mad race down to the valley below and allowed beavers to damn its flow, making a series of small ponds to mark the water's path. They built no fire that night but shivered quietly in their robes. Total darkness crept into their camp, and they lay, eyes open but unseeing, cowed by the gloomy silence around them. With the first hint of morning light, they again were riding, skirting the open glades where the river ran, preferring the company of the dark timber, until they could join the water again protected by the forest. Snow banks still lay heavy in the timber at these high elevations, but elk trails were broken through the drifts, and their horse's tracks mingled with the sign disguising their trail. By evening the river split, the flow much smaller now, awaiting the melting snow to swell its power. Lame Wolf continued on taking the left fork until it appeared to stop against a high cliff. Turning left again, the party rode next to the granite wall beside them and then turned down a steep muddy trail spiraling lower through the trees. Reaching the bottom, Lame Wolf stopped, warning the others to make no movement. Long minutes passed before a tall warrior stepped from the shadows into the trail. Lame Wolf raised his hand and signed the word for friend.

"We come seeking Red Willow. Tell him Lame Wolf asks for his audience and comes in peace, as all brothers who were initiated into the "Hair Shirts" should when seeking spiritual growth."

The tall warrior grunted, and then turned walking on down the trail. Behind them Prairie Dog and Flat Turtle felt the presence of others in the trees around them. Together they rode into a glade where teepees sat next to the edge of a small lake. The timber was gone now preferring to cling to the high rocks that surrounded the camp. Riding into the village, Lame Wolf dismounted and indicated to the two behind him to follow, before handing the lead of his horse's lip hackamore to a young boy. The tall warrior threw back the door of a lodge, signing that they were to enter. As the Blackfeet stooped through the opening, they saw two men sitting before the circle fire. Shadows bounced and swirled against the hide wall reflecting back on the pair that sat before them. Both were old, one with long braids of white hair and the other with braids of blue.

"Hello my old friend, Red Willow," said Lame Wolf to the white hair, "and hello Berdache, your beauty grows with the years," he finished. Blue Braids raised his wrinkled hand to cover his toothless mouth.

"Have you come to flirt, or do you wish to eat and rest first before you seek my favor?"

The next week the Blackfeet rested in the camp of Red Willow allowing their bodies to regain fat lost on their long trip. Their horses, mixing with the remuda of the Arapaho, also strengthened and regained their spirit, fighting for position in the herd. Lame Wolf explained to his fellow travelers that many summers ago, in the lowland river country the peoples of the Teton Dakotas held the Sun Dance during the summer. All tribes from the Teton came together, including their allies such as the Arapaho. The festival lasted for many days, and the best warriors from each tribe which included the Burnt Thigh, Hunkapa, Miniconjou, Ogalala, Oohenonpa, Sans Arc, and Sihapsa or Blackfoot, displayed feats of bravery and skills vying for attention from the young squaws and recognition from the elders. The rituals renewed the older brave's strength and initiated young men into the secret order of the Dog Warriors.

When Lame Wolf was young, Red Willow and Berdache always traveled to the north sharing their wisdom with the major chiefs of the

Teton people. All leaders respected Red Willow who was considered the most powerful Shaman of the tribes. Red Willow started Lame Wolf, or Swift Deer as he was called by his child name, on his first Vision Quest, mixing special plants with the blood of a wolf to help him see the path of his future. For three days and nights Lame Wolf sat staring at the hot sun until his spirit guide came to him and told him that to learn bravery and wisdom he must cut the smallest toe from his foot and carry it always with him. Like the lone wolf caught in a trap will chew through his limb rather than remain trapped, Lame Wolf was to imitate this deadly predator. All Sihapsa people knew that once trapped, no wolf would ever be caught again, as they became too fierce and cautious. Returning from his quest Lame Wolf spoke of his dream to Red Willow who directed Berdache to amputate the little toe from Lame Wolf. After this, Lame Wolf received his Dog Name and entered the warrior society. To this day the shriveled toe resided in the medicine bag around Lame Wolf's neck. On the last year that all tribes attended the Sun Festival, Lame Wolf's unrelenting fierceness earned him the place as a hair shirt among the Sihapsa people. This honor elevated the warrior to a Wakic'u who only took orders from their leader the Akicita or head shirt wearer. The Akicita was equivalent to a Chief of which there were usually up to seven in each tribe of the Teton people. The Akicita, being younger, still drew the blood of his enemies. Extremely secretive, this order and its members, the Wakic'u were feared and respected within their tribe.

The Teton peoples began to separate in the following years and with their nomadic nature drifted far apart only seldom coming together again for the sun dance. Lame Wolf had made the trip only once before, as he grew older, to Red Willow's home across the Rawah Mountains entering this hidden valley to visit with his mentors. Red Willow again was his guide, and Lame Wolf renewed his vows strengthening his soul before returning on the long ride home far to the north. Berdache supplied him with a magic elixir that would elevate his prestige among the Sihapsa Chiefs so that he might be appointed Akicita of the hair shirts. The trip was successful, and Lame Wolf was raised to this honor. Lame Wolf knew that the failure of his last raid would result in his removal from this place of honor within his tribe. Red Willow and Berdache must help him one more time.

As the days of spring lengthened into summer, Lame Wolf, Prairie Dog, and Flat Turtle lived with the tribe waiting for the longest day of summer when Red Willow would conduct the rights empowering them with the magic needed to overcome La Ramie and the trader. Life was easy among these high mountains in the summer. The camp of no more than fifty Arapaho found game plentiful and the Blackfeet mixed with Arapaho, hunting the elk in the timber and glades surrounding the village. At night they ate well using buffalo horn spoons to scoop huge platefuls of stew into the clay bowls supplied by Arapaho squaws. The young women cooked the elk meat in skin pits buried in the ground bringing the stew to boil by adding hot stones from the campfire. Prairie Dog and Flat Turtle found the women to be erotically beautiful with their tattooed lips and pierced ears strung with horsehair and beads. Upon occasion they lay with their feminine hosts in the soft grass around the lake, straining deep into the willing loins beneath them. The Arapaho believed that women should practice the skills needed to please their husbands prior to marriage. Prairie Dog and Flat Turtle quickly came to believe in this custom also.

Lame Wolf visited often with Berdache and Red Willow, smoking from the same sacred pipe and telling stories of creation and history. Berdache, a practitioner of the black arts, carefully instructed him on the new weapons that would be needed for his quest. Lame Wolf cut a bow from green ash, and with the raw sinews of a bull elk, bent and wrapped the bow, layer after layer until even his great strength was strained to draw it. From metal barrel rings, obtained in trade by the Arapaho, he fashioned points for new arrows, fletching them with the soft inner feathers of the mountain grouse. Two arrows he left without metal tips, hardening these pine shafts by heating them slowly over a wet wood fire and then burning the tips briefly in a hot pitch flame before rubbing the points thin and sharp. When finished, he showed the bow to Berdache, allowing him to enchant the weapon with accuracy. Berdache inspected the arrows and then coated the tips of them with liquid from a small pot, exercising great care not to touch them afterward with his fingers. From beneath the soft skins of his tent, Berdache pulled a long war club presenting it to Lame Wolf. The stone head, flaked on both sides, was held in place by rawhide applied when the skin was still wet. After drying the rawhide tightly bound the stone head to the three-foot handle. A whole was drilled with an obsidian awl through the bottom of the wooden handle and a loop of horsehair was braided there.

"This war club I made myself and have counted coup with it many times. It has magical powers and few enemies can stand against it. Take it and use it well, for it is a weapon for a true warrior, one who has seen the vision of an Akicita," said Berdache, his wrinkled hand stroking the strong muscles in Lame Wolf's wrist as he presented the weapon.

Lame Wolf thanked the shaman, taking care to show proper respect. He knew of the history of the twins having heard the stories many times around his own tribal fire.

Berdache and Red Willow were identical twins springing from their mother's loins over 70 winters before. A single organ of skin, the manhood of both, who only one could own, bound them together at birth. The midwife knew they must be separated quickly. Joined twins were a sign of bad luck for the tribe, and they would be killed if discovered. Choosing which was to retain his manhood, she cut them apart. She chose wisely, for as they grew, Red Willow became a strong warrior while Berdache chose the path of Man-Woman spending long hours with the village shaman, a withered hag who instructed her young pupil in the honored spells and wiles of a shaman. Not male, nor yet totally female, Berdache was both. According to the custom of the Arapaho, he was accorded respect, for God created all. Berdache loved flirting with the young men of the tribe but chose none for his mate. Daily he painted his face and braids in crimson and blues, wearing only the softest dresses and fur lined moccasins. Many young braves bestowed favors upon him to gain from his magic; as he grew older, it was to his brother that he was closest.

Both twins dreamt visions of past and future events, and as Red Willow aged, the twins grew even closer together, living in the same tent and ruling as one. Red Willow was the obvious leader, but Berdache whispered wisdom in his brother's ear. Red Willow's special gift was his ability to communicate with animals, using them to learn from the world around him. Few wished to confront either of the Shaman, and their enemies were scarce, having long ago traveled the hanging road because of the pair's magic. Of the two, Berdache, whose adult name meant non-gendered in Arapaho, was the more dangerous. He loved the dark arts, using potions and poisons to cast spells and enchantments. When angered, he could fly into a rage, and his frail looks belied his strength and quickness, much to the dismay of his enemies over the years. Red Willow was a shape shifter, and when in the form of an animal, could learn what that species knew. Together they brought fortune to their band. Long ago the Comanche of the south learned to stay far away from this corner of the mountains, and few Shoshone raiding parties penetrated the dark timber to the north. Food was plentiful, and the children of the tribe played fat and happy.

At last the long day of summer arrived, and Lame Wolf explained to Prairie Dog and Flat Turtle that together they would travel the path of the Sun Dance guided by Red Willow. Berdache told him that unless Prairie Dog and Flat Turtle experienced the test of the E-Tah-leh, or the path of the white bison, they would have little magic in battle, fleeing when confronted by strong enemies. Both Prairie Dog and Flat Turtle passed the trials of a Dog Warrior of the Sihapsa, but Berdache claimed their spirits were not yet pure. Lame Wolf would experience the greatest test, for he must match the magic of the white trapper. Early in the morning all three were led into the tent of Red Willow, made from 12 buffalo skins, a magic number, being the number of moons in a year. The walls were painted in bright blues and reds, and pictographs on the inside told of great deeds of the band. Geometric designs flowed across the walls in grouping of threes and sixes. Three represented the stages of man, these being childhood, adulthood, and old age. Six were the openings on the head, which allowed man to perceive the world around him with aide of a spirit guide. Two eyes, two ears, a mouth and a nose the Manitou gave man, and with the senses of hearing, sight, smell, and taste the true warrior could discern the world around him.

Once seated inside the tent, Red Willow dressed in his finest buckskin decorated with the tails of white ermine and fine quillwork from the porcupine. He spoke of a time long ago when Mahpfyato, the father of his people floated upon the waters of the world. Growing tired of no permanence, he called the ducks down from the sky asking them to dive into the water and bring up earth for him to rest upon. This they did, but only a small piece of land grew surrounded by water. Wanting more, he then called upon the great turtles, and after many years of hard labor this land around them was built. Here they reside till this day.

"You, Flat Turtle, are especially honored to bear the name of the makers of this land," said Red Willow. "From Mahpfyato, or Blue Cloud in the Sihapsa tongue, all peoples of the Arapaho came to be. Berdache and I are of the blood of Mahpfyato and respect the animals of this land for helping us find a home. That is why we share it with them."

"Today after purifying your souls in the sweathouse, Berdache will share with you a drink so that you may speak with your spirit guides. Heed their advice closely for they will guide you on a path of wisdom and bravery. Failure to follow your guide will bring about your demise in this land the turtles built."

All day the Blackfeet sat within the confines of a small earthen mound. Inside a fire burned, the smoke rising from a small hole in the top. Naked, the warriors poured water brought to them by Berdache onto the hot stones of the fire. Sweat dripped from their bodies, cleansing their souls of past disgraces. Boughs of green pine placed upon the fire filled the room with the fragrance of sweet resin. No water was allowed to touch their lips until by late that night Berdache entered ordering them to follow him. He led them back to his tent, and still naked, instructed them to sit in a circle in the center of the tent. With Red Willow watching on, he smeared a thick salve over their bodies made from the blood and fat of the antelope to give them speed and keen eyesight to see their enemies. He then gave then a dark liquid to drink.

Approaching Lame Wolf, Red Willow drew a sharp flint blade and cut through the palm of his own hand causing his blood to flow in slow drops to the tent floor. With his blood as paint, he drew a series of designs on Lame Wolf's Chest. Then taking the knife he cut two slits into the deep muscles on Lame Wolf's chest inside the designs he drew. Drawing an arrow shaft from a quiver by his feet, he broke the head and feathers from the arrow before pushing it through the cuts he made on both sides of Lame Wolf's chest. No emotion did Lame Wolf show, either from the knife or the arrow. A rawhide thong hung from the crossed poles above them tied to the top of the teepee. Securing this thong to both ends of the broken arrow, he told Lame Wolf to walk the path of his quest around the tent in a circle.

"During this journey your spirit guide will come, releasing you from your tether. Heed his advice for he is wise in the way of the white men, and with his magic you will be successful."

The long hours wore on, and Lame Wolf walked his journey, around and around the teepee. Beneath his feet, Prairie Dog and Flat Turtle jerked and twisted in their dreams, the dark liquid boiling through their blood. Through the wall of the tent a plaintiff call came from the forest, the howl of a wolf on the hunt, calling to his pack. With this, Lame Wolf collapsed to the floor breaking the shaft of the arrow as it tore through the skin opening raw wounds on his chest. His spirit guide had spoken.

With the morning light, Berdache and Red Willow helped the Blackfeet take nourishment as they were too weak from their vision travels.

"Now my brothers," Red Willow said, "tell me what you have seen, and where you traveled."

Prairie Dog was the first to answer, and still almost in a dream state, he told of his vision. He saw a large town of prairie dogs stretching across the vast plains. Amongst them walked a coyote, pausing at each burrow to ask if they would dance with him. Honored to be asked by such an esteemed member of the plains, many agreed and left the safety of their home to go dance with the coyote. Leading them to a great rock, the coyote told the prairie dogs they were to close their eyes and dance around the rock holding hands so all would be safe, cautioning them not to open their eyes, or danger would befall them. The prairie dogs, happy to oblige began to dance. Around and around they went, the coyote singing a sweet song. In a short while, the coyote ate the prairie dog beside him and continued to dance. When his song ended, the prairie dogs noticed one of the dancers was gone but were so caught up in the music they begged the coyote to continue. This he gladly obliged until he ate them all.

"Beware the treachery of your enemies," said Berdache. "Look beyond the promises of peace and understand the nature of whom you face in combat. You listened well, Prairie Dog."

Flat Turtle told of a vision he saw in which an old turtle decided he would leave the safety of his river and climb the rock cliffs to see what lay outside of his world, just once before he died. All day long he climbed the steep rocks until at last he reached the summit, and his heart's dream was reached. As he gazed over the rim, he saw another river below him. Attempting to climb back down, he fell back into his own canyon, slamming hard into the rocks when he reached the bottom shattering his shell. Without protection, the big fish of the river soon ate him.

"You too have listened well, Flat Turtle. A warrior must always fight with the weapons he knows, understanding that if he becomes too rash, defeat will be the outcome. And you, Lame Wolf, what did you see?" asked Red Willow

Lame Wolf paused before answering. His dreams were varied and confusing, and the burning in his chest was stealing his thought. Composing himself he began.

"I saw a white cloud swirling and flashing with brightness. The cloud changed into the form of a beautiful woman in white buckskin. She appeared before two warriors one day, as they were hunting buffalo. Lowering the buckskins from her soft shoulders she invited one warrior to take nourishment from her breast. The man did this and suddenly aged, turning to maggots and dust, swirling about her feet. She then turned to the second warrior and invited him to do the same. Having seen the fate of his companion, he approached with fear but complied with her request, sucking sweet nectar from the nipple she offered. After he fed, she gave him a pipe decorated as a buffalo calf and then slowly she changed into the form of a great white wolf and vanished as if by smoke back into the clouds from which she came."

Red Willow and Berdache exchanged looks before dressing Lame Wolf's wounds. They showed Prairie Dog and Flat Turtle to their sleeping tents and then returned to Lame Wolf. Finally Red Willow addressed Lame Wolf as he waited for guidance.

"What you have seen is the Daughterwind. She goes by many names and is a master shape shifter taking on many forms. She is the daughter of Manitou who he sends to the earth to test the hearts of men. Any man that harbors lust toward her is punished with his life. When she finds a man who respects her position as Manitou's daughter, she freely offers her love, giving her lover immortality as offered by the pipe of the buffalo calf. She goes by many names Walira, Daughterwind, and Vision Seeker are but several. Remember should she offer you herself, that she is not of this world, and if you fail to show her respect, you will diminish and disappear. The promise of immortality is tempting, through few have achieved this reward. Tell me what else did you see?"

"I saw a great bear in a cave fighting with many men. Although they wounded him greatly, they too paid a price. Perhaps none of them survived."

"This warns you," said Red Willow, "that the white trapper you hunt must be taken in a group. Last time you divided your warriors and allowed his strength to overcome small numbers. Do not make that mistake again."

"Two last things you must remember," Berdache joined in, "the trader that you seek is made from the elements. Thick river mud, water, and black iron are part of him and his brother of the earth, the hard metal, cannot kill him. He has no fear of death and at times has welcomed it. This is the reason I instructed that two of your arrows were to be untipped. From neither rifle ball or iron knife will he die. The poison on the wooden arrows will weaken him, and against the war club, he cannot stand, for it is made from obsidian. When this strikes, iron sparks will light a fire consuming him. Last night Red Willow and I joined in our power to protect and guide you. While you walked the journey of your quest, we enchanted this medicine shirt, and now present it to you. While you wear the Medicine shirt of the Inuna-ina or Arapaho people, no weapon made by man can take your life, Lame Wolf. The dream about the Daughterwind cautions you to be careful, for against her it has no power. When you attack the bear, do so during the time of his deep sleep late in the cold of winter. He is weaker then and less prone to vigilance. Until that time you and your warriors are welcome to stay with us. My braves grow restless and seek to make war against the Comanche to the south; we would welcome your strength in our group."

By July of 1811 Rodde's pregnancy was going well, and although she knew long hours of morning sickness, she appeared strong and healthy. She felt within her that she would carry this child to full term. With the other children, she experienced painful cramping and bled heavily until at last she miscarried, crushing her hopes to bear a son for Joshua. Joshua spoke little of it, fearing if he showed too much emotion this would somehow bring about another miscarriage and dash his hopes once again. Now that three months of her term were passed successfully, he found himself staying closer to her and the post. Most of the large run of furs was completed and warm weather would make any further fresh hides soft, causing the fur to slip easily, ruining the pelt. Piles of chores surrounded him in the post, and new shipments for the store were arriving weekly. These needed sorted, inventoried, and shelved. With out saying so, Joshua didn't want Rodde lifting heavy boxes or tiring herself overmuch, so he spent more time getting in her way at the post until at last exasperated, she lost her temper, banishing him to the work shed behind the post. He left, tail between his legs, with her sly smile lurking behind him.

Casting about in the shed, he finally decided that the large block and tackle, which was used for sledding heavy sledges on the keelboats, should be on the top of his list. The wooden rollers inside the tackle finally cracked from continual use. Joshua asked a furniture maker on Market Street to carve new rollers for him, and the craftsmen delivered them to the post the next day. All that remained was for Joshua to drive out the pins holding the outer casing, replace the rollers, and reassemble the wooden shell. The difficult part was getting the block together again. The wood shell was layered with thin metal bands and when pressed together they flexed open providing room for the ropes to slide smoothly through. Knowing the block was under a tremendous amount of tension, Joshua was very careful when he drove the last pin from the case. His caution was rewarded as the pieces sprung apart with incredible force knocking tools from his workbench. Gathering the parts together again, he replaced the rollers and this time placed the pieces into a wooden vise with a threaded turnscrew. As he closed the vise one turn at a time, the hardened wood and metal slowly meshed again, joining the block and tackle. Once, seeing the flat plates starting to slip, he released the tension several turns, pounding them straight again before reapplying the pressure. At last they were together, and he drove the pins in place bowing the block and tackle into a working tool. Completing his task, Joshua stopped for a minute. His hammer was vibrating slightly on the workbench as if some invisible hand was shaking the legs of the table. The hammer stopped its movement, and he returned to his work, thinking no more about it. Beneath him deep in the granite below his feet other blocks, gigantic in size were slowly being squeezed together also. Unfortunately no master craftsmen were available to readjust these plates or to relieve the pressure building behind them to prevent them from slipping.

The summer of 1811 was a particularly warm one, and clouds of moisture floated from the river. The residents of St. Genevieve complained daily about the humid condition, and during the heat of the day little activity could be observed on the streets. As evening approached, the avenues again became busy, bustling with commotion. People emerged from the shaded porches to visit in the street cafes and pubs lit by candle lanterns hanging from the towns sycamores. Whenever groups gathered, discussion turned to the deteriorating relations between Great Britain and the United States. No newspaper was yet established in St. Genevieve, but the downriver boats brought news, and the St. Louis Gazette arrived weekly speaking of growing hostility between the nations. Rumors concerning English atrocities had been circulating since 1793 when England and France went to war. Americans, still upset with the British from revolutionary times, were supplying the French with goods, both military and domestic.

The British in retaliation began seizing American shipping removing sailors suspected of desertion, making them sail under the English flag. America passed the embargo act in 1807, which confined American shipping to coastal trade attempting to deny British access, but this met with limited success. People in the southern areas of the United States wanted to go to war with England, but the populace of St. Genevieve was undecided. They were angered by England trying to monopolize the fur trade in the northern Missouri region, by stirring up the Indians. The lead merchants and saltpeter miners knew war would be good for business but feared the British might penetrate this far south disrupting the community they worked so hard to establish. Already settlers reported Saukees, Miamis, and Pottawatamie raiding parties were crossing the Missouri River and penetrating into the Meramec valleys to the north. Several families were found massacred. These tribes, allies of the British, needed little urging to plunder and burn.

The heat of summer continued to linger on into the fall, and Joshua constructed a small slew for Rodde, complete with a sail. She loved to sail, ducking into the waves along the shore of the river, sending sprays of water across the bow of the small boat.

"Joshua, do you feel the river to be alive?" she asked one day after returning from sailing. "Some days it seems the river plays with me, turning the boat one way and then another. My mother believed all things to be alive possessing spirits and souls of their own."

"My mother also. When she died my father committed her ashes to the river. She called it the river of life and wished her remains to mingle with the water," Joshua answered. "Perhaps they were much alike. I can still remember my mother's teasing when I was little. She told me I was born from a lump of the dark river mud she carried home in a bundle."

"Sometimes I think maybe she told you the truth," teased Rodde. "Maybe you should try warming your bed at night with river water; then you would appreciate me more."

"How could I handle another mistress?" Joshua pleaded, "I can't take care of the one I have at home. I thought once you became with child, you might give me some peace, but you're worse than before."

"As if you didn't want me to," laughed Rodde. "I haven't noticed you fleeing from the covers at night."

"That's because you have bewitched me," said Joshua, "I can never escape you."

"As it should be. I may have to have a talk with that river of yours, one of these days. I don't think I like sharing you with her, you're neglecting your duties."

By October the heat broke at last, and cooler air arrived bringing relief. The field harvest was small because of the heat. Rodde was forced to bring water to the house garden to keep it from wilting, and now in her sixth month of pregnancy, the routine was tedious. She pouted feeling she was fat, and it wasn't until Joshua would wrap his arms around her from behind, feeling the weight of her filling breasts and kissing the honey texture of her neck that she would she smile again, making him promise he still believed her to be the most beautiful woman on the Mississippi. He loved to slide his hands down across her swollen belly, trying to feel the life within.

In November, Moses Austin came to visit Joshua and stayed for supper. After a fine dinner, the men retired to the chairs by the fire. Moses in his grand manner complimented Rodde on the dinner she prepared.

"Absolutely the finest cuisine I've dined upon, Miss Rodde," he proclaimed. "Run way from this river rat and come live with me."

"Give me a few years," she laughed, "we have some unfinished business to complete."

Moses was buying shares in a new banking consortium in Herculeum, a few miles upriver. He wanted Joshua to join him and become a partner in the new bank.

"If war does come," Moses argued, "the price of lead and saltpeter will rise, shipping will increase on the Mississippi, and business will grow. There is much money waiting for those willing to invest in the future. I want you with me. You have proven to be a wise businessman."

Joshua promised to think about the proposition, and Moses left, promising to return later for Joshua's answer. Rodde was dead set against investing any money in banking, believing it to be risky.

"Joshua, what more could you want? We have food for our table, a warm bed, and each other. It is you I love, not what you own or what you buy. No one is better at the fur trade than you. Leave the banks to bankers."

That night as they lay together, he thought about her words. He trusted her advice and realized that she spoke always with his concern in mind. He was a fur man, that is what he knew, and here is where he would stay with Rodde and his son.

December 17th fell upon St. Genevieve cold and clear. Canadian air swept from the North Country meeting little resistance across the Madison and Jefferson Rivers as it pushed further south breaching the Platte and continuing on to the Missouri River. Here it paused regaining strength and then drove to the Mississippi touching all in its path. Trees hung thick with hoar frost, and only the power and current of the mighty mother river kept a channel free from the conquering ice. Near the banks the slower moving water was trapped and frozen. Two hundred river miles south of St. Genevieve, New Madrid residents clung to their down comforters, delaying rising, dreading the feel of cold floors on bare feet.

Rodde awoke early this cold morning unable to sleep. She knew her time was near; the midwife told her by Christmas if not before. Christmas Eve was only a week away, the night the Lord was born. Perhaps this was a sign of impending destiny. Their child was impatient for his birth, kicking and twisting within her. Realizing he would not stop for several hours, she left the warmth of the bed. Dressing in warm slippers Joshua fashioned for her, she drew his heavy capote around her body, loving the smell of him that swirled around her when she wore it. She fed the small red coals within the hearth, first with small sticks, and then seeing the flame catch, she added several larger logs. These also would soon be ablaze, bringing warmth to the room, melting the frost from the windows. Outside it was still, not a breath of wind disturbed the dusting of snow on her windowsills. She loved the snow, possibly because she never saw it when she was a child. With a sudden decision, she left the warmth of the room, knowing that Joshua would continue to sleep for another hour or so. This was a chance for her to talk to the son that waited so impatiently. She would show him the river that was to become his destiny. Taking extra precaution to be careful, she walked down the path from her home to the riverbank below. She knew just the rock she wanted to show him.

Our fishing rock, where I spent many hours with Joshua, she thought. And perhaps even the rock upon which you, little one, were made.

For it was here that she lured Joshua away from fishing that warm April evening almost nine months before, laughing at him while he tried to ignore her as she unbuttoned her blouse. She won him over, as she knew she always could, and they made love beside the river holding tenderly on to each other long into the evening.

In the sharp chill morning air, a sound arrived to the residents of New Madrid. The sound, difficult to describe, penetrated every house and every bedroom of the 400 residents. Like the tenor of a strong wind blowing, without the wind, it vibrated through the post walls of the houses. Reverberating and alive, the noise grew until people felt it within themselves as if their bodies were cellos across which a mighty bow was being drawn. Husbands and wives turned to each other, silently questioning in fear. Children began to cry, this strange feeling unnatural to their limited years when at last the sound stopped. The Mississippi stopped also; millions of gallons of water, a mile wide and 20 feet deep stopped, no longer flowing southward to the gulf. The river was confused not understanding quite why her flow was halted. Then slowly she sought a new direction and the mighty current began to flow upstream against itself, past New Madrid, past St. Genevieve and on by La Clede's landing in St. Louis.

The seiche effect from the grinding of the major faults 400 miles beneath the earth fooled even the greatest of waterways. Hell then opened up, and the earthquake began in earnest.

The noise and roaring came again, this time a hundred fold stronger than before. Within the next five minutes, every structure in New Madrid was shaken to pieces and from this epicenter a shock wave spread shaking the granite mantle deep within the earth for three hundred miles in all directions. The earth's mighty vise closed too tightly and unable to withstand the pressure, huge plates within the rock below slipped. Fracturing upward rupturing the earth above, huge chasms appeared where once level ground reigned. Solid stone seemed as if it were foam being shaken in a stone crock. Hillsides forested with thick timber disappeared deep into the earth, and islands miles in length including all fields and structures upon them vanished beneath the roiling river as it flowed north obeying the call of nature. Palisade after palisade of rocks fell into the water and canyons appeared where once only creeks ran. A huge burial mound on a hill overlooking the Mississippi sank slowly into the ground and was replaced with water becoming an instant lake. Over 1000 miles away bells tolled in Boston, sounding out the catastrophe to startled New England residents. Dark clouds of poisonous gases drifted across the landscape, and the roaring rose to a deafening volume. Within minutes all was quiet, but the landscape was changed forever. The Mississippi at last realized she had been tricked, turned southward again in huge waves, angry that she was fooled, trying to make up for the time lost.

Rodde felt the slight tremor through the hard rock beneath her. She looked down fearing the monolith was suddenly sliding into the river, but it was still stationary, guarding its location as it had done for thousands of years. She looked out toward the river, seeing the ice begin to pull away from the rock. River water lapped over top the ice near the edges. First it was only several inches, and then suddenly, it was the depth of a foot and gaining. Astonished by what she was seeing, she watched in amazement as the broken chunks beneath the water began flowing upstream, performing the impossible.

I must run and tell Joshua, she thought, he must know what was happening, he knew the Mississippi better than anyone.

She turned slowly, her awkward movement caused by the impending birth of their child and started to climb from the rock, fearful the water would raise this high and sweep her upstream. With her first step from the rock to the shore, the ground beneath her feet appeared to shimmer becoming almost gelatinous as it moved from side to side. She attempted to retain her balance but was unable to remain on her feet and fell hard to the ground. A sudden fear gripped her now, not for herself but for the unborn child within her.

"My God," she screamed, "protect me, protect my child. Take us not now."

Thrown about like a leaf in the wind, she wrapped both arms tightly around her stomach, trying as she might to protect what was within her. A roaring sound competed with her screams for Joshua, and she stopped unable even to hear herself. Above her the solid granite palisade began to loosen, shearing in slabs twenty feet thick, weighing a hundred tons or more. Rodde looked up to see the slow movement as the slabs began their descent to the river below. She tried once more to regain her feet, trying to flee for safety although she knew the distance could never be achieved in time. She ceased her struggle to regain her feet and turned away from the cliff behind her to look once more upon the river.

Accept us into your Kingdom, Oh Lord, and protect Joshua, was her last thought as the rockslide reached the riverbank, returning her and the child to the earth from which they came.

Not satisfied with the first attempt, larger sheets broke loose falling two hundred feet to guard the burial tomb, and then the ground accepted the sepulcher, swallowing the offering deep within its fold to hold them dear.

Daily, Night Wind's leg grew stronger. During La Ramie absence, Night Wind made use of her time to clean his cabin from top to bottom. The existing state of cleanliness seemed fine to Joshua, but Night Wind was sure there were vermin hiding in every corner. All the soft skins from the floor and the bed were removed and hung upon the corral poles to freshen in the spring air. She tricked Spotted Owl into beating the hides, telling him that all great warriors needed practice counting coup. Without practice she said, they would embarrass themselves when time for honor came much face would be lost. Spotted Owl took her counsel to heart and attacked each elk skin as if they were his fiercest enemy recently overcome in battle. Joshua delayed too long before making his escape to go fishing and soon found himself bucket in hand bringing fresh water to the cabin so Night Wind could scrub the split log floors, scouring several years of grease and dirt away until the finish of the wood was clearly visible again.

Just as Joshua thought he was going to be granted reprieve, she made him stake the buffalo hides, hair down, on the ground outside the cabin. Night Wind previously fleshed them when the hunters first returned but now she concocted a foul smelling brew and combined this with ashes from the fireplace. Once the hides were staked to the ground she poured liberal amounts of her mash onto the skins allowing it to melt into the still porous hide. After soaking for a day Joshua twisted the hides as tightly as possible tying of both ends to the porch of the cabin. Selecting carefully from the trees surrounding the cabin he chose two limbs and stripped them of their sticky bark. Night Wind then tied the freshly stripped limbs over the hides, putting one on either side before binding the newly fashioned pincers with rawhide. The work then began as Joshua pulled the limbs like a drawknife along the hides, breaking the hardening tissues throughout the length of the buffalo robes. Every time he slowed, she would assess his work and declare just a few more strokes were needed. Spotted Owl was smart enough to continue fighting with his elk hides staying far on the opposite side of the cabin.

That evening, Night Wind allowed Joshua to cease his labors and declared she felt strong enough to take a short walk across the glen to the notch where below she could gaze down into the canyon. Spotted Owl on one side and Joshua on the other served as her crutches, and the pilgrimage to the notch was accomplished. She marveled feeling the massive power of Joshua compared to her son beside her, knowing that some day Spotted Owl would grow into a man. Spotted Owl soon became engaged in throwing rocks to the water below trying to hit the foaming river with his missiles. As they laughed at Spotted Owls attempts, the evening closed in upon them, and for the few minutes the river canyon was bathed in a still light while the earth decided how best to expel the remaining luminescence from her home. Night Wind and Joshua grew silent acknowledging the bond as a palpable feeling between them.

"For the last seven years my life has been a trail," said Joshua. "I feel I have either been traveling to or running from something but never quite reaching it. Tonight it is different. I don't feel the need to do either. Somehow being here, above this river with you and Spotted Owl is enough."

"Your spirit is tired of travel," Night Wind replied, careful to keep her eyes from his face, not wanting to break his mood and allow him to escape within himself again."

"Last time we spoke," Joshua said, I did not share all with you that I felt. Many things have I been in this life, but dishonest has never been one. There was a woman on the road behind me. After the loss of my parents, I was angry with my God for leaving me a way to travel without the love and support of a family. She came into my life filling the void left there. Many years did we share, and although no children came to sit by my feet, we grew closer together because of it. With her love, all things in this world were granted to me. When at last she was to bear my child, her light was extinguished, and for many years darkness was all I saw."

"I am sorry for your loss," Night Wind replied very gently and softly, feeling the emotion in his words. "Does her spirit still reside with you; is it of her you think, giving your life meaning to face the challenges of paths you have taken?"

"I lost her spirit as I tried to strike against God for taking her from me. In Missouri, far down the river, there was a great war between mighty nations. The native people were forced to choose with whom to ally. I made war on all that did not join with my people, but looking back, I fought only myself. A battle I could not win. Instead of remembering her kindness and gentleness, I turned away and found revenge in blood. Being with you has reminded me, not of her, but that for many years I forgot what to be thankful for."

"And now whom do you see when you look upon my face?" asked Night Wind.

"I look upon your face and see myself as I'm reflected in your eyes," said Joshua turning to look at Night Wind. "For many seasons I cared not whether I lived or died, but now with you the dark dreams are swept away. When I look upon you, I see youth and beauty. I see a mother's love, a fierce love combined with tenderness. I see the woman I need to be with, not for remembrance of my past, but to share with me the future."

Night Wind felt the breath escape from her lungs, leaving her weak almost dizzy. That she loved Joshua she knew. She also knew from the darkness of his spirit that she must compete with another, a memory from his past. The battle would be hard, and his answer suddenly allowed hope to swell within her.

"I am a Vision Woman," she said, "and honesty too dwells within me. Far behind us on the trail I felt my love for you grow, but closely guarded it not wanting to stir the ashes of old pain. I could never be for you what once was, or share you with thoughts of another. For some it would perhaps be enough, but never for me. When I love, my soul becomes selfish. I had to know if your feeling for me was consuming, not just an attempt to regain another from before. What has gone earlier is always with us, just as I would die before choosing a way, different from the one, which made Spotted Owl grow within me. From pain and suffering, a new life sprang. The Manitou makes both the mountains and the valleys."

Unspoken her hand found his, locking tightly to the coarse roughness there, letting her feeling flow gently into him. The night recaptured its earlier tardiness, and fell quickly around them. Below the soft roar of the water falling floated to their ears. Above the Night Hawk, called for her mate along the rocky cliffs. The scent of fresh lupine hung pungent in the air as they returned to the cabin. The walk back was different than the journey there. Both felt the allure of a new beginning, risen from, not captive of the past.

Reaching the cabin, Spotted Owl soon drifted to sleep among the elk hides Night Wind returned earlier to the dwelling. Twitching slightly as he re-fought battles, counting coups won earlier in the day against imaginary enemies, he dreamt of himself as a great warrior never being forced to accept defeat. There was time for that in the seasons to come, learning that losses are inherent in battles as they are in life.

Together in the cabin Joshua and Night Wind completed their vows made earlier above the canyon rim, trusting in their confessions of love. No words passed between them as Night Wind shed the rainaments of her soft buckskin, standing proudly before Joshua, secure in her beauty, the burnished copper aureoles of her nipples flushed and dark, offering herself to him. Frozen in place as if enchanted, Joshua allowed Night Wind to draw him to her as she strained to embrace his strength. In the freshened robes of soft elk fur they laid together. Slowly at first they began the rhythm, older than the flow or the rivers to the sea. Not accepting his gentleness, her nature demanded more as proof of the bond between them, and fiercely she accepted him into her soul, making him part of all she was. Twice more she sought him before dawn first entered the window of the cabin making sure he thought only of her before falling asleep trapping him beneath her. Dusky in the morning light, he held her smooth skin as she rested against him, savoring the sensual aroma of their coupling. Her full breasts flattened against his ribs softly measuring her heartbeats. Thigh to thigh, knee to knee they melded as one, a complementing but inherent part of the other.

The next few days flowed by, night running into day. Amongst the rays of sunshine, Night Wind would blush when she caught Joshua looking at her, trying to memorize every nuance of her form and features, at night as if jealous of his sleep she possessed him, demanding full attention and homage to her love, binding him with her body and spirit. When her dreams came, early in the morning hours she searched for danger that would threaten their fulfillment but found none. Joshua appeared to her in the visions, not as a person but more enduring, a blending of the earth and water beneath her as she flew.

The cabin now meeting Night Wind's requirements, she allowed him time to fish in the swift waters of the river. He spent long hours exploring the lay of the land, striking out in all directions, ever mindful of danger that might threaten the safety of those he loved. He saw no smoke from campfires, and the only fresh tracks were those of animals coming to the water to drink. From his position high in the crevice of the notch serving as ingress to La Ramie's cabin, he saw a lone horse emerging from the river below late one evening. True to his word, the trapper worked his way up the steep hillside after being gone two weeks.

Reunited for supper that evening, La Ramie satisfied Night Wind's curiosity about her home and the safe return of her brothers catching her up on the latest new of the band. Painted Flower sent Night Wind her prayers for a speedy recovery and would await a chance to welcome her home. Although saddened by the loss of Kills-Crowe, Painted Flower was thankful of the boy's safe return and laden La Ramie with many gifts and presents in show of her appreciation. The greatest honor a Shoshone warrior could achieve was to travel the star road, secure in the knowledge he trained his children well, and this Kills-Crowe did. La Ramie stayed two days within the Shoshone camp and participated in the story dance to celebrate Lone Eagle's first coup.

"Uhnta-Wha and Little Eagle, now the ruling elders of the tribe will come for you, in two moons to escort you to the tribal council. Riders have been sent to all bands near the Sheep Mountains telling of Kills-Crowe's brave death. As the waning half of the second full moon departs, there will be a great council and a new chief will be chosen to steer the course of your people," said La Ramie.

249

Joshua immediately felt the sharp pain of her loss, but knew that duty would demand she leave him, counsel for her people must separate them for a time.

"Spotted Owl and I will make the journey alone when it is time. I am not a wandering virgin, unable to find my way to the water that boils," Night Wind's eyes flashed, as she answered.

"You underrate your importance to your people," La Ramie answered, knowing he had provoked her. "Just as we climbed the long ridge to the base of the Snowy Mountains we came across the tracks of three ponies. Their trail led to the south, away from the path to your people, but the tracks I recognized. They were those of Lame Wolf and two others. His vengeance toward you will not have cooled, and Running Horse knows this. A strong war party will insure your safety, and benefit the tribe as a whole."

"You speak the truth," she said more demure now. "Hidden here I forget my enemies that once were so close. Blackfeet traveling to the lair of the Arapaho does not bode well for our people. Deep in the mountains there live two Shamans, Red Willow and his brother the Man-Woman. Not even in my dreams do I fly above the land of the dark tall timber, for their power is too great, and I would become trapped and diminished. Special preparations need to be made to meet this warning. The friends of my enemy are always my foe."

Night Wind made no pretense to disguise her feelings for Joshua, now that La Ramie returned. She stopped often to check the mood of Joshua, speaking only to him with her eyes, touching him often as she passed near him. Later as Joshua helped La Ramie rub down his tired mount, he told La Ramie what had passed while he was gone.

"You never had a chance, boy," said La Ramie, "I done seen that right away. Like I said, once a Vision Woman sets her sights on something, she get it. Just the way of the world."

"I shall miss her when she leaves," admitted Joshua, "maybe in the spring I'll wander that way. Wouldn't do to go courting a princess without being rich."

"You're already rich, Joshua, it just took you some time to see it. I've got a pretty strong hunch that right after that big pow wow, Night Wind's going be right on her way back to you. We better get to work on adding another room to that cabin, so's I don't have to listen to her catawallin' all night long. Better start eating lots of meat boy, she's a handful of woman."

Very little escaped La Ramie's eye, either in people or the world around him, Joshua thought. It was as if he was part of the rocks and trees, observing all and judging none.

Within the week, a new room was added to the cabin, although small measuring only 12 steps each way in size. The newly tanned buffalo hides cushioned the board floors. Joshua constructed a small hearth and a window looking toward the north. Here in a sanctuary of their own, Night Wind and Joshua dreamed of road they would travel together sharing each other's souls, through body and spirit. Nightly they tried to drink their fill of each other, an impossible task as their love grew deeper, more elemental pending Night Wind's departure. Above them in the heavens, Manitou looked upon his work and called it good, knowing that the seed for the continuance of his people was planted, alive and growing, nourished in the womb of his daughter below.

Chapter 11
The Plans

By Friday afternoon Carrigan listened to 28 & 1/2 of the 35 scheduled class presentations. He learned facts about Wyoming and geology that he never knew before. Mr. James took time to talk to each of his classes expanding on the students' work, correcting them when they erred and offered new information when he detected a current of curiosity running through the students.

One topic the students found interesting was the discussion of the land and the way it was divided. Turning the learning into a scavenger hunt of sorts, Carrigan explained that a *section* of land was 640 acres and measured 1 mile square. He then talked about a *township*, which contained 36 *sections* of land and was 6 miles square. The next larger divisions were called *ranges* and this was composed of townships. He also broke down *sections* explaining they could be divided into *quarter sections, forties*, and *acres*, or in the case of housing subdivisions, even into *lots*. Most new subdivisions allotted 4 lots on 1 acre although some unscrupulous developers often tried to crowd twice that many building projects onto that small piece of land. The amazing feature was that each individual piece of land possessed a unique identity because of this method of surveying, no matter where it was located in the United States.

Choosing from the large quantity of topographic maps at his disposal, Carrigan would select a location and then provide this to the students. The first group to find it on the map received a prize, usually a slightly squashed candy bar from the bottom drawer of his desk--but the kids liked the game. As they got better at it, he used more complicated terminology such as the south half of the south half of the northeast quarter. By the end

A Wyoming Journey From Then and Now

of the day everyone got the hang of locating property and were attempting to describe the location of their homes in this terminology.

Carrigan also brought in the fact that when this system of surveying was adopted by the United States for the western lands, two sections in each township were set aside. These sections would be kept by the state but rented out to individuals who owned land around them. The rent of these lands would go into a special fund for the maintenance of the public schools. These two sections were numbered 16 and 36.

"Your education," he said, "is being paid for by pieces of land you have never seen."

Next week, Carrigan hoped to have time to talk about some of the early settlers in Wyoming, and the mountain men who blazed the trails following the rivers to the tall mountains and the cold streams where beaver could be found. He also owned an excellent film from the History Channel talking about the nomadic life of the Plains Indians as they followed the buffalo across the vast grassland. James said he would be back next week to tie it up with a lecture about the evolution of the animals that made Wyoming their home ranging from dinosaurs to horses. By Friday evening, Carrigan felt the thrill returning from teaching that he had not experienced for some time. It was easy for teachers to teach when kids wanted to learn. If he could just figure out how to make everything a little more relevant to their lives, both their respective jobs would be made easier.

The last bell of the day sent the kids scurrying for the hallways. The weekend promised to be a nice one and Carrigan left the school early so he could make it to the lumberyard before it closed. Stopping by his house first, Carrigan hooked his flatbed trailer to Gertrude's ample rear end. Between the pickup and the trailer he should able to haul enough lumber to finish his cabin's foundation. He bought twenty treated 6x6s to be used for foundation posts. Figuring the number of running feet around his cabin, he purchased an equal number to serve as the sills on which he could set the floor tresses. Carrigan meticulously selected the 2x10s making sure there were no cracks or knots on the boards. Carrigan finished his load with joist hangers, nails, insulation, and plastic sheeting--probably more material than he could put together, but the excitement was starting to catch hold and he wanted to make sure all the supplies were included. He parked the trailer upon returning home, changed clothes and thought about plans for the evening.

Tonight I'm staying home, Carrigan decided. Ben's Bar was just going to have to get along without him. Checking through his pantry the choices were assayed: macaroni and cheese (no, he had that last week), soup (didn't sound good), Hamburger Helper (too much like macaroni and cheese). Carrigan could cook something like Mexican food or jambalaya, but he really needed more time. Finishing off the last of a bag of stale potato chips, he finally gave up. Throwing some money in his pocket, and leaving the pantry door open Carrigan strode outside to the pickup. Gertrude didn't seem too perturbed at being kicked in action again just after she was put up for the night. Together they made the trip to Ben's Bar and Gertrude visited with her parking lot mates while Carrigan went inside to investigate the food, beer, and people.

Within Ben's the action was in full swing. Workers from the community just getting off shift crowded the bar, loudly jostling and teasing each other. Deeper in the lounge, professional people were drinking their mixed drinks, discussing business deals. Clear in the rear, the folks were chatting about friends with people who were mutually important in their lives. Some pairings were clandestine, others innocent. Whichever the case, the dimness of the light afforded them more privacy. Clear at the back table sat Chuck Attenby (the chicken carcass stasher) and Jenny Albright (the chicken carcass handler). Their heads were close together, either discussing matters or friends--Carrigan couldn't tell. Music education and physical education curriculums looked to be the furthest items from their minds at that minute. Jenny looked positively radiant and was wearing a dress with spring flowers as its pattern. Chuck was talking only to her and not the bar. She was never married--to Carrigan's knowledge--and both wives that once owned Chuck were far in his past. Everyone needs someone he thought, but he wasn't sure these two needed each other. The bar was full until Sheila noticed his arrival and from behind her, she slid a stool to the very corner of the bar near the cash register.

"Hi ya, Carrigan," she said. "I began to think for a while that you weren't coming in tonight. I even checked the calendar to make sure it was Friday, and sure enough it was; you were just late."

"I know, I know," he smiled, "I had some errands to do. Some of us have to work once in awhile."

"Tell me about it," Sheila fired back. "I'm stuck here behind this bar till midnight."

"With this crowd you'll be rich by that time," he returned fire.

Carrigan and Sheila shared some history over the last several years. Once or twice a month, when Sheila got off work, she would arrive at his house. At first just to talk, and then later the conversation would be continued in the bedroom. Neither of them seemed to mind the casualness of the relationship. They didn't have dinner together or go to shows. On weekends that she came over, Carrigan usually left early the morning after, fleeing civilization to wander in the hills, leaving Sheila as she murmured sleepy goodbyes. When he returned late in the evening she was gone, the bed made--waiting for her next late-night appearance. From deep within his being, this struck a familiar chord from earlier times, but he refused to analyze or compare it.

Sheila was attractive, in her early thirties, and had little ambition in life other than her present position as bartender. At that she was great, knowing enough about each customer to make them feel special. With her tight sweater and generous nature, she made a good living. Her only expenses were a little red sports car, the rent on a small bungalow, two Siamese cats, and Carrigan. She told Carrigan she was married once right out of high school and fully intended not to commit that error again. Carrigan didn't object to the relationship, but other than the physical nature of their affair, he found short periods of her were enough. She wasn't particularly well educated, didn't like to read, and was a little coarse. On the positive side, Sheila certainly wasn't promiscuous and told Carrigan she hadn't slept with anyone else since beginning her late night visits to his house. During the spring, the visits were becoming more regular. She was a loud talker, laughed often, touched people when visiting with them, and used terms Carrigan detested such as 'hon' and 'sweetie'.

Funny he thought, she would make someone a great wife, just not for me. He knew he should end the relationship, but found it difficult to end something that really wasn't started. How did one turn a woman away from the door when she came calling late at night?

A cold beer appeared onto the bar in front of him, "This one is on me," she said. "Are you going to be home later, I could bring over a six-pack and we could talk about the first thing that came up?"

Realizing that this was the time and now was the place, Carrigan stopped Sheila, holding her firmly by the elbow and looked directly into her eyes. "Listen, Sheila; I don't want you to come over tonight. It's like you told me last winter, what we do is just fun, nothing else. It has stopped being fun. I'm too old for you, and I just can't keep up anymore. Find somebody to love, make lots of babies with and get out from behind this damn bar. The kind of men you find in here, you don't want."

Fire leaped into her eyes, and she quickly bit back at him, "Sure, you started sniffing around that rich bitch last weekend, and now you're too good for me, Carrigan. You're a real son-of-bitch, you know that? We had something good and now you want to fuck it up. Well, screw you!"

The beer didn't taste quite so good after that conversation. Maybe he was in the mood for some Hamburger Helper tonight. Gertrude wished he would make up his mind, but she didn't protest as Carrigan drove out of the parking lot, headed back home where he should have stayed in the first place.

Carrigan slept restlessly that night; an unforeseen entity had stolen something from him, and no matter how long, or how hard he looked, he couldn't find it. Finally, unable to keep this dream from entering his thoughts, he arose, shuffling around the house garnering tools and material he would need for tomorrow. By six the next morning he was well out of town, leaving the sleeping city behind him along with his unmade bed, rumpled and empty, just the way he liked it.

Parking Gertrude and the trailer by a pullout near the river bridge, he threw rocks into the water as he waited for Nancy to arrive. Carrigan remembered floating sticks in the water, when he was young and then trying to annihilate them with rocky, cannon fire. His aim was much better as a boy, and today the armada survived without a hit, bobbing and twisting on down the river. Shortly after seven, Nancy arrived in a large SUV, with magnetic **Rainer Ranch** signs protecting the doors. Carrigan watched her exit the vehicle, taking time to look directly at her as she walked toward him. She had always been beautiful but now in her forties something else was there, perceptible but indefinable. Still slender, the designer jeans adhered nicely to her slim figure only hinting at the rounded firm body there. Sunglasses again held her locks of auburn hair from spilling down and across the gray eyes. Small lines were barely noticeable around her mouth when she smiled as she was doing now, knowing that he was studying her. A faded, blue, work shirt several sizes two large with the sleeves rolled up, showing a white tee shirt underneath completed her outfit.

"What are you throwing rocks at, Cowboy? Have the fish got you that frustrated?" she said by way of a greeting.

"No," Carrigan replied forcing his eyes from her, "just killing time; are you ready?"

"I was born ready," she laughed. "First let me introduce you to Stephen." Taking him by the hand she walked back to the SUV and opened the passenger side door to reveal a young boy sitting in the passenger seat, his brown eyes darting between his mother and Carrigan.

"Stephen, this is Mr. Carrigan," she said. "He is a very dear friend of mine. James, this is my son Stephen."

"Stephen," Carrigan said as he extended his hand to the boy, "your mom tells me you're a great carpenter. Just what I need today; thanks for coming to help."

The boy looked at the large rough hand and then back to his mother before extending his own small one. "Hi," was all he said turning to look out the front window again.

"My kind of person," Carrigan laughed, "a man of few words."

Turning his attention to Nancy again, Carrigan told her to follow him up to the end of the turn off and she could leave her vehicle there and get in with him.

"The road from there on might be a little rough on your paint job," he said.

Upon reaching the turnoff, Nancy parked the SUV and gathered the two bags and a cooler from the back of her car, throwing them on top of the pile of lumber being towed by Gertrude. She helped Stephen make the climb into the cab while Carrigan rearranged the coats, hats, and gloves to make room for the boy in the front.

"Is that a real gun?" Stephen asked looking at the rifle above the visors.

"Sure is, boy. Do you want to shoot it later?"

"Yeah," he said, "if my Mom would let me. Can I Mom?"

Nancy made a face at Carrigan, raising her fine eyebrows as she used to do when angry with him, and then turned to Stephen and said, "We'll see, maybe if there is time."

The rest of the journey to Carrigan's land was uneventful, and they chatted about the neighbors, the terrain, and the prospect for moisture this year. Twice Carrigan held Gertrude up to show Stephen the brown shadows of deer as the tanned shapes flashed in the trees. Nancy was able to figure out the wire gate opener at the school section and looked back at Carrigan as if to say, 'I'm a ranch girl you know.' Half an hour later, Gertrude lugged the trailer up the last hills and down into the glade near where the two creeks joined. The dew was nearly gone from the grass and everywhere it reflected the morning sun, giving a golden glow to the surrounding hills.

"Well," said Carrigan, "time to go to work. If you two would begin rolling those timbers off the trailer, I'll lug them over to the holes and start setting posts. Maybe we can get them all set before lunch. Stephen, I have a real hard job for you, but maybe you can do it, do you want to try?"

The brown eyes swung to meet Carrigan's face, "Sure, I will try, but I'm not very good at building things."

"Sure you are," Carrigan answered, "you just don't know it yet. Grab a shovel from the back of the pickup and after I set the timber in the hole, I need you to fill it half way up with dirt. Think you can do it?"

"I'll try sir," the small voice answered.

257

With Nancy rolling off the posts, Carrigan setting them into the holes, and Stephen throwing in a little dirt to hold them, all twenty were soon in place. Carrigan then leveled the corner posts both ways before stringing the lines to make sure he was square on all corners. One post he wasn't happy with and reset it several times until he was satisfied. When everything was right, he packed bags of cement from the trailer. After mixing it well in an old tub he'd brought, he finished filling the holes with a mixture of cement and dirt, tamping them tight with a heavy iron bar. Next he turned his attention to the center row, squaring these back to the corners, making sure they were dead set vertical. The sun continued to rise as the form of the cabin began to take shape. Nancy's arms burned from dragging the heavy timbers and whenever Stephen grew tired, Carrigan found a new task for him that held his interest again. Currently he was rolling up string from around the posts. Nancy stopped a minute to breathe and watched Carrigan rhythmically driving the metal bar deep into the ground around the posts. He worked steadily stroke after stroke, stopping periodically to lay the level on the post. Sweat ran in profusion down his face and arms, sticking the white shirt to his broad back.

Nancy admired Carrigan's heavy, thigh muscles as they swelled the denim of his pants with each thud of the bar. His butt always did look good in Levi's, she thought.

She marveled at the change in Stephen. Here in the mountains he was outgoing, running to do errands at Carrigan's request and peppering him with questions as Carrigan tamped the posts into the ground. What a change from the quiet, shy child she picked up from the airport earlier in the week. Watching Carrigan closely, Stephen also rolled his shirt sleeves up; when Carrigan stopped to wipe the sweat from his brow, Stephen did the same.

By noon, all the posts were set and Carrigan attached his straightest 2x4s to the outside edges, leveling them as he went.

"Let me chop these," he said, "and then we'll eat. Go ahead and wash up, I'll be right there."

Ripping the chain saw to life, Carrigan laid the blade flat on the 2x4s and cut the tops off each of the posts, making sure all were the same height. On the last three posts, he let Stephen hold the saw while Carrigan wrapped his arms around him, guiding the big chain blade as it angrily hummed through the treated wood. When finished the two carpenters went to the creek ducking their heads and hands in the water to wash up. Nancy watched them as they splashed in the cool water, rinsing the sweat, dirt, and wood chips from their faces and arms before coming over to join her for lunch.

In the cooler was a sack lunch for each. Thick slices of beef topped by tomatoes, onions, and pickles surrounded by sourdough bread. Chips, brownies, and fresh fruit also appeared from the cooler along with cold cans of lemonade. Stephen ate like a wolf and then eyed his mother's sandwich until she gave him half. Carrigan gave up his brownie and this, too, Stephen gulped down.

"I don't know if I could afford his help everyday," laughed Carrigan. "It would cost too much in food." Then turning to Stephen, he directed him to look behind the seat of the pickup where a fish net was hidden.

"Take that down to the creek and see if you can catch any of the brookies there," Carrigan said. "If you can we could cook them later in case you get hungry again."

Stephen pawed through the arsenal there until he found the net and then raced down below the joining of the little creeks, searching for prey. Finishing his lemonade, Carrigan told Nancy what they still needed to do to finish the foundation.

"You've talked to Stephen more in one morning than his father has in the last seven years," she said. "Thank you. This is the type of thing I want him to learn from Wyoming."

"My pleasure," he replied. "He's a good worker."

"Edmond always says that he will make more time for Stephen, but even when he takes him, he just leaves Stephen with his family. I haven't seen Edmond for several months now, although we do talk by phone. He's not happy that I'm spending so much time out here. If it weren't for Stephen, I would have left him years ago. He's everything I thought I wanted, until I got it. Regardless, from him I have Stephen and that is all that counts."

"You're lucky," Carrigan said, "he's a great kid. Don't ever let him lose that spark. So many kids I teach have lost their ability to care--about school or themselves. Somehow, their parents just stopped caring about them."

"No," Nancy said, "you are the lucky one. You said you were still looking for something, I think you found it. You have a natural gift with children; you treat them like they are important. More than that, you believe they are. Look at him wading in that creek trying to catch a fish just to please you. That's special, James; don't ever lose it. My mother used to talk about a saying, something like, 'A hundred years from now, no one cares how wealthy you were, or what you owned, all that matters is that you made a difference in the life of a child.' You have the ability to make that difference."

Carrigan didn't answer. He could tell that she was sincere, and maybe she was right. Maybe that's why he taught, because sometimes he did make a difference. Perhaps he thought too deeply about all of his students. Some of them weren't going to make it--in school or in life. The window to let someone care for them was shut, and could never be opened again. These were losses he needed to accept; strengthen the herd by culling the weak. This law of nature not even people were able to overcome. It was the job of the alphas from each sex to pass on their genes, insuring the survival of the species. The rest of the pack supported and protected these two, insuring success. Those members who did not contribute were culled, either by death or isolation. Maybe mankind was closer to the other species than they realized. Schools, peer groups, and other institutions were the process by which natural selection worked. Carrigan did his best to make sure all made the cut, but sometimes not even his skills were successful.

Stephen returned from the creek, smiling and wet, claiming a big one got away. Nancy and Carrigan laughed as he held out his hands showing the size, and told him next time he would be more successful. Carrigan, task driven now that the project was started, put them back to work. Using the rest of the timbers, he finished his foundation by laying them flat on the ends of the freshly cut posts. Making sure that all of them joined over the top of each post, he secured them by bolting the flat timbers to the posts with metal plates and lag screws. This formed three rows of supports. On this he then took sheets of ply board and secured them with ring shanks. This platform would keep varmints out of the bottom of his insulation. Next the tresses were set into place, each one nailed tightly with joist hangers and squared using the age-old method of Pythagoras, which postulated that the square of the two sides of a right angle equaled the square of the hypotenuse. This was the most time-consuming and in the hot, afternoon sun everyone was sweating freely. After crowning and nailing the last one in place, Carrigan used the straightest ones he had saved to nail the sill joists on to the upturned edges of his floor joists. The big rolls of insulation were kicked into the sixteen-inch openings between each joist. Even with clothes tightly buttoned and their sleeves rolled down, the fiberglass managed to work its way into every corner of their necks and arms.

As the last roll fell into place, Carrigan stripped off his shirt and raced to the creek, shouting behind him that the last one in was a rotten egg.

Stephen followed close behind him as both of them kneeled in the pool of water where the two creeks joined, gasping from the cold as they splashed each other, washing away the tiny threads of insulation.

Nancy, unable to resist, soon joined them, stripping off her denim shirt before scooping huge handfuls of water at the guys. Carrigan was struck motionless just after dousing her with a large wave, watching as her firm breasts outlined the wet tee shirt that now clung to her skin, molding itself to her lean flanks. Seeing the effect she had on him only caused her to laugh and she turned her attention to defend the attack from Stephen. Soon realizing she was overmatched, Nancy clambered from the stream. Turning her back to them, Nancy stripped the wet shirt off over her head before wringing out the water and squeezing back into it. Carrigan couldn't help watching the long muscles of her tanned back ripple before he, too, climbed from the stream.

Stephen, the winner of the water wars, followed last, his teeth chattering from the cold. Nancy hustled him to the pickup where she pulled fresh clothes for them both from her bags. Carrigan grabbed a different shirt from behind the seat, careful not to look on the other side of the pickup as they changed. His pants would soon air dry as he finished the last bit of work on the foundation.

Unrolling the plastic, he drew it over the exposed insulation, stapling the edges down securely around the sill frame, then he piled the remaining lumber on top of the plastic to prevent the wind from whipping it loose. Once the sheeting was laid on the floor he would be ready to stand walls, maybe even tomorrow if he could get into the lumberyard on Sunday to pick up the 2x4s. Carrigan was amazed at the progress they'd accomplished. The extra pairs of hands, even untrained ones, really made the project go much faster.

"And now little man," he said addressing Stephen, "let's burn some rounds through that rifle you've been wanting to shoot, if it's ok with your mom."

Unable to resist both of them, she relented and watched as Carrigan set out a plastic water jug against the edge of the hills to the west. Arranging a sleeping bag on the ground near the corner of the cabin to rest the heavy rifle on, Carrigan explained to Stephen about the bolt action and the scope. He found an old blanket to guard against the recoil and carefully watched to make sure Stephen didn't get his eye too close to the scope which could cut him when he fired the rifle. Carrigan selected some loads with lighter bullets and reduced powder charges he used for small game. These he loaded into the magazine. Talking Stephen through the trigger pull, the 270 erupted, kicking dirt up on the hill a foot above the water jug. Carrigan explained the rifle was sighted high and jacked another round in the chamber telling to Stephen to hold the crosshairs of the sight near the bottom of the jug. This time the jug exploded as the bullet tore through it, sending both the jug and the water high into the air.

"I hit it, Mom, I hit it," Stephen shouted to his mother. "Did you see? I hit it!"

"Yes, dear, I see," she shouted back, keeping her hands over her ears. The gun was really quite loud and big for such a little boy to shoot. Twenty rounds later the box was empty, and Stephen smoked every white rock on the opposing hillside. Carrigan left the bolt open as he put the rifle back in the rack.

"Man, that was great!" Stephen said, "Could we do that again sometime?"

"Whenever you want, but maybe we better find a little smaller rifle for you. Don't you have a .22 or a .223?" Carrigan asked.

"No, my dad won't let me; he says that all we need are laws, not guns."

"Well, out here, sometimes we need guns because not everybody reads the laws," Carrigan answered.

Gathering the rest of his tools, they packed up Gertrude and with a final look at a long day's work, they headed back for town. The sun fell, turning the hills a deep purple before they wound their way down across the school section. By the time they reached Nancy's SUV, Stephen was asleep, his head laying in Carrigan's lap and his feet stretched out over Nancy.

"Thanks for all your help, and for bringing lunch today," Carrigan said as he helped her carry Stephen to the vehicle. "I couldn't have gotten it all done without you."

Turning to face him, she stood on her tiptoes and kissed him, long and hard on the mouth. Catching him off guard, she withdrew before he could react.

"Thank you," she said, "for helping me to remember what an honest day's work felt like, and thank you for not judging Stephen by what I did many years ago. Today helped me put some things together in my life, and I'm beginning to remember what being with you is like. We're going up to the ranch in Cody tomorrow, but I'll call you when we get back, if that's ok?"

"Yeah, fine," Carrigan managed to answer, still a little shell-shocked.

"Trying to understand women, is just like tearing out a beaver dam," he said to Gertrude on the way back to town. "Just when you think you're making progress, you find a whole 'nother layer. It's a never-ending project." Gertrude perhaps agreed, but didn't say so, as her headlights followed the long curves of the road home.

That night Carrigan cleaned the 270, finished the wood with light oil and polished all fingerprints from the action. Realizing he was low on ammunition, he went down to the basement to load several boxes. Just as he completed sizing the cases the phone rang. Giving brief thought to ignoring it in case it was Sheila, he got up and padded over to it, speaking a brusque 'hello' in answer to its interruption.

"Mr. Carrigan, this is Roberta Lansing, Becky's mom."

"Hi, Roberta, what can I do for you?" he answered, glad that it wasn't Sheila.

"Well, it's about that project Becky is doing. She charged some stuff at the store, and I wasn't sure what it was for."

"What kind of stuff?"

"Oh, I don't know, a thermometer, deck wash and some weed killer, nothing special. I thought I better check with you because she got in trouble with her father last weekend when some girls came over, and I didn't want to ask him and get her in worse trouble. Does she know what to do with this stuff?"

"Well, I don't know; she showed the first part of her presentation last week and she and Tommy are supposed to make a model volcano to present what happened up around Jackson years ago, but I don't think she needs a thermometer for that. I tell you what, I'll check with her first thing Monday morning, and then call you back. Is that OK?"

"Fine, I just didn't want her to get into any more trouble with her father, especially if she was doing something for school. Thanks so much. I'm sorry to have bothered you."

"No problem," Carrigan replied, "it's all part of the job."

"Oh and one more thing, what's this prize that Becky keeps talking about winning?"

Carrigan thought a minute and then remembered the scavenger hunt game he played with the map locations. "I just gave prizes to the kids if they could find locations on a map. I didn't know it was that important to her; I'll make sure she gets one when we have class again."

The conversation ended, Carrigan returned to the reloading bench; "What in the world would Becky need a thermometer for?" he said to himself.

After all the cases were resized, he primed them with large, rifle primers and then ran them through the automatic powder measure before seating the bullets. He kept the loads light in case Stephen shot the gun again, double-checking after he was finished to make sure none of the primers were in backwards. Over the years he reloaded thousands of shells, but it always paid to be careful. Any time a person used gunpowder and explosives like primers, safety demanded checking everything carefully.

Saturday Tommy was finishing his project also. The previous week he finally gained most of the parts he needed. Now that he was this close he slowed down, carefully planning each step before going on. No one would stop him now. Seeing Becky with a girl finally pushed all feeling down deep inside him, deep enough that it could never escape again. Up until that point he drew most of his pleasure from planning. The planning was over. The volcano would fit perfectly into his preparation.

On Monday, he skipped all of his classes except shop. Taking the exact measurements of the gas canister hidden in his house, Tommy cut out a hole the exact circumference of the cylinder into the base of his project. Having practiced the pie cut necessary to shape the metal, Tommy took a fresh sheet and fashioned another cone fastening the edges with pop rivets. This he fitted over the top of his original project, checking to make sure it slid on smoothly. He got the measurement right the first time and the two cones stacked neatly together, one on top of the other. Using a can of stove-black paint, both cones were painted and allowed to dry before being meshed together again so they wouldn't stick. The top of his new project was just the right size to hold the little paper cup that the cafeteria ladies dispensed ketchup in on the days they served French fries. Into this cup, Tommy put a small amount of baking soda liberated from the home economics classroom. He practiced several times, adding lemon juice into the cup of baking soda. The resulting chemical reaction would cause the baking soda to expand, spilling out of the top of the volcano. With the addition of food coloring it would resemble lava flows. Together with the shop teacher, they even gave it several practice runs to make sure the simulation would work.

Becky was not in school on Monday. By now Tommy was used to the unexpected from Becky and he called her after school let out. Mrs. Lansing answered the phone, and after a bit of flustering, she put Becky on the phone.

"Did you get the stuff we need?" he asked. All preliminaries were now gone. He felt the need to finish this. This project was becoming part of him, not just something he was doing.

"Not yet I still need a few more things, Daddy is really, really mad at me. Some of the girls were smoking at my pajama party this weekend and he found out. He says I have to stay home until I can be good."

"If you win the prize, then Daddy won't be so mad anymore," said Tommy, his original harshness smoothing now, his voice becoming simpler, more factual.

"Maybe, but he was pretty mad."

"He might stay mad if you don't win, and then he wouldn't let you play with your friends for a long time. Do you still have the list of what we need?"

"Yes, I still have it. I'll ask Mommy if I can go to the store and get the rest. I've been real good today."

"When you get what we need, put it out back of your house on the stone fence, and I'll pick it up tonight."

"Ok, Tommy. Thank you for helping me so Daddy isn't mad anymore."

"You're welcome, Becky. Put the sack on the back fence tonight and I will see you in school tomorrow. Remember if you tell anyone, they might steal our idea and we won't win."

This time Tommy hung up the phone first. If she didn't come across this time, he would have to hurt her. It was important that she was the one that bought what they needed. No one would ever be able to trace it back to him. If she said anything to anyone, Tommy would deny asking her to buy the materials. Becky was easily confused.

After dark Tommy walked up the fairway from a different direction than his last approach. He didn't want anyone to see him near the construction site. The workers probably found the broken door today, the broken door and the missing cylinder that was right next to Becky's house--the same Becky that got the supplies from her dad's store. Sitting on the stone fence were two sacks (one much smaller than the other) and one bag of simple lawn fertilizer (the same brand that kept the backyard of Becky's house as luxuriant and green as the golf course that it bordered). Retracing his steps back down the fairway Tommy carefully carried his dreams; the prize was within his reach.

That night Tommy couldn't sleep, checking and rechecking his papers, making sure everything was right. On Tuesday Tommy again went to school, this time for only one afternoon class. In basic science Tommy sat through the dull movie watching from beneath his lowered eyes until he located everything he would need from the classroom. The set of cabinets against the far wall held the glass syringes, test tubes with rubber stoppers and beakers were scattered across the lab tables waiting their transference into his backpack. He looked at the Bunsen burner, but knew that his kitchen stove would work as well. He must be careful to not take more than he needed. The class bell rang and as the teacher left for bus duty,

Greg A. Garton

so did Tommy and his backpack, one step closer to the completion of his plan.

That night, enjoying the feel of the latex gloves, Tommy set the drug store sacks on the kitchen table. Following the directions from the library computer, he poured a small amount of the Karb-Klean mixed in equal parts with tap water that he boiled first on the kitchen stove, pouring them into a test tube. Slowly letting them swirl together, the H2O mixed with the calcium nitrate, which possessed water solulibility properties. Grabbing the cleanest kitchen towel he could find, he secured it to the top of another beaker with a thick rubber band. The once-white towel discolored even further as he poured the harsh chemical onto the towel, watching as it slowly dripped through the towel filter, pooling into the beaker below. He then removed the towel and attached it to a clean beaker from his backpack. Choosing a shot glass from his father's collection above the refrigerator he found the lettering on the glass funny and giggled as he measured out an ounce of the deck cleaner into the glass. He looked again at the miniature bucking horse surrounded by the words, *Wyoming a Great Place to Live* printed in gold lettering on the shot glass.

His dad might get a real surprise if he drank out of this one, he thought to himself.

Although he was still giggling, his lips didn't move. The strange choking sound echoed quietly in the little kitchen. Tommy laughed less often as he grew older especially after his father told him he sounded like a jackass when he did. Since that day, he made himself practice laughing without moving his mouth. It was a lot easier to practice when he could think about hurting something.

Taking the shot glass, he poured it through the stained towel, watching as it turned the towel instantly white as if by magic. The oxalic acid mixed with the residue of water and calcium carbonate on the towel before dripping slowly through the towel to the bottom of the beaker. This new mixture, nitric acid, tried burning through the glass that imprisoned it there, but unable to eat the glass with its corrosive nature, it finally settled, slowly foaming in its glass prison.

Tommy removed the towel, and being careful not to breathe the fumes, set the small amount of liquid on the kitchen window sill beside a plastic rose dusted with age, perhaps a remnant from his mother's presence many years ago.

Patience he told himself; within several days the water would evaporate from the beaker leaving a clear, white powder.

266

During the day on Wednesday, Tommy rested, visualizing the next step in his project. That evening he used a large kitchen pan to mix the liquid stove fuel with the lawn fertilizer, stirring the ammonium nitrate with his hands until the mixture was a soft clay. After inserting the gas cylinder into the volcanoes he brought home from the school shop, he rolled the dough out into a snakelike rope and then with torn strips from black garbage bags, he wrapped the satchel to prevent it from drying out and fed his venomous serpent into the mouth of the small volcano.

That night he stood on the trash can outside the school doors and carefully unscrewed the bottom of the twin emergency lights removing the 12-volt dry cell battery from within inside its protective metal box. It was important to him that the school donated their fair share of the material he needed for his project. After removing the battery, he replaced the screws and set the trash can back into place picking up several candy wrappers and throwing them into the can.

"Take Pride in Lakota High," he said, repeating the school slogan.

Thursday he was punctual in his attendance of school again, this time arriving early for the hot lunch program. He seldom missed lunch and was usually able to garner enough extra food in the loose pockets of his baggy jeans to eat a full supper also. He forged his father's signature on the application form for free and reduced lunch when he was a freshman. After the first year, no one asked him for a lunch card anymore. Today he even failed to respond to the sarcastic remarks from the jocks, taunting him from across the lunchroom as he sat in his corner table.

"Soon," he said to himself, "soon I'll wipe those smiles right off your fag faces."

Waiting until the last students left, he took up his empty tray and complimented the cooks on their lunch today. So impressed were they that the tired ladies gladly gave him a partially filled sack of powdered sugar he said he needed to take to the Spanish teacher for her cooking project.

He returned home after school to continue his project. Tommy boiled the thermometer in water on the kitchen stove and then removed it placing the heated glass in a cereal bowl. Holding an ice cube on the glass it sharply cracked in a loud pop. Tilting the thermometer, he poured the liquid metal into the bowl watching it gather in small balls. Here a little sweat began to bead on his forehead. He was watching very closely in science when the teacher gave demonstration of mixing acids with water and other reactive agents. The resulting flash and bang could be very impressive, but he didn't want anything to go wrong now. Taking the beaker from the windowsill he turned his head as he poured the mercury into the beaker of white nitric acid crystals. He watched the beaker, fascinated as the mercury absorbed into the powder changing it into small gray-white diamonds that reflected the dull kitchen light shining down on them. If the information was correct, these cubic crystals were now changed to Hg(ONC)2, or fulminate of mercury. There wasn't much there, barely covering the bottom of the beaker, but it was enough, he decided.

He gave up trying to find a measuring spoon in the drawers of the kitchen and taking the spoon from the sink he dried it before measuring several spoonfuls of powdered sugar in another kitchen bowl. Turning his head again, he poured one capful of Dandelion Dead, into the small bowl. The sugar immediately turned a light purple color reacting to the liquid by foaming and hissing as the sugar began to dissolve. If a little were good, a touch more would be better, he thought as he added one more capful of weed killer. In very small letters on the label were the words, 'Caution potassium chlorate, reactive oxidizer.'

By this time his hands were beginning to shake so he left the kitchen, not trusting his trembling fingers to do anything else tonight.

As he lay in bed that night he went over everything again in his head. Next week he would carry his hopes and dreams to the school and put them in Becky's locker. Everyone in class knew he was building a volcano and he packed it around the school for several days while building it until no one else was curious. If that sneaky bastard, Evans the resource officer, had a metal detector going at any of the doors, they would let him through when the metal volcano set of the buzzer. If Evans reviewed any tapes from the hallway cameras and saw Tommy carrying the metal cone in the hallway, he wouldn't think twice about it. This was a school project, after all. The outer shell of the volcano would slip right off the top once he set it in the locker and he could take the top one to Mr. C's room for the class presentation, knowing the baking soda and lemon juice would perform their assigned roles.

Meanwhile his real project would be safely in the school, setting in Becky's locker. This was a locker she shared with that queer, bitch Berti Eliza. Everyday after the last bell rang, all those fag jocks came laughing and joking to their lockers on both sides of this one. School was out at 3:35 by 3:45 they would be there gathered in a herd, ripe for slaughter. Three years of insults would be wiped out in a flash. It was a shame about Becky, but she deserved it, hanging out with those lesbos. The only thing left would be a few pieces of twisted metal, blown deep into the flesh of those he hated. They could never trace that back to him. The sheet metal he used was common and could be purchased anywhere, besides the volcano he built would be in Mr. C's room spouting its baking soda so Becky could win her prize. Becky would win the prize, he was sure. He personally would be the one to give it to her.

Friday he was calm again. Beside his bed was a small alarm clock. It was given to him many years ago when he was little and his parents were together. He could still remember the Christmas morning when he played with it. A Disney theme surrounded the little timepiece that had two small bells on top. When the alarm went off, Mickey and Goofy, hanging from a pole in the middle, would rapidly vibrate against the bells, taking turns clanging the alarm. At one time he loved the clock, time and time again setting the alarm and then waiting for it to go off jangling the bells. He would set the alarm one more time.

That afternoon he carefully shook the crystals from the beaker into the purple powdered sugar. Holding his breath he took a feather from an old duster in the closet and gently swished the two components together. He began to get dizzy and then he remembered to breathe again. He was almost ready. Gently scooping the mixture into a glass syringe, he pressed the plunger, expelling all the air from the tube. Next he took a piece of speaker wire and stripped the insulation from the end before inserting it through the needle end of the syringe till it touched the mixture. He repeated the process from the other end, throwing away the plunger and filling the remaining end with candle wax to hold the wire. Between the two wires, inside the glass tube, his blasting cap was completed. Tommy walked to his bedroom to get a pillow. After laying the finished project on the pillow he ran to the bathroom to piss. He never in his life had to urinate as bad as he had too right then. Saturday night he would tape the primer to his play dough, right next to the valve on the cylinder.

When the volcano was in the locker on Monday, he would attach one loose wire to a bell of the little clock, and the other loose wire to one terminal of the dry cell. The last piece of wire could be attached to the other post of the battery and then securely wound around Mickey and Goofy. When the tail was pulled down on Pluto, the alarm would be set. At 3:45 Mickey and Goofy would take a ride ringing the bell and completing the circuit. The sensitive primer wouldn't like the jolt of electricity and would show its displeasure violently, very violently.

Sunday morning Carrigan called the owner of the lumberyard begging him to come down so he could load some flooring and 2x4s.

"Carrigan, you're way too ambitious for your own good. Why don't you go back to bed and let the rest of us sleep, too?" complained the owner.

"Never put off what you can beg somebody to do today," paraphrased Carrigan.

"Oh, all right, I'll be down there in an hour," agreed the owner finally.

He hadn't forgotten that Carrigan helped his son graduate high school two years ago when everyone else gave up on the boy. The boy was now in the army somewhere in the Middle East, and doing great. Carrigan thought little of his efforts on the boy's behalf, but the lumberman and his wife were forever grateful.

Carrigan and Gertrude arrived early at the gates of the lumberyard and sat there listening to church hymns on the radio. A patrol car drove by, then stopped and backed up. Carrigan rolled down the window and recognized Sgt. William Evans of the Rockville Police Department. Evans pulled two shifts a week as the school resource officer and often traded war stories with Carrigan about the frustrations of being a police officer.

"You breaking in or out?" asked Evans, smiling.

"Haven't made up might mind yet. What are you up to this morning other than bothering me, interrupting my church music?"

"Not much. The boss is making us check everything out this week. Last weekend somebody broke into a trailer by that new house on the golf course, and now he wants us to stop everybody and find out what they're doing."

"Well, I'm just waiting to get some flooring. What did they take? I'll keep my ears open around the school for you."

"Just some welding gas, I guess. Idiots, they left the valuable canisters and took a little one, kids probably."

"Yeah I reckon; sometimes they just do shit to do it. I'll ask around and let you know."

"Thanks," Evans replied and drove off searching for other people out of place on a Sunday morning."

The owner soon arrived and Carrigan loaded the lumber, grabbed another cup of coffee and some Twinkies from the quick stop, and turned once again to the hills. Arriving at the cabin site he went to work fitting the flooring, making sure the ship lapping fitted on the joists in an alternating fashion, tying the whole unit together. He used ring shanks again to secure the flooring before cutting off the overhanging pieces from the outside with a battery operated circular saw. By noon the flooring was in place and he gathered the 2x4s on the flat floor of the foundation to begin framing the walls before standing them in place. While trying to decide where he wanted the windows and doors, he sat down with his back against the foundation to eat his peanut butter sandwich, washing it down with cold water from the creeks.

Something kept nagging him in the back of his mind. Mrs. Lansing's phone call made less sense the more he thought about it. He tried to make sense of the thermometer, deck wash, and weed killer, trying to see how Becky could fit them into her presentation. She couldn't use the thermometer for the volcano unless she just wanted to show how molten metal rose up a tube in the mountain. Maybe that was it. Deck wash contained acid or some other caustic substance in it and though lava possessed high concentrations of acid in its flow, he didn't want her messing around with those kinds of chemicals in his classroom. Weed killer was just plain poison, and made no sense whatsoever. What bothered him the most was Becky wasn't smart enough to mix any of that stuff together. He doubted if the brightest chemistry student could without blowing himself to bits.

Where was Tommy in all this? Becky said he would be in this week to finish their presentation. If Tommy did a good job Carrigan might even pass them both. That would be Tommy's only passing grade of his high school career. Try as he might, Tommy wasn't going to be one of those he saved, even if he gave him a passing grade. Something just wouldn't let Tommy change. Parents, peers, or just plain life--one or all of them permanently closed Tommy's window to the world. It was too bad, because although Tommy never did anything in school, intelligence wasn't the problem. Deep down Carrigan knew he was probably one of the brightest kids in school.

Carrigan started framing the walls, putting headers in where he wanted the openings. He would nail the top plates together after the walls were stood. The long walls he broke in half, joining them with the top plate after they were up so they wouldn't be so heavy to lift. Gauging his progress by the falling sun, he wiggled the last wall into place an hour before dark. Perhaps he should have cut the boards a quarter inch shorter, but square was square and it was a matter of personal pride in his building projects and his life. By the square and on the level, he tried to meet all men and perform all deeds. Grabbing a larger hammer from his toolbox, he pounded one side and then the other until at last the wall slipped into place, meeting flush with its neighbors. Permanently joining this wall to the others by nailing through the corners the entire length of the wall and then nailing down the overlapping top plates, he finished his job. Using the shorter scrap pieces and left over plates, he braced the wall from the inside by running the braces from the top of the wall down at an angle to the floor. This would prevent the wall from moving until he could set the rafters blending the walls into a complete whole. He again sheeted the floor with plastic to prevent rain from warping his flooring and ruining the insulation below. He was out of daylight and out of money. If he put in a rafter order this week they should arrive about the time of his year-end paycheck. Help would be needed to set the rafters but he would cross that bridge when he came to it.

Thinking about help made him realize that although the building went well today, he was lonely. Yesterday the cabin was fun; today it was work. The little glade didn't echo with Stephen's laughter, or reflect Nancy's beauty. Both enhanced his new home, and without them the studded walls looked bare and plain.

"Get used to it," he told himself, "you have a record of spending at lot of time alone, and it doesn't look like it's set to change anytime soon. All work and no play makes Carrigan a dull boy," he repeated aloud to himself. "Next time I come up I need to do something a little more fun, maybe I will go exploring for Otto's old still up Cherry Creek and maybe I'll just bring a book and fishing pole. I can fish all morning, and read all afternoon."

Carrigan was able to joke himself back into a good mood, refusing to allow any feelings of regret to creep in. Faithful as always, the old Ford backtracked down the mountain. Just before dropping off the ridge onto a steep switchback he paused to view the twilight flooding the plains stretching far to the east. On a clear day he could see almost to Scottsbluff in Nebraska, over a hundred miles away. To the northeast he thought he could just glimpse the bluish tint of the large lake damming the mighty Platte before she overcame this barrier to join with her sisters and continue flowing to the Mississippi. Evening cast the creeks and drainages in a mantled amethyst, dark and rich below him as they curved and twisted vainly trying to avoid meeting the Laramie River.

They weren't anymore successful than he was, he thought; she owned them all.

Carrigan could no more move from this country, away from his rivers and mountains, than they could move from him. Together they were part of each other, rooted for life, and realizing this, he felt more at peace than he had for some time. School was almost done, the cabin was started, and Nancy kissed him. He wondered if God would think her kiss as a sin, even if he didn't kiss her back. Somehow he didn't think so, just as he knew although his mother and father didn't attend church every Sunday, they surely were in God's heaven. Carrigan firmly believed God had his own way of sorting people, and high on His list were how a person treated his fellow man, and if they lived their lives trying to give instead of take. Somehow Carrigan knew God didn't care much for takers.

Back in town at last, Carrigan stripped clothes from his body on the way to the shower. He checked for ticks, finding two, before stepping into the hot water. They hadn't attached themselves yet and he dropped them into the fireplace, striking a match and burning them black.

"Damn bloodsuckers," he said out loud. "You may have a purpose, but I sure don't know what it is, and I ain't going to let you feed on me."

As the hot match burned the life from the hard-shelled vampires, something tugged again in his memory, like a flash. Try as he might he could make no further sense of it and he returned to the shower letting the hot water wash the day's work from his tired muscles. Wrapping a soft towel around his waist, he invaded the kitchen, throwing a steak from the freezer into a hot frying pan. Then covering the steak with onions and potatoes, he dumped in more grease than was good for him.

He then poured himself a large shot of scotch over two lonely ice cubes and descended to the basement into a dark closet in the back room and moved bottles around on the shelves till he found what he was looking for, a half empty can of deck cleaner. The lid was rusted and corroded, but he blew off the dust to read the label on the back of the can. *Active Ingredient Oxalic Acid* jumped out at him from the dirtied label. He scanned further reading the warnings about dangerous fumes and how it was an irritant to skin, but nothing else made any sense to him. Well, he always needed a question to ask James every Monday morning, what the hell was oxalic acid? He realized that he was going to miss Mr. James next year and maybe some more people, including various principals and young teachers.

At least Chuck and Jenny would be there next year now that they found each other. Suddenly he shivered as, unbidden, the thought of them being passionate with each other flashed through his mind--Chuck, still in his tennis shoes, and Jenny, her print dress cast aside, straddling him, the big saddle purse banging against her scrawny behind as they made love. "My God, you're one sick son-of-a-bitch," he said to himself.

He quickly put the can back on the shelf and closed the door. Upstairs he needed to turn the steak and stir the spuds or he would have to go to bed hungry. By the time he finished the scotch, steak, and potatoes, he felt much better. Carrigan considered getting back up to do some research in his library on whether oxalic acid could be used for model volcanoes but he gave up the thought. Sitting here he was just too comfortable.

His head just started to nod when the phone rang again. Picking up the receiver, he spoke a sleepy 'hello' to the caller. After a slight pause on the other end, the voice answered, "Hi, Cowboy. Did you get your house built?"

Chapter 12
The Final Battle

Summer appeared without warning, flooding the glade with green and purple as the lupine and bluebells burst into full bloom. Escaping from Night Wind's chores, La Ramie and Joshua walked the trails through the surrounding mountains near the cabin, planning the route of the trap line they would run next fall. They decided on two loops of five miles each. These would be walked daily after the traps were set to check for animals snared in the steel jaws. In case one of the men was detained at the cabin, skinning and fleshing, the other one could check the loops on alternate days. They found locations to set twenty traps on each loop, and as they traveled the streams and creeks branching from the river, they would often stop to watch the beavers working, fixing the dams and dragging fresh food to the earthen lodges protected by the still ponds.

The two men usually took Spotted Owl with them on the trails, helping him learn from the wilderness around him. Joshua gained even more respect for La Ramie's knowledge as he watched the trapper existing in his natural element. La Ramie pointed out many of the plants that were useful for medicine and which ones were poisonous. Rattlesnakes were daily occurrences, but following La Ramie's lead, Joshua stepped around them, leaving them to buzz in peace, their tongues forking the air to detect the men's presence.

"If I tried to kill everything I didn't understand in this world," La Ramie observed, "there wouldn't be much left that was interestin' to look upon."

Sometimes the men would laugh as Spotted Owl tried to capture the large Rainbow trout in the shallow backwaters of the ponds made by the beavers. The trout swam upstream from the river into the tributaries breeding there in the small creeks. When they attempted to return to the river, the fish found the way dammed by the beavers keeping them imprisoned in the high streams.

"Sometimes these ponds need thinned out," soliloquized La Ramie, "causin' them big fish eat all the little ones. Nature just lets them go, after them Rainbow eats all the Brookies, they just starve to death. Kinda seems like a waste. I like watchin' them Brookies a jumping for flies in the evenin' so I'se just kinda give them a hand and pull out them big Rainbows. All things need thinned out once in a while even people. That gives the young'uns a chance to grow and learn on their own."

Spotted Owl was in pursuit of a Rainbow as the men spoke, and sprays of water shot out behind him as his small legs churned through the muddy creek. In front of Spotted Owl, a ripple ducked and dived trying to avoid the windmill behind it. One minute Spotted Owl was at full speed, and the next he disappeared from sight as his chase led him into a hole of deep water. Bobbing up to the surface, Spotted Owl sputtered and spewed until Joshua waded in pulling him from the pond.

"Sonny Bitchin' fish," Spotted Owl, stated matter of factly.

"Whoa fish catcher," La Ramie laughed, "don't you go using my words no more. Night Wind will have my hide for sure. Next time you kain't ketch one say, 'Sonny Gun,' don't pay no attention to the words I use."

"Sonny Gun fish," Spotted Owl repeated, doing his best to copy the trapper. "I didn't wanta catch the 'God Damned' thing anyway."

Laughing so hard he could barely stand up, Joshua said, "Maybe we need to change some of our more descriptive vernacular, or both of us might not live to see beaver season."

The full strength of the summer reached the high plains radiating down along the canyon walls pooling the heat in the glade. At this elevation, the sun's ray burned the earth below during the hours of light. When darkness arrived replacing its brother, the air became chilly and cool. Late at night, their strength spent, Night Wind and Joshua would lie under the stripped Hudson blanket talking of the short time remaining before she must leave to travel to the council.

"Night Wind, I'm not very good a turning things loose," said Joshua looking out the small window of their sanctuary at the full moon hanging above the canyon rim.

"You're not very good at catching them either," she smiled. "It takes you a while to figure out what you have on the line."

"That's because they don't bite hard enough," he countered, "sometimes they just play with you," Joshua ended becoming quiet.

"Joshua, you could never turn me loose," she said at last, realizing he was serious.

"How can you turn loose of something that is part of you? When we first shared our bodies, I became a part of you, as you are unto me, together we became one. Whether I am by your side matters little, for that is only temporary. Should either of us leave, our spirit always remains. My body and spirit are yours forever, once coupled no force in the heavens or earth can rend them asunder. Now come here and I will bite harder, we'll see if you can handle what you have caught."

As Night Wind pulled him close, she wondered whether to tell him of the missed menses for the last moon, or of the sickness that made her head swim each morning. Not yet, she decided, for he would worry all the more. Within her their child grew. That this child was to be born and become a great leader of his people she had no doubt. Her visions had shown her the future.

With the second full moon waning sliver-by-sliver Night Wind and Spotted Owl readied for their journey. Night Wind's leg was now healed and although a slight limp spoke of the injury, she felt no pain. Joshua killed a large stag elk in the high timber above the cabin a week before she was to leave. Enormous in size, the bull had a deformed antler that rose straight above his head in a large spike, never branching, as did the antler on the other side. Perhaps from a fight, or an attack from a wild animal, the stag was castrated, the lack of testicles causing his size and deformed antler. When Night Wind saw what Joshua brought back, she was delighted, claiming the stag to be the best meat of any animal. That night as they sat upon the porch of the small cabin, the glade was immersed in moonlight, and fireflies danced their magic across the grass. Touching the couples' skin like velvet, the air had not yet caught the chill of the night. Holding the long spike of the elk antler, Night Wind bowed her head and whispered the Shoshone Prayer for the animal's loss of life.

"Oh great Elk, I give you thanks for your body, and your meat that will nourish our souls, may the Great Spirit receive you into his home with the honor that you deserve."

The quizzical look on Joshua's face caused her to explain the prayer. "With death comes life for others," Night Wind said. "The Shoshone way calls for thanks to be given. The elk must die to bring us food, but should we forget to be thankful for his sacrifice, Manitou will take his animals from us, and without them we would starve. Kills-Crowe told me when I was little, of a story from long ago when the Shoshone and The Comanche were one people with one home."

Five warriors left their village to hunt for game enough to feed their families for the winter. Across the Great Plains they traveled until they found a rabbit drinking by a waterhole. With arrows they slew the rabbit and then taking only the tender parts of the animal, they discarded the rest, claiming that the animal was not large enough to feed the tribe. The next day they traveled further and came across a deer eating the lush grass of a meadow. This animal they killed also, cutting from the carcass only the loins to roast on their campfire that night. The rest of the animal they left to rot, for it was not large enough to feed all their tribe either. Climbing high into the mountains they came upon the lair of the Great Bear. With weapons drawn they crept into the cave hoping to find the Great Bear sleeping, but he was not. The spirit of the rabbit and the deer had already flown to him, telling him of the hunter's waste, and the absence of thanksgiving for the sacrifice of their bodies. Please avenge us Great One, for there are five in their band, and we cannot take revenge upon them ourselves. With this knowledge the Great Bear laid in wait until the hunters were deep in the cave, and then he rushed out among them slashing them with fang and claw. The warriors were brave, and many arrows they shot into the Great Bear's body, but still he would not die, killing one warrior after another, until all the men were dead save one.

"Please spare me, Great Bear," the warrior cried. I was only trying to feed my family.

We all must eat or perish the Bear replied, but to waste any part of a creature you slay, or to fail to thank the animal for the ultimate sacrifice is against the law of the Great Spirit. For this you must die, and your family will starve.

I will return and thank the deer and the rabbit making sure that they are not wasted, pleaded the warrior. In the council fires at night I will sing of this law, so all men know of Manitou's command.

Pity then overcame the heart of the bear, and he let the warrior go. Soon the Great Bear grew weak from his many wounds and crawling to the back of his cave, he suffered for long days, the arrow wounds festering his soul before he died. The spirit of the Great Bear became vengeful that no one thanked him for the painful sacrifice of his life to avenge the deer and the rabbit, and he regretted helping them and freeing the man instead of killing him. To this day the ghost bear walks upon the face of the earth, his heart filled with malice toward all other living things because he died alone without thanks and praise.

"Oh great Elk, I give you thanks for your body, and your meat that will nourish our souls, may the Great Spirit receive you into his home with the honor that you deserve," answered Joshua, quietly looking across the glade bathed in the moonlight.

During the next few days, Night Wind carved upon the elk antler, making intricate designs the length of the horn, until a last she was satisfied, presenting the horn to Joshua.

"With the permission of the spirit of the elk, I have carved the story of our love here upon his horn telling Manitou of our bond," said Night Wind shyly. "Keep this with you, and I will always be beside you, my love protecting you from danger."

By noon the next day seven Shoshone warriors crested the notch above the cabin. La Ramie brought news of their approach as he witnessed their progress earlier from the tall cliffs beside the river. Among them was Little Eagle, war chief of the Shoshone.

"Even if the snows close all passes between us, it is here to you I shall return," said Night Wind, proudly displaying her love for the trader in front of her tribal leaders, so all would know the he was her chosen. "Let it be sung that Night Wind, Vision Woman of the Shoshone and Joshua, Larapihu Trader share the same lodge and from now one are one."

Spotted Owl tried to be brave, fighting back tears, in front of Little Eagle, until Joshua swept him from his feet, hugging the boy tightly, whispering quietly into Spotted Owl's ear, "Come back little one. I will not go fishing until you return."

Joshua moped around the cabin for several days till at last La Ramie could stand no more love sickness and put him to work constructing the fur press they would need for the winter. Joshua used these in Missouri and needed little advice on the construction of the new press. Using a broad axe, he stripped the limbs from a large tree blown down by the winds of last winter. Squaring the ends with the crosscut, he used a maul and wedges to split the tree. The inside he finished with the adze. When they were completed, Joshua set both ends of the two halves in the ground, cross-bracing them to prevent separation. A simple roof above the logs was covered with shake shingles Joshua split with a froe and mallet. The last step was to bore holes into the sides of the logs through which wedges could be inserted. As the finished furs were added, wedges were driven in to compress the furs into tighter and tighter bundles. After sixty furs were compressed, they were bound with rawhide making them easier to pack on the sawbucks.

While Joshua worked on this, La Ramie began making fresh hoops from green willow to stretch and flesh the furs upon. Once skinned, the furs would be lashed to this frame with rawhide. After fleshing, the furs would be transferred to wooden stretcher frames until dried and placed into the press. Within several weeks, these projects were completed, and the night air began to speak of the winter to come.

In the valleys the aspen trees exchanged their full green leaves for garbs of red and orange. High in the mountain, La Ramie and Joshua heard the bugle of the elk as males entered the rut, fighting for domination in the herd. The winners would gain the right to spread their seed, insuring the cows were bred by the strongest and most fit. La Ramie and Joshua oiled each trap and carried them in bundles, stashing them under rocks near the locations they would work later when the cold mountain streams turned slushy with ice. Here Joshua's skill matched La Ramie, for traps were his business. Joshua inspected the main beams and trip plates making sure they worked smoothly before moving to the next location for a set. Joshua preferred the double sprung traps, but these were more expensive, and he mixed them with La Ramie's older single step traps. Using nets and spears, the men caught baskets of carp in the river. Near the head of pond they placed the carp in covered stone crocks letting them bake in the afternoon sun making sure they were well covered with liquid. Within a week, the rotting fish turned to mush under the fall sun, and the odor would overpower any but the most brave. This stinking concoction would serve as their castorium until enough beavers could be caught to make use of the natural substance from the glands of the beaver. The putrefying odor would erase all human scent from the traps and cause the beavers to believe an intruder entered their ponds.

The trappers would set the traps just under the water in the streams, attaching a lead chain on a slide with weights. Hanging a stick doused in their carp castorium or the real castor after the run started, just above the trap, the set was made. When the beaver came investigating, he would step in the trap causing the iron jaws to close around his limb. Trying to escape, the beaver swam for deep water, the chain sliding smoothly behind him until the end was reached. Here the weight would prevent the beaver from surfacing, causing him to drown. The chain could then be pulled in, and the beaver retrieved.

Fall retreated, and winter began her coy appearance. The water of the creeks froze each night and falling behind in their tasks both men set to chopping wood they would need for warmth this winter. Joshua's skill with an axe soon reduced all deadfall into firewood around the cabin, and they were forced to go higher into the mountains, dragging more woods from these rough slopes by ropes and horses. By mid November the trappers were caught up with the chores, and La Ramie and Joshua rode from the cabin eastward searching for a route that would be shorter next spring when they returned to the fork of the Platte with their load of pelts.

Climbing over a high ridge to the east of the cabin, La Ramie led Joshua down into the lower edge of a box canyon that neither could see a way into. Circling the steep rim, they continued on to the next canyon, the lower end of which was the furthest leg of their trapping loop. Skidding down the loose rocks of the hillside, they found themselves at the bottom of a narrow creek. The walls of the canyon were fractured and veined with tall columns of stone collapsing against each other looking as if an ancient temple once sat here. As they followed the canyon upward, La Ramie stopped to point toward the hillside. Here in the tall pillars of granite, Joshua could see the opening of a cave, leached from the hillside long ago by the action of water and wind. Dismounting, both men tied their horses and climbed the loose rocks to investigate. Joshua could feel a draft leaving the cave as he stooped to enter. The floor was sandy and dry and within several feet of the mouth, the cave expanded to a large room bigger than La Ramie's cabin.

"I think we have found it, Joshua," La Ramie drawled.

"We found something all right," said Joshua, "but just what is it we've found?"

"Well, unless you want the cabin full of smelly beaver hides all winter, this here cave might just be the perfect place to store them once we get em bundled. If this draw leads on up to the east side of Blue Peak, coming out this way next spring will save us fifty miles. We kin stash the hides here and pick em up on the way through. If we cover them pelts with rocks, ain't no varmints gonna bother em. Coursin' we could always put them hides in your new room back at the cabin, and you could bunk with me, 'cepting that don't leave much room for Night Wind when she gets back."

"Couldn't agree with you more," Joshua said after thinking a short while, "ain't no use filling up the cabin when we've found a perfectly good cave."

La Ramie grinned at Joshua's back as the men left the cave walking back down to their horses. Behind them the wind from the cave billowed briefly blowing a sheet of sand from the floor of the cave, revealing the bleached whiteness of the bones that lay within.

The two trappers found the trail back down the canyon of the cave and followed it until it merged with the other creek coming from the box canyon. Here another glade, more secluded than La Ramie's, opened up before them. Joshua was struck by the natural beauty of the setting and sat his horse, taking in the grandeur of the panorama.

"Sometimes God just outdoes himself," he said speaking to La Ramie. "I must bring Night Wind here when she returns. If a man can't find God here, then I reckon he can't find Him anywhere."

By following a long draw the riders continued down to the river, stopping only once to view a towering pine leaning over the hill above them. The draw was filled with brush, but game trails allowed easy access for the men as they rode on. Once down to the river, they were able to return upstream before climbing the steep hill back to La Ramie's cabin, this time from beneath the falls.

Winter, growing bored with waiting, finally descended upon the mountains bringing days of snow and strong winds before breaking cold and clear. The work was nonstop as the trappers walked the loops, daily retrieving the beaver and muskrats from the traps. On the days when large numbers fell victim to the steel jaws, Joshua stayed at the cabin, skinning and fleshing while La Ramie traveled the circles. The cold weather set the fur on the animals making it prime and rich. The pattern varied little for the next month, both men falling asleep late at night over their food, bone tired from the hard work.

In December, La Ramie returned to the cabin, cussing a blue streak. Joshua could hear him coming up the trail from the pond.

"Has cabin fever struck so soon," asked Joshua when the trapper arrived, "that you talk to yourself this way?"

"For five years, I have that hat," La Ramie answered, "five years that fox skin brought me luck and kept me warm, and now the bent willow plans an ambush. Just as I was leaning over to stake the chain, the sneaky willow attacks me, slapping me alongside my head and knocking my fox skin into the water, under the ice. I chased that cap for two miles, but it made its escape. Damn near froze my ears off walking back. I cut that willow in so many pieces not even muskrats can chew it now. Sunny Bitchin' willow."

Realizing the trapper was in no mood for humor, Joshua was forced to turn away, biting his cheeks to keep La Ramie from seeing his grin. Going to his bags, Joshua retrieved his spare hat, a tightly knit blue cap, of the type much loved by the French Voyeurs, of the North Country.

"Merry Christmas, my friend" Joshua said, throwing the hat to La Ramie. "Although not as stylish as yours, this will keep your ears from freezing at least."

Grinning at last La Ramie, ceased throwing his tantrum, and helped Joshua fix supper, thanking him for his gift of friendship.

During the next week, Joshua began to feel an aching in his body. His head throbbed and chills invaded his sleep. After a few days, instead of feeling better, his condition worsened and La Ramie grew concerned for the health of his friend. Perhaps it was an infection from the beavers, or simply flu, Joshua was not used to being sick. When epidemics swept through St. Genevieve, he seldom even caught a cold. The long hours spent outside strengthened his immune system. But not this time. Daily he worsened until at last he lacked the strength to rise from bed. La Ramie made Joshua sleep in La Ramie's bed, so he could watch him during the night. Brewing pitch, with strong tea and honey, the trapper forced the bitter liquid down Joshua's throat, and with medicine sage, and the lining of aspen bark, La Ramie made a salve to spread on Joshua's chest. For a week it was an equal battle, with the threat of pneumonia always waiting for a chance to fill the trader's lungs. High fevers clouded Joshua's thinking, and he fought with old enemies, cursing and crying in his dreams. Visions of the great river and home swept in upon him forcing him back to the shattered remains of his past life, empty without Rodde. Unbidden in his fevered dreams, nightmares from his past in Missouri flooded through his searing brain.

Twice more the thrusts collided deep beneath the earth in the next several months following the December 1811 quake and the residents of St. Genevieve trembled in fear each time, but these were not as severe, and no more structural damage occurred in St. Genevieve. Columns of rocks loosened by the earlier quake finished their journey to the river below during these aftershocks, and few people went near these high palisades of stone. Joshua was the exception.

Thrown from his bed on that fateful morning of the first quake in December, Joshua ran through the house in search of Rodde. The shaking continued for some time and he was unable to find her. Panic and fear clutched Joshua's chest as he remembered that on mornings when the baby prevented her from sleeping, Rodde sometimes took walks along the river dreaming of the future for their child. Crying her name over and over again, Joshua ran to the river. Half way down the trail to their fishing spot, he stopped. Before him in the trail was a red ribbon. Clutching it to his face, Joshua breathed deeply trying to extract her scent from the crimson strip of cloth. The same piece of ribbon Rodde wore in her hair last night as she held him in their bed. Below him, where their fishing rock once was, the Mississippi formed a huge whirlpool of current biting against the hard granite rock. Where once the path ran, now only the dark muddy water swirled. Gone was the wide lane between river and mountain. Above were the stark scars where huge pieces of the palisade had broken loose and fell to the ground beneath driving this piece of earth below the waters of the river. Without going further, he knew now where Rodde rested, never to return to him. The river, rocks, and earth had taken her from him. All feeling left him as Joshua fell to his knees cursing God and all things He made.

Unmoving, Joshua stayed there upon his knees throughout the day, all hopes and dreams stripped from his soul, he looked out upon the river of life. When darkness fell, Joshua returned to St. Genevieve; walking along the street, he helped where he could. The damage, although far less than other towns suffered further south, still was extensive, and many residents were missing, either buried in the waters of the river or covered by the ruins of collapsed buildings. Search parties were formed moving the wreckage one post and stone at a time. As bodies were removed, Joshua studied each one, hoping against hope Rodde might still be found, but in his soul he knew different. The village surgeon Dr. Fenwick, who came to this small community many years ago from Boston, was killed in a duel earlier in the year but Madame Francios Carpentier Valle II or Madame Commandant as the locals called her, worked endlessly treating the victims of the quake, seldom stopping until all the injured were attended. She could not treat Joshua's pain.

Three days Joshua went without sleep until Justine found him against the door of her house. She accompanied him to the village parish several days later to file notice of Rodde's death, recording Rodde's name in the records of the deceased. No funeral would Joshua tolerate, and he would not enter the church. Justine went in his place, to light candles for Rodde, offering prayers of salvation for her and the unborn child in Joshua's place.

Joshua would not return to his home, the remembrance of Rodde's presence was too painful to endure. The post could not hold his interest either, and Joshua barred the doors shutting out that part of his life. Nights were spent at Justine's rock home, after returning from endless hours walking in the backcountry. Reports came to her of travelers seeing Joshua sitting alone in the forests, unmoving as if in a trance. Sometimes he was gone for days, returning worn and dirty. She forced him to take nourishment, but Joshua spoke little and refused any conversations about Rodde or his previous life.

Both Ashley and Henry returned to St. Genevieve spending long hours just sitting with Joshua letting him know they too felt the loss.

Jacques Bolduc sent food and offers of help, but Joshua barely spoke to him preferring to wander the hills alone.

By February of 1812 some healing of his soul occurred. Joshua reopened the post but hired people to run it for him on Jacques' recommendation. Joshua placed his home for sale and sold it by public auction, asking Jacques to retrieve only the weapons and clothes, all other items were sold with the house. Joshua never crossed the threshold again. The chapter of his life with Rodde in that home was closed. All proceeds Joshua turned over to Jacques, telling him to invest wisely.

"If I should follow Rodde with my death," Joshua told Jacques, "what we owned should go to your children. Renard, Jean, and Antoinette, for we loved them as if they were our own."

In March a Militia was formed and William Ashley was appointed colonel in the Missouri Militia. Joshua signed up with him and was appointed a militia scout. Knowing the malaise Joshua still labored under, Ashley established units of three men, each with an Indian scout. Information on enemy movements in the north could be gained by sending these patrols north of the Missouri River to gather information on the growing threat there. Ashley hoped the importance of these duties would engage Joshua and occupy his thinking rather than dwelling on Rodde's death.

Bands of Sauks, Miamis and Pottawatamies from the northland answered the call of the great Indian leader, Tecumseh, and made this area unsafe for all but strongly fortified positions and well armed patrols.

Tecumseh and his brothers Tenskwatawa and Chiksika were the sons of a mighty Shawnee War Chief. During a dream after drinking firewater, Tenskwatawa experienced a strong vision that clearly detailed the evil white men were bringing to the land of the native people. In his vision Tenskwatawa saw huge portions of land coming under control of the white man and claimed the 1795 Treaty of Ft. Greenville was causing the demise of all Indian Peoples. Tenskwatawa's dream told him the trinkets, whiskey and ways of the whites must be rejected, and the Indians must return to their former way of life.

Tecumseh, a tall handsome warrior in his own right, took up this call and traveled throughout all the Indian Nations asking them to come together to stop the white aggression. Tecumseh was extremely intelligent and studied the ways of the white man including the Bible and books on world history. Through his abilities, a village was established in an abandoned Miami Indian site of Tippecanoe in Indiana Territory. The new settlement was named Prophet Town in honor of Tenskwatawa's prophecies. Tribes from the middle and north countries joined there including the Shawnee, Ottawa, Huron, Winnebago, Potawatomi and Ojibwas tribes. Tecumseh established great respect in the eyes of these people for his fiery orations against white domination. They came to call him Shooting Star, after the flashing brilliance of a night comet.

Tenskwatawa foretold of an eclipse of the sun that would soon happen as a sign for all Indian tribes to rise up against the whites. This indeed came to pass, and the tribes believed his magic to be so strong they planned for war following his rites of performing ceremonies with sacred beans and medicine fires to make themselves invincible. Tecumseh chastised any tribes not allying themselves with Prophet Town, as having white blood in their veins. In one speech he brought the tribe to their feet, throwing hatchets high into the air in a sign of unison with him.

"Sell a country," Tecumseh cried. "Why not sell the air, the great sea as well as the earth. Did not the Great Spirit make them all for his people to use?"

As Tecumseh traveled building alliances, relationships between the red men and the white deteriorated. William Henry Harrison the Governor of the Illinois Territory decided to attack Prophet Town with 1,000 men while Tecumseh was away, feeling this was their best chance to stop the growing threat. Tenskwatawa led the warriors from Prophet Town against this army, secure in the knowledge that his magic would protect them from the white soldiers. Although the battle killed fifty of Harrison's men, many Indian were also killed, making the tribes realize for the first time Tenskwatawa's magic was fallible. The Delaware and Miami tribes left the alliance, and the other people of Prophet Town were forced to flee as the troops descended upon the town, burning it to the ground.

Tecumseh was furious with his brother for precipitating the conflict before he was ready. Tenskwatawa was driven from the flock and isolated in disgrace. Tecumseh then gathered his forces and began leading a border war in frontier areas far away from the organized resistance of the white armies. At the large council meeting of Tombigbee River, Tecumseh called for an all out war against the white man and although the Old Choctaw chief, Pushmataha, counseled conciliations, many tribes agreed with Tecumseh. Among the more warlike were the Sauks who previously enjoyed great success in destroying the isolated homesteads of northern Missouri. It was against these war parties that Joshua was sent, trying to find the gathered bands before they struck. If Joshua was successful, Ashley could lead a large force of men against them eliminating the threat.

After hugging Justine, Joshua bid farewell to his childhood friend Jacques. He then departed from St. Genevieve, which had been his home

285

for many years. Before leaving, he went again to the river where Rodde laid beneath the now still waters.

"From here I must leave," Joshua told her. "My soul withers and dies without you. Perhaps I ride to my death; sometimes I pray so, hoping to join you. Know this, that once I loved you more than life itself. As you told me long ago, the peace I am in search of lies far from here, but your memory will always ride with me."

Joshua and two other scouts, both young men from St. Genevieve, left on a cold gray spring morning, riding north, traveling a new road. None of them would ever return. With them rode an Indian, from the Tuscarora Tribe. An older race from the Carolinas, now dwindling in numbers, these peoples were allies of the Americans. Blue Feather he was called, and although Joshua knew well the country north to the Missouri, beyond the banks of this muddy river was unknown to him. Blue Feather trapped in those frontier regions for many years, and understood the lay of the land. William Jamison and Jourad Sewell rode with Joshua, and although the men were young, they handled horses and weapons well. Of killing and death, they were innocent, but this would soon change.

The four men would patrol the vast frontier of land from the Des Moines and Chariton Rivers as their north and western boundaries, south to the Missouri and the Booneville ferries. Blue Feather led them north, avoiding the well traveled trails, instead riding the older roads made years ago when Indian traders conducted commerce between the Mississippi and the Blue Mountains. Like ghosts travelers the men rode during the nighttime, resting in the dark thickets of cedar by daylight. Reaching the Missouri River, they waited until late in the evening before crossing the river into Booneville. The evening hours were spent gathering what information they could before riding on ahead of the dawn. The blacksmith shop in Booneville was established as their contact point. Should a large concentration of Indians be discovered, messages were to be sent here, and then relayed further south to Ashley's troops. The next three months Blue Feather showed the scouts the creeks and byways, introducing the riders to the friendly tribes living in small bands scattered in this rugged terrain.

Joshua made arrangements with groups of farmers on the forks of the Cuivre and Salt Rivers to always have fresh horses stabled and well rested in their barns. Exhausted from travel, the men arrived to the farmsteads by darkness, exchanged mounts, and then rode on. There safety lay in mobility. The fierce Sauks could not kill, what they could not find. In June word was relayed to the travelers. The information they gathered was now of great importance. War was declared between Britain and America. Worse news yet was that the British recognized the value of Tecumseh and made him an officer in their army. With the murder of settlers sanctioned by the English, over thirty tribes flocked to Tecumseh's ranks, including the Sioux from the far west. Farther north the entire Great Lakes region fell under British and Indian control.

Twice in the first year, Joshua's scouting was instrumental in saving human life and preventing the frontier from falling into English hands. Late in December through biting cold weather, the Kickapoos tried to attack Boonville, but Joshua's warning gave the residents plenty of time to mount a defense. With a break in the weather a gathering of Misquakies and Miami warriors moved south from the Butte des Morts to threaten settlements along the upper reaches of the Illinois River. Realizing word could never be sent south in time, Joshua was able to get a warning across the Mississippi at Saukenut to Harrison's forces who immediately routed the advance, killing many of the Indians as they traveled across the swampy meadows near the headwaters.

When Joshua returned to his patrol, Blue Feather told him that Jamison died when he was shot from ambush as the patrol tried to trade horses at a farmstead. Unknown to the scouts, the Sauk chief, Black Hawk, killed the farm family and waited for the scouts to arrive. Blue Feather and Sewell were able to escape back through the sycamore trees, a hail of lead chasing behind them. Disgusted by the abuses to the corpses they found there, Joshua returned with them, burying Jamison and the farm family. Black Hawk, fanatical in his hate for the Americans, made it his mission to track down and kill the wandering scout patrols.

Since the time of the declaration of war in June of 1812, Joshua heard little of the other battlefronts. More information reached Ashley, and when the old friends met for a few hours to exchange information or to re-supply, Ashley passed what he knew to Joshua. Originally American troops tried to push the British from Canada. These efforts did not go well, and the Americans were turned back by the strength of the fortified English positions. The only successful front of the war was on the oceans. The American Navy did sink numerous British ships. With pride, Americans talked about the Chesapeake and Constitution and what great fighting ships they were. As the conflict wore on, small successes were achieved with the battles of Lake Erie and Thames allowing American soldiers to push deeper into Canada. Tecumseh died covering the retreat of the British General Henry Proctor in the Battle of the Thames River. This weakened the Indian coalition but did not stop Black Hawk from his war. With the collapse of France in 1814, the British occupied Washington and burned the White House. Thomas Macdonough, a naval commander, won a major battle at Plattsburg Bay and stopped English forces from uniting with the other troops already on American soil.

Finally, in December of 1814, the Treaty of Ghent was signed, and both countries gave back land they had taken from the other. Not knowing the war was over, in January of 1815, Andrew Jackson and his troops whipped the British soundly in New Orleans, driving the last nail in the British coffin of American occupation.

Like Jackson, Joshua didn't know hostilities were declared over. Riding south to Boonville for a prearranged meeting with Ashley, the party crossed a covered bridge on Weas creek. Black Hawk's spies knew of their route and lay in waiting for them. Sewell fell mortally wounded with the first Indian volley. Blue Feather and Joshua retreated to the rock abutments returning fire across the small creek. Three times the Sauk warriors attacked their position, and seven bodies lay in testimony of the accuracy of the scouts' rifles. The Mide chants and charmed red war clubs offered little protection to the Sauk warriors. Knowing reinforcements for the Sauks would soon arrive, Joshua and Blue Feather planned to escape, floating downstream, leaving their horses behind as decoys, under cover of the night. As the fourth and final charge broke upon them, a war lance pierced Blue Feather's chest as he stepped in front of Joshua. Dragging his friend to deeper water Joshua dived deep into the muddy water, dragging Blue feather with him. In the darkness, they were lost, and five miles downstream Joshua crawled to the shore, Blue Feather limp within his grasp. Before walking on to Booneville, there on the banks of Weas Creek, Joshua buried his friend, in a grave dug by hands. Ashley told him of the war's ending and the disbanding of the militia. Blue Feather and Sewell's deaths were without meaning, the war was over. They died fighting for a country that knew nothing of their sacrifice by the hands of Indians fighting under a foreign flag to legitimize their hatred for the white man. These and a myriad of other thoughts cascaded through Joshua's mind, as he lay oblivious in the small cabin, guarded by his friend La Ramie.

The wind blew sharply as La Ramie left the protection of the cabin. The blistering snow was driven across the glade in sheets of ice, numbing any exposed flesh not wrapped tightly against the storm. Drifts were beginning to build in ripples much like the waves of a sea, constantly growing as each whitecap fed into another. Here and there as if berserk, the wind would suddenly spiral upward into the sky funneling a cloud of snow with it before shrieking to the ground again to race eastward attempting to leave the agony of the mountains behind. Looking behind,

La Ramie gave brief thought to returning to the protection just ten paces to the rear. Already the blizzard obscured the shape of the cabin making it appear ethereal and vague, its shape changing with each gust. The trapper had no fear of finding the way back as the glade was the only level bench within a mile of the cabin. By keeping the wind on the left check his course would intersect the structure behind him. With this much effort already invested La Ramie turned again to fight onward leaning heavily into the wind as it buffeted him, angry that anyone defied its fury. Perhaps the beaver set could wait until tomorrow, but an animal trapped and not drowned would chew through its own limb seeking escape. Although he trapped and killed for fur, La Ramie would let no animal suffer a slow agonizing death. By this code, he must face the storm to check the traps. La Ramie found the creek bed and started the journey leading downward by the pond following the trail to the river. He wished now the burden of the rifle was back in the cabin as both pistols would have been enough protection, but over the years his hand felt empty without it. At least the cold snow was not wet and the powder charges below the frizzen would remain fresh. The wind relaxed momentarily before drawing a huge breath to begin again and through the break in the snow, the pond appeared directly ahead.

Joshua would owe him supper and dishes tonight if he felt better; he smiled to himself, thinking about his friend.

The threat of the pneumonia taking Joshua's life was passed, but he still lay in the cabin weak as a kitten. The rising fever finally released its hold with La Ramie's last treatment, and now only rest and broth were needed to mend Joshua's weakened lungs. La Ramie didn't mind making the trip alone, all of his life he had been alone, enjoying the company solitude provided. This season with Joshua was a nice change, preventing boredom from entering the cabin when the long winter almost became unbearable. Joshua read to La Ramie stories of wonder from long ago about knights and dragons. La Ramie liked the tales about the jousting for honor, man against man. This was the way of nature, the strong survive, and the weak die.

Wars now depended on massed numbers of troops overwhelming their opponents. The skills of personal combat were becoming a trait of the past. Here on the high lonesome, a man's life was always on the edge, no cavalry would ride to the rescue. This somehow made La Ramie feel more alive, his senses more alert.

Stopping as he reached the pond, La Ramie turned his back to the wind, pausing to beat mittened hands against the sides of the bearskin coat, trying to drive the blood into his fingers again. Glaring suspiciously at the rough ice of the pond, he continued on. This cold snap came about suddenly, and it wouldn't be wise to try and shorten the route by crossing the slick surface. In this weather, water was an enemy. Once wet, the body would feel the numbing cold much more quickly. Toes and feet would freeze solid. Turning to face the wind again, La Ramie skirted the edge of the water searching for the notch that would allow access to the river trail. As he approached the opening, the wind escalated her fury, screaming a warning of danger. The warning, coming this late, was almost in vain.

Suddenly La Ramie knew what was ahead. Even before recognizing the figure of the enemy before him, he began turning away from the opening and the danger waiting there. Three rifles barked, attempting to stop La Ramie's retreat, their reports quickly carrying down the canyon away from his hearing, dispersed by the wind and snow. Another second earlier and he would have been able to make his escape; a second later and the trapper would have fallen where he stood. The margin between life and death was always very small in the wilderness.

The first rifle ball buried itself deep into the trapper's chest, penetrating through sinew and skin, into his right lung before stopping against the shoulder blade. Unable to complete its progress, the ball shattered the bone, its energy spent. As the first round entered his body, the second ball ripped through his side tearing a bleeding gash there, imbedding the fabric of the bearskin coat into the raw wound. The last round of the volley hummed its deadly flight passing within inches of his ear. La Ramie's reaction saved his life for a time. Staggered by the impact of volley, La Ramie turned away from the wind facing the pond, seeking escape from the rifle fire. From the safety of the rocks across the frozen ice he might be able to mount a defense.

How many were there he wondered. The shock of the wounds was already affecting his reactions, numbing the thoughts. Distance from the danger was the need; the rocks across the ponds offered the best line of retreat. Burning filled his lungs as La Ramie started across the pond, forcing the weakening legs to run. Sensing them behind, gaining on him, the rocks ahead were too far.

Have to slow them down, he thought, I need some time. Throwing himself to the ice, the heavy rifle steadied, pointing into the wind. The snow stung his eyes, and La Ramie closed them momentarily to let this gust pass.

The Arapaho felt the thrill of the hunt as he watched the big trapper coming toward them. For the last two days, high on the hill behind the cabin he lay with Lame Wolf, watching and waiting, making no movement that would betray their position. Patience was needed now, the time for killing would come later. The weather was cold and still and the smoke from the chimney below rose in a thin stream straight into the air. By first light they were in position, Lame Wolf and Running Horse, Arapaho war leader. Pride filled his heart that Red Willow chose him to go with Lame Wolf to the cabin of the white trapper. He would tell of this deed proudly upon returning to the village. Below them the white trapper came from the cabin to the creek, breaking the thin ice to draw water into a bucket and then returned back inside. Lame Wolf made no movement beside him.

The sun began to rise in the pale sky, and thin clouds gathered high above casting a shadow across the glade below. Finally the trapper emerged again, walking away from the cabin toward the pond.

"Let me follow him," he asked turning to Lame Wolf. "I will kill him in the river below."

"No," came the reply. "Red Willow said we must wait and watch, making sure this is not a white magic trick."

The day wore on and still they lay above the cabin. There was no sign of the trader. As hunger bore down on the two warriors, they saw La Ramie returning, making his way up the trail from the notch leading up from the river. Over his shoulder he carried two beavers. Their burden was heavy but did not slow the trapper's progress.

Lame Wolf is right, thought Running Horse. This white man is strong like a bear.

When darkness fell, the two warriors slid back from the hillside and returned to their camp where Prairie Dog and Flat Turtle waited for news with the other Arapaho braves, He Who Sleeps, and Drum Beater. Red Willow chose them to accompany Lame Wolf on his quest. Three Arapaho to join the three Blackfeet, making the party six, a strong number. Lame Wolf told them of what he saw while they watched cabin.

"We must wait until the white men are away from the cabin and take them one at a time," Lame Wolf instructed. "Away from the cabin their magic is not as strong. We will watch tomorrow and then plan what we must do."

Before dawn the next morning, Lame Wolf and Running Horse returned to the hill above the cabin. A chill wind was now blowing from the west, and the clouds raced above them building into darkening banks, gray and ominous. Again they watched the large trapper gather water from the stream, and again he left the cabin walking the route by the pond before going through the notch and disappearing below. Running Horse was numb from the cold, but kept still, matching the silent form of Lame

Wolf beside him. At last the trapper returned, carrying no beaver today. Below him La Ramie paused before entering the cabin, quickly scanning the hills looking directly where they were lying. Running Horse felt his pulse race even though he knew the trapper could never detect them in the midst of the trees, hidden by the green boughs, their faces daubed with the red mud. When night fell, the two warriors returned again to their camp. Snow was starting to drift on the wind, and the temperature continued to fall.

"Tomorrow," Lame Wolf said. "With the cover of the snow, he will walk right toward us. The notch is where we must wait. Prairie Dog will take his position above the round stones by the pond, and Flat Turtle will lie on the hill across from him. He Who Sleeps will stay with the horses waiting there in case we need him. Retreat to the cabin for the white man will be impossible. Tomorrow he is ours. When he is dead, we take the trader. Without the trapper, he will die easily."

By midnight the storm was upon them, and within several hours they walked the long circle down from the hills and around the glade. The growing storm would cover any tracks, and hidden behind the ragged rocks in the notch, they could see the trail down from the cabin. Each carried a buffalo robe to crawl beneath, letting the snow cover them, making their forms indistinguishable from the terrain. Three hours before dawn they took their positions, awaiting the trapper. The storm continued to grow howling through the rocks around them as it forced its will through the narrow passage. Lame Wolf gave no thought to the weather, the trapper would come, he traveled this way everyday. Cold weather did not bother a bear. He adjusted the bow loosening it in his quiver so it would slide quick and easy into his hands. The arrows nestled there, three tipped and two bare of metal points. With care the sharpened ends were turned downward so as not to risk a scratch from their poisonous tips. The war club hung from his shoulder by the horsehair band. He would use the club later on the trader.

Satisfaction came to Lame Wolf as between the sheets of wind driven snow he saw the trapper making the journey from the cabin. Lame Wolf held his breath for a moment when the trapper paused beside the pond, but then La Ramie continued onward walking around the ice instead of across it. A whirlwind kicked the snow high into the air and through the swirling white, the trapper appeared. Between the slits in the hide Lame Wolf watched, waiting, one more step, and it would be close enough. Suddenly the big trapper stopped, sensing the ambush ahead, and Lame Wolf knew they must fire now. The harsh cry of attach burst from the Blackfoot's throat, and throwing off the robe, he arose, centering the rifle on the white man's chest. The rifle kicked hard against his shoulder, and from beside him came two more reports as Drum Beater and Running Horse fired also. Lame Wolf watched in satisfaction as hair from the Trapper's heavy bear coat jumped, fur flying with the bullet's impact. The trapper pivoted and began to run sideways toward the pond, cutting down their line of fire.

How could he still run? Surely the other balls struck also, the range was too close to miss, thought Lame Wolf as he began reloading. He is hard hit and won't travel far.

Running Horse saw the trapper take Lame Wolf's round through the chest also. The wind blew Running Horses' rifle barrel just before firing, and he was sure the shot missed. Throwing the rifle down, he pursued La Ramie, wanting to be the first to feel the trapper's warm blood. Close behind him came Drum Beater, not allowing Running Horse to be the only one to share in the glory of the kill. Lame Wolf let them go, wounded bears could still be fierce, and he would wait, letting them corner the prey for him.

Pounding hard through the gap, Running Horse pursued his victim. He could see the trapper just ahead. Clearing the protection of the rocks, he staggered, allowing La Ramie to gain a lead. With redoubled efforts, Running Horse turned away from the blinding snow and followed as La Ramie began crossing the pond trying to reach protection on the other side. Running Horse must reach him before Prairie Dog shot the white man down, claiming the coup for himself. Head ducked, Running Horse concentrated on the footing trying to cut down the distance between predator and prey.

La Ramie opened his eyes again just in time to see Running Horse looming toward him. The trapper's big rifle boomed heavy and dull in the cold air, literally catapulting the Indian from his feet backwards, tearing a hole through Running Horses' chest large enough for two fists to push through. The Arapaho died before hitting the ground, never having seen the trapper lying in front of him. Rolling over and over in the snow La Ramie drew both pistols, and with effort struggled upright to sit facing the approaching storm. Where he lay, a large pool of blood was quickly freezing on the ice. It looked frothy, almost orange, and La Ramie knew he was shot in the lungs. Other than a burning sensation, he felt no pain.

Drum Beater ran behind Running Horse trying to keep up. Ever since they were small boys, Running Horse could best him in foot races, and try as he might, the results never changed. Suddenly he caught Running Horse, and passed him before realizing what was lying in the snow. Running Horse was sprawled, collapsed on his back, the snow behind was sprayed a wide crimson. A hard slap struck Drum Beater in his ear. Polestruck, the warrior slumped to the ice, the left side of his head imploded, with the impact of La Ramie's pistol ball. Bits of flesh, bone and brain floated momentarily in the air until they joined with the snow and wind fleeing the canyon rim. La Ramie fired from no more than ten feet and chose a head shot, not wanting a fight with a wounded Indian here on the slick ice. Swinging back to face the wind again, he waited, wondering if still others would appear out of the storm. Looking back at the bodies, he recognized the knotted grouse feathers of the Arapaho tribe. He watched briefly the feathers in Drum Beater's roached hair as they jerked violently in the wind trying to escape the shattered skull, before returning his attention to await more danger ahead.

Lame Wolf eased through the notch following Running Horse and Drum Beater. He looked toward the lake, but the whiteout conditions made it impossible to see more than several feet away. He paused to listen, but the wind carried any sounds away. Walking a few steps, he listened again before moving cautiously forward still hearing or seeing nothing except snow and the shriek of the wind across the glade. Something was waiting out there, he could feel it. Kneeling in the cold snow, Lame Wolf ceased his advance. Wounded bears needed time to stiffen from their wounds. This time he would be patient.

La Ramie could feel the blood running down his side, warm and wet. Realizing the bleeding was heavy, he knew if it weren't bandaged soon, weakness would overcome him before reaching safety.

I need to get off this damn pond, he thought. It's too open here, not enough protection. The weapons needed to be reloaded but in the wind it would take too long. He still had one pistol, enough. Behind the rocks, time could be taken to dress the wounds. Once the blood was stopped, he could make a run for the cabin. Perhaps there were only two attackers out there, and they both lay in the snow, their skins turning a bluish hue as the lifeless bodies stiffened. It took him several attempts to stand before staggering on, using the rifle as a crutch.

Prairie Dog thought he heard rifle fire, but the wind distorted the sound. The snow kept stinging his eyes, and the edge of the pond was barely visible. He kept turning to look toward the cabin, but it was impossible to see that far. Prairie Dog hoped the white trapper would come soon, his feet felt frozen. The rock offered little protection from the blizzard as the wind whipped over and around it finding every opening in the buffalo hide.

Lame Wolf has probably already killed the trapper and left me here to freeze he thought.

At last deciding that he would venture a short way across the pond to try and see what was happening, Prairie Dog moved cautiously from beneath the robe and stepped out on the ice. The force of the wind caused him to duck low, protecting his eyes from the white needles. The wind immediately attacked this new obstacle, trying to remove it from the ice. A sudden burst of snow danced across the ice swallowing him momentarily. As the blast moved on, Prairie Dog raised his head, spitting snow from his mouth. Before him a dark shape loomed out of the snow within arms reach.

"Lame Wolf," he asked incredulously, "why are you he...ahh," the words dying in his throat as La Ramie's knife blade sliced through his stomach tearing upwards deep into his breastbone, finding the heart within the protected cavity.

Prairie Dog's eyes focused on La Ramie, not comprehending what was happening until at the end he understood, that before him was the Great Bear, his white fur coat glistening with ice crystals. Struggling briefly before falling, Prairie Dog no longer felt the snow as it pierced his eyes. La Ramie attempted to pull the blade from the hard bone and gristle, but it was imbedded too deep. Leaving the knife, the trapper started again for the shore. As his foot met ice, the world collapsed around him. Far beneath him a warm spring brought water to the pond from deep within the earth. This warm water resisted loosing its form, and when at last it froze, the ice here was much thinner. La Ramie felt himself sinking, the cold water instantly forcing the breath from his tortured lung. Releasing the rifle, La Ramie kicked upward toward the shimmering light above. The heavy clothes saturated with water felt like a load of lead upon his back. Reaching the surface, he splashed toward the shore, trying to grasp the constantly breaking ice with numb fingers, before it too collapsed into the slushy water. Finally the trapper found thicker ice but was too weak to pull himself out of the water. Several times La Ramie tried, before harsh coughing racked his powerful frame, bringing bright bubbles of blood to his lips.

"I just need to rest a minute," he told himself, "just a minute, and then I'll get out."

Laying his head on the slick ice, he floated in the water while the storm roared above him. His thoughts turned to the green Canadian fields of a childhood, long ago and far away. The ice slowly refroze, capturing La Ramie, as he rested, no longer cold, at last joined for eternity with the land he so loved. The storm paused briefly paying its respect, but then hurried on again, uncaring where or when its road would end.

Lame Wolf finally tired of waiting arose and went on. Keeping the rifle pointed downwind, he circled the pond staying as close to the shore as possible, straining his eyes for signs of Running Horse and Drum Beater. The wind rose and fell in wailing moans around him, sounding like a funeral chant. This thought suddenly brought fear to Lame Wolf's heart and he looked behind him. Forcing himself to be calm, he stepped over a large rock and then paused looking down at the blue hand raised above the snow. Kneeling he swept away the flakes to reveal Running Horse, the dead lips drawn back in a grimace, the Arapaho's medicine shirt was gaping and bloody from the chest wound. Two steps away Lame Wolf found Drum Beater beneath the snow, his features unrecognizable accept for the grouse feathers still fighting valiantly against the wind. The Arapaho were warned of the White Bear's magic, but they hadn't listened, too confident of their own power, too vain and stupid. Somewhere between here and Prairie Dog, the trapper was still in front of him. Reaching the rocks on the far side of the pond, Lame Wolf found no sign of the trapper. The snow behind the rocks was tramped showing where Prairie Dog waited, but he was now gone. Lame Wolf started back into the face of the Wind.

Perhaps the trapper reached the safety of the cabin after all, but where was Prairie Dog, he wondered.

Lame Wolf took another step, suddenly feeling a wet cold through his moccasins. Looking down, Lame Wolf realized he was standing in slushy water. The pond was not frozen here; death would await him with another step forward. Changing the course around the slushy water, the Blackfoot saw what he was looking for. Throwing the rifle to his shoulder, Lame Wolf walked slowly to the clear ice a few feet in front, expecting the form of the trapper to spring any moment. Convinced at last, he kneeled staring at his enemy frozen in the water. Particles of ice clung to the beard, the face still and lifeless, the lapping of the water from below causing the only movement. A blue wool hat was still pulled far down over the ears, protecting them from the icy currents that seeped into the lifeless body. The trapper's hard eyes were filmed over, pupils dilated to pinpoints seeing only the clear pane between them. Pulled tight to the chest, La Ramie's hands pushed against the barrier that held him, unable to reach and stretch toward the light. Lame Wolf felt jubilation flood through him; honor was restored at last. Giving the dead trapper a wide birth, he went on a short distance before finding Prairie Dog still guarding La Ramie's knife.

Three warriors it had taken to kill the white man, and even then the water was needed to finish the task, Red Willows magic was indeed strong, thought Lame Wolf rubbing his medicine shirt beneath the robe.

Lame Wolf retraced the trail around the edge of the pond, heedless of the stinging ice striking his eyes. He would find Flat Turtle, and together they would finish the job. The trapper was waiting for them, still in the cabin.

The door to the cabin rattled slightly, rousing Joshua from his restless sleep. During the last week his fevered dreams floated between the cabin and the long years of fighting the Sauks on the Missouri frontier. Glimpses of past ambushes floated through his mind, faces of those he killed and close friends that died in his arms mingled together. At times he was cognizant of the big trapper forcing bitter liquid down his throat, several times he asked for Night Wind before remembering where she was. Awake now, he reached for Blue Feather to warn him of the sound. Together they would face the last assault, twice before the war party tried to overrun their position. Both he and Blue Feather were bleeding and wounded, this time perhaps they would fall, unable to stand the assault.

"Blue Feather, wake up, they're coming again, Blue Feather," Joshua rasped, his hoarse whisper louder.

Looking around the cabin, Joshua saw that it was empty. Blue Feather was gone, dying a valiant death many years ago on the banks of the Weas creek, dying to save Joshua from the Sauk war lance. Looking to the window, he could see snow still sifting through the shuttered frame, the fireplace was cold. How long he was asleep, Joshua didn't know. La Ramie should have been back by now. The wind buffeted the door again, and Joshua watched as the leather drawstring was slowly pulled upward. The Sauks weren't outside, but something was. Frantically Joshua searched for weapons, relaxing when his hand found the grip of the pistol beside him in the bed. Looking further Joshua saw La Ramie's shotgun leaning against the wall at the foot of the bed. Retrieving this weapon, he quickly checked the pan making sure of the powder charge. Dizziness overtook him again and lying back with the shotgun covering the door, Joshua waited, watching the rest of the drawstring retreat through the latch.

Counting heartbeats, Joshua forced his breathing to slow waiting for the door to open. As if by command, the wooden entrance slammed inward, a wave of snow billowed in seeking the interior of the cabin. Through the snow charged Flat Turtle, screaming the shrill war cry of the Blackfoot warrior. The darkened interior of the cabin momentarily caused Flat Turtle to stop his charge trying to find the enemy within. The shotgun exploded the charge of mini-balls across the room, spinning Flat Turtle in a blood spiral as he crashed into the table, scattering plates and spoons across the cabin floor. The light from the door darkened as Lame Wolf appeared, bow drawn seeking his prey within.

Joshua fired the pistol as the arrow left the bow, each instrument of death passing within inches of the other. The arrow sliced through the thick muscles of Joshua's shoulder shattering its deadly wooden tip into the elk horn headboard of the bed. The pistol ball punched through the porcupine quills of Lame Wolf's medicine shirt just burning the skin on Lame Wolf's ribs before smashing into the quiver of arrows staggering the Blackfoot back against the door. Horrified that he missed, Joshua rolled from the bed, crawling for Flat Turtles' bloody rifle lying by the fireplace. With a cry of rage, Lame Wolf sprung after him, raising the obsidian war club for its downward stroke on the trader's head. Hearing the cry, Joshua rolled to his back just in time to see the stone club descending downward seeking to smash the life from his body. Throwing his head to one side, splinters from the wood floor stung his cheek as the club bit into the pine flooring. Rolling once again Joshua stretched to reach the rifle, his hand closing instead on the elk horn Night Wind decorated with scrollwork. Lame Wolf grunted as he tried to pull the club from the boards, cursing the trapper by screaming "Sakarita," dog eater. With the remaining strength left in his fevered body, Joshua lunged driving the elk horn upward with both hands into the crotch of Lame Wolf standing above him, feeling the sharpened horn penetrating through the Blackfoot's manhood and deeper through the pelvis and into the small intestines. Hunching, with a grunt of pain, Lame Wolf snarled, fumbling for the knife at his belt. Joshua scrambled to his feet, jerking the war club from the pine boards before spinning to slash the obsidian blade down upon the exposed neck of Lame Wolf hunched over before him. The sharp blade cut through skin, severing the spinal cord, rupturing the Blackfoot's throat. The magic of the war club made by the Man-Woman overcame the enchantment of the Arapaho medicine shirt that protected Lame Wolf no more. Shaking, Joshua stared down at his enemy, no longer a threat, killed by two weapons, not made by the hand of man. Staggering to the door Joshua pushed it shut against the howling wind and pulled his rifle from the rack over the door. Returning to the bed he laid down watching the door.

"Blue Feather," he said, "get ready, they may come again."

Visions swirled through Joshua's mind again, blending the future with the present and the past. The trader felt his body floating, the poison from Berdache's arrow slowly finding its way into his bloodstream. Several times his consciousness returned, and he saw flames leaping in the fireplace. Once he heard chanting, the soft voice reminding him of Night Wind. At the foot of the bed, a small owl sat looking at him, the black feathers on her breast resembling long braids of shining raven black hair.

Chapter 13
The Preparation

Carrigan entered the teacher's lounge early Monday morning. This was the last Monday of the year he would check his mail box, sorting through the various announcements, advertisements, and late assignments from students that crammed the small cubbyhole. The pile was thick today, and he eyed the trashcan close at hand, debating whether to heap the whole mass deep into the bottom of the receptacle. Responsibility overtook him, and he laid the pile on the nearby table, sorting through the paperwork. Late assignments and student papers he clipped together, giving them the highest priority, and then he buried them back in his box. Advertisements for textbooks, flyers announcing good deals for teachers, and requests for information from sales reps on the classes he taught were all blindly thrown over his shoulder. He called this game mailbox basketball. With each shot, he listened to see if the material made the lip of the trash can, scoring points for his team, or if they were air balls to be retrieved later. Judging from the sound, he was shooting fifty percent from the field. Good enough to win this game. The last group of papers was school announcements concerning which day each class would be taking the state exams, the protocol for graduation, and a listing of students and staff who owed books to the library. Glancing down the rows of names on the last paper, he was relieved to find he wasn't among the rogue's gallery. This bundle he also filed in the trash.

Mrs. Libby, the school librarian, was a fierce little thing, tenacious as a bulldog. Carrigan didn't want her reminding him to set a proper example for his students. Last year she attributed a missing video to his library card, and for three months afterward, he received her venomous stares every time he entered the library. She finally found the video in her office from among the piles of her projects stacked there, but never offered apologies for the evil thoughts she harbored toward him. Secretly she believed he broke into her sanctum and placed that video beneath those piles of paper just to spite her. Carrigan was sure two grudges were held against him, one for theft and one for breaking and entering. He therefore made sure not to annoy her again, realizing she would put a contract on him for a third offense.

The last piece of paper was a handwritten note from Jan Rudoff. the principal, asking all teachers to attend a meeting before school tomorrow. The last few words caught his attention, "please plan to attend." Missives from the administration usually arrived with clip art, couched in educational jargon; somehow the handwritten copy conveyed importance. Just as he finished reading the note, the door behind him clicked open, and the author of the note entered. Close behind him, Trisha Collingworth followed, listening to Jan's speech. Looking backward, his head turned over his shoulder, Jan ran directly into Carrigan staggering them both.

"I knew you cared," Carrigan commented, "but you don't have to show it."

"I'm sorry, I'm sorry," Jan replied, "I wasn't watching where I was going?"

"That's fine, my broken bones will mend sometime this year, and what are you two planning this morning," Carrigan asked.

Trisha reddened and turning, left the break room, while Jan looked around Carrigan to see who else was in the room. Finding it empty, he swept both hands through his hair as if to compose his thoughts before speaking.

"Carrigan, you're a real wise ass, but I know that if push came to shove, I could count on you. I'm turning in my resignation tomorrow and plan to announce it to the staff. I don't think I can be effective here any longer. Marge and I have talked long and hard about it. I can get on as an assistant principal in Sioux Falls. Marge and I both have some family there, and we just felt it would better for both of us."

"Well," Carrigan drawled, giving himself time to compose his thoughts. "I'm glad you and Marge talked. It's none of my business what you do, but I will miss you. I think you've been good for this school, and you have supported me, which I really appreciate. We still need to get more hands-on classes for the kids and move away from strictly a college prep approach, but that's a battle to be fought next year. Strange I gave some thought to not signing my contract either. I don't expect you want me to say anything until tomorrow, is there something else I can do for you?"

"No, not really. I did tell Trish that you usually had some good common sense advice, and told her she needed to talk to you before she made any decisions. I hope you don't mind."

"Not at all, my advice is usually worth what people pay for it, which is nothing, but I don't mind giving it away. Maybe someday somebody will listen. I might even follow it myself, if I thought it would do any good. Tell her to stop by anytime."

Remembering that he promised Mrs. Lansing that he would talk to Becky, Carrigan left the work area and scanned the hallway outside asking several students if they had seen her. Finally the persistence was rewarded, and one of her friends jerked a thumb over her shoulder indicating the door to the library.

Great, thought Carrigan, I have to enter the lair of the tiger.

Peering inside the door first, Carrigan located his nemesis. Ms. Libby was standing with her back to the door straightening pencils in the cup on her counter. Walking as quietly as possible, he entered the den and searched the computer banks and tables looking for Becky's blonde hair. Far in the corner, he saw a pair of sandaled feet, and as he looked further around the bookcase, Becky's features came into view. She was sitting at a table concentrating on a magazine open before here. Actually she was kneeling on the chair with both hands supporting the fine-featured face as it frowned, deeply engaged in thought. Walking over to her, Carrigan paused before interrupting her.

"What are you studying so hard, Bec?" he asked.

Seeing him beside her, she flashed a quick smile, "Hi, Mr. C. I don't like these pictures any more;" she said her lower lip pouting outward. "The book says the picture on this page has three things different in it than the other picture, and I can only find two. I think they cheated. See here, the troll has a club in his right hand, and in the other picture it's a spear. This castle has two chimneys, and the first castle only has one, but I can't find anything else. Do you want to help me?"

Carrigan glanced briefly at the pictures in the "Highlights for Kids Magazine." "No, Beck, you don't want me to help, I'm totally blind. Your mom asked me to check with you. Did you charge some stuff at your dad's store for your project in my class?"

Carrigan almost felt her body stiffen, and Becky began to hum tracing her finger over the pictures on the page.

"Beck, did you hear me?" Carrigan asked again. "She didn't want your father to be mad at you if you did it for school. I told her I would ask."

"Daddy is real mad at me," she answered. "Sometimes he lets me buy things at the store. All I have to do is sign my name. Last week I got Mommy some aspirin."

"Did you charge anything for your project last week, Becky?" he persisted.

"Just some stuff for Daddy."

"Did you get anything for Tommy?"

"Tommy said if we win, we get a prize," said Becky, turning to him. "Is that true Mr. C.?"

"Did Tommy have you get some things, Becky, so you could win?"

"Tommy said not to talk about our project so people won't steal our idea. If we do good, Daddy won't be mad anymore."

"Ok, Becky, I'll see you in class tomorrow," Carrigan sighed, realizing he wasn't going to win this round.

Checking the clock high on the wall above the stacks of books Carrigan decided he needed to find Tommy and question him a bit further about the project before he called Mrs. Lansing back. The best place to find Tommy was outside the west door. As he crept back by the front desk, Ms. Libby turned quickly trapping him before he could leave.

"May I help you?" she asked.

"No, Ms. Libby. I just needed to talk to Becky."

He imagined feeling the cold stare penetrating deeply between his shoulder blades as he escaped through the exit into the hallway. Glad to have survived again, he walked briskly to the west doors. Avoiding the gyrating young ruffians racing up and down the halls, he made it to the portals and popping them open with his hip, stepped out into the morning sunshine. As he suddenly appeared, kids froze, staring at him. Here the kids congregated passing cigarettes and listening to rap music anytime class wasn't in session, and a lot of the time it was. Quickly realizing they were busted, cigarettes disappeared behind backs, under hats or were quickly flicked into the street. Spying Billy Lenz standing among the group, Carrigan aimed his attention at Billy, spearing him before he could flee.

"Billy, come here," Carrigan said, knowing the subtlety wasn't an effective tactic on Billy. Billy looked around for help but the other students wouldn't meet his eyes and then drawn by Carrigan's magnetic stare Billy found himself ambling closer to the teacher.

"Billy, have you seen Tommy, I need to talk to him, and I know you two hang out sometimes,?" Carrigan asked, speaking slowly and clearly.

"Nothing," Billy said, "we didn't do nothing."

"Billy, listen to me. I know you didn't do anything. I just need to talk to Tommy, have you seen him?"

"We just drove around, and then Tommy ate all my bread," Billy answered, "we didn't do nothing."

Some days were just like that Carrigan thought. He was batting two for two. Maybe he should practice talking to a mirror. He didn't seem able to get his point across this morning.

"Billy, if you see Tommy, tell him I need to talk to him. And Billy, wipe your nose before you go to class."

Billy swiped his nose with the sleeve of his black shirt arcing a long green tendril from his nostril to his sweatshirt. Carrigan retreated back into the sanity of the school and headed for his classroom. He would take another crack at finding Tommy during lunch. The class bell rang before he made it to his room.

Tommy didn't make it to school Monday morning. On Sunday he completed his project carrying it into his bedroom where his secret nature caused him to throw a blanket over the metal cone. He then bagged all the scraps and left over cans with double bags and walked several blocks away before throwing them in the dumpster behind a vacant house. The battery he put in his backpack before setting them both by the front door. He didn't want the battery and the volcano in the same room, not yet.

Just as he was thinking about making the rounds for supper Sunday night, the front door burst open, and Tommy's father blew into the room dragging a big duffel bag behind him. Tommy didn't remember if it had been two weeks or maybe more since his dad was home last. He knew that Joe was making a run on the west coast, and Tommy hadn't expected him for several more weeks. Glancing toward his bedroom door, Tommy was glad that it was shut. Joe Columbo was short, prone to dressing in cowboy hats with Wranglers pulled low below a big gut. Like Tommy, Joe wore a chain also, from his front belt loop to the large wallet in his back pocket.

Sometimes on the road Joe felt a little guilty about leaving Tommy at home, but Tommy needed to learn to make it on his own, just like he had, he thought. The boy was too much like his mother anyway. She would have done them both a favor if she had taken the boy when she went.

"Howdy Thomas, my boy," Joe said, "how's it hangin'?"

Tommy thought briefly before speaking. What approach should he take this time? He could slip into his angry role and disappear until Joe left again, but this left his father alone in the house with his project, or he could play along until the old man blew town again. Number two he decided; maybe the old man would buy some groceries before he took off again.

"Hi, Dad," he answered, "you're home early, did you have a good trip?"

"Great trip kid, I picked up a full load in Frisco, and they already paid me to take it all the way to Baltimore. Don't have to be there 'til Tuesday. Run out to the truck and bring in the beer, there's a whole case out there. Let's have a few," Joe said, pleased that Tommy wasn't ignoring him. Tommy made the round trip bringing in the beer from the seat of the big conventional parked outside, putting it down on the kitchen table. The cans of Bud were still in six-packs, gleaming with moisture.

Bud wasn't his favorite but as long as the old man was buying what the hell Tommy thought.

Tommy quickly checked the kitchen with his eyes making sure that nothing was out of place before sitting down, popping the top on a cold one as Joe talked about the west coast.

"Dad," I'm hungry, Tommy said after his second beer. "Could I have some money to go eat?"

"Sure thing, buddy boy, bring me back some tacos. I just need to relax a little while, been driving all day."

Tommy knew relax meant finishing the case. He blinked twice when Joe handed him a twenty but didn't question his good luck. He worried a little about leaving the house and his room alone in the care of the old man, but knew that soon Joe would be passed out at the kitchen table, and he wouldn't have to worry about it. Hunger growled in his stomach. Tonight he would go through the front door of the Mexican restaurant and not have to look in the dumpster behind.

When Tommy got home later that night Joe was indeed still at the kitchen table snoring loudly. Tommy put the extra tacos in the empty refrigerator before going to his room. After putting a chair under the doorknob, just in case his dad got up in the middle of the night, he relaxed. He was too close now to let anything go wrong. His last thoughts before falling asleep were of fire burning brightly and hot, cleansing feelings of humiliation from his soul. When Tommy arose the next morning, he carefully checked under the blanket before leaving his enclave, shutting the door tightly behind him. Joe was still at the kitchen table, but awake now, eating the cold tacos from the fridge. Evidently one beer survived because Joe finished this off before licking the last bit of taco sauce from his fingers, belching loudly when he finished.

"Gotta go, Thomas my boy, the road is waiting for me. Have you been getting along all right?"

"Fine, Dad," said Tommy, for once glad to hear that the privacy of the house would soon be his again.

"How's school, you still going everyday?"

"Sure, no problems, beats hanging around here. Could maybe you get us some groceries before you go?" asked Tommy.

"No, don't have time buddy boy, but here's a big one," said Joe, dragging out his wallet, chain and all. "Sorry I didn't leave much last time, insurance was due, you know how it is. Get what you need, I shouldn't be gone longer that a week or two. When I get back, you'll be outa' school, then you and me can make some runs. How would that be?"

"Fine Dad," Tommy said looking at the hundred-dollar bill, Joe was offering to him. Tommy never saw a hundred before, and he counted the zeros twice before taking it from his father.

"Don't spend it on anything I wouldn't," laughed Joe.

"Yep, Tommy was going to be all right," Joe thought. He was starting to grow up. It would be good to have Tommy with him in the truck this summer. Make a man out of him. He was glad Thomas was through with his mad phase. Growing up was hard work.

Quickly as he blew in, Tommy's father was gone. Tommy looked around the kitchen at the beer cans scattered across the floor and the empty sack with the greasy spots staining the brown surface.

The house felt quiet and a little lonely, he thought. At least I'm rich now. I'm going to eat good this week.

After cleaning up the kitchen, Tommy walked back into the living room and saw his backpack sitting by the door. The black bag, and the battery inside suddenly brought his attention back to reality. Today was Monday, the day he was going to take his project to school. With his dad coming home, the project from last week seemed so long ago. He had money now; he could do anything he wanted.

Did he still need to take his assignment to school, he wondered He didn't have to hang around here anymore. With a hundred dollars he could go anywhere he wanted. Far away from the assholes around here. He could blow this town maybe take a bus down to Denver.

Continuing on in to his bedroom, he drew the blanket off the volcano resting quietly on the floor. Sitting down on the bed, he spent the next hour just looking at it. He liked the way the black paint solidified the cone making it appear powerful and heavy.

Carrigan's first period class was filled with juniors and half an hour into the period they were called out to take the math portion of the final exams. Two seniors were left sitting in the room that seemed barren without the press of squirming bodies. Both of the seniors completed their class presentation last week so he only let them beg for five minutes before allowing the pair to start a jigsaw puzzle on a back table. The period passed quickly, and between the three of them the puzzle began to take shape. The cover of the box said it would be a green dragon attacking a small hobbit in the castle of a mighty wizard. The problem was everything in the puzzle was green. At this rate in five or six years all the pieces would be joined. The two kids promised to return when they could as the class ended. Second period started, and Carrigan was relieved to escape from trying to fit all the parts together. It was starting to give him a headache.

Pausing to collect his thoughts for a minute he tried to remember if he had planning next period or if that was tomorrow's schedule. The days of the week lately seemed to blend together. His question was answered as students began pouring in his door. He gave brief thought to trying and to find Tommy in the milling mass of humanity outside, but pushed the idea away. It wouldn't be wise to leave his room unprotected this late in the year. Senior pranks were a constant hazard.

This second period class was full of juniors complaining about the math test. The English portion wasn't until Tuesday, giving them a little reprieve till they played "fill in the blank" again. Carrigan never understood why the state department of education thought there was any validity to the testing because the kids owned no stake in the results. A few students tried, but most spent the hour making elaborated designs by filling in the squares with pretty patterns. Huge grants of money were awarded, new programs added, and reliable courses eliminated based on the results. Further adding to the comedy of errors was the results were compared year to year on different classes of juniors. This was like saying the teachers did a better job of teaching last year's oranges than this year's apples.

Go figure, he thought. Mine is not to question why.

Carrigan made this class suffer through his history of Wyoming in thirty minutes or less, giving them just the facts, before letting them call it a day and attack the green dragon waiting for their nimble eager fingers. Shortly before the noon bell rang, Tommy appeared in his door.

"Hi, Mr. C., I heard you were looking for me."

Surprised, Carrigan had to think a minute before he remembered what he wanted to ask.

"I just wanted to check and make sure you Becky were going to be ready tomorrow with the rest of your presentation."

"We'll be ready; in fact if its okay can I leave this model in here. I don't want to keep it in my locker, somebody might mess with it," Tommy asked, showing Carrigan the black volcano.

"Sure," Carrigan replied, "just put in under the table over by the TV. Nobody will bother it. I missed you both classes last week."

"Ya, I know, my dad came home for a while, and I spent some time with him. I don't get to see him very often any more. We just did some father son things. It was great."

"Good," Carrigan replied, "sometimes we all need to do that. I talked to Becky earlier; she said you had her pick up some things at her folks store for your presentation. Something about deck wash and weed killer. I wanted to check and make sure you didn't bring anything potentially dangerous to class. How were you planning on doing the presentation?"

Carrigan closely watched Tommy's eyes, trying to see if he struck any raw nerves with his fishing expedition.

"Naw, nothing dangerous, just some baking soda and lemon juice with a touch of red food coloring. No deck wash, heck Mr. C, my dad and I don't even have a deck to wash. The weed killer would come in handy. Our whole yard is full, but Becky didn't give any to me. Is that all you needed?"

"Yes, Tommy thanks for checking with me, Oh, one more thing. Keep your eyes open. I talked to Sgt. Evans last weekend; he said some kids stole some stuff from a construction trailer. If you hear anything let me know will you? I don't want to turn them in, it's just the some things found around construction sites could be dangerous and I don't want anyone to get hurt."

"Sure thing Mr. C., see you tomorrow," Tommy finished without a pause.

Nothing in Tommy's answers or his demeanor looked the least bit out of the ordinary. Carrigan wouldn't bet Tommy wasn't involved in the break in, but if he was, Tommy was a very smooth liar.

Five minutes before lunch, Carrigan feeling particular magnanimous, and wanting to retrieve some aspirin, let the students out of class. The kids, unused to such generosity from him, looked at each other and shrugged, filing out the door, disappointed because they were denied a chance to plead for an early release. Carrigan ransacked the administration office until the secretaries plied him with Midol, claiming it was "good for what ailed him." Grabbing two pieces of pizza from today's lunch crew, he went in pursuit of Mr. James to ask his question of the week. A quick search of the science teacher's classroom found it to be empty, and Carrigan penetrated deeper through the lab room into the ecology area behind.

Here he found, whom he was in search, and plopped down on a wooden bench beside James as the science wiz was slowly flipping pellets of food into a small pond.

"Want some pizza?" Carrigan asked.

"Nope, brought my own lunch today," James answered, tossing another pellet.

"What do you know about Oxalic Acid," said Carrigan launching right in.

"It burns, and the FDA hasn't approved it for use with contacts."

"No, really I need to know."

"Why don't you ask one of the teachers that will be here next year teaching Chemistry?"

"I would but they don't put up with me like you do; besides you owe me. I left my bear fossil to you in my will."

"God, Carrigan don't you ever give up," James asked, conceding he lost the game. "Oxalic acid is used by the chemical industry mainly in areas of wood fiber cleansing and preservation. A strong acid compound, it has proven to be an economical way to produce pure sulfuric acid because when combined with calcium sulfate the calcium ion in the sulfate has a much stronger affinity for oxalate, and so the sulfate ions, along with the H^+ from the oxalic acid, can be removed by washing them with water. All that then remains is to evaporate the water, and you'll have sulfuric acid. In your terms Carrigan, a cheaper acid is used to make a more expensive one."

"Thanks," Carrigan replied, "now why don't you eat some pizza and let me feed the fish. Food and fish are things I know a lot about."

Third and Fourth period arrived and passed, during which Carrigan gave his short lecture on facts about Wyoming, hoping that somewhere deep in the recesses of their little minds some of the information might stick, waiting there until some day far in the future it could be recalled and used.

"Many different countries have controlled Wyoming over the years," he started, "including France, Great Britain, Mexico, Spain, Texas, and the United States. The state nickname is the equality state, the population is roughly 450,000 people, and the land area is about 98,000 square miles. Indian Paintbrush is our state flower, Meadowlarks are the state bird. Cottonwood the state tree and Buffalo or Bison is the state mammal with Cutthroat trout being the state fish. People have lived in Wyoming for over 12,000 years, and many tribes of Indians called Wyoming home. John Colter was one of the earliest white explorers back in 1807 when he found

Yellowstone Park. Many people traveled through here by wagon train following the Platte River. Later the promise of gold brought many more. The army established several forts and fought fierce battles with the native people for control of the land. Buffalo were once thick on the plains, but cattle now graze the broad grassland. Women in Wyoming were the first to vote anywhere in the nation. Wyoming became a state in 1890 and is the 44th state. Our state capitol is Cheyenne and the main industries are agriculture, the mining of minerals, and tourism. Now go forward in knowledge and finish my dragon on the back table."

By the end of the day, the dragon was really starting to take shape, most of him anyway. His tail was still unassembled, but the fierce head breathing long incinerating plumes of fire was finally pieced together. Before leaving school that afternoon Carrigan checked out the model volcano Tommy brought into his classroom earlier. The model stood about a foot and a half high, was made from sheet metal and then painted black. The seams were pop riveted, and it was nothing more than a metal cone with a small white paper cup sitting in its mouth.

"Nothing too dangerous here," he decided. Sometimes he let his imagination get carried away. It really was time for a long, long summer vacation.

After school, Carrigan ran by the lumberyard again, placing his order for the roof tresses. The clerks told him it would be seven to ten days before they were delivered. Once he hauled these to the hills, the cabin would really start to take shape. He also priced several different types of shingles, deciding to wait on these before he ordered any. Finishing with the lumberyard, Carrigan drove by Assisted Living to check on his friend Otto. It had been several weeks since he stopped to visit. Although Otto lived among many other seniors, he was always glad when Carrigan came by. It was from Otto that Carrigan bought the mountain property, and he wanted to tell the old German about his start on the cabin. Otto was on the porch of the facility when Carrigan arrived, and Carrigan sat down beside him as evening shadows began to flicker and streetlights snapped to attention guarding the avenues.

"Started the cabin last week," Carrigan offered.

"Ya vat is goot," Otto replied. "Always vanted one of my own, but vhisky and cabins didn't mix. Revenuers vould know vere to find you."

"Maybe in a couple of weeks after school is out, I will drag you back up to the hills, so you can show me where the still used to be. Might want to build one of my own."

"Yavol," Otto answered. "Ve might take some fixings vith us, driving in the hills is thirty vork."

Carrigan stayed several hours asking Otto questions about the legends surrounding the land, and where the best fishing spots were on the river. Some of the answers he knew already, but Otto enjoyed telling the stories and the two spent a pleasant evening together before Carrigan headed for home. He still needed to make a call and finish some paperwork before tomorrow.

"Vatch oot for the cave," were Otto's last words. "It isn't vise to look too deep in dark places. Ven ve go, I vill show you vat I found there."

Carrigan nodded and stepped off the porch where Gertrude awaited him. Supper that night at Assisted Living was toasted cheese sandwiches, and the aroma made Carrigan hungry. He thought he might just fix some for himself when he got back to the house.

After supper of toasted cheese and tomato soup, two of his favorites, Carrigan returned a call to Roberta Lansing. After several rings, Becky answered and Carrigan heard her calling for her mother on the other end.

"Mommy it's Mr. C.," Becky yelled, forcing Carrigan to remove the phone from his ear.

Roberta came on the line after a short while, and James told her about his conversation with Becky this morning, explaining that he didn't think she was going to use any deck wash or other chemicals in the presentation, just lemon juice and baking soda, but he asked her if she had the receipt of exactly what Becky bought. Another pause ensued before Roberta came back on the line, reading from the receipt. One sack of lawn fertilizer, deck wash, weed killer, carburetor cleaner, a thermometer, and some liquid stove fuel.

"Reed is out of town at a convention till Friday," Roberta said. "Becky claims that her dad told her to get this, and I believe her. Thank you for your concern; you know how protective I get over Becky. I'll check with Reed when he gets back, but I feel much better now, knowing she didn't take this stuff to school. Thanks so much, Mr. Carrigan".

"No problem," like I said it's all part of my job. What time does the store close, I need a few things myself?" Carrigan asked

"Now that it's getting warm we stay open 'til eight in the evening."

"Goodnight Roberta, thanks for the info," said Carrigan.

Checking the time, Carrigan realized he had a few minutes left before eight, so he drove downtown to Lansing's Drug Store. The store was a nice fit for Rockville, and although it was called a drug store, much more could be purchased inside. Taking advantage of the fact that large discount stores wouldn't come to a town this size Big Reed stocked clothing, sporting goods, automotive supplies, and a line of home and garden materials. He also had a large pharmacy in the rear of the store. Prowling the aisles, Carrigan found the items from Roberta's list, and he made notes of the active ingredients from each of the projects, jotting them down in a small notebook he carried in his front shirt pocket. A habit left over from his days in law enforcement.

Once a cop, always a cop, he thought to himself.

Returning home to stay for the evening he thought about watching some television, but decided against it. In the closet he still had several unopened boxes from his parent's home that he packed up before renting the small ranch several years ago. He always planned on going through them, but every time he started, he would get sidetracked on some small piece of memorabilia, and the boxes still remained mostly full sitting on his closet floor.

"Tonight I'm going to make some progress," he said out loud.

Kneeling on the floor, he opened the first one and carefully looked through a sheaf of old newspaper clippings he found. Probably cut out by his mother. She had always been a great one for saving articles of interest to her.

A short ways into the pile he came across an article on the Wind River Indian Reservation, and he retreated from the closet to the comfort of the couch before studying the yellowed paper. He read and then reread the article looking for some connection to her, but found none. The clipping was written primarily about the reservation and the Shoshone Indians who lived in central Wyoming. The reservation was also home to the Northern Arapaho people. The tribes operated as two separate tribal governments. The reservation covered 2,268,008 acres and about 2,650 Shoshone tribal members lived there. The tribal headquarters were located near Fort Washakie, Wyoming. The per capita income was $2,340. Almost 50% of the residents graduated from high school, but only 4% went on to finish college. The clipping was over 20 years old, and Carrigan hoped the numbers had improved since then. That wasn't a lot of money to support a family. Returning the clipping to the archive Carrigan decided to call it a night. The boxes weren't hurting anything sitting in his closet, maybe this summer he would have more time to go through them.

The next morning Carrigan dawdled in the kitchen washing dishes and tidying up until he remembered the meeting called by Rudolf. Fleeing out the door, he hurried on his way to school. Just as he was locking the door on his pickup, before going to the meeting, he kicked something on the floorboard that skittered out the door and into the gravel. Stooping down to pick it up, he realized it was a shell casing from the .270.

Probably one that fell out of the cartridge box last weekend, he thought.

Not wanting to take the time to unlock the door again he thrust the shell casing into his pants pockets and jogged over to the prep area arriving just in time as Rudolf began to address the other teachers. Rudolf's message was short and sweet. A few of the teachers afterwards hugged him and several shook hands wishing him the best. Jan Rudolf was a good principal. Most of the time he kept higher-level administration off their backs and let them teach. He handled the discipline cases fairly and didn't try to push all the administrivia onto the teachers. His personal life was none of their business, but most were sorry to see him go. There were far worse principals out there in the educational field, and all veteran teachers realized one of those types might be at the helm here next year.

Trisha Collingworth stopped Carrigan just as he was leaving the meeting. She chatted a minute about what a shame Jan leaving was, and then appearing a little nervous, asked Carrigan if he had time later for her to ask him a few questions.

"Sure, come on over," Carrigan replied. "First period wouldn't be good, I have a full class, but second period I have planning. Stop in then."

"Thanks," Trisha replied looking relieved. "Jan said your bark was a lot worse than your bite. I appreciate you making time for me."

First period came and went, with Carrigan repeating his Wyoming speech again before letting one more group do a presentation on Kimberlites found in the mountains south of Rockville. The discussion about diamonds led the class into how all women wanted was to be married. Carrigan realized there were no logical answers to this discussion and changed the subject before making the kids go to work on his jigsaw puzzle. Only three days were left, and he wanted to complete the puzzle before school ended, but a thousand pieces of green were a lot to put together. The students, by the end of class, finally assembled the Hobbit. He looked very diminutive against the wrath of the dragon with only a small shield to deflect the firestorm breathed by his evil foe.

Trisha arrived half way through his planning period. He was glad for her interruption as he was trying to make sense from the chemical symbols he was doodling on the notepad laying on his desk. Chemistry class in college was a long time ago, and like the 1000 piece dragon, the combinations of elements were causing his headache to return.

"I guess what I need to ask you is if you consider me an asset to the school or a liability," she asked him coming directly to the point. "I've been thinking of quitting and leaving town. My secretarial skills are good. Maybe education isn't where I need to be. The last several weeks have been pretty tough, and I feel sometimes like I've lost all respect from the kids, and worse yet my peers."

Carrigan eased back in his chair studying her before answering. Trisha appeared a little "blonde" upon first inspection but during the year, observing her teach, he knew her background to be solid. She was extremely well read, and she strongly encouraged her students to read also. They constantly complained about it in his class. Several times he was aware that she spent long hours of individual time with students, going over and over projects until the format was correct. These were characteristics that showed she cared, the kind of care that wasn't taught in educational classes, but rather came from the person. That she was young, naïve, and too attractive for her own good, were other parts of the person that worked to her disadvantage.

"Let me tell you a story," he said. "Maybe it will be some use to you. If not, then I'm not the right person to talk to."

"Long ago there was a young coyote. Her name was Kalina, and she was the youngest and prettiest in the pack. She wasn't happy with her youth and beauty, but wanted the pack to recognize her for her worth and intelligence. She thought everyday on how to accomplish this.

One day early in the spring while she was out roaming the grassland looking for a juicy prairie dog, she came across an old Bear named Bemu. Now Bemu was very old and crafty having lived many years. He knew of Kalina and invited her to help hunt honey with him. 'After we get the honey,' he growled, 'you can take your share back to the pack, and they will think you are very wise and important.' Together they soon found an old honey tree in a great field of Clover. Bemu hoisted Kalina up and told her to take the honey from the tree. Sensing a thief in their midst, the bees became very angry and swarmed against Kalina stinging her many times causing her to drop the honey and run for her life. Bemu ate all the honey ignoring the bees. What were a few stings to something as old and tough as he was? Kalina ran back to her pack swollen from stings and barely alive.

The pack laughed and laughed at her for being so stupid as to trust a bear. Not able to stand the humiliation, she left her home and family in search of another pack, but wherever she went the voices of the pack preceded her, and they too laughed at her stupidity making buzzing sounds in their throats when they howled. Finding no sanctuary, she returned home dejected and heartbroken. As the days of spring turned into summer, she watched the world around her day after day. She saw the bees gathering honey and her pack hunting, barely finding enough food for all the members. Finally one day she left and climbed the mountains to visit with the Great Wolf to ask him what she should do. Finding him she explained her plight. He said only, 'Look within yourself. You are young and beautiful, and coyotes are very crafty, use what God has given you." Disappointed Kalina left the mountains, and as she returned to her den she came across a herd of buffalo. Using her sweetest voice she told the buffalo about a huge field of clover near her home that was the sweetest in the land. Naturally the buffalo followed her, and she showed them the clover surrounding the old tree and the bees. The buffalo ate for days and days until at last all the clover was gone and the earth was brown and bare. Then Kalina waited and watched the bees. At first the bees couldn't believe all their clover was gone, and they could make no more honey.

Finally realizing the tree did not have enough stores of food for the winter, they flew together in a great swarm and left the plains moving far to the west where there were fields of clover the buffalo had not eaten. After they were gone, Kalina climbed the tree and removed all of the honey the bees could not take with them and brought this great bounty back to the pack. With the honey, there was food for all, and the pack lived through the winter growing fat and sassy. Each night they paid homage to Kalina calling her wise and brave, yipping about her glory to all the other packs. And thus Kalina found her place."

Trisha leaned her head back, listening as Carrigan told the story, smiling several times at his description of the young coyote.

"I can tell Kalina needs to be very careful not to ask advise from the wolf too many times," she said when he was finished. "Next time the wolf might just devour her because she was so silly. Thank you, James, I can see why Jan likes you."

Carrigan felt a little silly after Trish left. It was his experience that beautiful women tended to do whatever they wanted anyway, and the world had to keep up with them.

I feel a grease attack coming on he thought. This would be a good day to go to the diner. The noon bell rang, and Carrigan left the school. It had been a while since he visited with Traci anyway.

Tommy was busy also that morning. Yesterday he brought the project to school finally deciding to keep it in his locker. No one shared the space with him. He didn't like to be this close to his work, but he feared Becky might mess with the project if he put it in her locker.

Time for that later, he thought.

Billy told him that Mr. C. was looking for him, and at first he panicked. Practicing his answers in case Becky squealed, he calmed himself, trusting in his ability. He removed the outer cone of the volcano and carried it to Mr. C.'s room. Just as he feared, that bastard Evans was making a nuisance of himself again, but he released just a bit of his boyish charm he kept for times like this, and Mr. C. didn't suspect a thing. Still he needed to be careful. He didn't like the way the teacher looked at him sometimes, almost as if he could tell what he was thinking. Finding Becky he told her that he was going to put the volcano in her locker tomorrow and that he would take it to the classroom for her presentation. Becky was worried about her daddy finding out she picked up things from the store without his permission, but Tommy coached her and kept reminding her how happy Daddy would be when she did well on their presentation.

Tommy quickly ate lunch on Tuesday and then removed the inner volcano from his locker carrying it nonchalantly to the end of the hall, the jock's hangout area, and put it gently into the bottom of her locker. He was sweating heavily when he finished, and he wiped the sweat from his face, drying his hands on his pants before continuing.

He almost lost his nerve on Sunday after his dad was here, but this was his one chance to make up for the last three years. Should anything go wrong, he still had the hundred dollars buried deep in his pocket. He could leave town in a hurry if he needed to. He used the last of his dad's taco money this morning to buy some lemon juice and baking soda for the presentation. He wanted everything to be perfect. Connecting the last wire he paused a minute before completing his project. Very slowly and carefully, he pulled down on Pluto's tail setting the alarm.

Carrigan was late again today, arriving back in his room after most of the students were in class. Knowing some of them would be leaving to take the English part of the state exams, he called on Becky and Tommy to finish their presentation before the other students left. Before allowing Tommy to load the volcano, he checked the small box of baking soda, feeling a little stupid when he tasted it before allowing Tommy to continue. The food coloring and lemon juice were new bottles that never had been opened.

"Heartburn from lunch," he said to the kids who laughed at him when he tasted the baking soda, screwing his face up from the bitter taste.

They were used to him doing stupid things in class, sometimes he seemed more like one of them than a teacher. With a flourish, Tommy added the lemon juice and on cue the volcano bubbled and spewed frothy red foam down the sides of the black model. Even Carrigan had to admit that it looked very realistic, and Becky danced around the table clapping her hands and laughing. Tommy finished by reading a short paragraph on lava talking about the temperature that rocks melted and how fast some flows moved.

"Nice job you two," he said. Remembering his promise to Roberta, Carrigan came up with a couple of slightly dented Snickers from his bottom drawer and gave them each one.

"Oh, Tommy, thank you, thank you, that was so much fun, and we won didn't we," she said throwing her arms around Tommy's necks and giving him a big hug.

The rest of the class giggled until Tommy glared at them, and then he shuffled to his usual seat in the back of the class. Carrigan didn't think Tommy looked very happy for just receiving Becky's praise and passing his first class in three years. Tommy was a funny kid.

Most of the class left to take tests, and Carrigan put the others to work on the jigsaw puzzle. Tommy didn't participate with the group, but then he never did. Carrigan went back to his desk listening to Becky's childish laughter as she found a piece of the puzzle that fit. Several minutes later, looking up from his own puzzle, Carrigan found Becky standing in front of his desk.

"What is it, Becky?" said Carrigan, surprised by the interruption.

"I forgot," she said, "I have a cheerleading meeting now. Can I go put my books in my locker?"

"Sure" Carrigan answered, "just don't goof around in the hallways."

"I won't, I promise," said Becky.

Carrigan returned to the puzzle on his desk only to be interrupted again as Tommy flashed passed him.

"Going to the bathroom, Mr. C., be right back," Tommy said over his shoulder.

"Thanks for letting me know," Carrigan said to Tommy's back as the student left the classroom.

He was relieved that Tommy and Becky's presentation was over; he didn't know why he was nervous about it, probably just because it was the end of the year. Still something in the symbols in front of him kept drawing his attention as if they were runes, which when once deciphered would open a magic door. On the page he had noted the active ingredients from the supplies that Roberta Lansing read to him. At the top of the page was written the word thermometer and near the bottom he wrote fertilizer. Try as he might, they just wouldn't go together. Near the middle of the page he wrote Oxalic Acid and beneath that were the symbols he was playing with arranging and rearranging. Something was looking back at him, but it took him just a minute to realize it. If Oxalic acid combined with sulfates to form sulfuric acid, wasn't it possible that Oxalic acid or deck cleaner could combine with calcium nitrate, or carburetor cleaner to form nitric acid. Excited now he scribbled the symbol for nitric acid

317

and paired it with the other words on his page, pausing a minute as he looked at the KCIO3 before moving on letting his pencil rest on the word thermometer. Thermometers didn't have active ingredients or maybe they did, what was in them. Mercury of course, a heavy metal, poisonous like the rest and then he remembered a time when the professor embarrassed him in class many years ago because he was looking at Nancy instead of the black board.

"And what do you get when you mix mercury and nitric acid, Mr. Carrigan?"

He still remembered the professor's look of disapproval when Carrigan realizing he was on the spot answered, "A mess."

The class laughed but not the professor and in his stern voice corrected him, "No Mr. Carrigan you get very unstable explosive compound, fulminate of mercury."

Carrigan quickly reached into his pocket and pulled out the .270 casing, examining the end where the firing pin struck the primer igniting the powder inside. Quickly checking the rest of the words on the list he looked again at the weed killer $KClO_3$ Potassium Chlorate, now he remembered it from the MERC manual. Along with being an effective herbicide, the chemical was also used in matches to make them flare when struck. Combined with fulminate, the two would form a primer capable of a flash explosion. These two would burn hot and fast enough to ignite more inert ingredient like fertilizer $NH4NO3$ especially if the fertilizer was mixed with fuel oil making it a compact mass rather than loose grains. Carrigan felt a hot wave of nausea climb into his throat. His hand shaking, he reached for the telephone, and when the office secretary answered asking him to please hold he shouted at her, "Get Jan on the phone, now Damnit." Stunned the secretary put the principal on the line.

"Carrigan quit hollering at my secretaries," said Jan.

"Listen to me," Carrigan said, he voice trembling, "don't ask questions, don't interrupt, just listen. We have a code red in the school. Evacuate all the buildings now, I will take care of rooms on this side, don't announce it, just do it now. Take everyone to the football field at least a quarter mile from the school, and if you see Tommy Columbo, don't approach him, just let him go. Call 911 and tell them we have a bomb on campus, but start the evacuation first. Do it Jan, for God's sake do it now."

The students working on the puzzle couldn't help but hear Carrigan on the phone, and they looked scared as Carrigan led them from the room. Carrigan burst into the classroom across the hall, saying just the words "code red" to the teacher as she looked up to see what the interruption was to her lesson.

"Take my kids with you and go to the football field," he said. "I will tell the others."

Down the hall, Carrigan entered every classroom saying only two words to each teacher, sending them to join the other lines of teachers and students leaving the building. These evacuation drills were practiced many times, and the kids joked and pushed each other moving quickly to the exits. Carrigan scanned the lines of youngsters passing him looking for Becky but was unable to find her. There was no sign of Tommy either. The last room in this wing was Trish Collingworth's and with the look on his face, she needed little urging to get the kids moving down the corridor. At the end of this annex was a short hallway; Becky's locker was in this wing along with the "chosen others," mostly preppies and jocks. Barging into the bathrooms, he checked each stall making sure they were empty before pushing back out the doors headed for the end of the hallway leaving the doors swinging behind him.

Becky felt better about herself today than she had for some time. She didn't feel quite right about not telling Mommy the truth, but she did what Tommy told her and sure enough the volcano blew up just like he said it would.

Much better than when Daddy did it, she thought. His was just made from paper. She didn't know how Tommy used all the stuff she gave him, but now she didn't care. Mr. C. must know how Tommy put it together because he said they did a good job. She didn't really like the kind of candy bar Mr. C. gave her, but it was fun to win anyway. She couldn't wait to tell Daddy when he got home from his trip.

Just as Becky found the right piece for the face of the wizard in the dragon puzzle she was putting together, she remembered the cheerleaders were supposed to meet concerning a car wash to raise money for uniforms. She didn't really want to go, but she didn't want the other girls mad at her either.

Puzzles were fun, something she was good at. Somehow she just knew when a piece was right, and never had to try fitting it in the hole like the other kids did. She looked one more time at the wizard; his long beard and flowing gown were such a pretty color of white. He was sprinkling a magic spell over the little guy who was fighting with the dragon.

Becky wasn't sure whether the wizard's spell would help the little guy or the dragon but maybe she would understand better when the puzzle was done, she thought.

As she left the classroom Becky began to run down the hall so she wouldn't be late. Passing the bathrooms she thought about how long the meeting might be. The other kids teased her because she went pee so often, but Mommy always told her to go when there was a chance. Becky turned quickly and ducked into the bathroom just to make sure she didn't have any accidents later.

Tommy was suddenly alert as Becky abruptly left the room. He hadn't even seen her leave the puzzle. He was still thinking about the hug she gave him and the way her breasts felt when she squeezed up tight against him.

"Where was she going," he thought? There was still time left in the period, and Becky never went to her locker between third and fourth period. He watched her everyday and knew her routine. After third period, she always turned left out the double doors and went straight to life skills.

Jumping from his chair, he followed after her just to make sure she didn't go to her locker. He didn't want anyone messing around in there now. Telling Mr. C. he had to go to the bathroom, he flew down the hall. As he turned the corner, he stopped short. The hallway was empty before him. Looking behind, he checked the doorways to the other rooms but they were shut and quiet. He couldn't believe she disappeared from sight that quickly. Slowing down, he stopped directly in front of the bathrooms trying to decide if he should check in the girl's bathroom but deciding against it he walked on down to the end of the hallway. He could wait by her locker, and if she came he would divert her attention so she didn't try and open it. As Tommy turned the corner into this isolated part of the school, he was overcome by feelings of indecision.

Why did Becky hold on to him so tightly back in the classroom? Maybe she was starting to come around and was beginning to realize that she would be a lot better off with him than those lesbo bitches. He still had the money; he could take Becky out to dinner, or buy her something she would like, his fantasy continued.

Suddenly the knowledge came to him that he didn't have to blow anything up. He could if he wanted to and still might if anybody gave him any more shit, but things were going pretty good right now. He could turn off the alarm, go back to Mr. C's room and get the other volcano and put it in the locker just in case Becky looked in it after school. Meshed together again, they could be carried back to his house and hidden after school was over. He wouldn't throw them away just in case a need developed in the future.

Maybe I better get rid of the battery too, better to be safe he thought.

Arriving at the locker, he opened the door pausing to appreciate his project, thinking about all the time he put into it.

It was too bad he couldn't show this to Mr. C. This was quality work and Mr. C. was all the time talking about trying your hardest and doing your best. This was good.

Kneeling down Tommy lifted the switch that turned the alarm off. Next as he began to unhook the battery, Tommy realized for the first time how close the wires were together. Somehow he never saw this before. There was less than an inch between the striker and the bell. Perhaps because he assembled this part first and then attached the last end to the negative end of the dry cell. Holding his breath, he started to turn the plastic cap on the negative terminal of the battery when he sensed someone behind him.

"Hi Tommy, what are you doing?" said Becky, holding her books tightly to her chest.

Tommy looked back at her, and then turned his attention to loosening the wire again.

"I thought the volcano was back in class, how did it get in my locker. Oh, silly me, I went to the bathroom. That's why I didn't see you carrying it. We sure did a good job, didn't we?" she asked.

Tommy didn't answer. The threads on the screw of the terminal were rusted and he was having trouble taking the cap off. He didn't want to put both hands around the battery, fearing he would bump the clock while it was still attached to the battery. He looked over at the bells on the clock thinking it might be easier to take the wire from there, but it was wound around tightly and was very close to the striker.

"Why are you putting wire on it, Tommy?" Becky asked.

Just then Tommy heard the sound of students in the hallway. Doors were opening behind them, and voices of students laughing and joking echoed to this end of the hallway. Knowing he was about out of time before somebody else saw him, Tommy decided he would just pull the wire from the test tube, shut the door and then come back when nobody else was around.

As Carrigan turned the corner, he saw two students in front of the banks of lockers. He started to raise his voice to direct them out of the building when he realized the girl standing with her back to him was Becky. Kneeling below her reaching into a locker Tommy was trying to work the duck tape loose from the top of the volcano, so he could break the line of communication from his blasting cap. Suddenly Carrigan realized where the last piece of the puzzle was.

Licking his lips before trying to talk, Carrigan shouted down the hallway, "Becky Lansing, I need to see you," hoping she heard him over the growing commotion behind him caused by the students leaving the building.

Becky turned to look in his direction. Tommy looked up also. Carrigan switched his attention to the dark pools of Tommy's eyes. Now Tommy knew what the noise was down the hall, people were leaving the building because of him. Seeing Carrigan's expression suddenly brought the seriousness of what was before him to a higher level.

This wasn't a game any longer; somehow he hadn't quite been careful enough. But how did he know, Tommy wondered. Just five minutes ago, Mr. C. was all happy, throwing candy bars at him, and now he just stood there looking at him, looking down on him, staring at him with a mixture of fear and disgust.

Becky began walking toward Carrigan her hand pointing to her ear indicating the she couldn't hear what he was asking her. Tommy thought briefly about grabbing her, holding on to her, preventing her from leaving until he got out of the building, but he didn't want to get any nearer to Carrigan who was running toward them.

Oh to hell with it he thought, giving up on trying to work the tape loose. Let them figure out what to do. He could duck behind Becky, and Mr. C. wouldn't be able to get a hand on him.

Turning loose of the tape Tommy reached out and pushed down on Pluto's tale, resetting the alarm clock. Perhaps Tommy bumped the blasting cap as he pulled on the tape, or maybe the elements inside the test tube suddenly became destabilized. Whatever the cause the tightly combined chemicals inside their glass container performed the task for which he created them. Tommy heard a slight hissing sound as he finished setting the alarm. The glass tube beneath the tape seemed to flare briefly, and then as if in slow motion Tommy watched his hand disappear from his arm. He had the briefest glimpse of what appeared to be his finger bones white and stark without flesh on them, like the negative of an x-ray, and then his vision was extinguished as the bright flash expanded filling the locker with a burning heat. The second flash occurred milliseconds behind the first. The soaked fertilizer exploded transferring its energy into flame and expanding gas rushing toward any obstacles in its path. The force of the explosion rushed through the top of the volcano erupting instantly and blowing the metal valve completely from the gas cylinder. The red-hot flame ignited the flow as it rushed to escape the heavy metal confines. Tommy felt himself floating as if carried on a current of flame as the massive force threw him across the hallway. His journey was interrupted when he slammed hard against the opposite wall, broken, blinded, and burned.

Carrigan felt Tommy's decision like a will of communication that flowed between them and knew that he arrived too late. Within several steps, he met Becky and locking onto her wrist with an iron grip dragged her behind him as he reversed directions, running for the safety of the corner just in front of him. Jerked from her feet, Becky's legs floated out behind, leaving her sandals on the floor where she was standing. Beside them the lockers blew open in a quick series one after the other, flung outward from the force of the pressure traveling from compartment to compartment. Carrigan felt the heat chasing him, relentlessly close as he dove for the corner of the hallway frantically pulling Becky with him till he could wrap his arms around her tiny waist. Behind them her sandals melted into the carpet where seconds ago she was standing. Forcing himself on top her he clutched her to him, attempting to crawl further down the hallway away from the heat. As suddenly as the cloud of flame appeared, it was over and as pages of books and smoking papers rained down upon them, Carrigan beat the smoldering sparks from his clothes before throwing Becky over his shoulder as he ran on down the hallway past his room to the double orange doors and the fresh air beyond. Inside his room the concussion knocked ceiling tiles from their hangers dropping them on the tables. The jigsaw puzzle pieces were scattered re-scrambling the hobbit with the dragon into a myriad of green pieces. The wizards spell that Becky completed, although broken but successful, protected them from the dragon's fire. Tommy's presentation was over.

Chapter 14
The Council

Night Wind sat before the fire, the tent walls around her were decorated with Kills-Crowe's many exploits written in layers of years. His daughter read them from left to right and top to bottom. She paused a minute with the notation of her birth and the sign for Maxpe or far seer noted in red pigment, many seasons ago. Prior to her notation were descriptions of the days both of her older brothers, sons of Morning Ray were born. Each brother now had wives. Reading further she paused when she came to the name-glyph of the death of her mother, Morning Ray, the paint pictures in black, a color her people seldom used, showing his sorrow. The story went on switching to blue, the paint told of Kills-Crowe's marriage to Painted Flower and of the birth of Lone Eagle and Little Dog. She noted with satisfaction the picture sign for the battle with the Sioux late in Kill-Crowe's life. For years since she was attacked and raped by the Sioux, while with the small hunting party, Kills-Crowe hunted for those responsible. At last they were found and slain, slowly over the course of several days, layers of hide were removed from their bodies, strip by strip until the nerve endings could stand no more.

Painted Flower gave to her the sacred bone feather pipe that guided Kills-Crowe's plans for everyday life and for battle. While he was chanting and dreaming alone in his tepee, the pipe would speak to him, charting the course of action for his tribe. Now Kills-Crowe was gone, and a new leader would be chosen. Night Wind's ride home across the plains was uneventful, and climbing the long hills leading from the plains, she remembered how much she loved and missed the snowy mountains. The party of Shoshone crossed the high passes riding beside the cold lakes still edged with snow, before descending into the valley. Spotted Owl was quiet, and she knew he was thinking of Joshua and La Ramie, as was she. By the second night without him, alone in her robes, she felt cold and bare, and only the stirring in her womb brought her comfort. A few tribes from the north were already gathered by the time Night Wind arrived at "the water that boils." Here thermal activity deep within the earth brought hot water to the surface of the valley, and mud pots bubbled beside the spring, smelling of sulfur and minerals.

The Sheepeaters were delayed, finding hunting hard in the Wind Mountains far to the north. This tribe of Tukadika lived within the great Absaroka Range, and the trail for them would be long and hard. Even longer was the route for the Ventres or Green River Bands, arriving from the west. Among them would be the three pillars of the nation, Ink-a-tosh-a-pop, Fibe-to-un-tu-wat, and Washakie. From the southern ranges would come the two brothers Pah-dasher-wah, or Strong Bear and Moh-woon-ha the Moon Follower. From among these warriors, a new chief would be chosen. Perhaps even Little Eagle would figure in the decision before the council was over.

A medicine wheel would tell the time for the council to make a decision. Each of the 28 spokes, one for each tribe of the Shoshoni Race, came together without ending, forming a stone circle of life, divided yet harmonious. On the shortest day of the winter season, a decision would be made by the tribes for a leader to be chosen. When the wheel showed them the day, the ceremony would begin. Night Wind, as Vision Woman, must tell the tribes what she saw of the future and the past, to help the elder chiefs in their choice. Although her recommendations were not binding, the elders listened closely to her prophecies, interpreting the visions for the best of the tribe. Soon she must purify herself and then retire to a fasting bed high in the mountains around the valley, and pray for guidance to come. Alone and naked, she would dream, flying between what has been, and what is yet to come. This was her purpose, her place as Bu Hagant of the Shoshone.

Night Wind feared little that walked upon the earth, but in the mountains high above the valley were stories of the Nunum Bi, small spirit people reported to be evil and cruel, aligned with O-kee-pa, a demon within the rocks. No person who saw one, returned alive to the land of the living, and from this evil, she must protect herself. A few mummies of the Nunum Bi were found by the tribes over the years, discarded shriveled shrunken shells of their former selves. From these remains Night Wind knew they existed, waiting for her.

In the tepee of Kills-Crowe, she thought back to the quilling society her mother hosted, when the moon was near it smallest sliver. Morning

Ray would cry to the village of the meeting. All the women from the tribe would come, bringing robes and clothes to work upon. Night Wind loved listening to the stories the women told and the rumors about other tribe members. In late afternoon, the women would assemble, burning sage to call forth the spirit of the Double Woman, to aide them in the process of attaching the quills and paint to the projects. The older women were more skilled and held higher ranking than the initiates, and Night Wind thought with pride of the time she completed her first doll, earning the honor of mugua. The Double Woman was devious, though, and she would whisper in the ears of the young women, that the work was too hard and they should quit, letting others do their work. Night Wind learned well from Morning Ray not to listen to this advice, and always labored long into the night completing her designs. After the death of her mother, she no longer took part in the ceremonies, her visions setting her apart from the other women. They were frightened of Night Wind's powers and nervous in her presence. Only Painted Flower still sat with her, talking of times long ago, and working on the intricate designs.

"Of what do you dream second daughter," asked Painted Flower as she came into the tent.

Smiling upon her stepmother, Night Wind motioned to the painted life of Kills-Crowe before them on the tepee walls. "Of Kills-Crowe," she said. "I think of his blood that runs within my body, of his stories, but mostly of his love."

"All this and more, we will miss," said Painted Flower. "He was a good man, and a wise leader. Stay with me tonight, Night Wind. Tell me of your journey from the rendezvous, and of this trader. Tonight we will quill, calling upon the Double Woman and honor Kills-Crowe."

That night in the tent of Kills-Crowe, his daughter and his wife honored him by making a scroll to hang upon the walls of the tepee, dying the quills with vermilion and arranging them on the soft deer skin so all might know of Kills-Crowe's life. Through this, he would live on. As they worked, Night Wind told Painted Flower of her journey and the growth of her love for Joshua. She told Painted Flower about the great bear of a man who held her with such tenderness, of his dark moods, and his kindness to Spotted Owl. Night Wind shared with Painted Flower of the child that grew within her and of her plans to return to Joshua after the council. Together they planned their work and wrote of Kills-Crowe's bravery on the meadow as he fought with Lame Wolf and the Blackfeet. As in life, the quills of the porcupine were used for defense, the women's work defending Kills-Crowe against the loss of his memory among the people of the Shoshone.

As the days of fall passed, more tribes gathered, bringing information from across the mountains, uniting old friends in the valley. Strong Bear spoke with all the arriving tribes, making sure they were aware of his greatness. His brother, Moon Follower, met with small groups of warriors telling of Strong Bear's great deeds, persuading them that his brother was the chosen one. Washakie spent the days hunting in the hills surrounding the valley bringing in meat to feed the rapidly growing lodges. Little Eagle allied himself with Ink-a-tosh-a-pop, and Fibe-to-un-tu-wat spending time equally with both in case either should be chosen.

The first snows of winter threatened in the gray skies, and Night Wind could delay no longer, she must seek the visions to help the race. With the aid of her sister-in-laws and Painted Flower, she spent the day within the sweat lodge sipping water mixed with honey until her pores held the aroma of sweet clover. That evening Night Wind fasted alone within a tent erected just for her. Spotted Owl stayed with his uncles. At first light, she left the village, climbing into the mountains to spend the day and night alone divining wisdom. By mid morning she was seated on a granite bench overlooking the valley below. Night Wind watched the smoke rising from the tepees, feeling the chill bite of the cold air, and tightly wrapped the blankets around her, letting her mind relax, seeking the place deep within her. Throughout the day she sat, sipping only small drinks of honey water, until at last, Apo, the sun fell, bringing the valley into the darkness of the night. By midnight Night Wind's head drooped, and she felt herself drifting, beginning the flight on the winds that carried her across time.

The earth beneath her receded, and as she flew the ground changed. She saw the great Oblayela or wilderness, and the earth swarmed with grasshoppers. Men tried to drive the hordes of insects into holes in the ground, but there were too many, and they swarmed over the men passing on in great waves. Flying on, she saw ships with white canvas rolling across the seas of the great plains, passing through huge villages of prairie dogs. Behind the ships, the tribes of prairie dogs, sickened and died, their bodies untouched and rotting. A great tepee appeared to her, half red, half black each side painted with symbols of the bear and the moon. Suddenly fire spread across the plains, and smoke rose high into the skies driving before them vast herds of animals fleeing with tribes of her people into the mountains, and through the fire came the spirit of Pono-Kamila, the horse spirit, father of all horses. Astride him sat Washakie, chanting and shaking a rattle to the sky. In answer, the clouds opened and heavy rain fell, drowning the prairie fire, leaving the landscape blackened, smoking and burned. The rainwater gathered into a huge lake and flowed toward the mountains of the wind pooling there unable to go further, and then darkness descended upon the land. Shortly before Apo rose again in the east completing his circle to awaken the new day, two eyes looked down upon the sleeping form of Night Wind as her spirit still floated. Narrow and wicked, the gaze sought her, feasting on the fullness of her body. Hunger ate into the evil soul, and the creature moved to slake the need. Light suddenly flashed bright and brilliant drawing the creature's gaze to the veiled form of the tsoap watching over the lush body of the woman being before him. Snarling in frustration, the eyes retreated burned by the bright light, afraid of the strength in the old ghost warrior guarding the spirit woman. The morning sun flooded the valley, and Night Wind arose, weak from her journey to return to the village below.

Painted Flower awaited Night Wind's arrival and welcomed her to the warm morning fire, rubbing heated oil into Night Wind's limbs, restoring circulation to the cold flesh. Night Wind ate of the warm tinpsila stew made from prairie turnips before crawling beneath the warmed robes to sleep again, this time to restore strength to her body. Tonight she would appear before the council of the elders to speak of what she saw. Before falling asleep, she looked upon the soft deerskin scroll honoring Kills-Crowe, Painted Flower hung above the willow pinned door of the lodge, protecting all who slept within.

That evening the camp was quiet and still. Night Wind approached the council tent and was bid to enter. Seated before the fire were all elders of the assembled tribes of the Shoshoni people. Most of them she recognized, others she knew of by reputation. She remained silent as the warriors passed the pipe between them, not speaking until the pipe completed the circle of leaders. She looked at the silent face of Washakie, seated with men twice his age. Even with his limited season, the reputation of his fame was well known amongst her people. Born of a Flathead father, his mother was of the Lemhi Shoshone, in the Green Mountains. His child name was Pina Quanah, or smell of sugar. Washakie's father died when Washakie was very young, killed by a Blackfoot ambush. His mother returned to her people.

When Washakie was raised to a warrior, he chose to live with the western tribe of the Bannock Shoshone, a fierce cruel tribe, skilled in the arts of war. Here he learned the ways of battle, counting many coups while living among them. The Bannocks hated the white men above all, and never failed to drive the white trappers from their land. Washakie then moved to live with distant relatives among the Green River Snake Tribe.

His war name of Washakie came from his habit of shaking a rattle made from buffalo hide as he went into battle. The Sioux called him Shoots-on-the Run, and of all the Shoshone warriors, Washakie was the most feared. Stories told of his pursuit of a band of Sioux who stole horses from his villages. Three moons Washakie pursued them, to the joining of the Great Platte and Missouri Rivers before cornering them. He killed them all in single combat hand to hand before returning to his village with the horses. Strong Bear and Moon Follower looked down upon him because Washakie always dealt fairly with the white trappers he encountered, a strange custom considering his training with the Bannocks.

"What have you seen, spirit daughter?" asked Little Eagle speaking at last. As chief among the valley Shoshone, he directed the council. "Tell us of your far sight."

Night Wind spoke of all she saw, describing her visions slowly, adding the sights and sounds from her dreams. When finished, she sat again silently as the men once again passed the feathered pipe around the circle, searching for understanding in her dreams.

"The Vision Woman no longer thinks clearly," said Strong Bear, "Her alliance with the white man, makes her dreams false."

"All know that Strong Bear should become our leader," agreed Moon Follower; "she talks of Washakie because he is drawn to the whites, always begging their favor. She only wants protection for her white lover. Send her from the lodge she is no use."

Night Wind's face flushed with anger, and she bit her tongue, forcing her words of anger down inside her. Anger now would only confirm Strong Bear's words.

"Night Wind speaks truly," said Two Waters, the oldest member of the council. "Many years have I known her, and her visions are true. When I was young we drove the plagues of grasshoppers into deep holes, burning them with fire, their bodies providing food for the winter. She speaks of the grasshoppers because they are as the white men. This I have seen in the lands far east of the Pawnees, they come, more and more, never ending. They ride in the white ships always driving the native people before them. With them comes the dying. The pox they bring killing the native people, so the Indian may be more easily driven from their land. The fire speaks of the wars between us and the Cheyennes, Sioux, Blackfeet, and Arapaho. As we have been driven to the mountains, soon the game will diminish, and we will fight amongst ourselves. This is the plan of the whites, always making us weaker. Pono-Kamila has chosen Washakie to lead us, uniting us for the wars to come. She cautions you Strong Bear, against a division between yourself and Moon Follower, your brother. If we do not stand together, the fire will burn us from this land."

"Thank you, Night Wind," said Washakie, turning his dark gaze toward her. "I too have dreamt of the great fire, always it burned around me. With your sight, I now understand what I must do."

Her task completed, Night Wind left the tent. The council would continue for many days before a decision was made. The Vision Woman's honesty made enemies of Strong Bear and Moon Follower, and against their influence she must always guard herself. She must also warn Joshua for it was against him they might strike, seeking revenge for her dreams.

The long days wore on, and Night Wind spoke to Spotted Owl telling him to prepare for their trip through the high passes and across the plains. She felt a need to be with Joshua and longed for his touch and shy words. She sought him constantly in her dreams, but only mist appeared, as if some stronger power hid him from her. The few feelings she could gain of his spirit were in the hard granite of the mountains and in the running water of the river that flowed through the valley, reminding Night Wind of Joshua's laugh. The child Night Wind carried was active, and although she showed little signs of the pregnancy, she knew he was strong and healthy as the child rolled within her. Tavendu-Wets he would be named, child of the white man. He would be born into a time of great change for her people, and with a foot in both worlds, Tavendu-Wets would grow brave and wise, advising even Washakie in the years to come. In her dreams, she saw him before the gathered tribes of her people, upon his head a bonnet of eagle feathers, trailing long and full. Beside great water, deep within the mountains of wind, he would lead his people. No longer would she keep him from Joshua, together they would raise their sons, teaching them the ways of each world, red and white.

As the full moon of winter emerged, the temperature fell and the council called forth the tribes to announce their decisions. Unable to reach consensus, they decided on a duality. Two chiefs would rule, where once there was one. The regions would be divided. Strong Bear with Moon Follower at his side was to rule over the Western Shoshone. Washakie, supported by Ink-a-tosh-a-pop and Fibe-to-un-tu-wat was to reign over the Northern Shoshone from his lodges in the Absaroka. The decision made, the tribes started preparing for return to their own camps. Little Eagle and his band would stay in the valley of "the water that boils."

Dark clouds loomed on the horizon, and Night Wind knew that she must leave soon or the snowy range would be closed preventing her return until the warm spring winds melted the deep snow. She told only Painted

Flower of her decision, and on the night before she was to leave, her brothers arrived at the tent of Kills-Crowe.

"Painted Flower told us of your planned return to the canyon of the white men," spoke Black Crowe, the oldest of her brothers. "Buffalo Shield and I will ride with you, as would have our father were he still here."

Relieved, Night Wind spoke only thanks to her family. Although Kills-Crowe was gone, his lean features were reborn in their looks. They too felt Washakie was not seasoned enough to be their chief and supported Strong Bear, but Night Wind was family, that was enough. The trail through the mountains would be made shorter by their presence. Even the Nunum Bi would not face two Shoshone warriors in the high passes. Spotted Owl was excited, remembering Joshua's promise to teach him of the iron traps by which the trappers caught the beaver. By first light, the family was mounted, riding single file toward the snowy range far above the valley. As they entered the trees, Black Crowe pulled up suddenly, alarmed by three riders he saw sitting their horses quietly in the drifting fog of the low timber. As the mist cleared, Night Wind recognized Washakie, Ink-a-tosh-a-pop, Fibe-to-un-tu-wat waiting for them. The three chiefs were outfitted for a long trail and were dressed in the warm furs of the wolf.

"With Night Wind's permission, we will ride with you across the plains, through the long valley and down the creek of the cottonwoods. The trail beside the Platte will be open, and by this way we shall return to our homes," said Washakie. "Perhaps we can talk more of your dreams about the mountains of the wind."

Night Wind merely nodded, recognizing the honor the chiefs bestowed upon her. Not even O-Kee-pa would leave his kingdom of rock beneath the earth when Washakie rode through his mountains. That night they camped high in the Snow Mountains, cupping their hands around the warm bowls of broth Night Wind prepared. Her brothers took ashes from the campfire burying them beneath the earth for Night Wind and Spotted Owl to sleep upon, heating their robes and protecting them from the brutal cold. As they rode on in the morning, the wind began rising to their backs and by nightfall they camped beside the river of the Arapaho, near the bend were it fled from their mountains, seeking what protection they could from the round rocks.

By morning the storm worsened, and the wind screamed around them as it swept from the high mountains behind. Sixty miles of the plains were before them, offering little protection 'til they reached the Blue Mountain chain far to the east. Washakie then took the lead, tying all horses together, tails to bridle, and they started across the rolling grassland, now white with drifts. No light from the sun was visible, and only the gray landscape was revealed when the wind paused before gusting again. On they rode until the horses were too tired to push further through the growing drifts. Here Washakie made them wait while he went ahead. Spotted Owl left his pony to ride with Night Wind, sitting in front of her folded under the heavy robes, his back against his brother, yet unborn.

Washakie returned, just as Black Crowe grew restless, and led the family to the south, slashing their horses with his quirt when they lagged until they dropped into a deep ravine washed by spring floods. In front of them, a red overhang of sandstone loomed, formed by the whirlpool action of raging water. Underneath this roof, they stopped. Picketing the horses by the front edge, the Shoshones made camp under the overhang. Fibe-to-un-tu-wat and Buffalo Shield fed the horses with corn from their bags, rubbing the horses' backs with handfuls of blue sage while Night Wind built a fire from the driftwood lodged in the back of the overhang. Above them the blizzard continued, worsening into the night. Night Wind shivered suddenly, hearing the sound of death in the storm. She spoke quietly to Tavendu-Wets, assuring him of the safety of his father, yet a day's ride from them. The fire grew, reflecting heat from the sandstone walls, warming the space within. In front of the horses, the drifts rose, providing a wall from the storm outside.

"Tell me more of what you see of the mountains of wind I love," asked Washakie. "Long have I lived among those rugged peaks, and there is no great water, only the north running river."

"There will be great rains, and this water will join together fighting to enter the river as it runs through the mountains of wind. Here you will live beside the great water, protected from the white man, not even their magic may enter there. I also see many squaws and children of the Arapaho seeking refuge with you, from what I do not know."

"Arapaho," Washakie said, spitting into the fire. "They are the murderers of my father. With them I will grant no refuge."

"Against the whites, all native people must stand," said Night Wind. "Those who do not will be swept from this land."

Washakie never answered but turned to look into the fire, wondering at the Spirit Woman's words, fearful but excited by the future she saw.

That night outside the walls of sandstone, the plains were buried beneath blankets of heavy drifting snow. Night Wind knew they would be unable to continue until the wind abated, and she could only pray for the safety of Joshua, hoping he was warm and protected.

"Oh Manitou," she said, "watch over the life of Joshua, protect him and do not yet grant him a place with you until he holds our child within his hands."

Morning came, and with the light, the wind slackened. The wall of snow between them and the bright world outside glistened as if embedded with crystal. Black Crowe and Buffalo Shield slashed through the wall of ice with their bows and walked out into the chest deep snow of the ravine. By mid morning, they left the deep draw and worked their way eastward again, taking turns breaking through the drifts so the others could follow. Progress was slow, and the river canyon was still far ahead.

By nightfall Lame Wolf still had not returned, and He Who Sleeps grew tired of waiting. The storm still raged around this protected location in the trees, and the horses stood, heads lowered, tails to the wind. Lame Wolf is probably torturing the trapper and neglected to return to include He Who Sleeps, he thought.

He wished he were home in the warm tents with the doe eyed squaw to keep him company. The thought that five warriors would have trouble killing two white men never entered his thinking. Dragging more wood to the fire that valiantly fought against the cold wind, he rolled back into the buffalo robes. If Lame Wolf had not returned by morning, he would climb the hills behind the cabin, to find the rest of his band. Nothing would bother the horses and he would only be gone a short while.

Morning arrived, and neither Lame Wolf nor any of the others returned. Angry now at the way he was treated He Who Sleeps shook the ice from his robes and fought through the deep snow to the ridge top above him. Following the ridge that was barren from drifts because of the strong winds, he climbed the last hill pulling himself up tree by tree to look over the top of the timbered hill at the trapper's cabin below. Beneath him smoke still rose in a slow spiral from the chimney of the cabin, but there was no sign of life. The glade was still and pure, covered in a deep white blanket. No tracks led to or from the cabin. Looking carefully, He Who Sleeps could see several large drifts lying on the pond near the entrance to the notch and another one by the rocks near the south edge.

A coyote appeared through the notch cutting a fresh trail through the snow, his nose sending out plumes of powder as he hunted for signs of food. Suddenly the coyote stopped and circled the large drifts on the pond. Bravery finally filled the heart of the coyote, and he began digging in the drift, exposing the brown patch of hair. As He Who Sleeps watched, the brown patch grew until at last, He Who Sleeps recognized what lay beneath the robe. The Arapaho now knew the snowdrifts as imposters, and he slid back from the hillside disturbed by the thought of his fellow warriors lying frozen in the snow below. For a moment he thought of stalking the cabin to finish what his band started, but again he envisioned

333

the warm lodges and the doe eyed squaw. Returning to his horses, He Who Sleeps gathered the halters of his horse and Running Horse's mount, now ownerless, and began the journey home, breaking through the drifts headed toward the west. This was the Blackfeet's quarrel, let Lame Wolf finish it, if he was still alive. He Who Sleeps was wise enough to know that he should be far from here. Behind him on the hill a large white wolf, watched as the Arapaho left the mountains. The wolf could still smell the horses below, food was hard to catch in the deep snow, and today the hunting would be better.

Washakie stopped the party by midday. Cutting a trail through the white powder was tiring for the horses, and each rider exchanged lead positions every hour, letting a fresh mount break the trail. Ahead Washakie could see the tracks of two horses angling across the whiteness in front of him. He carefully scanned the flatness around him, but nothing was visible even to his sharp vision. The trail of the two horses lead to the south into a broken range of low hills and looked to be very fresh. From the snow splatters one set of tracks appeared to be from a riderless mount. Washakie was torn; behind him was the party he was leading. He could follow the trail of the two horses in front of him in case the tracks were those of an enemy. If they were enemies, Arapaho or Sioux, the owner of the horses would die, turning the white snow to crimson with their blood. He could backtrack the trail in an attempt to learn where the horses were coming from and determine if they posed a threat to his party, or he could continue on their present course riding to the head of the large river. Turning to look backward, he scanned the faces of those behind him, pausing on the visage of Night Wind as she sat patiently waiting for his decision. Concern reflected back from Night Wind's coal black eyes, and he knew she wished only for speed toward the camp of her trapper. Once she was there safely, there would be time for investigation, and a death trail would begin if the tracks proved to be those of his enemy, the Arapaho. His decision made, Washakie motioned the party forward. The Great Apo overhead was now trying to make amends for his absence earlier, and the snow became moist as it started to melt in sheets of water across the wide prairie. The last several miles to the head of canyon were soon traveled, and the party paused before entering the canyon walls. The river was frozen in spots, but where the water ran fast and deep no ice dared to invade the rushing stream. Before reaching the falls, Washakie turned to Night Wind for guidance, and she pointed across the river and toward the steep hillside. No further sign was needed and Washakie pushed his mount into the cold torrent. The horse snorted and plunged, breaking the ice with both feet rather than with single strides.

Long ago the war pony learned how to smash the frozen water beneath its sharp hooves rather than trying to walk on the glass like surface. The steep hill was slick and the wet drifts of snow provided little traction, but eventually all the horses made it to the top where Washakie paused to let the horses blow before riding on to the gap ahead. Upon reaching the gap, Washakie signed for Night Wind and Spotted Owl to stay, while the five warriors crested the hills to scan the flat whiteness below them searching for signs of danger or a possible trap. Washakie surveyed the scene below him, noting the coyote tracks in the fresh field of snow around what appeared to be several bodies, stark and unmoving in the white expanse in front of him. He knew Night Wind's first response would be to fly down to hill to her trapper, but the smell of danger was still strong in the air, and he again signed for her to stay while the Shoshones rode down the hill, fanning out upon reaching the meadow, riding slowly trying to make reason from the scene.

Two bodies lay half way across the small plateau crumpled close together, and another still form guarded the eastern side of the basin close to what appeared to be open water. Circling the lower edge of the basin, the riders checked two frozen pale bodies laying a short distance from the opening for the trail to the river below. Neither Arapaho was scalped, but both were lifeless victims of large caliber weapons from short distance. Washakie dismounted upon reaching the edge of the frozen pond, not trusting his mount to the slick ice, especially with the visible open water lapping against the ice on the far side. There must be a warm spring within the pond, which prevented the water from freezing, but also posed substantial danger should anyone walk near it. Washakie circled the southern edge while the other warriors waited for him, their eyes vigilante on the cabin on the northern edge, watching for any sign of danger.

Upon reaching the east edge, Washakie gently tested the ice with his foot before walking the short distance to the other crumpled form lying there. The warrior was from the Blackfeet tribes, and his still open frozen eyes held a look of wonderment as if death was a surprise. Death came to this Blackfoot by a large knife that still protruded from his chest clutched by both of his frozen blue hands. Just as he was turning, Washakie's eye fell upon a tip of blue near the edge of the open water a short distance away. Walking slowly, Washakie tested each step until he was close enough to see the cause of the three dead braves lying in this field of white. Washakie recognized the face gazing through the clear ice. As he took another step closer, the body within the clear prison bobbed sharply in the water, and then with a sharp crack in the still air, separated from the harder ice and with only a trailing flow of bubbles to show its passage, floated a short distance before sinking into the open water.

"Goodbye my friend," Washakie said as the weight of the heavy wet bear coat pulled the body of the La Ramie deep into the waters of the pond.

The stream of air bubbles was the only response, and Washakie chanted a slow death song about the bravery of his friend La Ramie before cautiously backing from the pond's ice to return to his other warriors waiting on the far side. Three braves lay dead here on this death ground of white. What lay before them in the cabin Washakie didn't know, but feared what he would find. If Joshua was still alive, there would be tracks from the cabin, but the snow around the structure was unbroken and still.

The five warriors surrounded the cabin, listening for signs of a trap within, but all was silent. At last Washakie pulled the latchstring and gently opened the door, careful to keep his back to the outside wall. Nothing stirred within, but even the darkened interior could not hide the blackened frozen blood on the pine cabin floor. Lowering to a crouch, Washakie slid within the door, his rifle cocked, expecting the shrill cry of attack, but none came. He paused to survey the interior of the cabin, a lone pine fagot burned still within the cold interior, its small red coal threatening to extinguish before the slight breeze entering in the door. Half way across the room, the shredded form of a Blackfoot brave lay sprawled across the floor. Near the fireplace, knelt Lame Wolf. His head was partially severed from the body, hanging by a few tendons and skin, the black eyes looking upside down and back towards the open door. The once fearsome enemy appeared to be skewered on an elk horn driven deep into his crotch. And on the bed beneath the blankets of soft elk, lay Joshua, his white hands still gripped upon the stock of a rifle pointed toward Washakie and the open door.

Washakie was sure the trapper was dead, until he saw two small spots of red upon the trappers milk white face, as if the Joshua was barely clinging to life like the small pine knot alone in the fireplace. Washakie dispatched Night Wind's brother to bring her and Spotted Owl to the cabin. If life still lay within the trapper, she could nourish the flame, perhaps the ember would die, but the trapper fought well, and if possible, he should live to sing his own war songs of bravery. Then with the others Washakie dragged the bodies from the cabin before retrieving the bodies of the three warriors by the lake. Although they were enemies, they appeared to have fought bravely in battle. The scalps were not Washakie's to take, so he left the bodies untouched before helping to load the stiffened corpses on horses for burial in a rock cairn in the high cliffs above the river.

Lastly Washakie returned to the frozen pond circling it searching for La Ramie's body, but the dark waters kept their burden, and Washakie suspected that perhaps the body had been pulled down into the earth through fissures in the bottom of the pond, never to surface again.

After taking care of the horses, Washakie reentered the cabin to find Night Wind chanting beside the still form of Joshua. Her brothers built a fire in the fireplace and helped Night Wind heat water in a large kettle. With this water, she mixed herbs and medicines from her medicine bag and bathed Joshua's face and chest. She found the discolored tips from the shattered arrow in the bed and pulled slivers of the arrow from Joshua's wound. Washakie did not need to tell her that two of the dead warriors were Arapahoe from the enchanted mountains south of the Snowy Range. Poison from the arrow was deadly, and it would take all of her skill to save the father of her unborn child. Washakie made a mental note that someday he must climb through the enchanted forest and permanently eliminate the threat posed by Red Willow and the Man Woman so their poisons could not spread to his people. Night Wind attached a poultice to Joshua's arm before meeting Washakie eyes offering him silent thanks for his efforts in her behalf.

"The trail of the last Arapahoe grows dim with the melting snow. I must leave now before the last member of the ambush can return to the safety of his mountains. Whatever the future holds, you and your trapper are always welcome in my mountains of wind. If the trapper dies, ride North with your brothers to the Absaroka. With your vision, the Shoshone can build a fortress against the coming threat. If he should live, I will pay homage to his bravery next year with the rendezvous.

"My brothers will stay until Manitou decides the road the trader will travel. Thank you for your help across the plains. Should the father of the child within my belly travel the hanging road, I will ride to the Windy Mountains. I fear he would not be welcome back across the plains, and perhaps Strong Bear and Half Moon would work against me because of my visions."

"Should the trader die, your child is always welcome within my lodge. I will tell him the story of this battle and how Lame Wolf died. Good-bye now, Apo is melting the trail I must follow."

Night Wind watched the three pillars ride from the basin toward the plains to cut the trail of the lone Arapahoe. She had little doubt they would ride through the night if necessary until their enemy was found. If the warrior stopped upon the plains to spend the night, Washakie would interrupt his dreams.

That night on the flat hills of La Ramie's country, He Who Sleeps, followed the pattern of his naming as his spirit soul rose toward the Hanging Road. He died swiftly, never hearing the Shoshone warriors when at last they found his campsite. They left his body for the prairie wolves, contemptuous of his courage because he ran homeward rather than die fighting back at the cabin of the trappers. Washakie, Ink-a-tosh-a-pop, and Fibe-to-un-tu-wat turned north again with first light, a fresh scalp adorning Washakie's war saddle.

Throughout the long dark hours, Night Wind sat beside Joshua. Spotted Owl fell asleep in front of the fireplace, glad to be back in the cabin, confident that Night Wind would return the trader to him. Through his fever, Joshua thought he heard chanting again, and his thoughts raced over mountain ranges and across time. He felt as if he was fighting to escape something or some feeling that gripped him. As the poison continued through his system, he remembered flashes of his life after the war before his journey to the Blue Mountains.

When Joshua returned to Booneville and learned the war was over he felt no feelings of jubilation. During the years of constant danger and traveling, his once powerful frame was reduced to a lean skeleton, and his eyes were murky and troubled. Joshua spent days in an undersized room of a boardinghouse, staring out the small second story window for hours at a time. All pay Joshua accrued from his commission with the Missouri Militia was held until the end of the war and Ashley approved through a local bank to deposit Joshua's money and establish credit and payment for his friend's room and board. Ashley also arranged for a Presbyterian minister to meet with Joshua to try and lift his spirits and bring him back to the world of the living, away from his dark thoughts and gloomy moods.

Booneville was established enough to have several denominational sects or preachers and a few who claimed to be non-affiliated. Terrence Narthman arrived in Booneville from Northampton, Massachusetts along with his new bride Elisha. Both were of Scots-Irish descent and were raised on the viewpoint of the Great Awakening, Presbyterian beliefs of piety, suspicion of wealth, and a dislike for worldliness and ecclesiastical pretension. With the arousing of their religious fervor, Terrence felt the frontier was his battleground. Here Native Americans and the rough frontiersmen would receive the word of God, and free from the restrictive bounds of Catholic teaching or other rigid church doctrine, these "savages" would be receptive to salvation. Narthman's following in Booneville was small but growing. Ashley met the preacher before and thought him to be a decent person and with deep concern for his friend Joshua, Ashley hoped the young preacher's words would help Joshua realize that the guilt of the present could never change the past.

Narthman agreed to meet with Joshua upon Ashley's request. Narthman felt that human volition was the key to salvation, and within each individual, there was a desire to "Choose God" and through this, personal salvation would arise. Each soul was in charge of its spiritual destiny. After leaving Massachusetts, Narthman served under the Springfield Presbytery in Kentucky. Here he was witness to the height of revival fever and preached to conventions where over 20,000 people flocked to hear the word of the Lord. In the midst of preachers of Lutheran, Methodist and Baptist denominations, these men of God believed that rather than adhering to the tenants of a particular faith, convergence of the soul was utmost, not which hierarchal system was chosen as the messenger. In all things essential, unity was the goal and in all else freedom. Barton Stone was a mentor and guiding light for Narthman, and the young preacher soon rose in the ranks of God's elite. During these revivals, bizarre manifestations would exhibit themselves within the listeners. People would begin to shake and jerk, sometimes undergoing severe seizures. In other instances, they would begin to bark and take on traits of animals. The orthodox Presbyterians disapproved of these visible displays of God, and pressure came to bear upon the ministers participating in these revivals. Those who encouraged this type of fervor would find a limited future among the rulers of the church. Unable to rectify his beliefs with the rigid structure of the church, Narthman left Kentucky traveling deeper into the frontier where he could disassociate himself from doctrine and reach the more fundamental Christian soul. Before leaving, in a small civil ceremony, Narthman married the daughter of the most prestigious rector who held to the rigid beliefs of the Westminster Confession. Together they fled Kentucky and followed the Missouri River to Booneville to preach the word of God.

Following Ashley's personal request, Narthman went to Joshua's room and asked Joshua to speak of the war and his feelings that arose from constantly living on the edge of death. Rather than ignoring him, Joshua told Narthman of the constant fear, the days of riding and hiding, never knowing where or when the next ambush might appear. He was also open with the young preacher about his loss of faith although he said little of Rodde, only that his wife was killed by an act of God in St. Genevieve. Narthman could feel the pain in the frontiersman and spent hours talking of the churches' beliefs about God's love, and said that Rodde's death and the war were the results of events, unplanned, random and non-intentional.

Joshua listened politely and then would turn to gaze out his window. Joshua did consent to attend a revival held by Narthman the following Sunday.

Terrence and Elisha followed the pattern of revival meetings began in the south of using Sunday revivals as an event to socialize where people gathered from widely scattered settlements. The preachers of God's word, hoping some part of the message would survive in the collective memory the next day, tolerated alcohol consumption and rowdy behavior. Baptisms, weddings, and salvations were included in the service, regardless of previous affiliations. Elisha took an active part in these revivals, preaching the word of God on the pulpit beside her husband, rather than sitting demurely in the background. This perhaps above all was why she fled the stodgy confines of her orthodox background. On the frontier, women understood God just as well if not better than men.

True to his promise, Joshua aroused himself from his dreary routine of dreaming of the past alone in his room and rose early the next Sunday. Trudging down the stairs, Joshua retrieved hot water from the common bath area and retired again to his private domain. Here the sweat from his sleepless nights was washed from his body, and Joshua shaved, refusing to meet his own eyes in the mirror above the small washstand. Thanks to the landlady's attention to detail, clothes were laundered and waiting for him in the small closet of his room. By the time Sunday's first light of renewal filtered into the small room, the trader was ready, ready to leave the self imposed prison, ready to bury the ghosts of his past, ready to see what his Maker held in store for him.

Although Narthman's words did little to relieve the emptiness within his soul, they did have the effect of clarifying Joshua's own thinking. His entire life seemed to be a constant road of loss. Everything Joshua ever cared for was taken from him, his parents, his wife, unborn children, and close friends who trusted him. Their faces a constant reminder of what was gone, a continual dream each night as he slept alone in his bed. This Joshua could accept, this pain was familiar, almost a comfort for his loneliness. What he could not handle was any more losses. Realizing this, the answer lay before him. If he refused to allow anyone to enter his life, Joshua would forestall any future pain. No one's loss would ever hurt him again, because he would not allow closeness again. Perhaps by leaving people behind, this would be easier. The road must lay to the west, alone. The healing wind of the far mountains might begin to salve the frontiersman's injured soul. Let Narthman's cruel God, do what He might; Joshua's own death would only be a release. Fortified, Joshua left his thoughts behind and descended to meet the morning, ready to travel the road that lay ahead.

The streets of the small community were already beginning to bustle with activity. Wagons moved along the rutted tracks, hauling the necessities of civilization. Small boys raced along with the wagons, shouting with glee, although the oxen and teamsters ignored the distracting shouts. A few couples strolled down the plank boardwalks, dressed in their Sunday finest, sometimes trailed by a watchful matron to insure innocence. Lost only to each other, these couples paid no attention to the lean figure that passed them on the streets almost shadowlike. Little did they know the sacrifices that were made on their behalf in the northern frontier. Joshua smiled at their naiveté, hoping their dreams would never be shattered as his were.

Buying a fresh loaf of golden bread, Joshua broke his night's fast and accepted the cold tin cup of cider pressed on him by the young street vendor.

"It's good to see a man eat," the young girl said, "it's an honor Mr. Coural."

"How do you know my name?" asked Joshua

"Everyone knows you. They call you the ghost."

"Why, do I scare the town's people?"

"Oh, no," laughed the girl, "Mr. Lisa and Mr. Ashley say the Indians could never find you, they thought you were a ghost, and they feared you. Now that you have been here in town since winter, we never see you either; still many people respect what you did during the war. But you do look like a ghost; you should get outside in the sun more often."

"You're right," laughed Joshua, "I should get outside more."

He walked on, enjoying the flavor of the bread, and the bite of the cold cider. The sound of his own laugh, echoed in his mind, as he realized that this was the first time he found amusement in a long time.

Toward the east end of the street, a small creek that murmured a spring tune, flowed gently beside the swaying trees near its banks, which bordered a large field. Already a tinge of green showed across the grass as winter slowly began to fade from this small frontier community. Here in this field the Sunday revivals would be held later in the day. A few people were already there, but the preaching would start later, timed so the farmers from outlying areas could finish their chores and have time to travel to Booneville. Some traveled downriver, and others up, coming to the revival in wooden pirogues. A few families came from the north across the rough terrain fighting the muddy rutted trails in wagons pulled by slow moving oxen. After Sunday services, they would buy or trade

341

for supplies and return to their farms, hopeful for a wet spring and good bounty on their crops.

Joshua jumped the creek and strolled on across the field until he found the curved shaped of a large tree that fitted the small of his back. Here he sat to watch the arrival of the people and the preparation for the revival. Joshua felt detached from those around him, but he enjoyed the spring sunshine on his face. Perhaps the young girl was right; he was a wraith that walked this world only to watch other people's happiness, never to enjoy his own. He went over in his mind an earlier conversation he had with Manuel Lisa, one evening when Joshua left his confines to eat in a small pub just down the street from the boarding room. Lisa was staying in town buying fresh supplies for a trip upstream the Big Muddy, to his trading post, the new Fort Lisa.

Lisa had spoken of the New Fort Lisa, he established far up the Missouri in 1812 and told Joshua of the Great Plains with herds of buffalo and wild game. Forced to abandon his first fort in Montana located on the Big Horn River because of the pressure from the English soldiers and the Indians, Lisa established another post a short ways north of Bellevue on the western bank of the Missouri River. Lisa received an appointment from the government in 1814 as sub-agent for all the Indian tribes along the upper Missouri, and during the last year of the war was able to prevent some of the Teton Dakota tribes from becoming British allies. He was just returning from St. Louis where a council of forty-three tribes met to negotiate treaties with the United States.

Lisa told Joshua that the gunpowder plant between Postosi and St. Genevieve finally became reality during the last several years of the war, and would welcome Joshua into that business also, but the descriptions of the Omaha, Oto and Pawnee tribes and the land around Council bluffs stirred feelings inside Joshua that were repressed since the death of Rodde.

Lisa's other proposal was that Joshua would journey north with him to a place called Bellevue thirty miles to the south of Fort Lisa, and then on to the fort to run the trading post. This location was nearer to the Platte River and would become a junction point for furs traveling down this waterway. Lisa would supply the outpost with boatloads from St. Louis. This post also would be further from the more hostile tribes of Sioux further to the north. Lisa believed Joshua could establish positive relations with the friendly tribes, and the fur merchant wanted someone who could be fair but was willing to provide a strong defense should that be needed.

Bellevue was a natural point of meeting because of the confluence of the two rivers a short distance away. If Fort Lisa post proved successful, it would serve as a preemptive strike against Lisa's main competitor John Jacob Astor who founded the American Fur Company in 1808.

Astor gained a monopoly on fur trade in the Great Lake's trade and was trying to expand into the reaches of the upper Missouri area. A child of a poor German butcher, Astor was growing into one of the wealthiest men in American from his shrewd business dealing in the fur trade and his real estate investments in New York City. Astor used his investments from the fur business to buy prime locations of property in New York and then waited until the city expanded and his property became extremely valuable. Astor also used shipping to transport furs to China and then bought Chinese goods back to American for sale, often making over $50,000 per voyage. Astor's trading post, Astoria, near the mouth of the Columbia River was established in 1811. Because the shrewd trader owned vast resources of cash, he loaned the American government money to finance the war of 1812 and doubled this money again when the war was over and the bonds came due.

Lisa knew that if Astor established a post in Bellevue this would undermine his business further to the west and the north. In Lisa's dealing with the Omaha Indians, a word meaning "the upstream people," he found them a friendly industrious people, and he feared losing their trade to Astor. Lisa traded furs with them for many of the accoutrements of the white people and also encouraged them toward a larger agricultural base by providing seeds for pumpkins, turnips, and potatoes. The more warlike Mountains Indians and Teton Dakota tribes looked down on trapping as a way of life, but the Pawnees, Otos, and Omaha tribes were becoming very adept in the white man's ways of gathering fur. The fierce Sioux lived for war and fighting and very seldom could be trusted in business dealing. Lisa could acquire fur from these regions by sending out parties of trappers in large enough bands to fight off the advances of the fiercer tribes to the north. As Joshua thought about his conversation with Lisa, he realized that St. Genevieve held no interest for him. Escape from death and the grim reaper's reminders were what he craved, not a return to Rodde's grave.

Lisa promised to return with the winter's trade from the northern reaches and contact Joshua on his return trip. If Joshua were interested, he would arrange for Joshua and a boatload of supplies to make the trip north. Something about this morning cleared the webs from Joshua's mind, and he realized he intended to take Lisa up on his offer. Bellevue wasn't as far as he wanted to retreat, but it was a start. Relieved by his decision, Joshua relaxed against the tree as people continued to gather on the field. Young people passed by waiting to be married, saved, or blessed, all of them oblivious to the silent figure sitting there on the ground. Like the grass and trees around him, he was part of their world, unnoticeable, sharing in none of their happiness.

By noon the preaching began. Narthman used a technique of call and recall in his sermons, where he asked questions of the assembled, and then answered their questions for them; always leading them in the direction he wished the sermon to go. Narthman, although appearing frail, possessed a strong voice, which carried far out over the field. Joshua could clearly hear him, even seated at the back of the throng near the tree line.

"Does the Devil, care about your soul?" Narthman quested rhetorically.

"No," came the massed response.

"Who does care for you?" came his call again.

"Jesus," the masses answered.

"Would Jesus want you to drink and fornicate?" came the question

"No," came the response again.

"Who tempts man with the sins of flesh and drink?" Narthman shouted.

"The Devil," the crowd agreed.

"Then leave this road of sin, and come into the house of Jesus."

If only it was that easy, thought Joshua.

Who steals your wife and children, said Joshua to himself.

Jesus was his answer.

Who leads you to the well of hope, only to leave you dry and parched, Joshua asked again. Jesus was his reply. If the Devil did these things, why didn't the Lord God stop him, perhaps there were no Devils and Gods, only man, he thought to himself.

After an hour, Narthman stopped speaking and turned the podium over to his wife Elisha. Joshua studied her as she spoke to the crowds. Her voice was much lighter than her husband's, but the crowd stilled when she spoke, and Joshua could hear her words clearly. Elisha spoke of virtue and purity; she spoke of the feminine soul and how it was a woman's duty to help men avoid the road of sin. She looked the part as she spoke. Elisha was almost taller than her husband, with striking white blond hair. Her skin was snow pale, and blue eyes pierced the virginal face. Beautiful, thought Joshua, but cold somehow as if she was disdainful of those less featured than herself.

By late afternoon Elisha finished, and several weddings were performed, and the young couples blushed as ribald cries echoed from the crowd. Narthman again stepped to the podium and began calling for sinners to repent and forsake their evils in the name of the Lord. His voice rose and fell like a whirlwind, at times his speech was rapid and ringing, while at other times, he spoke slowly and low. The crowd began to demonstrate signs of agitation. Amen's rang out across the field, and people raised their hands and swayed as if blowing in the wind. As Narthman again denounced evil, several women in the crowd fell to their knees barking like dogs, two young men ran through the masses spinning in circles bumping one into the others. Like a beehive, the crowd began to chant and sway. Narthman called for sinners to come forward and be saved, and slowly, as if pulled, hundreds of people surged forward to the stage. Here Narthman and Elisha passed among them laying hands upon shoulders and heads. Often the repentant collapsed as the couple passed by. Within an hour, it was over, and Joshua shook his head, trying to recover from the trancelike state he found himself. With a sudden realization that he was famished, he rose from his tree and walked toward the stage. The Narthmans were still in front of the stage speaking with several men dressed in suits and three matronly ladies clothed in full calico. Terrence Narthman's eyes fell upon Joshua as he approached and a smile fell arose across his slender face.

"Thank you for coming, Joshua," the young minister said. "I might say you look healthier here in the open, rather than the confines of your room."

"Must say, I feel a good bit better," replied Joshua. "That was quite a revival you put on."

"Yes, we do what we can," Elisha said, extending her hand to Joshua. "Terrence spoke of you. Thank you for coming. We were just retiring to our tent to picnic on the fine food these people of God have brought us, won't you join us?"

"May I present my wife, Elisha," said Terrence. "She very seldom waits for an introduction, and yes please join us. I'm afraid all of this service to the Lord has made me quite hungry."

Elisha refused to release Joshua's hand, and he found himself walking with her to the rear of the stage where a small tent was pegged into the grassy field. Lanterns were already lighted, and it gave the canvas a warm glow as Joshua entered the tent. Tables and chairs were scattered in a random fashion, and the smell of fried chicken and cornbread, emanated from the woven baskets on the tables making Joshua's knees weak and his mouth water.

"All Christians need nourishment," Elisha said, "if not for their soul at least for their bodies. Come eat and tell us of your plans for your future. I think God has provided you to us, and we must never waste what God allows."

Joshua and the Narthmans visited long into the evening, until all the chicken was finished and only two lone pieces of cornbread remained. Only politeness kept Joshua from finishing these off, as he still felt a hunger within him that was not yet filled. It was if his body suddenly felt the need to replenish, having long fasted from his human needs. The conversation turned to stories of the frontier and Manuel Lisa. Terrence explained that they too had met with Lisa during his last trip through Booneville. Lisa told them of the vast plains and the Indians tribes that inhabited the great frontier.

"Terrence and I have prayed about this many nights," said Elisha quietly, "and the answer was revealed to us. This must be our calling. Every savage we can bring to the light of God drives evil further away. Lisa is providing transportation for us to Bellevue and will arrange contacts so we may meet with the leaders of the Indian tribes. This is what God intended for us to do. Manuel said you may make the trip also, and what a valuable resource you could be for us. The boat trip is probably long and arduous, not to mention the dangers. I felt God intended for you to travel with us. Won't you consider it, Joshua?"

Joshua felt the touch of her hand again, as she looked into his eyes. A thousand reasons why they shouldn't go flooded his mind, and then withdrawing his hand, he remembered his promise to himself. Only to himself would he be responsible. The Narthmans could travel where they would. He had no hold over their lives, nor would he ever become part of their lives. Alone to himself he would stay.

"Yes," he heard himself say, "I am planning on going to Bellevue, and would never argue with anyone so sure of his or her destiny."

"Excellent," Elisha cried. "We have many plans to make in the coming days, while we wait for Lisa's return."

"Glad to have you on board, old man," Terrence said, wringing Joshua's hand. "What an excellent adventure it will be."

Joshua eyed the last of the cornbread as he left the tent that evening, but decided against taking a piece to eat on the walk home. The field was dark as he walked back toward the town, now quiet in the spring night. The images of the buildings were vague and dusky, and the boardwalk to his room appeared soft and yielding as if covered in moss. Joshua walked close to the inside, near the buildings almost as if he was unsure where the edge was, not wanting to fall from his path, now that it was revealed to him, even if his final destination was unclear.

Unsure of where he was Joshua slowly opened his eyes, was he back in Booneville? Slowly the room began to swim into focus, and instinctively he reached for the weapon near his hand only to find small warm fingers intertwined among his. These fingers flowed with strength almost like a charge of lightning, causing him to gasp as he felt vigor flowing through his body. Blinking again, Joshua focused on the dark brown eyes locked to his with their fiercely protective gaze, and he realized Night Wind sat beside him, holding him, letting her love and soul flow through him, chasing the poison and nightmare securely into the deep caves of his memory. Seeing him returning to this side of the Milky Way, Night Wind then locked the caves within his mind, releasing the father of her child from the torment that had gripped him during the past days. Unable to speak, Joshua simply allowed himself to be pulled into her gaze, feeling his soul joining with hers, trusting that where she lead him would be safe. Long into the night they remained thus, melded in spirit, locked forever by the joining of their souls, forged eternally under the watchful eyes of the Great Manitou who sees all.

Chapter 15
The Aftermath

The silence following the blast echoed more stridently across the campus than the roar of the percussive explosion. Carrigan observed the panorama before him, scanning the strange scene of frightened students and stunned teachers, suddenly becoming cognizant of the ringing in his ears. Students were lying scattered across the green of the open campus area. Another group of students, those earlier out the doors, stood poised in route to the football field, awestruck looking back toward the school. No one was talking, their vocabulary couldn't express the presentation they witnessed. Hearing a gasp Carrigan remembered the slender form of Becky slung across his shoulders, momentarily forgotten after his race down the hall. Setting her feet to the ground, he maintained the grip on Becky's shoulder until she made eye contact.

"What happened, Mr. C., why was there all the fire?" asked Becky.

"It's all right, Becky, it's all over now. Are you okay?" Carrigan asked, fighting to keep the adrenaline in his system from making his voice shake.

"My wrist hurts a little. I didn't know I could run so fast. Thank you for helping me. Please, Mr. C., will you make sure Tommy is okay?"

"Yes Beck, now walk over with Mrs. Collingworth and go with her students to the football field."

"Sure Mr. C., but tell me when you find Tommy."

"I will, Beck."

Carrigan paused a short while to visit with Jan and the resource officer, telling them what he knew. Evans radioed this information to the police units arriving on the scene directing them toward the corridor that sustained the explosion. By the time Carrigan returned to the hallway, the sprinkler system was performing its task even though no fire was evident in the school. Sirens were screaming as disaster management, additional police, and fire rescuer units rushed to the school. Evans entered the building behind Carrigan, and they started down the hall together ignoring the cascade of water falling around them.

"Is there a chance we need to look for more devices?" asked Evans.

"I don't think so, the amount of material he used wasn't a large quantity, but I don't know for sure, HAZMAT officers need to get the dogs in here and check everything. I'm not even sure if there was anyone else involved," Carrigan answered.

By the time both men made it to the end of the hall and turned the corner, they saw the first officers on call had already secured the hallway. Two policemen knelt beside the burned figure of Tommy. The coroner and ambulance units had been called, but there was no rush. Tommy was dead. His clothing was burned from his blackened remains, and much of the flesh was charred from his body. Inhuman, Tommy lay, blackened and alone, the only victim of his attempt for revenge. Carrigan crossed himself and said a short prayer for Tommy's salvation.

The containment of the explosion in the locker area minimized the damage to the school's walls and ceiling. All glass was pulverized from the skylights, windows, and doors, and the brick and tiles were darkened from the flames, but no cracks in the flooring or walls were visible. The metal lockers were distorted, resembling Tupperware baked in an oven.

This corner of the hallway filled with students was a vision too grotesque to contemplate, and Carrigan felt only relief that the hallway was empty, except for Tommy. It was far better that one was sacrificed, rather than what might have been. With a final shudder and glimpse toward the melted carpet on the flooring, Carrigan turned from the scene. The professionals were on hand; he would be needed far worse as parents began to arrive to pick up students. Carrigan would answer the same question, the same way a thousand times before the day was over. "I don't know, I don't know, I don't know." Evans reminded Carrigan that investigators would need a statement from him before the day ended. Carrigan nodded his assent and left the building, walking toward the expanse of green grass, and cool breezes flowing from beyond the double orange doors toward freedom from the wet smoky hallways of the school.

By five o'clock that evening, all students were returned to the care of their parents. Several groups who missed class for a skip day to a nearby lake were finally located by their frantic parents and forced to account for the whereabouts to police and their parents. Carrigan wrote his statement for the police investigators about Tommy's school project and how he finally made the connection to Tommy and the bomb. The officers impounded the remaining model volcano and obtained search warrants for Tommy's house and school locker. No one had been able to contact Tommy's father, and the burnt remains were transferred to the county morgue pending notification. Tommy's locker held only a few girly magazines, some cigarettes, and a slightly stained Barbie Doll with deep scratches inflicted by the words "lesbo" written across the pale vinyl skin in blue ink. Carrigan locked the door to his room, leaving the scattered papers and puzzle pieces strung across the floor, unable to deal with the mess this evening. Groups of teachers were still huddled together discussing what they knew and making assumptions about what they didn't, but Carrigan felt no desire for company and left for home. Deep within him, guilt bit harshly into his soul, for his inability to foresee the senseless tragedy and somehow erase Tommy's self inflicted pain.

Three beers later his guilt worsened, and Carrigan turned to scotch hoping the higher proof would provide a remedy. It didn't. Near midnight Jan called to tell Carrigan that school was to be cancelled for the rest of the term for students. Grades would be closed at the time of the explosion, and the year was declared officially over. No one wanted to return to the building after the events of the day. Jan expressed his appreciation to Carrigan for his detective work in discovering the coming explosion.

"Because of you," Jan said, "the children were all out of the building, and the bomb didn't go off near the start or end of school. The loss of life during either of these two times would have been horrendous. Broken windows we can fix, broken bodies are something none of us could have lived with."

"There was one broken body, and I don't think I will ever be able to handle it," answered Carrigan.

"I know," Jan returned, "but we all sow what we reap, and Tommy just plowed too deep a furrow. There is nothing you could have done, more than you did. The glass is full Carrigan, not empty. Sadly Tommy won't be missed, and the world will go on without him. Come in Monday morning, I need to talk to you about where we go from here. Now go to bed, and quit beating yourself up."

Retiring at last for the night, Carrigan was unable to sleep and stared at the bare ceiling, making a mental note to check the class grades and make sure Tommy received a passing grade. Somehow Carrigan wanted a permanent record that the boy's life was not in vain. He held no malice toward Tommy, only a deep feeling of regret and sadness.

Indeed the sun arose the next morning, and Carrigan woke feeling little better than the night before. His sleep, when it finally arrived, was filled with images of Tommy's broken body. Hell could offer little more than Tommy already faced. After placing a call to the police department, from which he learned nothing new, Carrigan decided the further he could run from Rockville, the better he would like it today. On a whim, he called Otto at the Senior Center to ask the old German if he wanted to take a drive to the hills. Carrigan wanted company, just not company that would remind him of the events of yesterday. Sensing his mood, Otto said little on the phone.

"Do ve need to bring our own viskey, or vill you have some for the road?" the old German asked.

"I'll bring enough for a week," said Carrigan, "who knows we might not want to come back."

"Das is goot," Otto answered, "see you in a vhile."

Carrigan appreciated Otto's quiet support. He never questioned Carrigan about the events of yesterday, although the news was sure to have reached the Center. Probably there wasn't anybody in the state of Wyoming that hadn't heard of the bombing in the high school. This was a small state, and usually this type of event happened in the big cities, not places like Rockville.

Carrigan thought back to the long evenings Otto sat with him beside the bed of his father. James Senior fell suddenly ill during the first year Carrigan taught at Lakota High. His father's balance seemed to fail, and he fell several times during the course of a few days. At first the doctors thought James Senior was experiencing some sort of seizure disorder until the cat scans revealed the truth. A malignant tumor was found, and the rate of growth was an indicator of the viscous nature of the disease that soon robbed his father of mobility and dignity. Chemotherapy and radiation were attempted, but only served to further depress his father's ability to fight for his life. Death as the outcome was conceded, and only the time of the finality was in question. For over a month, his father fought, until at last, too tired to struggle longer, James Senior gave up.

During these trying times, James Senior would brighten and visit a few minutes with Carrigan, expressing pride in his son and words were exchanged between the two men, something that always was lacking before. During the periods when Carrigan's father slept, the strong narcotics temporarily relieving the pain, Otto's door to his room would open just down the hall and the old German would appear, to sit quietly beside Carrigan, sometimes talking when Carrigan seemed receptive. Otto lost his leg to diabetes and was hospitalized recovering from the amputation. The hospital nights were lonely for him also. Together they kept the silence of the night at bay and gave each a foundation to discuss the unexplained nature of life.

"The var is loost, the hount is dead, and the frauleins vill smile tomorrow," said Otto, which was his way of telling Carrigan; life is what it is, nothing more, and nothing less.

On a chance, Carrigan called the lumber company to see if the roof tresses were in before going to pick up Otto. They were, and Carrigan left the house to hook up the trailer to Gertrude. As Carrigan was leaving the phone rang, and he hesitated before choosing to ignore the ringing and continue out to the pickup. The last thing he wanted was to talk to a newspaper or television reporter about school. Let them try to get information from the school board.

Nancy let the phone ring ten times before giving up. Carrigan must have left the house early this morning, or else he was not answering any calls. Nancy had been fortunate and found a connecting flight for Stephen in Cody bound for Salt Lake, and then eastward on Rocky Mountain Air. This saved her driving over to Jackson or back down to Casper. Stephen would finish out his last several weeks of school and was looking forward to coming back to Wyoming and helping work on the cabin and hopefully getting to shoot again. She called her husband, and he promised someone would meet Stephen on the other end. Nancy was just returning to her corporate offices when news flashed on the radio telling about the explosions in Lakota High School. Fear clutched her throat until she finally got through to her attorney in Rockville. He told her that one student had been killed but that everyone else was okay. When Nancy asked if he heard anything about Carrigan, she learned that one teacher was some sort of hero and managed to get all of the students safely from the building before the bomb went off. That's Carrigan she thought.

Checking back through her prenuptial agreements filed with the corporate law offices in Cody, before her marriage to Edmond, relieved her mind. Edmond was not entitled to any of her corporate stock should they be divorced. During her last conversation with Stephen's father, Edmond told her that unless she was on the plane home with Stephen, he was filing for divorce. Nancy would never have taken the first step, but since he placed the ball in her court, she wanted to make sure she was ready to play the game. Wait 'til Edmond tried to deal with her corporate lawyers. He would learn what rough and tumble was all about. Edmond may have sired Stephen, but he had never been his father. Nancy was surprised when she became pregnant as they coupled infrequently without warmth or passion as if Edmond was closing a business deal and speed was of the utmost concern, leaving her feeling used and unattractive.

She was surprised by the way Carrigan looked at her in the creek last weekend, as if he enjoyed what he saw. Carrigan would never fit into the high society crowd of Washington, but he was all man and possessed an uncanny ability to connect with young people.

Carrigan, Gertrude, and the trailer rolled into the lumberyard, and soon every spare inch of space bristled with tresses. The men in the lumberyard tried to discuss the previous day's events in the school, but Carrigan only nodded and hummed as they loaded the rafters, giving out no information with which to fuel further speculation. I'm getting pretty good at this he thought. Becky was a good teacher.

Becky nodded and said nothing yesterday when Carrigan released the young girl to parental care after telling her that Tommy was dead. Huge pools of tears filled her eyes. Compassion wasn't something Becky was deprived of at birth.

Otto was waiting impatiently for him on the porch of the center when Carrigan arrived, trailer in tow.

"I thought you vere building a hoouse, not carrying one up to the hills," said Otto.

By the time they crossed the Laramie River Bridge, Carrigan finished explaining to Otto in brief terse statements what happened the day before and about the guilt he felt for Tommy's death.

"This old world is hard to understand, maybe the Lord made it that vay on purpose, so ve couldn't try to meddle in his affairs."

The rest of the journey passed in silence as Otto realized Carrigan preferred to think rather than visit. That was all right with the old German. The morning was beautiful, and he still loved the hills and the rolling plains leading up to the slumbering peak, deep blue in the morning light. Otto laid his head back and enjoyed the trip, remembering when he first arrived in Wyoming full of piss and vinegar, ready to take on the world.

Otto was born in Chicago on the first day of the New Year in 1925. His father, a machinist, arrived from the old country several years before in 1923 and managed to find employment in the growing Chicago factories. German was the only language spoken in his home until Otto attended a school when he was six. In the next few years, Otto learned English and a few facts and figures although he never did learn to read very well. By the time he was ten, Otto became a machinist helper, working long hours with his father setting dies and doing repetitive tasks such as turning threads. The depression affected even men with skilled trades, and life was hard for the family, but at least they were working. Between them, the family made four dollars a day. When Otto turned fourteen, he saw a wild west show in the Chicago Coliseum and knew immediately Chicago was not where he wanted to live the rest of his life. With a few dollars saved from his work and two clean shirts freshly laundered and sewn by his mother, Otto left home.

During the next year, Otto worked his way from Chicago to Kansas City and further west to Omaha before finally arriving in Denver in 1940. In each city he would work odd jobs, always dreaming about the west. While in Denver, he took a job with a freighting and construction company, learning to handle the heavy equipment and cable dozers. War came to the United States, but with his thick accent and German heritage, Otto knew he would never be accepted into the Army. Trying to move even further from the growing population in Denver, Otto applied his skills in the small rural communities in northern Colorado, never staying in one place long.

When Otto was twenty-five, he was notified that both his mother and father were killed in a tenement fire in Chicago. Otto sent money for burial expenses but never went east for the funerals. An only child, he was now truly on his own. After the end of the war, Otto went to work with a large company hired to work on irrigation canals in southern Wyoming near the small town of Rockville. Rockville needed to expand its ability to irrigate the growing acres of hay and crops, and the older canals were not deep and wide enough. Water was brought from the Laramie Plains into a series of reservoirs where it could be stored before being pushed down the Laramie River and then into the creeks and canals in the Rockville area. After a year of dangerous work in the steep mountain terrain and the fertile flatlands, Otto knew he was home. When the construction process was over and the company moved on, Otto stayed.

With the money saved from his wages, Otto purchased a small garage that adjoined a pool hall. Over the years he had learned how to fix almost anything with a motor. In 1951 Otto's Repair was born. When business was good, Otto worked day and night repairing heavy equipment, haying and farming machinery, cars, trucks, and anything else that came through his doors. During the winter months when business was slower, he played solo, a gambling game, with the other card players in the pool hall. During the summer months, Otto fished every inch of the Laramie River. Otto didn't fly fish, he used whatever means was necessary to catch the wily brown trout that swam in the swift blue waters. Playing fair wasn't important to him after growing up in the Depression. Worms, Clorox and even sometimes dynamite were lures he used to fish with. Otto usually caught his limit.

Otto's favorite story was about a local game warden that always tried to catch him using explosives to catch fish. Knowing he was under surveillance by the Game and Fish, Otto invited the game warden to go with him one day. Realizing this was his chance to catch Otto breaking the law, the game warden readily agreed. Together they rowed in a small boat out onto one of the reservoirs on the Laramie Plains built to hold irrigation water. When they were far from shore, Otto explained to the game warden that he would now show him his secret method of catching fish. Reaching into his knap sack, Otto pulled out a stick of dynamite and lit the fuse with his cigar. The game warden immediately began to rant and rave about how long Otto was going to spend in jail, and gave Otto a full lecture on the illegalities of fishing with explosives. Otto smiled and handed the lit stick of dynamite to the game warden just before it was about to explode. Grinning like a Cheshire cat toward the stunned warden and with his thick accent Otto replied simply. "Ve vill deal vith that later, now are you going to talk or fish."

"That game varden vas a pretty good fisherman," Otto would always tell his listeners. Needless to say Otto never had any trouble with that particular game warden again.

When a local rancher went broke after the harsh winter of 1953, and was unable to pay his machinery repair bill, Otto bought the rancher's mountain property high in the Laramie Mountains. With it, Otto acquired the right to lease the adjoining state land, section 36. Both sections joined the Laramie River, and at last Otto was a man of property. From this land he could go fishing anytime he wanted to. Most weekends this was the German's escape from the repair shop. The residents of Rockville became accustomed to the sign on his door, "Gone Fishing" every weekend beginning at noon on Friday. Forty-five years later Otto never regretted his choice of moving to Wyoming. Failing health and his diabetes forced Otto to realize that he could no longer trek the mountains, and he applied for housing in the senior center. The housing was expensive, and before Otto could get in he had to sell his mountain property. After visiting with Carrigan, Otto knew here was a person that loved the land as much as he did. Carrigan promised Otto the land would never be sold and broken into cabin sites, nor would Carrigan ever turn it over to a large corporation. Carrigan would use it just as Otto had, to fish, to enjoy, and to replenish the soul.

When they arrived at the unfinished cabin, Otto commented on the long hours of work already involved.

"It is vhere I imagined you vould build it," Otto said. "Das is the right place. Sometimes I used to think das vas the center of the vorld vhere God came to rest vhen he vas tired. You've done vell, my boy."

Throughout the rest of the morning Carrigan stood the tresses against the side of his frame walls and then used Gertrude and a rope to snake them on top of the walls. From here he tied a rope to the crown of the rafters and with a block and tackle pulled the joists upright before tying the rope to Gertrude's trailer hitch. One at a time the backbone of the cabin rose and was hammered into place on sixteen-inch centers before being nailed into place with hurricane anchors. By noon the job was done, and Carrigan awoke Otto from his nap in the shade of the pickup to eat lunch. The two men feasted on sandwiches, pudding, and a whole bag of cookies. Carrigan teased Otto that if he kept eating cookies his other leg would fall off, but Otto only laughed and joked that it was better his legs than other parts of his anatomy. Otto always liked to drink Jack Daniel's Whiskey, and Carrigan mixed it half and half with water while the amber liquid was still in the bottle. Retrieving the bottle from the cold stream, they polished off the smooth brown brew while Otto told Carrigan about his days as a moonshiner. Carrigan heard the stories many times before, but with every telling Otto added new details, and Carrigan closed his eyes, imagining what it must have been like in the early 1950's.

Otto said he learned moonshining from a man he worked with in Denver. During the years of 1919 to 1933 the manufacture, distribution, or consumption of alcohol was made illegal by the 18th amendment. Very few people in the west paid much attention to the law, and people just made their own alcohol. Sometimes organized crime moved in and brought in whiskey and rum from either Canada or Puerto Rico, but most of the alcohol came from stills set way back in the hills away from the prying eyes of law enforcement. Sometimes the police were paid to look the other way. Moonshining continued on after the repeal of prohibition in 1933 with the 21st amendment because it was cheaper than store bought liquor, and some people preferred the taste. The rancher from whom Otto bought the land, told him there was an old still up Cherry Creek that was used off and on for the last thirty years. When Otto bought the land, he went exploring and found the cave a mile up Cherry Creek and also found some of the copper boilers and condensing tubes from the still. Knowledge met opportunity, and Otto began hauling corn mash off the flats up to the hills, converting the corn to a high-grade moonshine. Sometimes when the repair business was a little slow, Otto would trade his concoction for food or repair parts. Jack Daniels was the only whiskey he claimed which could come close to his home brew.

Once ground, the corn meal would be mixed with rye, yeast and sugar before putting the mash into big vats. During the summer the mixture would ferment in about three days, but during the winter the process took longer. After his mash was fermented, Otto would cook it in a boiler that caused the alcohol to rise off in a vapor. This vapor would run through a coiled copper tube routed through a barrel with cold water flowing through it. This caused the vapor to condense, and he would catch the final product in quart jars as the clear liquid dripped from the end of the tube. Otto said the clear mountain spring water of Cherry Creek made the best whiskey around. Sometimes in the fall he would take some special orders for chokecherry liquor that the housewives in Rockville were partial to. Otto never charged the women, and they kept him supplied in canning jars. After the whiskey aged for a while in the cave, Otto would haul it to town and trade it or sell the fiery brew for a dollar a gallon. A gallon of whiskey would last quite awhile considering it was close to 100 proof. Otto claimed the left over mash was good for fishing also. When Otto poured the mash into the deep holes in the river the fish would just come floating to the top, plumb drunk.

There were other stills around Rockville, but people trusted Otto. Some of the other outfits used battery acid to speed up the fermentation process or lead pipes instead of copper. If the whiskey didn't kill a person, lead poisoning might. Otto said one moonshiner always put dead muskrats in the brew, claiming this was the secret ingredient to great whiskey. Otto called the whiskey forty-rod because that was how far some people could run before passing out after drinking the white lightening.

"After your done vorking, I vill show you the cave," Otto said. "All the years I stored the viskey in there it gave me the chills. Give me an hour head start, and I vill go there vith you. You must see for yourself."

"I don't think anything can bother me after yesterday," Carrigan answered, realizing that for a whole morning he hadn't thought about school. I brought bedrolls and thought we might spend the night if it's all right with you. I could catch some fish and fry them for supper. Tomorrow you can show me the cave."

"Yavol, that makes me hungry already. Hope you brought some more viskey, all das vork makes me thirsty. Right now I need a nap. Let me know vhen the fish are frying."

Carrigan just smiled. He had more whiskey but knew better than to reveal the location until evening came. It was nice to have company around even if Otto wasn't any help with the cabin. That afternoon Carrigan leaned sheets of plyboard against the walls of the cabin then climbed the roof pulling them up and nailing them on the newly set tresses, alternating the seams to tie the structure together. As darkness began the stealthy approach through the canyon, Carrigan nailed the last piece of sheeting on the roof and climbed down the ladder. Otto still wasn't stirring, so Carrigan grabbed his pole and headed for the river to catch supper before darkness closed in around him.

That night after supper of Rainbow Trout, fried potatoes, and more whiskey, Carrigan stoked the fire in his outdoor fireplace before retiring with Otto to the unfinished porch were the two men spread the bedrolls. The moon was full although slightly tinged with red as if issuing a warning. Across the canyon coyotes sang their lonely lament, and in the timber near the edge of the glade, Carrigan could hear the noise of a large animal moving through the underbrush fulfilling its role as predator or prey, he knew not which. As he drifted off to a restless sleep to dream of fiery explosions, Carrigan was aware of the plaintiff calling of an owl as she flew through the night air searching for something or someone.

With the first light of morning, Carrigan was again on task nailing the remaining sheets of plyboard to the wall of the cabin. Here he was glad for the eight-foot height of the wall. Two sheets applied in shiplap fashion covered eight feet of the wall, and with the preplanned dimensions, he soon covered the exterior. Once finished, he used a battery saw to re-cut the framed doors and windows, using spare pieces to seal the eaves and ends. By noon this job was finished, and Carrigan's thumb was too sore from missed hammer blows to work anymore. Otto offered constructive comments and kept a supply of nails close to hand. The two carpenters made lunch from the remaining food, mostly lunchmeat and potato chips.

The heat was beginning to reflect from the canyon wall, and they began the slow process of walking up Cherry Creek to look at Otto's cave. Carrigan drove Gertrude as far as possible, but the last quarter mile was too rough even for her tough frame, and they went on foot from here. Otto wasn't fast on his artificial leg, but with the aid of a crutch he made fair time, stopping often to rest on the large rocks adjacent to the creek. After an hour of patient travel, Otto stopped and pointed up the hillside toward the fractured granite wall. From forces applied long ago, this rock was piled into tall columns like pillars of a temple, leaning crookedly together resting each upon its neighbor. Beneath two of the larger pillars, an opening appeared. Otto just pointed, too out of breath to speak, and Carrigan clambered up the steep slope of loose rocks to the entrance to the cave. As he approached the opening, being careful not to tread on any early season rattlesnakes, he could feel a breeze blowing from the mouth of the canyon. Ducking through the narrow opening, Carrigan could see the room open into a large cave with a sandy floor and rough-hewn walls. Near the entrance were several large wooden tubs, the lumber warped and aged. Near these a large copper boiler sat, turned on edge, badly corroded from long years of use. The interior of the cave was dark, and Carrigan didn't want to penetrate the quiet interior further without a light source. Carrigan left the entrance and walked back down the hill to where Otto waited on a rock.

"It's pretty dark in there, but it felt a lot cooler than it is out here. We should get some light and go back in it to get out of the heat," Carrigan said when he was down the hill.

"I thought so too one time many years ago," Otto answered. "I vent in clear through the big room. There it gets real narrow. I vas just fixing to get down on my hands and go through the opening vhen I looked down in the sand. Right there staring at me vas and old vhite skull, the eyes looking right at me. Skeered me to death, I jumped back and fell down in the sand. Vhen I got up, there was another skull, eyeing me vith those empty sockets just like his partner. I left that cave a running, and it took me three veeks before I vent back."

"I don't blame you," said Carrigan, "I'm not sure I would have gone back."

"Vell I finally told myself that old bones veren't nothing to be skeered of, so I vent back in with a shovel. I started sifting through the sand and found more heads, and lots of bones all over the cave floor. I also found some strange arrowheads, long fluted points, like spearheads, but they didn't look like anything I found around here. They vere vhite just like the bones. Some of them vere human bones, and some veren't. One of the bones vas as thick as my thigh. I never did go into the rear cave. I just stored the viskey, right in front. I thought the men and the other animals that died there should stay undisturbed. Gave me the chills every time I vent in that cave. After avhile I gave up making viskey and left the boilers in there."

"Last week I found the head of an old bear down by the cabin," Carrigan said. "Seems like there was a whole lot of death going on around here a long time ago."

"Vell, if you find any more, just leave em lay, right vhere you find them. Nothing good vill come from messing vith graves."

"All right, Otto, I'll just let them be. Now let's get back before it gets dark. There might just be some moonshine left for us to get home on."

Returning back down the canyon, Carrigan and Otto picked up all the scrap lumber and piled it inside the cabin to be used later for soffit and fascia on the cabin. Next trip up Carrigan would try to get shingles on the roof and side the cabin walls. Then he could start on the interior and the windows. On the drive back to town that evening, Carrigan felt better. Something about the hard work, or the beauty of the surroundings helped sooth his mind, putting perspective on the events of last week. Here in the mountains he didn't have to worry about fixing anybody else. Here he could allow the mountains to restore peace to his soul.

Carrigan dropped Otto off at the Senior Center promising to return and take the old German to the hills again after the cabin was finished. Carrigan ran Gertrude through the car wash, allowing the hot water to wash of the miles of the trail from her metal flanks. After air-drying her, Carrigan drove to his house, tired from the weekend labors. His right arm was stiffening from the repeated hammer strokes and Carrigan knew by morning the aging limb would be of little use. It's hell to get old he thought, but it sure beats the alternative.

After a hot shower, Carrigan dragged the box of his parent's belongings from the closet vowing not to get sidetracked tonight. He was doing well until the phone rang, and he was forced to stop. Carrigan was surprised to find the caller was Reed Lansing. Not quite understanding the reason for the call, Carrigan was guarded until he could discover the motive. Lansing talked again about how grateful he was to Carrigan for getting Becky from harm's way and then talked about the constant pressure of the media trying to get more information about the incident. At last Lansing came to the point, and Carrigan asked him to repeat his question, not understanding the meaning.

"The board wanted me to call and offer you the position of principal for next year at the high school," Big Reed explained again. "I know you're certified for administration. We would rather have someone from the district instead of bringing in an outsider. There is a lot of healing that needs to be done, and we think you're just the man to do the job. What do you say?"

"Well, I don't know," said Carrigan, realizing he heard Lansing correctly. "That's something I will have to think about. As of Friday, I didn't think I ever wanted to teach again, let alone be a principal. When do you need to know by?"

"Jan's contract expires June 1st, and we'd like someone on board by then, to start cleaning up the school and rebuilding. Think about it a couple of days and let me know, and thanks again for watching out for Becky, she's pretty special to me."

Carrigan returned to the couch and his project, feeling every muscle ache in his body. Now he was going to have a headache to boot. He always swore the one position he would never take was principal of a high school, but maybe in that position he could make the changes he was always whining about. He was going to need the Absorbine Junior and a bottle of aspirin tonight.

Carrigan stopped when he came across another clipping about the Wind River Reservation's formation. There was no date on the clipping, but it was yellowed with age similar to the first one he read. The article told about the year 1878 when the Arapaho and the Shoshoni first came to live together in the Wind River area. Chief Black Coal of the Arapaho met with Chief Washakie of the Shoshoni people. The Arapaho were pushed from Colorado by the whites. Disease and the Sand River Massacre, where American soldiers killed many children and women by attacking a peaceful camp, decimated their tribe. Chief Black Coal's heart was heavy, and he knew he could never return to the Fort Collins area. Swallowing his pride, Black Coal approached Washakie to ask for land to live on and for a peace between their peoples. At first Washakie declined, knowing the long years of hatred between the two tribes, but after hearing council from one of his Shaman, a powerful sub chief named Tavendu-Wets, Washakie relented, realizing the position to deal with the white politicians would be stronger if the Arapaho tribe dealt alongside the Shoshonis against the white man. Thus the deal was struck. Blood enemies for over a hundred years came to occupy the same land, each vowing they would make no more war on their kinsmen.

Carrigan paused a minute to reflect on the article. It was possible with inspired leadership to heal divisions among people, especially if they could be united against a common cause. In the case of the Indians, the common cause was the white man. What could be used in a school to unify the student body? A common cause was needed so that no one would be picked upon and humiliated to the point of breaking, seeing violence as their only way out. Strong leadership would be needed from someone with a foot in both worlds, someone who understood the hopeless and the hopeful.

Feeling his eyelids beginning to close, Carrigan replaced the paper back in the box. As he picked the box up a corner of the cardboard ripped and it fell from his hands to the floor coming to rest on its side. In the very bottom Carrigan could see an old envelope sealed in wax, along with what appeared to be an elk antler. Surprised that he hadn't noticed these items before he knelt to investigate when he heard someone knock on the front door.

Now what, he thought. There seemed to be a conspiracy afloat this evening to prevent him from resting his tired body. Whatever it was it couldn't make his head ache any worse he thought, as the throbbing continued to escalate. Carrigan padded to the door and threw it open. There in the cool night air stood Sheila, six-pack of Fat Tires in hand and a wide smile of forgiveness on her lips.

"Thought you might need a backrub. I tried to call you earlier but when you didn't answer I figured you were in the mountains working. I brought some beer. A couple of cold ones and some TLC would make you feel a whole lot better."

Carrigan tried to remember what he said to Sheila that confused her about his intentions last time they talked. Actually a back rub would feel really good this evening and a cold beer might even help his headache.

"Okay," he said, "two beers and a backrub, nothing else. I meant what I said, about you finding someone else."

Carrigan was asleep five minutes into the backrub lying on the floor of his living room. Sheila finished the beer she opened for him before putting the rest into the refrigerator. Gathering a blanket from the bedroom she covered him then lay down next to him curving her full body, spoon like to his back. Carrigan was funny, she thought, somehow she felt better just laying next to him.

When Carrigan arose the next morning, Sheila was gone, and only her perfume on the blanket covering him showed that she was there, and he wasn't just dreaming. I shouldn't have let her in he thought, but he was too tired to throw her out. He would have to speak more clearly the next time. The backrub felt good, at least the part he remembered of it. Best-case scenario would be they could remain friends without sharing the same bed. He made a start on that last night. Feeling the urge to return to work on the cabin, he arose, dressed, and left for a run to the lumberyard. He stopped by the school to visit with Jan, somewhat surprised by how quiet the campus was. Carrigan's wing of the building was still closed with yellow police tape, but the office area was open, and the secretaries smiled at Carrigan when he walked through the door. Bantering a minute, Carrigan collected his summer's paycheck and strolled in to harangue Jan. The principal was bustling around the office, sorting papers and collecting photos and certificates from the walls. Carrigan told Jan about his conversation with Lansing, and Jan echoed the idea, stating he too thought Carrigan would be good for the school.

"Hell, I thought you would try to talk me out of it," whined Carrigan. "Since when did you agree with the school board?"

"Ever so often they make sense. It's time you stopped hiding amongst the kids and find out how much fun administration is."

"I already know, besides I think I'll just quit and go live in the mountains, chasing bears and hunting beavers. I don't like people well enough to be a principal."

"That's why you're perfect for the job, now get out of here and let me pack. Call me when you make up your mind."

Carrigan deposited his paycheck in the bank and rolled Gertrude into the lumberyard. Inside the lumber store, he drained the coffee pot while waiting for them to load his shingles. Carrigan kept eyeballing a small chromed wood stove on display in the store until at last he splurged and told the guys to load that also. Together with the stovepipe, flashing, and roof cement he spent more than he wanted to, but all cabins needed a good stove. Just as he was finishing his last cup of coffee, he looked up, surprised the see Nancy standing at the counter.

"I thought you were in Cody, chasing Buffalo Bill around," Carrigan quipped.

"Naw, he's too old for me, no challenge there. I really came looking for you. Gertrude told me you were hiding in here."

"Where's Steven?"

"I flew him out of Cody. He still has a couple of weeks of school left, but he's really looking forward to helping you again. Don't get it all built 'til he gets back."

"No danger in that" Carrigan laughed. "I'm just getting shingles today."

"Do you need any help? I'm a union carpenter now," asked Nancy.

"Love to have you come along, if you can spare the time. Shingling isn't my favorite job."

"That's why I worked all week so I could have time to play a couple days. Pick me up at Ben's, and I'll order some lunches to take with us. Do you want any beer?"

"No, ice tea only, Otto helped me yesterday, and just being around him gives me a hangover, see in half an hour."

Nancy was ready when Carrigan arrived and loaded the cab with more food than the two could eat in a week. She'd taken time to change clothes and wore shorts and a halter-top. Her long waves of hair were braided and hung in a thick ponytail down her back. The scuffed hiking boots she wore looked out of place against the designer shorts with only the long expanse of her willowy brown legs to separate them. Carrigan looked at the thin white scars on her knee from the repaired ACL. Nancy caught his gaze and smiled flexing the leg.

"Good as new," she said, "though I swear it aches every time we get a heavy rain. Makes me think another flood is coming."

After several minutes of silence on the way up Carrigan explained about the events at the school, knowing that Nancy would never repeat what he told her. She was silent as he talked, letting him tell the story, smiling when he downplayed his role, and crying when he talked about Tommy.

"How can anyone as big and tough as you, be so forgiving," she asked when he finished. "Thank God the boy didn't take you and Becky with him."

"Someday," Carrigan said, "we need to build a school where everyone makes it. But enough about school, what did you do in Cody?"

Nancy told Carrigan about her trip, omitting the part concerning Edmond's threatened divorce. Nancy enjoyed the relationship with Carrigan just as it was, and she didn't want to put any pressure on it by bring in her husband or ex-husband, whatever the case might be.

The miles seemed to fly by this morning, and soon they arrived at the cabin site. Carrigan backed Gertrude next to the walls, and from the pickup bed began throwing tarpaper and shingles onto the roof. While the morning was still cool, they roofed the cabin, starting near the bottom edge and working upward. With Nancy setting the shingles in place and Carrigan securing them with nails, the small roof was completed by noon. Carrigan wanted to continue working, but Nancy threatened him with a union strike if she didn't get a lunch hour, so he relented, and they ate lunch near the y of the two creeks. Nancy undid the laces on her work boots and kicked her slender feet in the gurgling creek, enjoying the feel of the cold water flowing between her toes. Carrigan wolfed down a sandwich then laid back in the grass with a cold bottle of ice tea and told Nancy about his visit from Reed Lansing and the job offer as principal for Lakota High.

"You'd make a great principal," Nancy concurred. "Isn't that what you've always wanted to do, blend a college prep program with alternative offering for the kids that aren't going to college?"

"Yes, it is. Statistically only about 17% of all high school students graduate from college. Sometimes in high school we don't do a very good job for the other 83%. We need to teach and offer classes so they will be prepared for the military, apprenticeships, job training, and the trades. We offer three sections of British Lit and no sections of technical report writing. Doesn't make sense does it? The state tests the kids on chemistry but doesn't ask any questions about electricity or plumbing. Our priorities are catty wampus, all mixed up."

"Haven't you answered your own question?" she asked.

"I know, I know," Carrigan conceded. "But my fear is, I will get stuck in the middle. I won't be teaching anymore, and the school board and the state won't let us change the curriculum, so the kids will loose out all the way around."

"Well, sleep on it a few days, maybe the answer will come to you," Nancy concluded.

Carrigan finished his tea, and reluctantly left the creek, hating to leave the comfortable grass, honest conversation, and slender brown legs flashing through the water. Returning to the pickup, he planked boards up to Gertrude's lowered tailgate, and dollied the stove down the plank boards and into the door of the cabin. Carrigan unstrapped the small stove and maneuvered it on top the flat rocks placed earlier on the cabin floor. Returning again to the roof, he inscribed a circle three feet from the northwest corner and cut an eight-inch hole through the roof. Nancy pushed the joined sections of triple wall pipe up to him from the inside of the cabin until he estimated the height was right to form a good air draw from the stove. Carrigan flashed the pipe and coated all the edges with roof cement. As a last step, he attached the rain cap and clambered from the roof. Once inside the cabin, Carrigan finished the job by securing the bottom of the triple wall pipe to the top of the stove. When he had more time, the corner would be rocked with moss-covered flagstones from the surrounding hills. The result would be beautifully natural and fireproof. A fire could be built now to ward off the evening chills, but it would be safer once Carrigan put the flagstones in place. Satisfied with the completion of his projects, Carrigan quit work for the day and geared up for a trip to the river. Nancy needed little urging to tag along. The afternoon heat spread across the glade as the grass in the meadow relaxed, enjoying the promised coming of summer. Nancy's laughter echoed from the canyon walls as she teased Carrigan about his attention to detail with the fishing tackle.

Watching the man and woman walking down the draw to the river, the cabin remained behind. Centered in the glade, built but unfinished, the structure stood, a natural example of what could grow from a solid foundation. The abode rose to guard the meadow but many hours of work remained before the structure would meld into the wilderness. With time, patience, and attention to detail the home like a relationship would mature, becoming an integral component of the rich mountain earth to which the dwelling was joined.

Later that evening the couple sat within the walls of the cabin sharing a bottle of wine as they finished the fresh trout Carrigan barbecued in tinfoil. From one end of the room, the flickering glow of a small Coleman lantern reflected the pair's shadows against the opposite wall. A small fire snapped brightly in the new chrome stove sending its glow of illumination to compete with the lantern before breaking through the shadows to form a contrasting silhouette on the far wall.

"I reckon we'd better get on back," Carrigan said at last, suddenly being struck by how much he felt like staying where he was.

"Up to you," Nancy said softly. "I don't have anywhere to be, and no one is waiting for me."

"I don't reckon Edmond would want his wife spending nights with strange men, even if they were old friends. I wouldn't if I were in his shoes."

"Edmond hasn't cared what I did for a long time," Nancy explained. "He told me last week he was filing for divorce. I put a lot of thought into it the last several days. If he doesn't, I will. Being here with you made me realize that Stephen and I belong in Wyoming."

"So where does that put us?" Carrigan asked.

Rising, Nancy turned down the flame in the lantern until the small light sputtered and died leaving only the amber flickering from the wood stove.

"In the dark," she said.

Slowly the shadows on the wall lost their separate identities melding into one, dancing and moving in cadence across the framed partition. Occasionally the pitch in the stove would crack sharply sending out a flare of light, and the room would glow brightly before returning to a slow steady radiance. By morning the fire was only a bed of red embers, all energy from the wood consumed by the hunger of the flame that burned throughout the night providing warmth to the newly built dwelling. Above the small cabin in the still darkened sky, the Milky Way began to withdraw its illumination from the earth below, the assigned task of the Great Manitou now completed.

Carrigan arose early, shedding the protection of the bedrolls to hop about on one foot trying to pull on his cold Levis. Nancy watched staying within the warmth of the covers while he stoked the fire before setting the coffee pot on the stove to heat. Waiting until she had his full attention, Nancy braved the cold room to dress in one of his work shirts and an old pair of pants several sizes to large for her narrow waist. She buttoned the shirt slowly, enjoying his gaze and the power her femininity held over him. Together they slipped beneath the covers again to drink the thick rich coffee, blowing on the heavy cups to cool the steaming brew. Neither spoke, but each was cognizant of the deep feelings of satisfaction and peace that flowed within them. Carrigan knew that here in the mountains a lifetime of searching was ended. Perhaps Otto was right, it was to this glade that God came to rest, granting peace and serenity to his children living there.

Later that morning Gertrude was loaded with supplies before Carrigan and Nancy started back down the trail to town.

"This wasn't one time magic, was it cowboy?" Nancy asked breaking the silence.

"Well, there isn't much doubt it was magic, but I would have to die before I would allow last night to be a one night stand. You always did enchant me, and I won't let you go again."

Nancy never answered except to lay her head against Carrigan's shoulder as he maneuvered the big pickup down the trail leading from the school section. She watched the tall trees flow by enjoying the security of Carrigan's arm around her, protecting her, making her feel vulnerable and needed. Behind them in the western sky, clouds began to gather, rolling into dark gray thunderheads indicating a coming storm. The wind freshened, and the hint of moisture tinted the breeze as it sighed through the evergreens before continuing down the canyon. Nancy rubbed her knee, feeling a dull ache within from the old injury.

Carrigan dropped Nancy off at Ben's to get her car. Nancy offered to fix supper for Carrigan that evening. She needed to check in with the ranch offices to gather any messages and handle any problems. Carrigan wanted to pickup some windows and a door and return to the hills. If he could install these, the structure would be weather tight and protected from any storms until he could finish the interior and caulk the cracks.

Promising to reappear by seven that night, Carrigan left the parking lot thinking momentarily about returning to hold Nancy against him one more time, but realized she would think he was acting like a teenager again. Carrigan made it to the glass company and picked out three windows and a door, bracing them with cardboard in the back of the pickup so they wouldn't break on the return trip to the mountains. On a hunch he swung by the school, parking in his accustomed spot. The breeze was chilling the air now, and he slipped on a jacket before running in to see if Mr. James was in the science lab. The room was empty, but he left a note on James' desk asking for a return call. If Carrigan took the principal job, he wanted James on board in some capacity working with the "at risk" students. The man's talents were too great to just allow him to retire. After writing the note, Carrigan saw his fossilized skull still lying on the lab table. Grabbing this on the way out, he threw it into the pickup, kicked Gertrude up to full speed, and headed into the wind back to the hills before the rain started.

By early afternoon, Carrigan parked the pickup next to the cabin and started setting the window frames in his precut openings. He was glad now for the time he took earlier making sure all the openings were square. The windows fit well, and he screwed them to the frame openings before filling the cracks with aerosol foam insulation. When finished, he checked the windows to assure they slid easily and weren't bound or jammed.

After Carrigan finished the last window, the rain, which no longer waited patiently for him to finish, began to fall, the drops huge and slushy as if trying to decide whether it wanted to be snow or rain. Carrigan drug the door inside and stood it against the cabin wall. Grabbing a sheet of plywood Carrigan nailed it against the opening of the door. This would keep the rain out until the sun chose to make its reappearance. He didn't want to stand in the rain to install the door and was afraid if he worked on it now, the wood might become too wet, swelling the frame making the fitting impossible.

Checking the time, Carrigan realized he still had an hour before he needed to get back to Rockville to meet Nancy for supper. He dug the yellow slicker from behind the seat of the pickup and grabbing the fossilized bear skull, he headed down the draw toward the river. Half an hour and he could throw the skull into a deep pool in the river, returning the fossil to the elements from which it came. He had been thinking about this for several days now. Reburying the skull in the glade didn't seem right to him, and he thought about taking it up the Otto's cave and throwing it in, but he wasn't comfortable with that option either. In his dreams the last several nights Carrigan remembered brief dreams of bears, fires, and children trying to escape a burning school. His rational intelligent mind told him removing the bear skull from the ground beneath his cabin was in no way responsible for the bombing in his school, but something deeper inside either derived from the Shoshone blood or perhaps flowing with his Celtic heritage told him differently. Thousands of years of superstitions and legends won out, and he knew the skull must be returned to the river beneath twenty feet of water where it could settle into the soft silt finding peace for the next eternity. He didn't view his decision as superstitious, merely prudent, after all what could it hurt.

The rain fell heavily now, but visibility was still good as Carrigan slipped and slid down the game trail catching himself by grabbing willows and buck bush beside the trail. Reaching the river he paused a minute before walking up the river where the canyon narrowed and the granite walls stretched to close together. Here the water rushed high and fast, bursting through the opening. The high canyon walls were starting to stream with water from the gathered rain, and Carrigan was glad he wouldn't be near the river's edge long in case flood stage was reached. Pulling himself up hand over hand, Carrigan reached the top of a granite hummock. The river pooled itself deep and dark below him, waiting its turn to rush through the narrowed channel before it. With the rain, the water was starting to swirl battering hard against the granite wall.

Carrigan paused long enough to say; "Only thy Maker knows your name. May he receive you into his waters there to abide into eternity."

With that, Carrigan threw the skull into the water. The heavy bone fragment fought briefly against the current resisting the pull of the whirlpool until it sank deep into the nadir swirling down to the deep muddy bottom buried forever until its maker saw fit to bring it toward the light again. With this task done, Carrigan started down the river again until he could turn up the draw and back to Gertrude waiting beside the cabin. Not even the gloominess of the day could repress his spirit. Carrigan felt as if all aspects that he searched for so long were finally coming together. He would take the principal job and begin making the school a place for all children regardless if they were athletic, college bound, or simply trying to get by. Any life he shared with Nancy would fill his soul with peace. Last night they loved each other as if they were two halves of the same spirit finally united. No matter how he moved, she seemed to sense his mood and shifted to meet the changed rhythm, each climbed the hill together reaching the top at the same time, only to discover they both had the will and strength to go further. Long ago Nancy told him she felt they were fated to be together, now he understood what she meant. This summer Carrigan would finish the cabin, and here at the very center of the Maker's world would be a retreat to replenish his being when the world closed in too tight around him.

Lastly there was Stephen, and although Carrigan realized the boy would spend some time with his natural father, Carrigan would teach the boy the beauty of the land, reverence of nature, and how to flip a yellow humpy on the backside of a rock where the sleek brown torpedoes lay in wait. Life just didn't get any better than this, he thought. It had been a long journey, but now he was home.

Nancy realized she didn't have anything in the freezer but hamburger, so after checking the time she called Ben's, asking them to set out two of the thickest steaks they had in their meat locker. She could swing by and get them before Carrigan returned from the mountains. She wanted to make sure he ate well tonight because he was going to need his strength. Something inside her awakened, and now she needed to answer the calling. Nancy decided she would wait until Carrigan appeared before putting the steaks on, maybe he would be wet and cold and in need of a hot shower before supper. Yes, she determined as she left the house to go pick up the steaks, a hot shower was definitely what he needed. After Nancy picked up the steaks, she turned to leave and almost ran into the bartender coming down the hallway. Nancy remembered her from previous evenings spent in the lounge but couldn't remember her name.

"Cooking supper for someone tonight," Sheila asked seeing the thick steaks wrapped in clear paper.

"Well, yes," Nancy replied, trying to be friendly.

"Great" Sheila replied, "as long as it isn't Carrigan. We've been together a long time, and I would hate to see anyone moving into my territory."

Nancy immediately felt anger flushing through her; just who in the hell did this woman think she was?

"Carrigan is a big boy; he has the run of any territory he wants," Nancy replied curtly. "Now excuse me, I need to get home."

"Well," Sheila said to Nancy's retreating back, "he seemed to like my side of the river night before last when I slept with him."

"Bitch," was all Nancy said as she left Ben's, running to her vehicle to avoid the heavy rain.

Carrigan found the entrance to the draw leading up to the glade before he turned to look at the river behind him. Already in the last thirty minutes the water was appreciably higher, and whitecaps were starting to shoot over top of submerged rocks. As he started up the trail, a large bolt of lightening splintered rocks in the canyon across from him. It was early in the year for a real gully-washing flood, but the rain didn't seem to be letting up any.

He needed to hurry up the draw because the road home would be slick enough to delay him even with Gertrude's sure-footed ability. Ten minutes of sliding, falling, and cursing the gumbo mud brought Carrigan half way to his destination. Already water was starting to pour into the draw from the valleys of the mountains above, and Carrigan was forced off the trail several times to avoid wading in the waist deep water. The thick brush caught the wooden debris washed down from above, damming the water even deeper.

Suddenly something flashed across the trail in front of Carrigan, close enough he could feel the air disturbance caused by the swift passage of a body in front of him. Through the gloom, he couldn't tell what the animal was other than it was fast and appeared dark in the thick rain. As Carrigan stopped trying to peer into the brush and dirty water below him, in the draw another rent of lightening split the sky, torching the air with ozone, clearly showing the massive head of a bear swimming strongly across the water filled draw.

The bolt struck the top of the large tree leaning over the canyon, exploding bits of wood like a bombshell hundreds of feet in each direction. Blasted from its hold in the rocky soil, the tree tumbled end over end to the canyon below. His ears ringing Carrigan swung his vision away from the bear to see the ancient pitch battering ram rushing to meet him. One step carried him away from the tip of the three foot diameter log as it slammed into the muddy trail just behind him, the concussion throwing him from his feet, sliding him down the trail face first in the slick mud. Suddenly tremendous pressure slammed against his left leg as a large limb from the falling trunk met the earth, driving a sharpened pitch pine stake through Carrigan's thigh.

Held tightly against the mud Carrigan struggled to raise his head, choking from the ooze. Breaking branches with his hand he managed to turn halfway over trying to determine what was holding him. Horrified he saw the stake nearly the size of his wrist driven through his leg and deep into the ground below. Strangely there was no pain, only a tremendous feeling of pressure as if his limb were squeezed in a vise. Forcing his mind to be calm, Carrigan attempted to lift the huge limb that was still attached to the dead pine log. Realizing he was trying to lift the entire tree weighing many tons, he next attempted to use his good leg to kick through the tough wood. By the second blow, the pain began to arrive, pulsating upward across his back like burning knives.

First things first, he thought. Opening his slicker, he tore the front from his shirt and then tried to pad the area around the wound. It would do him little good to attempt freedom if he bled to death first.

The pain passed momentarily, and he finished bandaging around the pine spear. Next he thought of the pocketknife. Biting his lips to keep from screaming, Carrigan retrieved the knife from his pocket. Sweat now beaded his forehead mixing with the rain and mud. By turning partially around again, Carrigan attempted to saw through the wooden dagger. The small blade snapped after a few minutes having barely scratched the iron like surface of the pitch pine. Great he thought, now I can't even cut my leg off, laughing at the vision of him amputating his own leg with a broken pocket knife. I'd walk around like Otto, no wonder the old German drinks so much whiskey. Together we couldn't whip anybody in an ass-kicking contest.

Carrigan thought about Nancy. She knew he was supposed to return by seven, and if he didn't show up, maybe she would send someone looking for him. Maybe, that was a long shot.

Glancing around, Carrigan was startled to find the water in the draw had risen dramatically while he was struggling to free himself. The muddied current was less than a foot away from his outstretched hand. If I don't think of something I'm going to end up as bear bait he thought. He let the feeling of death enter his mind for the first time. Anger now filled his thoughts, and Carrigan raised himself with both hands, fighting against the pain as he lunged with all his strength, trying to tear the impaled flesh from its prison, but the leg held, and Carrigan passed out from the pain.

He awoke again shortly, feeling lightheaded and sick to his stomach. Water was running in his mouth, and Carrigan quickly raised his head. How long he was out he didn't know, but the current was running in a fast stream beneath his head. Only by holding himself upright with both arms could Carrigan keep his face from the water. Soon his arms weakened, and taking a deep breath, he allowed his head to drop into the cold water while flexing his arms to gain strength again. This time he pushed himself up to find that his chin barely cleared the current. Sticks swirled by striking him in the face, cutting his cheek.

The cold water numbed the pain in his leg, but his arms began to betray him again, and he took another breath, plunging his face in the water to allow the quivering muscles to rest. This time as he raised himself he could find no air, and he arched his back, trying to raise his head higher, gagging as the cold water flooded his throat and lungs. Suddenly the current surged and between waves, air flooded his senses as he gulped greedily.

A strange odor hung heavy in the air almost like wet fur, and Carrigan started to look for the source when his arms gave out for the last time, collapsing him back into the current. More water surged through his lungs, and this time he didn't gag, the water seemed suddenly peaceful, and his mind floated.

Before him he could see a long river running through broad flat lands. The river twisted and turned growing in size until it at last joined another. Together the waters flowed through low hills covered with thick trees until this water joined even a wider river. As far as Carrigan could see, the river flowed past tall granite cliffs and stately trees, finally reaching a long shoreline where waves pushed against the mighty tide to no avail.

Beside him Carrigan thought he felt something warm, and he had the sensation of floating above the canyon walls higher and higher until he reached the base of a stairway. A bright light beckoned him upward, and slowly he began to climb the hanging road of the stars.

Nancy was furious by the time she reached home with the steaks. She felt betrayed and used, Carrigan thought of her only as another bimbo like that floozy back in the bar. Then slowly her thinking cleared, and she remembered what she felt last night. Together they shared much more than just a late night fling after a bar shift. Calming herself even more, she remembered Carrigan telling her he was so tired from the weekend he fell asleep on the carpet of his house night before last.

That Sheila and Carrigan slept together before she had no doubt, but in her heart she knew it wasn't when that floozy bartender claimed.

Why did she even feel jealous, hell she was still married, on paper at least, if not in spirit? Relieved, she felt like a teenager again. After a hot shower, thick steaks and a night with her, Carrigan wouldn't even remember how to get to Ben's Bar.

Outside the lightening flashed huge jagged bolts, and Nancy felt her level of concern growing. By seven a cold feeling gripped her chest, and by half past Nancy felt as if something was being torn from her soul. Somehow she knew he was in trouble. Crying, she pulled on her coat and ran into the night, determined to drive the road to the hills.

Forcing herself to be calm, she called the Sheriff's office from her car phone, pushing the jeep hard on the slick roads toward the west. Between flashes of lightening she could make out the mountains dominating the dark skyline. Towering above them all, Laramie Peak's outline served as her beacon as she drove on her journey through the rain.

The River North
Chapter 16

Slowly during the next few days with Night Wind's nursing, Joshua began to regain his strength. The ravages of his fever and thoughts of the desperate fight with Lame Wolf receded, allowing his body and mind to begin to heal. Night Wind's temporary repression of his memory gave him a small measure of peace. Buffalo Shield and Black Crowe hunted the ragged crags leading down toward the cabin, and they returned with a mule deer from which Night Wind made a hearty stew.

At first Joshua could only sip the broth, but by week's end, he was able to keep down the boiled meat and tubers from the stew. As the weather broke with the rising of seven suns, so rose Joshua, and he began to wander about the cabin ordering the sequence of past events, and gradually healing the pain he felt from the death of his friend La Ramie. Joshua searched within his being for feelings of guilt, but realized that the life and death of La Ramie were inexplicably linked together with each only being stages, much like the spring that would follow winter. Night Wind fretted so much about Joshua's indoor amblings that Joshua fled the cabin with Spotted Owl to wander down to the river in search of open water where they could at least pretend to be fishing.

Finally after two weeks, Buffalo Shield and Black Crowe mounted their warhorses, and after bidding farewell to their sister and nephew, started the long trail westward back to their families and the warm springs of their homeland. Both vowed to return during the early fall buffalo hunts to visit the new baby due in the summer.

Night Wind promised to bring many treasures for them from the Rendezvous she would attend with Joshua when the deep drifts of the mountain's snows allowed them passage down the long tributaries of the river. Joshua soon felt strong enough to return to the trap line and continue adding to the cache of furs he and La Ramie had established. Joshua and Spotted Owl, weekly transferred the furs to the cave after pressing them, but with Night Wind's growing pregnancy, he did not allow her to go with them to the cave, fearing her horse might fall on the ice slick granite talus slopes.

"Next summer," Joshua would say, "I will show you where we will build our home, in a place even more beautiful than you are."

Night Wind chided him that she was jealous of anything that Joshua though more beautiful than her, but never said anything about the feelings she had when Joshua left with furs for the cave, only telling him to be careful. Secretly she wondered if the black thoughts she sensed were caused by her mood and pregnancy. At night when Joshua was asleep, she soared above the river in her dreams, searching for her signs of danger, but just when she thought she might discover something, a cloudiness enveloped the canyon, and the vision woman could never discern what made her uneasy. Night Wind remembered her dream of a trapper in a blue hat beneath the ice and how she was wrong to think it was a prophecy of Joshua's death. Perhaps these feeling were the same. Joshua was strong and healthy again as he demonstrated each night beneath the robes as the couple tried to make up for their time apart. Within Night Wind their baby tumbled, vibrant and alive, free spirited and waiting for the warm winds of summer to be born.

"I'm worse than the old women of the lodge house," she thought, jumping at shadows and fearing the worst. Never in her existence had she been so happy, so content with her life and her mate. Never the less, she worried every time until Joshua and Spotted Owl returned from the cave. By March the canyon winds were noticeably warmer, and the river showed long stretches of clear blue water before it disappeared again beneath jagged flows of ice smashed together in broken shards. The fur began to slip and loosen on the beaver's rich pelts. Joshua discontinued the trap line and no longer made his morning rounds, unwilling to kill anything that would not be of value. Soon new beaver kits would begin to appear from beneath their mud lodges. Joshua smiled as he thought of La Ramie's term "seed stock" for future years. Already in the cave was a load of furs that would tax the strength of even La Ramie's horse when they began the long trek back to the rendezvous. Late one evening after Joshua greased the last of the traps before hanging them from their long chains along the cabin wall. Night Wind beckoned him to sit beside her on the warm elk furs. Holding his hands between hers, she asked Joshua to tell her of his journey from Missouri, and how he arrived at the rendezvous to steal her heart like a spirit in the night.

"Once shown to the sunlight and shared with my love," she said, "these memories would remain as a gentle part of you, not torments that chase you like demon wolves on the wind. Let there remain nothing between us that darkens my dreams of our future. In the times that your spirit hung between this world and the next, I felt you shudder as you ran. Tell me of these dreams and thoughts. You have already shared with me the pain you hold for a past love, what other sorrows have your footsteps seen before entering my heart and soul."

With this entreaty from Night Wind, Joshua shared with her throughout the night the story of the latter stages of his life, of Blue Feather and his journey to Bellevue and beyond, always traveling toward the Great Blue Mountains. Joshua told her of Lisa and the Mountain Men and also about the Narthmans. Night Wind listened and held him, glad at last that her mate shared with her all that once was.

Joshua spoke of his feelings after the war, of the long depression, which he suffered through, and his vow never again to become close to anyone or anything. He talked of the friendship of Ashley and Lisa and how they never abandoned him during the long bleak periods in Booneville when he could find no reason to carry on with his life, and no God to whom he could appeal to for help. Night Wind noticed the transition in his voice, as he talked about the long boat trip upstream on the Missouri and his agreement with Lisa to help at the fort and in Bellevue.

The ride from Booneville to Bellevue had passed quickly for Joshua he explained to Night Wind. Days were spent rowing, or rather pushing with heavy poles, the craft further north and west up the slow flowing waters of the Missouri. Often the crew made 20 miles per day, and on some days the sail was unfurled to catch the variant winds. Joshua took his turn poling, enjoying the feel of sore muscles, and the strain in his thighs from honest labor. Many times had he done the same thing as a boy along the edges of the great Mississippi. The Missouri was much smaller and offered far less dangers to watch out for than those presented by her big sister. The landmarks, first charted by Lewis and Clark were checked off behind them, and the boat sailed past Grand River, Fort Orleans, Condor Bend, and Fire Prairie.

Lisa re-supplied with fresh meat and eggs when the party arrived at Fort Osage, and Joshua shot a fat buck deer swimming the river near the Bear Medicine Island that he jerked and shared with his boat mates. It wasn't until Grand de Tour that Joshua spent any evening time with the Narthmans, but lured by Elisha's promise of cornbread, Joshua dined with them in their tent near the riverbank. Both the Narthmans were in exuberant moods, and Terrence spoke of his early childhood and a special calling from God to spread the ministry of the Lord to the "heathens of the west."

"I fear for the souls," Terrance said, speaking about the Indians tribes he would meet near Bellevue. "More so, I fear for what the wrath of the Lord may deliver unto them if they fail to heed our words now. Already the heavens darken, and they may face destruction just as Sodom and Gomorra faced. The patience of God has limits."

"I always thought that living a life that brought no pain to others, and endeavoring to help one's country and fellow man in times of need ought to please any god," Joshua replied. Most Indians only fight with one another because they feel threatened with the loss of their own families and lifestyle. They treat their children far better than we do the orphans that wander the streets of St. Louis. Many children starve in the streets while men and women of means step over them like so much refuge. Accepting God doesn't make someone a good person, only his or her actions reveal that."

"But Joshua," Elisha countered, fixing Joshua with her deep gaze. "These people we go to help, have the ability to understand their choices. Surely when presented with knowledge of the true God, they will chose the path of righteousness. If they turn away, they are no better than animals, and deserve to feel the wrath of God. For in Ezekiel 21:33-37 it is written: As for you, son of man, says the Lord GOD against the Ammonites and their insults: A sword, a sword is drawn for slaughter, burnished to consume and to flash lightning, because you planned with false visions and lying divinations to lay it on the necks of depraved and wicked men whose day has come when their crimes are at an end. Return it to its sheath! In the place where you were created, in the land of your origin, I will judge you. I will pour out my indignation upon you, breathing my fiery wrath upon you, I will hand you over to ravaging men, artisans of destruction. You shall be fuel for the fire; your blood shall flow throughout the land. You shall not be remembered, for I, the LORD, have spoken."

"Surely God doesn't want it both ways," Joshua persisted. "If Indians are no better than animals, how can God condemn them for not following his written word? Does he send a flood to kill the coyotes, buffalo, and badgers? How could a loving God destroy his creatures that have only tried to live their lives that He set out for them? They are following their natures given them at creation. Why would God care, he does nothing to intervene, when innocent women and children die. It's bad enough he turns a blind eye to the suffering in this world, without trying to destroy more of his creatures."

"Oh Joshua," Elisha sighed. "Let God enter your soul to heal what your life has wrought. Hold not onto this righteous anger and rise above to the live his plan for you."

Joshua didn't reply, knowing that further argument was futile. The cornbread didn't taste nearly as sweet in his mouth, and for the first time he was aware, that blind adherence to the preaching of Elisha without the application of common sense could result in tragedy for her.

He thought of the Bible quote: Proverbs 24:14 Know also that wisdom is sweet to your soul; if you find it, there is a future hope for you, and your hope will not be cut off.

God, unfeeling or not, gave man the ability to reason. Blind faith only resulted in steep falls down the mountains of life.

Bidding the Narthmans goodnight, Joshua took his leave to lie with the other boatmen, watching the spinning of the Milky Way in the black night holding the heavens at bay, hoping that the feeling within him was wrong as he reviewed her words his last thought was: "Do not judge, or you too will be judged. For in the same way you judge others, you will be judged, and with the measure you use, it will be measured to you."

During the next few days as the party progressed on past Solomon's Island toward the Bald Hills and Nebraska Territory, Joshua sat with Lisa, quizzing him about the history of Bellevue and his expected duties there once they arrived.

According to Lisa, Joshua explained, there were a few hardy souls already in Bellevue when Lisa arrived. No one living there knew just when the first white men settled near the banks of the river. Manuel stated he climbed the sloping hills from the riverside where his boat lay moored and as his eye swept that wonderful panorama of forest, hill, and river, he exclaimed in French, "Bellevue;" he then staked out his fur trader's cabin in the valley below and thus began the first settlement.

Lisa remembered the year to be 1810. Wanting easier access for fur traders from the northern reaches, Lisa traveled another 20 miles upstream and established an outpost that he called Fort Lisa to accommodate the early voyageurs. This was mainly a barracks for his trappers and a staging center for his furs before they were carried downstream to Bellevue, there to be loaded on large boats for the trip to St. Louis. This also served as a supply post for the Astorians who traveled upriver. Lisa didn't want their competition in his area, but realized the wisdom of selling them supplies, sometimes receiving payment in furs. Lisa claimed that during the last four years he found there was often more money in supplies than in fur.

By early 1815, Lisa's trading post in Bellevue was established and doing well.

The government also opened an Indian agency called the Council Bluffs Indian Agency, at Bellevue. The Omahas, Otoes, and Pawnees came there to trade. It was easier for the fur traders and Indians to meet at Bellevue than at any other post on the river. The smooth valley of the Platte made a natural means of transportation, and the rock foundation of the hills sloping to the riverside made excellent docking places for boats. With groves of trees and fresh water nearby, homes and buildings could be established. The Platte and the Missouri came together just downstream and offered unmatched views of the wooded valley.

Bellevue was the stopping place for all the early adventurers, trappers, travelers, missionaries and soldiers who came to this region. By 1812 Lisa convinced Lucien Fontenelle to operate the post in Bellevue for him instead of opening a competing post. Joshua would work part time at Fort Lisa and then escort the furs downriver to the main store in Bellevue and assist Fontenelle in grading, sorting, and bundling the furs for continued shipment to St. Louis. Missionaries were already making their first attempts to civilize and Christianize the Indians, and both Terrence and Elisha, Lisa claimed were excited about the prospects that lay before them in Bellevue. Joshua wondered what they would feel if they failed to win over the stoic Indian tribes.

Toward the last week of the journey, Elisha made it a point to seek out Joshua in the evenings, apologizing for anything she said before that hurt his feelings. Joshua relented to her persuasions, enjoying the sound of her voice, and listened to stories from her childhood and how excited she was to have found Lisa as a benefactor. She filled in more history about Lisa that Joshua never knew. Elisha told Joshua that Lisa kept his wife and family in St. Louis but also loved an Omaha Indian girl named Mitain. Among the Indians it was common for a man to have more than one wife, and the early Indian traders often married a wife in each tribe to gain alliances and to further trading interests.

Elisha spoke of a daughter Manuel sired at Fort Lisa. The baby was named Rosalie. A son named Raymond was also born to the couple. Lisa wanted Rosalie to go to St. Louis and become civilized, but her mother had refused so Lisa made frequent trips to be with his Indian wife and children before returning to his other family in St. Louis. Joshua could detect no tone of sarcasm in Elisha's story and was somewhat amazed that someone of her missionary zeal would not look down on the dual marriage. Elisha also stated that Mitain and the children were baptized Christians; perhaps this helped in Elisha's mind.

Late one evening the party's travails were suddenly over as the keelboat rounded the last big bend, and Bellevue came into view. The next few hours were occupied with unloading the Narthmans and all their associated baggage. Lisa ordered several of his men to help them establish their new accommodations and promised to return shortly to welcome them to the new community. He briskly ordered which supplies were to be unloaded at his trading post here and which would continue making the trip upriver to Fort Lisa.

Joshua tallied inventory sheets and moved the remaining freight to a more central location, keeping the boat from leaning in the water. Long ago he understood the importance of this when pushing boats upriver to St. Louis. Terrace shook Joshua's hand before wishing him well in his new position, and Elisha hugged him fiercely, making Joshua promise that he would return with Lisa to have dinner with them at their new home, which waited in Bellevue. Soon the parties were split, and Joshua with the remaining boatmen set out upriver. All were anxious to reach the final destination. The night was clear, and with a small breeze, the sail was unfurled. By morning, the crew could reach Fort Lisa and rest the following day. Many of the boatmen had Indian women and families awaiting them, and like all men of their ilk, when a job needed done, they just pitched in to complete it, regardless of the long hours involved. True to the boatmen's prediction, they reached Fort Lisa just as the sun's first streamers reflected off the dark waters, bringing a new day into the lives of the small party.

Joshua too, was glad to reach another destination in his journey away from that which was, and toward what would be. He hated to admit to himself that he was secretly glad to have left the Narthmans behind. At times the fanaticism in the preacher's eyes struck a chord too deep inside him. Although he blamed God for the misfortunes in his life, he did not feel that had he adhered to the Holy Scriptures as closely as they, the events of the past would have turned out differently. He could have read the Bible every day, and Rodde would still have died when the quake pulled her into the swirling current. Joshua did not believe that God would make an exception for one life, regardless the level of religious fervor.

Joshua rested a minute as the heavy boat glided the backwaters before bumping into the landing pier. Lisa had not exaggerated the beauty of the setting. The small post was nestled between earthen dirt works in a grove of trees. Near the front door, a small creek threaded its way through the front yard before ending its journey into the turgid waters of the Missouri. The top of the protective earthworks were tipped with split rails of pine, woven together and supported by crosspieces through which gaps presented themselves, enabling anyone behind them a concealed place from which to direct musket fire. Several heavily built doors connected the earthworks, forming a defensive perimeter around the fort. Joshua saw the doors were open, but he noticed several heavily armed men near the apertures.

Breakfast that morning was roasted antelope, turned and cooked on large spits in the center of the parade yard, and Joshua jostled with the other trappers cutting off large steaks which he washed down with a tankards of spring cold ale dipped from stone crocks buried in the mud of the small creek. Lisa introduced him to his company of fur men and other than slow smiles and nods; they gave no notice that he was a stranger among them. Joshua immediately felt at home. These were men no different from those he led and fought with in the war, men who dreamed his same visions and wanted only the wind to their face and to feel untrammeled ground beneath their feet. The day passed swiftly as the remaining cargo was provisioned in the fort, and Joshua inspected the ledgers and accounts for which he was responsible. Surprised by the quick passage of time, Joshua realized it was growing dark, and he joined the other men for a communal supper eaten at the long tables adjoining the trading room of the fort. Bowls were heaped with hot stew filled with meat along with hominy, loaves of coarse bread, and butter squash.

Within an hour the men could eat no more, and they drifted from the room to their own barracks to perform tasks such as the mending of equipment or telling stories of accomplishments amongst their peers. As the last of the sparks drifted lazily into the starlit night from the big fire pit in the parade yard, Lisa showed Joshua to a small room in the rear of the post that would serve as his personal quarters. The cell was bare except for a small table with a pitcher and bowl, a long low-slung willow bed covered in Hudson Bay blankets, and a tri corned stool near the door. The floor was clean swept earth, and a small open window allowed the muted trickling sounds of the brook outside to gently swirl throughout the room. Joshua felt the peace of the room immediately, and he soon lay down and drifted off. No visions of violence or death disturbed his slumbers this night, as the stream guarded his dreams, allowing nothing of his past to enter this sanctuary.

The next several weeks passed smoothly with Joshua quickly becoming once again accustomed to the rhythms and rules of a fur trading post. Furs were bought, goods were sold, and hundreds of other transactions consisting of mixed variations of the two, were conducted on a daily basis. On the frontier, there was little actual cash money, and barter was the economic activity of choice. Joshua sometime gave away foodstuffs, and clothing for information, a valuable commodity to all traders. Of particular interest was the continuing debate over slavery and admission of new states to the Union based on whether they were slave states or free ones.

As Joshua's love for Rodde first grew back in St. Genevieve, his abhorrence for slavery grew with it. Missouri was a territory that allowed slavery, but no decision was yet made on the issue of the other western territories. Most of the black trappers that Joshua traded with were born free men, and Joshua pitied anyone that attempted to enslave these wandering men of the prairie and plain. The merchants that Joshua talked with believed that Alabama territory would soon apply for statehood, and along with this southern province; Missouri would attempt to become a state also. Because of a gentlemen's agreement in Congress, it was decided that the number of free states and slave states would remain equal to preserve power between the north and the south. Illinois was set to join the union within a year, and this would give the free states of the north more voting power, but Joshua worried that the union would be torn apart if both Alabama and Missouri were allowed in as slave states, and perhaps even if they weren't.

There was talk that James Tallmadge of New York was offering a compromise that would rectify the problem in the future, but many of the traders Joshua spoke with were against this plan, nicknamed the Missouri Compromise. People from the lower reaches of the Mississippi were already beginning to talk dis-union. They claimed they would become a new country before allowing the north to dictate the issue of slavery for them. The south was also afraid if they offered any latitude in their discussions, the blacks might rebel against their owners as had happened in the Dominican Republic. Joshua knew that a million black slaves in the south could be formidable army to overcome if revolution broke out. He also remembered the heartache of the War of 1812 and understood that a war between the states would be a long lasting and brutal conflict of neighbors against neighbors. His internal feelings were beginning to grow even stronger, that he must flee from this strife and escape to the solitude of the mountains to the west.

Joshua was surprised one day when Lisa announced they would be returning to Bellevue the next day and from there, Manuel would travel back to St. Louis. Joshua was now officially in charge of Fort Lisa. Another phase was reached, and Joshua confidently looked forward to the challenge.

A long morning's ride brought Lisa and Joshua to the outskirts of Bellevue and the large low-slung mud chinked structure that was the

Missouri Fur Trading Company's main place of business in Bellevue. Lisa's trading post run by Lucien Fontenelle brought a stream of reminiscences flooding back through Joshua about his own store, many memories and miles downriver.

During the next several days, Joshua lived within the confines of the post, learning the ins and outs of this portion of the trade chain. Stocking patterns and sales were the same as Fort Lisa except on a larger scale. The main difference was the refinements. Many of the trade goods stocked here were of a household variety, planned for use by the residents of Bellevue, not the basic needs of Lisa's free trappers.

Within these walls, gathered a wide variety of Indians and hardy frontier souls. Here the Kansa tribes of the south came to trade furs and beadwork from the northern Arkansas River drainages. Mixing with them were the sallow faced Pottawattamies, the taciturn Otoe braves, and, of course, the Pawnees who loved to bargain and trade even if they eventually acquired something of limited use to them. The game was in the trade not the acquisition. Coursing among these tribes were the Osage, Ponca, Arikara, Mandan, and, of course, the Omaha. Although many of the languages were similar, often there was enough difference to cause confusion in the trades, and sign language was used to work out the differences.

Occasionally even members of the Santee Sioux from the north mingled among the smells and sounds of the post, although they were always quiet and suspicious, often with good cause. Conflicts between the many tribes of the Sioux and the southern tribes were always flaring to the surface. Pitched battles and small wars would erupt without warning, and then just as mysteriously they would settle quarrels, and trading between the tribes would resume. Hunting was very good north of the Loup Rivers along the Cedar Creek and Beaver Creek tributaries. All the tribes assumed this to be their special province, and many battles broke out when one tribe discovered another hunting or trapping within this area.

Fontenelle had also taken a wife from the Omaha tribe. She was the daughter of an important leader, Big Elk, and this alone helped trading because the Omaha tribe flocked to this location believing Lucien to be more honest than many of the small ramshackle posts along the lower part of the Missouri.

Amid the Indians walked frontiersmen whom Joshua had heard of by reputation but never met and some whom he worked with at Fort Lisa. Coural spent hours seated upon the large wooden barrels of flour listening to Joseph Dickinson, and Forest Hancock and, of course, John Colter who traveled this country with Lewis and Clark. These men, the true Coureurs de Bois, or pioneer men of the fur trade, told of sights unimagined in the far west. Many times their lives hung in the balance when meeting the Blackfeet and Western Sioux tribes. Colter told of boiling mud, huge waterfalls, and erupting geysers of hot water in the Yellowstone area far to the west.

The trappers told stories of beaver so thick that they fought with each other to fall into the hands of the mountain men. Colter and Lisa worked together in 1807 further up the Missouri near the Big Horn and Yellowstone Rivers. It was from this location that Colter claimed to have struck even further west finding the Absaroka Range, the Valley of the Wind and a pass descending toward the Pacific slope following the Snake River on through the Grand Tetons. Colter also recounted how the Blackfeet had captured him and forced him to run a race for his life, naked across 150 miles of prairie, until he reached the safety of Lisa's outpost on the Bighorn River.

Although Colter spoke very highly of Lewis and Clark, Joshua noted reticence in Lisa's voice when he mentioned the famous men. Joshua did know that William Clark was the president of Lisa's company, but it was apparent there was no love lost between them. Lisa's plan of outfitting large groups of trappers to winter behind barricaded fortification, running long trap lines, resulted in Manuel's fortune. Unlike some of the English fur companies that relied on only Indian furs, Lisa held little regard for the trapping abilities of Indians, and always claimed their natures prevented them from working the hours needed. By 1810, when Lisa opened trading operations in Bellevue, he came to realize that ventures further north were unprofitable because of the fierceness of the Blackfeet. For now he was content with working only as far north as the Big Sioux River and the southern Dakota Region.

Lisa's fortunes further expanded when he ran a newspaper ad in the Missouri Gazette in 1813, soliciting brave men, and from this recruitment came his legion of trappers that filled the post with furs. A hardier or rougher bunch of men could hardly be assembled. Amongst their ranks were men such as Jed Smith, young Jim Bridger, Tom Fitzpatrick, and Hugh Glass, the Sublette brothers, James Clyman, and Edward Rose. Ashley always claimed within a few years he would reclaim the North with these men and reopen that vast area of riches. Andrew Henry and William Ashley were close partners with Lisa also. Seldom did a week pass when letters from these two had not arrived to cheer Joshua's long and lonely days in Booneville.

Every fall these fur men would leave Fort Lisa, spreading out in groups of twos and threes with little else but their traps, their Hawken rifles, shot, bullet moulds, one set of extra clothing, knives, and tobacco. Amongst their possession were often trade beads and salt with small amounts of coffee and tea. On these meager provisions, they would live a year, returning in the spring, rowing flat-bottomed canoes filled with furs. Traveling with them were their squaws to help with the camp work. Some relationships lasted for years, while others lasted only the season, with the Mountain Men purchasing new wives, by trading acquired horses, or perhaps gallons of whiskey. Joshua's conversation with them helped him understand what desires drove each of them. Fontenelle cautioned him to stay away from Edward Rose, a Cherokee-Negro, who was once a river pirate on the Mississippi.

"Just as soon kill ya, as look at ya," Lucien told him. "Life has no value for that man."

It was Colter who cautioned Joshua away from Bill Williams. Colter claimed that during the long winters, Williams had gained a taste for human flesh. None of the other trappers would partner with him. Joshua encountered him several times striding down the middle of the muddy streets, his long tangled gray hair flowing behind him as he walked, shaking his fist and shouting verses from the Bible toward the heavens. Even without Colter's warning, Joshua would have given Williams a wide path.

This spring had been an especially profitable season for the trappers, and many of them had earned over a thousand dollars for their efforts. These same furs were worth four times the price in St. Louis, but the trappers were happy. St. Louis wasn't their type of town. Here in Bellevue they bought copious quantities of whiskey and women. They didn't even complain about Lisa's mark up on coffee and sugar that he purchased in St. Louis at seven cents per pound and sold to the mountain men for two dollars per package.

Joshua especially liked it when several of them would gather in the store at the same time. Stories would begin to flow, with each tale getting more improbable but with these men, who knew; perhaps some of the accounts were true.

The morning of Joshua's planned return to Fort Lisa, he entered the trading post to wish Fontenelle good-bye and pick up a few necessities for the trip. Just as he was about to pull the leather latchstring, the door exploded outward. Sleeping Blanket of the Otoe tribe, dragging a young Otoe girl by the arm, brushed passed Joshua. The old Indian appeared in to be in a hurry, and the girl's feet bounced along the boardwalk behind the grim faced Indian. Lecturing sternly as he walked, Sleeping Blanket never looked back as he talked. The young girl resigned herself to fate, and allowed herself to be drug limply along, following in the older Indian's steps. Joshua recognized the girl to be Snow Bird, Sleeping Blanket's daughter, and he wondered what the girl did to incur the wrath of the normally complacent Otoe. Upon entering the store, Joshua found Elisha Narthman standing there white-faced and visibly shaken.

"What did you do to Sleeping Blanket, he usually doesn't get so riled up?" asked Joshua.

"I told him the army of the Lord would be coming to his village, to slay the non-believers unless he let his daughter be baptized in the name of God."

"Elisha, it none of my business, but it seems like in the short time you've been here you've got more Indians riled up than all the Sioux attacks did last year. Don't you think you should take it a little easy for a while until they get to know you better? Even Christ didn't stir up all the non-believers this fast."

"Joshua, there is never enough time to save everyone. It was important to save her because she is yet innocent. Heaven knows how long that will last. I merely told them about God's words as is stated in Numbers 31:7-18 when under Moses' orders his followers attacked the Midianite: The forces of the lord killed all the men. All five of the Midianite kings – Evi, Rekem, Zur, Hur, and Reba – died in the battle. They also killed Balaam son of Beor with the sword.

Then the Israelite army captured the Midianite women and children and seized their cattle and flocks and all their wealth as plunder. They burned all the towns and villages where the Midianites had lived. After they had gathered the plunder and captives, both people and animals, they brought them all to Moses and Eleazar the priest, and to the whole community of Israel, which was camped on the plains of Moab beside the Jordan River, across from Jericho. Moses, Eleazar the priest, and all the leaders of the people went to meet them outside the camp. But Moses was furious with all the military commanders who had returned from the battle.

"Why have you let all the women live?" he demanded. "These are the very ones who followed Balaam's advice and caused the people of Israel to rebel against the LORD at Mount Peor. They are the ones who caused the plague to strike the LORD's people. Now kill all the boys and all the women who have slept with a man. Only the young girls who are virgins may live; you may keep them for yourselves."

"Elisha, if you keep that golden hair of yours through the winter it will be a miracle. Why don't you come up to Fort Lisa and preach to those trappers. Now there is a bunch of sinners who could really use help from the Lord."

"Maybe I will, and thanks for the advice. I don't think Sleeping Blanket wants me talking to Snow Bird anymore."

The seasons at Fort Lisa flowed one unto the other, and Joshua found that he had little time for sulking alone in his room. A steady stream of furs arrived during the fall and winter months that he roughly prepared for shipment down to Bellevue. On the odd days that he wasn't logging in furs for the company books, he would make short trips up the various tributaries to meet with the leaders of a variety of tribes to gather furs from them. These tribes never understood the idea of credit on the books, but always insisted on immediate payment. Some days Joshua would exhaust his entire supply of trade goods at the first encampment he met. At other times, especially during harvest festivals or spring buffalo hunting times, Joshua would return home with few furs, having packed huge crates of trade knives, brightly colored beads, blankets, traps, and firearms complete with shot, powder, and tools across vast stretches of river and plain for nothing.

Maintaining a steady supply of inventory with which to trade was the hardest part of his job, and invariably after he sent an order downriver to St. Louis, he would find he was running low on certain items. Lisa disliked keeping items in inventory for long periods of time, complaining constantly about how he much money interest costs hurt his credibility with his investors back at the parent company.

With the first spring thaws of 1817, Lisa informed Joshua that he wanted him to make a trip westward along the Platte to gather furs from the small stations along the way before reaching the far Pawnee encampments, inviting one and all to a huge celebration to be held the first full moon of August. Lisa was sending ten men with Joshua, each leading two pack mules. Joshua found his excitement growing as he prepared for the trip. At last this was his chance to see what was beyond the vast prairies and perhaps glimpse the far Blue Mountains that still haunted his dreams.

Joshua's fur buying upstream along the Platte went well, and the trader met many clans of the Pawnee tribes. The party stayed south of the Loup River and spent several days exploring along the Little Blue streams before continuing westward. Within a month, the pack train arrived in a beautiful valley called Ash Hollow. Jacques was amazed to find accommodations here, and several Spanish men living with Pawnee women had established a small outpost.

The next day a group of trappers lead by Jules de Munn arrived from the south. They were planning to follow the Platte eastward until they could find a fur post and re-supply. de Munn was ecstatic to meet Joshua. Combining the remaining food from de Munn's party, along with the provisions from Joshua's group, the men held a large feast that night. Several jugs of liquor were brought out and passed around after supper as the two parties swapped stories and tall tales about their travels.

That night around the campfire Joshua listened to the tales of exploration south of Ash Hollow and the California crossing. Jules de Mun told of his travels southeast to the Arkansas and Canadian Rivers and then due south near Huajatolla, the great cones of rock so named the "Breasts of the World" by Spanish explorers. de Mun had taken leadership of a group of trappers from Joseph Philibert. Philibert and his group angered the Mexican government by working the river basins near the south end of the Rocky Mountains in 1815. Mexican soldiers seized the trappers, and all of Philibert's furs were confiscated. The company was forced to spend a winter in a Santa Fe prison. Hearing of their plight, Jules paid the fines, reorganized the party, and sent them out again with the idea that all the trappers were to meet at a certain time, near a certain locations along the headwaters of the Huajatolla River, near the high ruins of ancient Indian Pueblos.

de Mun was backed by money from Auguste P. Chouteau. Many Spanish garrisons in the south continued to deny that Spain had ceded any country from the Louisiana Territory, and they were fearful if they allowed trappers into the area, American troops would soon follow. The trappers continually played cat and mouse with Mexican troops throughout the next few years, but the rich harvest of furs made the expedition worthwhile. de Mun also told of Edwin James, a doctor in his group who climbed the tall mountain named for Zebulon Pike in the Colorado territory. Pike scouted this area in 1806 but believed the mountain too tall to climb. James claimed to have found eagle traps near the top of the peak placed there by the Ute Indians so they could gain feathers for their sacred ceremonies. The tall mountain was visible for many miles eastward as explorers crossed the broad plains leading to this portion of the Rocky Mountains.

During the next several days, Joshua traded furs with de Munn, replacing the meager rations for the explorers from his foodstuffs. Joshua was particularly drawn to one of de Munn's trappers Jacques La Ramie. La Ramie had just rejoined the party after spending a year in the mountains to the west along a river he called the Arapohay. Jacque's stories of the deep river canyons, and high blue mountains struck a chord within Joshua. By the time the de Munn party turned south again, La Ramie accompanied

Joshua back to Fort Lisa where he planned to catch transportation to St. Louis.

"Might'n be the last time I see any cities for a while," the older trapper said in his drawn slang, "and I've a hankering to see fer myself what this country is becomin'."

During the long days eastward back to the Fort Lisa, La Ramie described the location 50 leagues west of the California Crossing where two rivers met. Here he claimed were streams full of beaver, broad plains of buffalo, and scenery more beautiful than heaven itself.

"That would serve as a good place to meet next spring; I could talk to the Shoshone, and a few clans of the Sioux. Along with them injuns and some of the other trappers and we could have a grand ol' pow-wow. Meeting there once a year, word about the rendezvous would spread and befur' long Lisa would have more furs that he could shake a stick at. This ider' has been workin' fine for de Munn. Sure would save some distance, getting paid for the furs, and stocking up agin, without havin' to go clear south to Pueblo or all the way back east to Lisa's post."

Upon reaching Fort Lisa, Manuel and Jacques agreed with the trapper's plan, and a time was established next spring for Joshua to take a pack train to La Ramie's meeting place. Wishing Joshua well, La Ramie set out downriver accompanied by Lisa headed for St. Louis. La Ramie was already shaking his head about how many people were moving to Bellevue.

By Christmas of 1817, Joshua received a letter from Lisa that arrived by dispatch rider sent from Osage. Joshua set down onto the narrow surface of the loggerhead in the trading post and opened the dispatch from Lisa. He noticed immediately the Manuel's tone was somber as he told about current events in St. Louis and the fluctuation of market prices of furs and supplies. By the second page, Joshua discovered the reason for Lisa's tone. He wrote tersely about the death of his wife during the summer. He also wrote of plans by the United States government to send a party back into the northern regions of the Missouri protected by soldiers.

Lisa claimed there were now steamboats capable of navigating the shallow waters of the Missouri, and the government party should arrive with the first warm currents of spring. The government corps would be making stops in Bellevue and then continue on to Fort Lisa. Manuel thought they might winter there while sending out further explorations north to establish an appropriate site to build a fort, garrisoned by U.S. soldiers to prevent raids by the hostile Indian tribes of the north. Lisa said the post was to be named Fort Atkinson, and he hoped this would stabilize the region, allowing even more trade to flow through his post.

Lisa did return in the spring of 1818 followed close behind by a company of soldiers. Manuel was very pleased with Joshua's efforts in the post and was excited about the venture to meet La Ramie. He agreed to stay and run the post while Joshua left to meet La Ramie for their first rendezvous. Lisa felt Joshua should take even more pack mules and men to assure the safety of the party.

La Ramie, true to his promise, met Joshua, and all of the extra mules were loaded with furs and trade goods from the Shoshone Indians. Their beadwork and quilling was the most exquisite Joshua had ever seen, and he was sure these items would sell well in Bellevue. This trip had proved a defining moment in Joshua's life. Although he enjoyed his duties running the trading post, the time he spent with La Ramie convinced Joshua, that his destiny was to be in the mountains not on the river plains. La Ramie invited him to spend a winter high in the Blue Mountains trapping and working as an equal partner, a free trapper, whose only masters were God and himself. The last several years helped Joshua to accept the losses in his life, and he began to understand that by fulfilling his destiny, through him all those that loved him and died would travel with him in memories and dreams.

Joshua's arrival back in Bellevue was tempered by the news he heard upon arrival. Prior to his leaving, Joshua spoke to the Narthmans, and they related their plan to visit a Ponca village north of the Loup River. Joshua made them promise to be careful, and after learning that a wagonload of parishioners from their church would accompany the missionaries, he felt better about their going. Anxious to visit the village, the Narthmans rode out a day ahead of their escort. Thirty miles north of Bellevue, their church members found them alone, naked and tortured, staked to the bare plains. Their deaths appeared to have been slow and agonizing, and Joshua hoped that their faith carried them through in their last hours.

He would miss his conversations with the couple and their dinners together, but both died following their dreams and beliefs. Apparently the markings on the arrow-ridden bodies were from the Blackfeet. Bellevue was now an armed camp, and vigilante committees were being organized to pursue the raiders. Joshua could only hope that no peaceful tribes would pay the price for the missionaries' deaths. Remembering Terrence's sermons back in Booneville, Joshua felt that the young couple truly had left this "road of sin upon the worldly earth and entered into the house of Jesus."

Manuel Lisa had already written to the families in Kentucky, notifying their next of kin of the couple's good works in Bellevue and of their deaths. Both Elisha and Terrence were buried together in a large stone cairn, out among the grassy hills of the Nebraska Territory, a monument to their vision of bringing God to the wilderness.

The spring of 1819 was slow to meet her cue this year and demurely showed brief glimpses of herself, before retiring behinds curtains of sleet and snow. Today Joshua was unable to determine if she would make an appearance or continue this game of hide and seek. Low dreary clouds veiled the horizon, and a hoar frost hung heavy on the men's beards as they unloaded the latest barge of supplies sent by Lisa from St. Louis. Along with the supplies was a dispatch addressed to Joshua from Lisa, and Coural drained the last drops of the thick coffee in his battered mug before opening the letter and reviewing its contents. Shortly into the first page of the letter, Joshua's brow began to wrinkle, and he studied and re-read Lisa's written instructions to him. Joshua hated being a go-between. This was several times now in the last few months that Lisa sent dispatches addressed to Joshua and then included postscripts for translation to Mitain, Lisa's Omaha Indian wife.

Why couldn't Lisa simply send a message to each of them and keep Joshua the hell out of the middle.

By the second page, Joshua learned that Lisa had married a young woman named Mary Hempstead Keeney, and within the month the couple would be making a trip to Bellevue. The acquisition of a new wife was not a major surprise for Joshua. A man in Lisa's position needed a mother for his children and a hostess for the rounds of entertaining that occurred in St. Louis. When a company depended on large amounts of investor funds, it served well to set a good table and invite large numbers of people to frequent parties. Sometimes Joshua missed the balls and parties he attended in St. Genevieve. These galas were always a good time, and it was fun to hear about the lives of others instead of always being reminded of personal misfortunes.

Lisa wanted Joshua to choose several special presents from the post in Bellevue for Mitain, and after presenting the gifts, Joshua was to relate Lisa's specific instructions. Mitain was to return to her family tribe, the Upriver Omaha. The children were to go also. Lisa would contact Mitain there, but he did not want his Indian wife around Bellevue when the new spouse arrived on the scene.

Joshua thought to himself that this situation probably could get a little sticky as Mitain had a reputation for being tremendously jealous and more than a little hot headed. Other than Elisha and Madam Lajoie, who arrived early in Bellevue's history, the new Mrs. Lisa would be one of the first white women to travel this far north on the Missouri. Joshua wished that Elisha was still here and had the chance to visit with another white woman, and perhaps hearing some words from civilization about fashion trends, and other women stuff before she met her fateful end on the broad prairies. The last few times Joshua had spoken to her, Elisha seemed quiet and withdrawn, fearful that she was unable to save those she preached to. At least she would have died knowing she made a difference in this world.

The morning sun had yet to warm the chilled spring air within the compound when Joshua left the post headed for the stables to saddle up and begin his ride to Bellevue following Manuel's written instructions. Joshua wouldn't speak to Mitain until returning with the presents and then packing would begin for the return to her parents' lodges where Mitain was to wait until Lisa could find time to go there. Mitain would complain sharply in the nasal whine of the Omaha tongue to Joshua, or "Moon-jah" as she called him, when he told her about Lisa's orders, and then muttering all the way, she would comply. Sometime when she was especially angry, she used the term "Too-nea" which meant snake, but that was usually only when she was intoxicated. Moon-jah meant black bear, of the Huhanguia Bear Clan, and though this was a lower clan, than the Higinee of which she belonged. Joshua always thought that wasn't bad since he was still rather new to the country. Joshua would make sure he found Mitain something nice and vowed to himself to make no mention about the new wife.

Mitain could have a real short fuse when she was angry as Joshua found out several times in the last few years when he evicted her from the post for meddling in company business. Often the maiden would prowl the store looking for places where Joshua kept the liquor hid, and upon finding the cache, she would confiscate the entire hoard, remaining drunk for several days. Remembering this, Joshua returned to the post and locked the door to the back office, just in case Mitain came by before his return. Sober, she could be reasoned with, but when drunken, Mitain would pose a real threat to him, Lisa, and any other unfortunate victims that wandered too close. Satisfied that the liquor was secured behind solid locked plank doors, Joshua left the doorway again, headed for the stables.

His first indication of danger was the deathly quiet swish of the arrow fletching coursing by his left cheek, twisting and snarling as it embedded itself into the front newel of the porch support. Diving for the front door, while several shots rang out behind him, a he could hear Clyman's call for men to man the palisades. Several times in the last few years the post had been sniped at with bow and ball, by passing factions of drunken Indians, but something seemed different this time. Frantically Joshua tried to think of the number of men in and around the fort, had those in the fields outside had enough warning, who and how many Indians were attacking him, and a thousand more instant concerns. Grabbing horn and bullet pouch along with two rifles from the racks just inside the door, Joshua ran low and hard for the protection of the palisade walls, noticing with relief the front gates to the fort were swinging shut. At least there weren't any enemies inside the walls, and if there were, the men inside the fort would make short work of the intruders.

Already powder smoke began to curl thickly around the fort's firing portals, and Joshua thrust his rifle through a small opening searching for danger. Beside him Bill Williams fired, and Joshua jerked his attention back to the low row of locust bushes just to the left of the front gate. Suddenly a warrior, clad in the rainaments of the Sioux tribe leaped to his feet, aiming an oversized musket toward William's rifle smoke. Joshua caught the head and the long greasy braids of the Indian in the vee of his rifle sight, and began lowering his aim as he squeezed the stroke of the trigger. The rifle exploded the projectile through the throat of the warrior who fell slackly back into the sharp thorns of the bushes. Changing rifles, Joshua looked for further threats but could not detect any.

Suddenly another person was running for the fort, and Joshua sighted again on the fast moving head and began to squeeze his shot when he recognized the face as that of Mitain. In her arms she was carrying her son Raymond, and the awkward cradleboard swung wildly as she raced for the gate. Evidently she had been working in the garden near the walls of the fort when the first attack came, and she lay in the rows of dirt until the first volley cleared and now she was making a break for the fort.

"Hold yer fire," Joshua screamed, afraid that another wall defender would make the same mistake he almost had. "It's Mitain. Open the gates."

As Mitain reached the gates, no one had yet released the catches to swing them inward, and seeing her standing before the gates was too tempting for several attacking Sioux near the potato cellar on Mitain's left. Two warriors jumped up and fired, resulting in one rifle ball tearing a large section off Mitain's shapely calf from her slender leg, causing the flesh to swing loose like a dripping red wolf pup biting on the flank of an elk.

"Mah-sjeen nea, bastards," screamed Mitain, which seemed slightly out of kilter to Joshua as Mah-sjeen meant white rabbit with pink eyes, and then he remembered that white rabbit was the favorite food of the Omaha Bear Clan. A powerful insult indeed.

Both rabbits paid the price as a volley of at least 20 rifles from the fort literally tore the two Indians to pieces misting the potato cellar in a fine spray of red. Again the countryside went quiet.

The fort's gates were not yet open, and Joshua started to leave the wall to open the portals when Mitain screamed again, begging Joshua to listen to her.

"Please Moon-jah, catch Raymond, next time they will kill him not me," and without waiting for agreement, she slung the cradleboard upward over the palisade.

Barely having time to react, Joshua dropped the rifle, caught the cradle, and stood there amazed as Mitain then ran in a limping shuffle east around the corner of the palisade headed for the smaller gate. Perhaps she thought this access would open more quickly.

Joshua stayed on the palisade walls another hour, waiting, as the morning sun drove the chill from the log walls. No more intruders were sighted, and the trappers began dismounting from their post to search for wounded in and out of the fort. No trappers were injured in the attack, but five Sioux braves paid with their lives for the aborted attempt to catch the men in the fort unawares. This was a heavy price, and Joshua understood why the attackers had withdrawn into the wooded hillsides around the fort. Not wanting to leave in case another attack came, Joshua appointed three trappers to make the ride to warn Bellevue of the renegade Indians, and posted sentries in shifts for the rest of the day. Suddenly remembering Lisa's request for presents for Mitain, he instructed the trappers to bring back the three prettiest presents they could find in Bellevue. He sincerely hoped it wouldn't be two bottles of whiskey and a whore. The post surgeon soon had Mitain's leg sewn together again, and everyone bragged about her bravery. This story would circle the country for a long time. Mitain had shown the truest love for her children, regardless of the danger she faced herself.

The next several weeks passed normally without further attacks, and life returned to common duties around the post. By mid May, Joshua again organized that pack train of mules that would carry supplies, whiskey, and trade goods to the rendezvous near the junction of the Arapohay and the Platte River. He looked forward to meeting La Ramie and hoped the season went well for all the trappers in his company. With each passing day of spring, the feeling grew stronger in Joshua that he wanted to be on the other end of the supply chain. At this year's rendezvous, he would speak to La Ramie, gather a list of supplies he would need, and plan to accompany La Ramie next year. Joshua had saved most of his pay, and if he worked one more year, he should be able to purchase everything he needed to spend a year in La Ramie's mountains.

By July, after a successful rendezvous, Joshua made the now familiar journey back across the long plains of Nebraska, following the windings of the Platte River, allowing the mules to take their time and feed on the lush vegetation of the broad prairies. Leaving the rendezvous this year had been extremely hard, and only the knowledge that when he returned next spring he would no longer be a trader, kept Joshua to task. Joshua purposefully had taken his assistant with him this year to show the route and the daily routine. Twenty armed men were a formidable opponent, and although they often saw roving bands of mounted Indians, none of them offered the pack train any resistance.

Next year he would trek to the joining of the Platte and Arapohay, conduct trade during the rendezvous, and then leave with La Ramie. This would be a culmination to his dreams, dreams that pursued and haunted him since he was a small boy running beside the vast waters of the Mississippi. Winter would pass slowly for him this year, but Joshua vowed to start preparations early to help pass the time. Fort Lisa would become his jump off point, and not the edge of the frontier as he once imagined. Perhaps someday Joshua would follow the Arapohay in the far mountains and beyond the passes of the Tetons to search for the lands of the Pacific. Past losses were forgotten, and only the promise of the future held his dreams. Another destination in his journey was reached, and the trail beckoned him ever onward.

Joshua's retelling of his last six years of life to Night Wind did ease something within his being. Perhaps it was only that the story of his life was not totally contained solely within memories anymore. Should anything ever happen, Night Wind could share with his son some history about the man that already loved this child very much. Joshua thought in terms of masculine because Night Wind was so sure the babe that grew within her womb was a boy. Perhaps on the long ride to the rendezvous, Joshua would talk of the story of his mother. Joshua never realized before how Night Wind's gentle and caring love reminded him of the love his mother shared with her family and through her to him.

Some day he would like to take Night Wind and their children down the long stretches of the Missouri and show Night Wind St. Louis and even perhaps further downriver to the origin of Joshua's birth. Although Joshua described the size, power, and majesty of the Mississippi, no words could convey the feeling the mighty river engendered. Only standing beside the mother of all rivers could impress upon a person the sense of grandeur and oneness.

Slowly the early spring days passed until when he awakened one morning Joshua listened to the chirp of robins outside the cabin, and the slow dripping of ice releasing its grip from the small cabin within the vast fold of wilderness. No light yet filtered in the small cabin, and the feel of

Night Wind's warm muscled thigh felt reassuring as he planned the day. Together with Spotted Owl, they would take all of the horses, making the trip to the cave to load furs, beginning the trip from these mountains of La Ramie. Even La Ramie's mount would be needed, as the packhorses could not bear the entire load, especially in this rough terrain. Following the drainage of the Arapohay might lead them downward toward the Platte. Joshua never traveled the complete length of the long canyons below La Ramie bastion, but the older trapper said it was possible although several places were narrow and dangerous. La Ramie did tell him by backtracking to the plains to the west after a day's ride, he would run across the starting of another drainage that also led to the Platte. Although a longer route, La Ramie told him the passage was much flatter and that this stream consisted of three forks that eventually joined the Arapohay several leagues above where the Arapohay joined the Platte. Smiling to himself, Joshua vowed to call this body of water after La Ramie who still guided and instructed Joshua's trail.

Joshua thought briefly of returning the way of their arrival to this lonely outpost, but he remembered Night Wind's fall and instinctively knew the drifts would still be too deep. There were many trails to these mountains of La Ramie's, but all of them were dangerous to the unwary traveler. Joshua would lead his family west and south until the easier way could be found. Night Wind's pregnancy needed no disruption now. Joshua lost one family because of nature's disasters and vowed no act of his would cause this to happen again.

Night Wind's face was composed and silent as she breakfasted her two men. Carefully she hid any of the fears that roiled inside her. Many nights had she prayed to the Great Spirit, and she was secure in Joshua's competence. Her family would be fine; perhaps it was just the long isolation in these mountains throughout the winter that made her jumpy. Joshua and Spotted Owl left the cabin anxious to begin the trip, but when they checked the corral, Joshua noticed immediately the top rail of the small horse corral was splintered and broken. The piebald and La Ramie's huge bay horse stood hip shod within the corral along with the mounts of Night Wind and Spotted Owl, but one of the two packhorses was gone. A quick check of the tracks confirmed the escapee had jumped over the broken rail and managed to disappear during the night. Perhaps wolves prowled too close, or maybe a fracas between the horses happened, whatever the case, without the extra horse, all of the furs could not be taken from the cave.

"Spotted Owl," Joshua said, running his hand over the rough whiskers on his face, "Ain't no use heading down there unless we have all the horses. Saddle up your paint and find that damn packhorse. I will head out with the other horses. I can tie them single file and make it down the trail all right. Follow along when you find him. If it's later than noon, wait 'til first thing in the morning. I don't want you wandering down that trail in the dark. If I don't see you by evening, boy, I will spend the night and look for you first thing tomorrow morning. And don't let your ma come with you; I don't want her on that trail. Now vamoose and find that horse, I'll see you tonight or first thing in the morn."

Spotted Owl, feeling emboldened by Joshua's confidence in him, raced to find his hackamore and blanket.

Turning to Night Wind, Joshua placed both his hands on the taught stretched skin of her stomach, waiting to feel the movement of his other son within.

"Damn horse anyway," Joshua said, "should have let him drown in the Platte on the way here. I'm going to load him so heavy he'll be too tired to run away again. Now don't worry about me, I'll be fine. If I have to spend the night, I'll be back by noon tomorrow. Don't let Spotted Owl start out today if it gets too late. I love you. When we get back we can start packing here. Tell my boy a story tonight if I'm not back."

With a fierce bear hug, Joshua was gone, and Night Wind watched the procession of horses winding their way to the east out of the protected glade of the cabin. Momentarily Night Wind's sight blurred, and the blue sky turned gray as she absently noticed the silence that enveloped the park as if time and season changed around her. The baby kicked sharply, bringing her back from the reverie of thought. When Night Wind's vision cleared, Joshua was gone, and she was alone. Chilled by the icy wind blowing off the snow-covered mountains, the Vision Woman turned and went into the cabin. There was much to do if they were leaving on the morrow.

Mah-toe, the huge bear, ambled slowly up the slick slope. He could have dug deeper into the thawing earth utilizing the six-inch long claws to gain a firmer purchase, but that would have taken too much effort, and he preferred to go slowly this morning. By crisscrossing along the hillside, he used his keen nose to detect the wide variety of scents clinging to the loose soil. Mah-toe had no need of urgency this morning; yesterday he came across a bull elk in the dark timber and killed it with one blow from his mighty forepaw. Leisurely, the great Ursus dined, until only bits and pieces of fur remained on the carcass. Great had been his hunger, but now the vast quantity of food made him lethargic and satisfied.

Traveling by instinct, with no planning of the route, the great bear slowly made progress toward the meadows above the river. He would return to the rocky crags above the cold waters of the fast running waterway. How many years he returned here was un-remembered. He was old, older than even his own recollection. No memories of parents or siblings remained, only a generally bad disposition coursed through the thoughts of his small mind. His many years were a collection of aches, pain, and wounds that further shortened his already sour temper.

Large beyond belief, a throwback to eons before, he stood over ten feet tall, and his jaws were capable of crushing the head of a full-grown elk. One incisor had split and broken when he bit a pine tree in half because it dared to impede his progress, and the sharp pain was a short fuse for his mighty rage. Seasons came, and seasons passed, he killed and ate, that was all. The undisputed ruler of these mountains, no force, seemingly not even time argued his reign. Winters were spent far to the north and with the warming of spring, the predator traveled south. Mah-toe liked it here; somehow within his small brain he understood, like the salmon returning to their place of birth, his ancestors were of this mountain and river also. When the hot days of summer caused him discomfort, he would lay in the cool sand of a deep cave here, until hunger and thirst forced him to action. Life wasn't good or bad for him, it simply was.

Mating wasn't something Mah-toe cared about anymore, but last fall a young female grizzly dared to approach him, whining and shuffling, unsure of the instincts that drove her. He coupled with her fiercely, even biting deeply into her throat as his seed flowed, but the tooth flared a sharp burst of pain through his being, and he released her, thereby saving the life of the young female.

Hana was she called by the forest, and she too awoke from her slumber a day after Mah-toe. Within her new life grew, soon to be born. This would be her first birthing, and Hana was restless and uncomfortable as she overturned logs, looking for grubs and the small brown mice that used the fallen trees for protection. Suddenly she caught the remembered scent of her mate from last fall, and pushing aside the hunger, the young female bear followed this trail. Soon she came upon the remains of the elk Mah-toe killed, and the young female chased the angry magpies from the remains before cracking the bones to suck out the sweet marrow within. Her hunger somewhat satisfied, Hana again picked up the trail of the huge bear and quickened her pace, hoping to find further food along the trail.

By late afternoon Mah-toe reached the crest above the box canyon and lay panting in the cool afternoon sun before he started down the trail into the canyon and the small meadow below the cave. Instinctively he rumbled a low growl deep within his massive chest, someone or something had invaded his lair. Normally Mah-toe would have rushed down the trail eager to kill anything that dared to challenge his domain, but a strange aroma arose from below, a scent different than any in his recent memory. Years and age stirred the caution within him, and the bear continued to growl softly until he could further detect the source of his enemy. When darkness closed in, suffocating the tall canyon walls in darkness, the predator moved slowly down the trail, each step now brought the intriguing smell of horses, more clearly to his keen senses. Once many years before Mah-toe dined on horseflesh, and he remembered the meat to be sweet and fulfilling. The other strange smell, the odor of danger was still in the air, mingling with the horses and the faintest tinge of Hay-jaay, the beaver.

Mah-toe halted at the border of the dark timber just at the edge of the open meadow. His small eyes, although red and bloodshot, could discern movement beneath him even in the darkness. His nose already told him what was before him. The smell of danger was a man creature, much like others he had killed before, but strangely different. Several times he ate of man's flesh, but found it stringy and tasteless. This being's scent exuded the sharp tang of the cold river mud, and the dull heavy scent of the hard black rocks that Mah-toe sharpened his long claws upon in the high mountains.

Once many seasons past, Mah-toe found his great bulk mired in the soft mud of the river. The greater his exertions, the deeper he sank into the black mud until even his great head was forced beneath the water into the thick dark ooze. With a last desperate effort, he freed himself and struggled to the riverbank. Even now he was careful never to drink or fish in the fast waters of the river unless he stood upon hard rock beneath the stream. Mah-toe wanted to taste the blood of the horses, but the scent of this being of iron and mud instilled caution deep within him. Hunger had not yet made the marauder careless, and the big bear could bide his time. Throughout the night, Mah-toe watched the campsite, growling softly when the yellow light of Pageji, the fire, flared, reaching into the shadows. Once the man being moved from beside Pageji but then returned. The horses shifted restlessly, but the wind carried no scent of the giant bear to them. Dozing Mah-toe rested, his huge head on his forepaws as the last of the elk meat coursed through his system, feeding the body of its master, a master perfectly suited to rule this wilderness of stone and water.

Although morning had already broken, little light yet penetrated the canyon walls. A cold fog hung heavy in the air allowing only brief visions of the rocks and trees before the gray mist closed in again. Mah-toe rose at last and began working his way toward the campsite below. With each step, the smells grew stronger, and this morning his rage returned. No beings challenged him in this, his domain.

The cold air caused sharp pains to shoot through his eyes from the nerves of the splintered tooth, and the great beast's anger was fueled even further by the slow gnawing return of hunger. He broke into a rolling humped run, eating long reaches of ground beneath the dagger like claws of his feet. Suddenly the fog betrayed the charge, and a small amphitheatre of luminosity showed the campsite. The biggest horse snorted and reared snapping the lead ropes of his picket, reaching high in the air, the stallion waved sharp hooves in warning. Mah-toe heard the shrill scream of another horse, and then he was among them. The big horse dodged the bear's charge, wheeling sharply to lash out with both hind feet catching Mah-toe on the left hip. The great bear felt something shatter within his massive muscles but continued the assault, smashing a smaller horse into a rock outcropping. Before the stunned horse could struggle to its feet, a crashing blow broke the horse's neck, and the sharp claws penetrated the hapless throat sending a jetting spray of blood through the fog to splash against the rocks. Roaring loudly, the huge predator stood to his full height watching for life in his prey, ready to crush any movement beneath him, but the horse's struggles were slowing rapidly.

Again the fog closed in, and the bear fell to all fours, suddenly feeling a blinding surge of pain in his rear hip. Hearing movement behind him, Mah-toe reversed directions and again rose to his full height to peer with blood-tinged eyes through the fog. The pain in his hip was forgotten as the rage of his charge still coursed through Mah-toe's body, the small red orbs searched for another being to destroy. Again a shift in the fog showed Mah-toe the cause of the sound. Before him stood the man, puny in size, but the scent of mud and iron wafted strongly to the bear's nostrils. Momentarily the great bear paused, caution rising in his consciousness, and then the fury of the bear's rage won out, and Mah-toe dropped for the charge.

As the bear's feet hit the ground, the grip of the fog exploded with a flash of light as a rifle ball slammed through the enormous muscles of Wah-toe's chest, through his lungs, cutting the major arteries surrounding the great heart. Already enough air was stored in the beast's brain that he raced the remaining steps to crush the little man before him. Together bear and man collided and collapsed, extinguishing the flames of Pageji as two forces of nature jarred the earth with the force of their fall. Mah-toe roaring loudly, finally felt the man's body between his great jaws and with the last of his strength the bear closed the jagged rows of teeth upon the frail body, crushing bone and tissue like porridge caught in the orifice of a great trap.

Twice the man's arm rose and fell driving a knife deep into the internal organs of the great bear, but the rife ball had already stolen the victory, and the ruler of this wildness twitched in the throes of death. Again the fog fell heavily over the campsite, settling slowly on the still forms, as the blood of man and bear mingled together before soaking deep within the earth. This earth knew not their names, only the Great Maker knew who lay still and unmoving on the cold chilled gravel, but uncomplaining the soil took into her bosom the life-forces that once ruled the vastness of their kingdoms and now returned to their origins.

The packhorse continually chased the next bite of grass from hill to hill. After pausing a bit to graze, he raced on to the next patch enjoying his freedom after being penned for so long, and it wasn't till late in the afternoon that Spotted Owl finally caught up with the escapee. The pack horse actually seemed glad of the company, and appeared slightly ashamed for his actions as he trotted, neighing softly up to nuzzle with Spotted Owl's mount. The boy slipped a rawhide loop over the straggler's neck and started back to the cabin.

"Damn horse," said Spotted Owl, in his best imitation of Joshua, "I'm going to beat you to death for running away, and then kick you twice for dying."

In actuality Spotted Owl was glad for the morning's ride, he felt important being able to track the wayward horse, and he sympathized with the horse's feelings of wanting to roam the hills and enjoy the beginnings of spring. By the time Spotted Owl reached the cabin, it was late afternoon, and he tied the horses in the corral after rubbing the mounts with handfuls of fragrant sage. Night Wind was quiet and spoke only in one-word answers to his questions as they ate supper and lay down in their robes for the evening.

Next morning Spotted Owl was up early, ready for his departure to meet Joshua, but to his surprise his mother was already arisen and had warm grain gruel ready for his breakfast. Spotted Owl saw both his and her mounts were blanketed and ready for travel.

"Joshua worries too much," Night Owl said, before her son could repeat the trader's words about Night Wind not being allowed on the trail to the cave. "You need help loading the furs, and I can at least hold the horses. Now hurry up and lead the way to this beaver skin village of yours."

What Night Wind didn't tell Spotted Owl about was the vividness of her dreams during the hours of darkness and how she knew Joshua was in terrible danger, danger from a spirit being that was more a force of nature than the will that drove the man she loved. Pushing the mounts hard and exhorting Spotted Owl to hurry, she pressed her horse firm and fast down the trail to the east that led to the rough ledges above the box canyon and the cave of Joshua's and La Ramie's where the season's worth of furs were stashed.

Night Wind cared naught for the furs, only that she could reach Joshua in time to warn him of the danger she felt. Behind her Spotted Owl was silent, feeling the urgency in his mother's haste. By the time Night Wind dropped off the rim of the box canyon, a thick fog swirled in around her, and she was forced to slow the pace. Once during the descent, she thought she heard the sound of a rifle shot, but after pausing a moment to listen, no other sounds penetrated the thick fog. When the pair reached the bottom of the draw, Night Wind paused to look imploringly at Spotted Owl. The young boy understood that he must lead the way, and suddenly his confidence was shaken, all the terrain looked the same in the heavy mist. At last he could make out the edges of a small stream, and he turned up creek knowing this would lead to the cave and the plateau where Joshua would camp. Within a quarter mile, the ghost form of La Ramie's horse appeared out of the fog, dragging a broken picket line covered in drying blood. With a silent scream of anguish, the Vision Woman spurred forward into the fog, leaving Spotted Owl to catch the ghost horse, and follow rapidly after her. Cursing the big bay fighting his return back up creek, Spotted Owl suddenly rode into a campsite that was scattered, torn and broken. One horse lay stiffening and dead against a pile of rocks, and beside the cold campfire lay two broken bodies. One was the largest bear Spotted Owl had ever seen, bigger yet the beast appeared in the fog. Hugging the other still form rocked Night Wind, Vision Woman of the Shoshone. A high keening wail broke from her lips as she held the dying body of the man she loved.

The scene Night Wind observed when first reaching the campsite was not a surprise, her vision was true last night, and her only hope had been to arrive in time to warn Joshua. When she first reached him, she thought him dead already, but as she pressed her lips to his cold pale mouth, she heard or rather felt a small breath leave his body.

Blood flowed heavily from jagged wounds in his chest, but with a will of effort, he whispered softly, "My love is yours forever; hold close what we have made. Look for me at night when I will fly with you until the end."

Ripping open her soft leather blouse, Night Wind tried to staunch the flow of her lover's blood by pressing her flesh tight to the torn wounds but not even the sharing of her spirit and warmth was enough, and Night Wind felt his spirit pass through her, rising past the fog to the stairway of heavens above. Night Wind began the funeral song, and the Great Manitou heard her anguish on the wind as it echoed through the high mountains and across the plains of time.

On the edge of the forest glade, Hana watched the scene of death below her. She had no experience with man but felt no sentiment of danger. Her keen sense of smell identified the woman and the young boy. She also smelled the death of Wah-toe and another smell what was, what would be, and from these lines, the web of time and life would be changed because of the births of both offspring. of strongly pungent iron and earth. She knew this was the presence that killed the great bear and that somehow this essence was steeped into the earth all around her. Her keen senses could also tell the woman was with child, just as she herself was about to give birth to new life. Both Hana and the woman carried within them seeds of future generations of this land. Content, the young grizzly turned back into the forest to find a warm safe place for the unborn cub.

In the coming days, Joshua was laid to rest in the canyon he loved. Night Wind and Spotted Owl left these mountains of Joshua's and La Ramie's never to return. After traveling to the rendezvous, Night Wind told of the bravery of La Ramie and Joshua. From here mother and sons traveled north to the Mountains of the Wind where Washakie benefited from her wisdom. Here Tuvantu-Wets was born, as were his sons and daughters, as they will continue to be until the Shoshone no longer live in the Land of the Wind Water.

High in the far Blue Mountains near the great peak of La Ramie's another ancestry lives and dies and is reborn again. No longer vengeful against man, the bear clan rules there yet. The Great Manitou looks down upon the circle of life that is his creation and calls it good. The ebb and flow of life are interrelated, and all of The Maker's creations are tied to the land from which they draw their sustenance. This was the simple truth of life Joshua learned; at last as his destiny was fulfilled.

Chapter 17
New Beginnings

Nancy fidgeted in the tight black dress. Once upon a time this would have been her attire of choice, but things had changed, she had changed. People do that sometimes because life forces them too, she thought. Perhaps this was the life she had chosen for herself, and it perhaps it chose her, whichever, she was just starting to find a sense of contentment that had been missing for a long time. Now she wished only for the comfort of her worn Levi's and the soft touch of a flannel shirt rubbing lightly over her tanned skin. The gymnasium was packed with parents, aunts and uncles, and cousins of all varieties. Most wore their best attire, which in Rockville could range from Wal-Mart synthetics to Dior designer outfits.

Graduation was always a time of celebration, but also a time to register a sense of loss, loss of its youth from the small community. Many of these young people would be leaving Rockville, some never to return again. Colleges, apprenticeship programs, military branches, and jobs would now fill their needs. Their time at Lakota high was done. Hopefully the education these seniors had received, both socially and in the classroom, was enough to provide for them a basis to expand their lives. Wistfully, Nancy thought back on words she heard Carrigan say hundreds of times about how he wished the young would seize the future, instead of merely becoming trapped by time, forever frozen into choices they refused to take. Decision not made, were decisions all the same. Life waited for no one, it simply was, and each person could grow to be an active part of it, or become flotsam, directionless, allowing life's current to determine his or her destination.

"There is no need to reach high for the stars. They are already within you - just reach deep into yourself! Explore the splendor of the heavens, and you will find your beauty within."

The speaker's words brought Nancy back to the present, almost as if they were aimed specifically at her, rather than the class of seniors waiting impatiently in their hot starched robes for the principal to finish speaking to the class. Somehow graduation speeches were usually best after they were reflected upon awhile, sometimes years. This group of squirming bodies wanted only the clean white diplomas and a running head start toward the graduation parties that awaited them. Nancy looked more closely at the students seated in front of her. Perhaps she was too harsh in her assessment. Many of the students were listening to the speaker. It could be because of the speaking skills he possessed. The voice from the podium rose and fell in intervals, not loud but sincere as if he was speaking to everyone in the gym individually, giving friendly advice rather than lecturing. He spoke to his audience, not at or above them.

Amidst the graduating seniors, Nancy recognized Billy Lenz and Becky Lansing. Sitting together, their attention was focused on the stage. It was hard to imagine a year ago that either one would be among these students here today. Billy had been removed from his home and placed in foster care on a tip from Trisha Collingworth, his English teacher. Billy came to her after Tommy died and told of the activities he was involved in prior to the explosion. Although many of the brain cells Billy eradicated from his long period of chemical abuse would never come back, a year of intensive work through family living and social etiquette classes did much to transform Billy into a different young man. At least he had enough sense to trust Trisha.

That was what every young person needed, thought Nancy, just one person they could trust, when all else in their world was going to hell. Gone were the blank eyes, the constant use of drugs, and the stream of mucus from Billy's nose. His diploma showed he graduated under a special exemption, but it was a sign of progress all the same. Through a work-study program Billy worked with Jimmy Sickles in the school transportation pool, and with Jimmy for an example of hard work and attention to detail, Billy began to like the duties assigned him. The school district even wanted Billy to stay on next year and was sending him to a local junior college to complete a six-week program in mechanics. Billy was going to be okay.

Becky also graduated, partly because her father was on the school board, but mainly because no matter what class she was in, she tried her best. Her long brown legs didn't hurt her any either, thought Nancy to herself. Becky didn't understand very much of what the speaker was talking about, but she smiled and nodded her head. There would be no shortage of customers as Lansing Pharmacy with Becky behind the counter. Hopefully someone else could take the orders and make change. Her looks would be enough for someone soon, and she could start her life as a young wife and homemaker, in a house next to the golf course. There were worse ways to get along in this world.

As Nancy continued to study the seniors, she noticed many other young women in the audience who were paying particular attention to the podium. It helped that the speaker possessed a certain amount of boyish charm; his tanned rugged features looked more at home in the rugged hills, visible through the open doors of the gym, than they did standing as a symbol of the educational facility he represented. The suit hung well from his strong shoulders, doing little to conceal the lean frame beneath. Several times the speaker tapped a hardwood cane upon the side of the speaking platform to accentuate his comments. He spoke to the students about the values of morality and honesty.

Nancy was carried into his story as the speaker used a segue about a young Indian maiden who persevered through a harsh upbringing to become the leader of her people and found immortality in the stars of the Milky Way because of her honesty. Slowly the speaker wove his themes into the Indian legend.

Once many years before Lakota High School came to stand upon this location there was only a large Indian village situated here. Nameskeek' oodun Kuspe it was named through the land. In this place lived a supreme being who was invisible -- a mighty hunter, whose dodem (teeomul) was the bear. He was the Deity of the spirit world. He would only become visible to those who were pure of heart and lived their life in honor. Therefore there were indeed few who actually saw him, but many young people claimed to, hoping the Deity would reward their young lives with many fortunes.

"Cogoowa' wiskoboosich," the voice would ask sounding like the soft breath of the wind. Speak of the clothes I wear in your presence.

At other times the Great Spirit would inquire about other things such as, what is the color of his fur? The young people would give answers as to what they perceived a Deity would wear as they described clothing and fur of the richest hue. Always they were wrong.

"Na Cheir so titte ma," would return the answer on the wind, "you have not yet learned the lessons of our people as you do not truly see me. Return and study harder, so you may become leaders of our nation."

Now in the village there dwelt an old man, a widower with three daughters. The youngest of those was very small, weak, and often ill, which did not prevent her sisters, especially the eldest, from treating her with great cruelty. The second daughter was kinder but did not stop the older sister from burning the youngest one's hands and face with hot coals. The youngest daughter's whole body was scarred with the marks made by torture, so that people called her Oochigeaskw' (burnt-skin girl). When her father, returned home each night, he asked what it meant that his youngest child was so disfigured. Her sisters would promptly say that it was the fault of the girl herself, for having been forbidden to go near the fire; she had disobeyed and fallen in.

Now it came to pass that it entered the heads of the two older sisters that they would go and try their fortune at seeing the Invisible One. So they clad themselves in their finest, and striving to look their fairest, they went to visit with the invisible being.

"Cogoowa' wiskoboosich," came the voice.

The oldest sister explained that he was wearing a shawl of bright red and blues, and that around his neck was a golden symbol of the sun, for this is how she imagined a great Deity would look.

"No," shouted the second sister, "you wear the robe of the great white bear of the north and your leggings are of the finest elk hide, chewed and tanned a golden brown."

"Return to your father and send your youngest sister to me," the Deity answered "for you do not truly see me, your voices speak of jealously and deceit."

When the two sisters returned home, they told their father of their visit and the Great Spirit's request to see Oochigeaskw', the burnt-faced girl. Hearing of the command from the Great Spirit and having no clothes beyond a few blankets, the youngest sister went into the woods and cut sheets of birch bark. From this bark she made a plain dress. The sisters and the tribe laughed at her, but she paid them no mind. From a discarded fur of the woodland deer, she made leggings and new moccasins, and thus clad, she set out to see the Great Spirit.

The Great Spirit observed she was dressed in the style of his people from long ago and was pleased that she dressed plainly and did not try to hide her scars and burns. By this the great Deity understood that this noble girl knew more than the mere material things, as the world knows them, and he respected her for dressing herself plainly rather that hiding herself behind gaudy baubles and rouge. He recognized that she knew honesty, and morality and genuine respect for other people were more important than any of the vanities of the world.

407

As the brown of the evening sky became black, the Great Spirit spoke to her, asking what she saw when she looked at him. The young girl replied with great reverence and fear, "I see the evening rainbow."

"And where does this rainbow lead, little one?" asked the Great Spirit.

"High into the Ketak'soowowcht, the Spirits' road, or the Milky Way," answered the little burned one.

"Then you can truly see me, and for your honesty, you will become the leader of your people."

The Great Spirit then gently bathed her, and as she was washed, all the scars disappeared from her face and body. Her hair grew again so that it was very long and like a blackbird's wing. Her eyes were like stars shining in the night sky. In the entire world was no such beauty. It was a great marvel to behold. Then, having done this, he bade her take the wife's seat in his wigwam.

"You will become my wife upon this earth, and during your time here you will lead your people so that all will prosper, the rain will fall gently on these lands, and the game will multiply as far as the eye can see. You will teach your people what you already know, that only through compassion for others, spoken with honesty, and lived through morality can one's spirit find the path of the Hanging Road. You will also teach them that cruelty and deceit must always be punished, just as your sisters will become tendrils of moss to wave forever in the stream, watching as life passes them by."

Oochigeaskw' begged him not to transform her sisters, but the Great Spirit would not relent, and the two evil girls became just as he said, and remain such even until this day. Oochigeaskw' became the wife of the Supreme Deity and ruled her people wisely until the time she passed from this land and rose to the heavens to shine like a star living with her husband in the night skies.

The graduation speaker paused before continuing, "Respecting each spirit and soul in this world will provide you more satisfaction in life than all the material goods or fame you acquire. Remember and use this story of Oochigeaskw' as you leave this gym today. I leave you today," the speaker continued, "with a quote from Susan B. Anthony who fought tirelessly to make sure all people, especially young women, were treated fairly.

'Sooner or later we all discover that the important moments in life are not the advertised ones, not the birthdays, the graduations, the weddings, not the great goals achieved. The real milestones are less prepossessing. They come to the door of memory unannounced, stray dogs that amble in, sniff around a bit and simply never leave. Our lives are measured by these moments.'"

Nancy's memory did open then, unannounced, and thoughts returned of the torrential rain that inundated Rockville a little over a year ago. She remembered her frantic drive into the mountains and shuddered when she realized how close she came to being swept away by the massive wall of water that rushed down the Laramie River as she crossed the river bridge on her way into the rain swept hills to search for Carrigan. Only Nancy's fear saved her life. She pushed the jeep hard on the wet roads, and it was this speed that allowed her to cross the bridge before it shattered into pieces behind her, as the flood, bearing tons of water, logs, and debris smashed the steel girders into tinfoil and metal shards. The next day when she returned to town, she could only marvel at the destruction the river had done to the tresses. Sadly she knew other people downriver were not as lucky, and for these souls she mourned. The river exacted its toll in human life and then satisfied, its muddy tide receded once again to become the slow rolling stream it was before.

Twice this river came close to claiming her life, and twice she escaped. Strange, Nancy thought, Carrigan played the role of savior both times. Her rescue from the whirlpool of Devil's fireplace by rope up the slick canyon walls clinging tightly to Carrigan seemed fresh in her mind. Hugging herself tightly, she could still feel the strength of his body as he pulled her slowly, hand over hand, up the granite cliffs. Why she left him then, she didn't know. A deep sadness still filled her when she reflected on all those years that she could have spent lying next to him, loving him, and she never was able to explain, even to herself, the answer to this question.

And then again years later, the fear for his safety pushed her past the bridge and death that was close behind her. Deep in her core she felt perhaps the price was paid by a different person, the river having taking someone else so she could be spared. Perchance this exchange was fate, or perhaps it was the sacrifice of a different person long ago that was connected to her and this land who paid her price. Other events from a year ago she still kept locked away, deep within the recesses of her essence, fully understanding the fear and pain were more than she could examine at this time.

During the last year, Nancy did examine what the significance of these close calls meant to her, and how Carrigan's love for her helped shaped her decisions. She finalized the divorce with Edmond and moved her and Stephen's household to the ranch near Rockville. Her home and family were now here. She ran a successful campaign to become a school board member and immediately set about making changes in the educational system that had produced a Tommy. No child should be pushed to the limits he endured. For in a community, when one is in pain, all suffer. Changes were needed to recognize this pain, and soothe it.

Schools and their programs couldn't fix everyone, but that didn't stop her from trying. Wryly she reflected that many of the changes were ideas Carrigan had pushed for. With Ranier money as financial backing and her voice on the school board, programs moved from ideas to reality. Lakota High could be something for everyone, and at the very least, all students would feel someone here cared about them and their dreams. For dreams make reality, and without dreams only nightmares can be found.

After a pause to let the audience consider his remarks, the speaker concluded his speech and the roll call of names began as each graduating senior was called to the podium to receive his or her diploma. Pride reflected from the faces of family members assembled within the gym. Every graduate owed something to the people seated here. No one achieved a hallmark in his or her life without the help of someone else. Nancy used to believe that that individuals were responsible for success or failure on their own, but Carrigan helped her realize that people, time, and the very earth itself are tied together, dancing to a complicated rhythm with the outcome known only to the Maker himself. Maybe this was why she had been separated from Carrigan's strength for so long; maybe it was all part of some grand plan.

After the last graduate made the trek to the stage, the principal dismissed the ex-students.

"Remember," he said, "to reflect upon these statements you have heard today as you leave these doors. Graduates, for by that appellation I address you, you are now free to begin the rest of your lives."

A loud roar erupted as hats flew into the air, and classmates hugged each other, congratulating each other on this part of the journey they had finished together. Nancy mingled with the crowd shaking hands and conversing with parents and students alike. During the last year she had come to know many them, somehow instinctively this was something she knew Carrigan would have wanted her to do. Suddenly a smiling familiar face appeared before her. Jan Rudolf had returned for the graduation, and she found herself hugging him tightly before he held her at arms length looking deeply into her face. During the last year Nancy spent long hours on the phone with the ex-principal trying to understand the tragedies that occurred here. As they visited about the school and Carrigan, Nancy began to understand why Jan and James were close friends with a deep respect for each other. She, too, now counted Jan as a friend.

"How have you been my dear?" he asked, the humor in his voice, never far from the surface.

"Well, like everyone else, I'm hanging in there," Nancy replied. "I'm so glad you came back for graduation. Carrigan wanted that."

"Wouldn't have missed it for the world, I wanted to see how Lakota High was surviving a year later; there sure have been some changes, and many of them for the good I think."

"I think so also, more teachers, smaller classes, and a much larger variety of offerings for the kids to take. The freshman academy worked out well this year, and only three freshman failed two or more classes, and maybe next year we might manage even to drag these kids along also."

"The new principal filled me in this afternoon on the novel programs being offered for "at risk" students, how on earth were all of these financed?" asked Jan, shaking his head knowing that Nancy would never admit to infusing millions of dollars into Lakota's High's aging infrastructure.

"Well," Nancy replied, "money does more good in schools than in bank accounts. Did you have a chance to tour the new shop for auto mechanics or the culinary facility yet?"

"Nope, but those are next on my list, and I plan to bring some of my school board down to look at Lakota's electrician and plumbing classes. It's great that students can begin working toward apprenticeships while they are still in high school. It looks like the college prep programs are doing well also; three National Merit Scholarships were awarded to this class of seniors."

"You get the credit for that, Jan. Those advanced programs were all started while you were here. Enough of that, how the hell have you been?"

"Great," Jan beamed back. "I'm working some as a principal, some as a teacher, and spending a lot of time with students, just listening and learning. I miss the school here, but up north there are plenty of challenges to meet. My wife and I spend more time together. It's almost like we're getting to know one another again. The change has been good for us. I'll call you next time I'm down; maybe you can buy me lunch at Ben's."

"Maybe not Ben's, some of the help there doesn't appreciate my smiling face," Nancy said, "but we can scare up something to eat somewhere. Please do call. I like talking about old times with close friends."

Visiting with Jan chased away the last remnants of dark thoughts that eddied in the backwaters of Nancy's mind all afternoon. She finished talking with several families as the massed assembly slowly thinned, with parents and students flowing outward heading toward the graduation parties in the town and toward the warm spring night from the open

411

orange doors of the gym. Nancy walked out into the spring evening air, still warm and musky from the afternoon sun. Near the corner she noticed Chuck Attenby and Jenny Albright visiting together, laughing and teasing each other about some private joke. Carrigan had told her about the rocky relationship between these two teachers, but at least for the moment, they genuinely seemed to be enjoying each other's company. The teachers of Rockville always attended graduation, to survey their handiwork of the previous four years. This was a nice thing, and she hoped the students appreciated the extra effort. Nancy also hoped the new teachers would learn from this example, teaching wasn't just a 9-5 job, and anyone who entered the profession with this illusion, soon became disappointed and bitter. Instructing young lives demanded constant attention, even on weekends and nights.

A brief stirring on the evening air slowly wafted the gentle scent of sage down the avenues leading to the school parking lot. Immediately the smell caused a stirring in Nancy's soul as the familiar scent allowed her to think of the mountains that watched so peacefully in the west. The last rays of the sun still peeked over the massive blue bastion of Laramie Peak, intensifying the vibrant hues of the distant range. Somehow the colors brought a measure of peace to her, reassuring her place and direction in this time and setting. A wasp lazily made slow circles high in the ceiling of the gym before suddenly changing course and flowing like a leaf caught in a swift current, flew out of the doors and into the twilight air.

Nancy finally located Stephen visiting with some of his friends near the playground outside. Seeing her, Stephen's face brightened, and he waved back before turning to tell his friends goodbye. He was her firstborn and the pride of her life. Here he would learn the values of being a man and grow into his heritage and station in life. She once again gave a small prayer of thanks to whatever caused her to awaken and return to this small corner of the world.

Several hours of work remained as Nancy needed to meet with the rest of the school board to sign the diplomas for the students. Few of the graduating seniors realized the paper they received this evening was not valid until all signatures and seals were attached. The principal would verify the completion of any final course work and with this endorsement, the originals would be mailed to the graduates. Stephen waited in the lobby of the boardroom, deeply engrossed in a book about wizards, dwarves, and elves. He liked the magic of fantasy and could read for hours. Nancy was much the same way when she was young, and she never denied him reading time. Carrigan always told her this was the single greatest factor of academic achievement. If kids could read, and read well, all other educational subjects would open up for them. Nancy looked for the principal to congratulate him on the evening's speech, but he was attending the myriad of parties held throughout the small community. Just part of the job, the human connections were at times more important than any of the academia that crossed his desk. Finally everything was signed, and Nancy gathered Stephen from the lobby, book in hand, and left the boardroom and went into the night air.

Nancy and Stephen crossed the street toward the parking lot near the administration building. Waiting patiently, a large Ford pickup sat in the center of the pavement. Empty parking places were evident on both sides of Gertrude's doors, but she didn't seem to mind the absence of company, in fact Nancy thought this vehicle was a lot like Carrigan used to be, only allowing a select few to be close to her. Driving this large truck gave Nancy a sense of security and sometimes she even imagined she could smell a familiar scent still in the interior. After making sure that Stephen was secured in his seat belt, she double-checked the car seats to make sure they hadn't worked loose. Four people in the cab were a tight fit, but Nancy didn't mind, at least she didn't have to turn around to check on the twins if she needed to. She had left the twins with Tracie prior to coming to graduation, and now she needed to get back there before they drove Tracie crazy with their constant need for attention. Tracie's daughter Katie loved playing with the twins, and Nancy was appreciative that she could drop them by anytime she needed to.

Missy and Joshua were born the end of February, and at three months of age, were already exhibiting many characteristics of their father. Nancy was probably the most surprised person in Wyoming when she missed her period in July.

After the birth of Stephen, the doctors told her Stephen would be an only child and that she wouldn't be able to have any more children. Following that, she never used birth control, not that it would have mattered, as she and Edmond hadn't slept together for many years now. There must have been something in the water or the mountain air when she lay with Carrigan in his newly built cabin a year ago. Thinking deeply, now she recognized the babies for what they were, miracles. Her pregnancy was an extremely smooth one, and somehow she wasn't even shocked when the doctor told her there would be twins. Something inside let Nancy know, one would be a girl, and one would be a boy. Joshua was wiry and blonde, while Missy was dark with bronzed skin. The Indian blood that ran through Carrigan's veins seemed to come full measure in his daughter, and her eyes were unfathomable pools of rich chocolate that looked deep into Nancy's soul every time she held her daughter, rocking and murmuring to the small babe when she was restless.

Many times during the strong storms that blew outside the windows in the late winter, she held the babies to her full breasts letting the feeling of completeness wash over her as the infants suckled and nuzzled her nipples. How she could have ever felt her life was full without them, she didn't know. They somehow completed a circle of meaning within her and allowed her to understand her place in the circle of life. It was through her that these children came into the world, replacing and enriching unfinished fragments of the humanity around her. They were part of her and part of Carrigan, and together the infants completed an intricate web of life that Nancy felt swirling in her inner being.

The big truck roared to life, and she pulled out of the parking lot, letting Gertrude warm up before accelerating the pickup out onto the street and starting westward toward Tracie's house. She couldn't help glancing at Carrigan's house as she drove past. Perhaps it was just her imagination, but she seemed to feel the pickup's engine slow slightly as if anticipating this house to be her final destination. Shaking off the feeling, Nancy shifted down and revved the engine to let Gertrude know she wouldn't be stopping here tonight. She thought back about the first time she went into the house after her return from the mountains that wet and rainy night a year ago.

She had returned to the house, Carrigan's house, a year ago, hoping somehow the structure could provide strength she knew she was going to need for the coming days. She was sure that within the confines where Carrigan called home, her anxieties and worries could somehow be lessened, or at least compartmentalized and structured to allow her to handle them. Her trust was rewarded, and she did feel better the minute she entered the door, sensing the peace and tranquility within.

As Nancy entered the house, she was struck by the familiarity of the surroundings. The house, like the man, was simple yet refined in its tastes. Several rooms appeared almost Spartan, containing only the bare necessities. These necessities though, showed their value and worth, through the craftsmanship of their form. Nancy realized that all the furniture and decorations were of the earth. There was a complete absence of polished metal or plastic. The furniture was solid and simple, mostly of a mission design, fashioned from oak and pine. The fabrics were woven cottons and wools blended in earth tones, with occasional splashes of color giving the rooms the appearance of a forest meadow with hints of a rainbow or sunset peaking through.

Centered on the mantle of the granite fireplace were several pictures and a small stone figure. The picture frames were made from aspen and appeared handled and worn, as if someone held them often. The first was a picture of James Carrigan Senior and his wife Melissa, Carrigan's parents, standing in front of a large bay horse. Seated bareback on the horse, a young boy grinned proudly from beneath tousled blond locks. Nancy recognized the horse and the boy. Carrigan always loudly complained that Joe liked her better than him, and Nancy never told Carrigan about the pounds of rock candy she snuck to the horse when she was in college. She doubted if Joe had ever betrayed their secret relationship either.

The second picture was of her. Nancy wasn't even aware the picture had been taken, although she recognized the location as being at the rodeo grounds in Lamar, Colorado, many years ago. Her hair was windblown as she stood staring off into the distance, leaning against a horse trailer. The photograph was excellent and appeared to capture the wistful vulnerability within her that she had almost forgotten once existed. What was she thinking her future would be many years ago when she was the young girl in the picture?

In front of the fireplace, beneath a coffee table a large box lay on its side, the contents flowing out onto the hardwood floor. Nancy seated herself on the floor, cross-legged Indian style, and began searching through the papers, being careful not to tear any of the yellowing newspaper clippings and paper documents. She felt almost as if she was spying into a secret world, as she began to piece together the story the ephemera told.

Many of the articles on top detailed the early history of the Shoshone people, describing them as one of the first tribes to obtain horses with which they hunted across the Great Plains. Other documents were photocopied from historical journals and were written about the decimation of the Indian people by the diseases brought by the white man as they traveled through the homelands of the Shoshones. The Shoshone Chief Pah-dasher-wah, who was reputed to be a close ally of Chief Washakie, narrated one article. In this narration, Pah-dasher-wah, or Strong Bear, which was his English name, told of a famous spirit woman of the Shoshone people who predicted this wave of destruction.

She told us of a vision she saw in the great Oblayela or wilderness. In this wilderness, she saw ships with white canvas rolling across the seas of the Great Plains, passing through huge villages of prairie dogs. Behind the ships the tribes of prairie dogs, sickened and died, their bodies untouched and rotting. A great tepee appeared to her, half red, half black, each side painted with symbols of the bear and the moon. Suddenly fire spread across the plains, and smoke rose high into the skies driving before the flames vast herds of animals fleeing with tribes of her people into the mountains. Through the fire came the spirit of Pono-Kamila, the horse spirit, and father of all horses. This spirit horse spoke to Chief Washakie and told him to limit contact with the white people and to burn and bury any robes of anyone who became ill with this great sickness. Washakie protected his people by gathering them in the valley of the Great Winds and making the white eyes promise to stay away from this sacred ground. Because of these words of advice, the Shoshone people survived the diseases of the white man. The name of this female prophet was not mentioned and apparently was lost over time.

Her vision indeed was prophetic, and Chief Washakie was very wise to listen to her, thought Nancy.

Nancy finished with this article and rising, she wandered into the kitchen. Within the refrigerator were several cold root beers. Confiscating one of these, she returned to the box of articles, aware that although she had many other obligations, she felt compelled to continue reading here, as if she was destined to continue looking for answers to questions that Carrigan had searched for.

The next clipping talked about the 1863 Treaty of Friendship between the United States Government and the Shoshone people. This was the basis for the establishment of the Wind River Reservation that was finally granted on July 3, 1868. The reservation was situated between the towns of Camp Auger, which is now named Lander, and what would become Riverton, Shoshoni, and Thermopolis. Nancy found a picture of Washakie posing for the camera with a rifle and a peace pipe that signified the duality of his nature. Under his leadership, his people made and maintained successful treaties with the United States government. Fort Auger was built at Washakie's request because he hated and feared the Sioux and the Cheyenne Indians and believed the fort would offer protection for his people. Washakie ruled his tribe with a firm hand and listened only to his closest advisors. Under him, the Shoshone people learned the ways of agriculture and survived in the world of the whites.

In one picture, an aged Washakie posed with a much younger man, who at first glance Nancy assumed to be his son. Upon closer inspection, she realized the other figure in the picture had decidedly white features, with lighter colored hair and eyes. Turning the picture over, she could make out the name, Coural, written in pencil, by a woman's hand.

Another article had been underlined in several places, and Nancy recognized Carrigan's handwriting in the margin in numerous places. Mention was made here about Washakie's decision to allow the Arapahoe tribes to live on the reservation in 1878, but the Shoshoni people did sue the federal government for back rent, and in 1938, they won a settlement which was divided among all members of the tribe.

Nancy also came across a time line in Carrigan's writing which made note of the Brunot Cessation which guaranteed the Shoshone people $5000 worth of young cattle yearly, and the 1897 accord which returned the northern part of the reservation to the United States for a cash payment of $50,000. This area contained a massive hot springs and would become the location for the town of Thermopolis. In 1906 Riverton was built upon lands obtained from the Indians, and schools for the Indian children were built at the Saint Stephen's Mission and at Fort Washakie.

Here again Carrigan made notes in the margins and circled the parts of the story that told of Indian children being forced to abandon their native language and speak only English in the schools. They were also forced to dress as the white man, their hair was cut, and they were beaten if they failed to follow these rules.

No Indian children could write or speak of the Ghost Dances of the Piute leader Wovoka, who brought these dances to the Indians as a way of bringing back past ancestors and driving the white men from the lands. The Sun Dance was also banned in formal legislation by the United States government for fear that this ritual would lead to hostilities. The names of the Indian children were also changed to make them appear "whiter." For example, the name Lone Bear would be changed to Lon Brown. This made the tracking of Indian heritage much harder, because later historians would suddenly lose a line of an original family clan.

Carrigan had noted that in 1899 Washakie's health began to fail, and he died in his home in 1900, living to be over 100 years old. Two of Washakie's sons, Dick and Charlie were mentioned, and the notations stated they were well traveled, even visiting England, appearing in movies and plays about their people. Again Nancy came across the name Coural who was described as a half-breed, but was mentioned as the best negotiator for the Shoshone people when they had any dealings with the whites and was the driving force behind the many of the concessions the Indian won back from the federal bureaucracy.

Near the bottom of the box, folded in a linen envelope was a fragile peace of paper written in the same woman's hand as on the picture of Washakie. This envelope was still sealed with wax, and instinctively Nancy knew that Carrigan had not read this letter yet. Nancy realized that this writing held the key to Carrigan's search, and that all the other information was merely collaboration for this text. Before reading it, Nancy returned to the refrigerator for another root beer, but after letting the cold air flow across her face, she changed to a juice instead before returned to read the old letter that she assumed to be written by Carrigan's mother, Melissa.

Seating herself as before, Nancy ruptured the seal and gently unfolded the foxing paper before slowly beginning to read the letter within.

Dear James, for it is by this white name, the name of your father, I shall name you, although your Indian name will be Fis-tow-a dep or strong one, when you are born into this world. Perhaps the day will come when you wish to know more about yourself and your heritage. This will help you to understand should I not be here to tell you myself. I was born in 1920 near Pavilion, Wyoming. My father was of German Irish people, and he worked hard and loved his family, but fell ill and died when I was young. He never had many chances in life but was a decent God-fearing man. His love for my mother was his weakness, and because she was Shoshone, he was never given a chance to rise above his station. In Pavilion, he was known only as the squaw man. Indians near the reservation were thought of to be beneath or inferior to white people, and even my mother's people disapproved of the marriage. After my father died, my mother remained separate from her people, unwilling to return me to the poverty and desperation on the reservation.

Your father also knew of my heritage but laughed at my fears that we would be treated the same as my parents. It is for his ability to make me laugh that I love him. I am glad that we moved here to Rockville, although I fear for you and

418

hope that you will never be called the names I endured. "Half breed", and "dog eater" were constant taunts I faced when I was young. You are born from a family with a long and proud tradition. Always remember this and know that you are of the earth, nourished by her, and will forever have the blood of my people running through your veins.

In my visions, the totem of the great bear will guard you, for I am from the Tissura'ti ti line or vision people and can foretell your birth, just as you will one day be able to see parts of your future. The bear will give you strength and courage, but it will also make you aloof from other people and distrustful of their motives. Guard against this in your life, or you will be lonely and without joy

We of the Shoshone, or lodge grass people, track our heritage through the maternal line, for it is in the women that the vision runs the strongest. My mother Little Wing was born in the canyon of the great wind in the year of the Treaty of warm springs. She served her people as a vision woman while she was on the reservation before her marriage away from the tribe. Tri-Van-Ta-Wae or Soft Feather, her mother, served as Vision Woman before her. Warm Breeze or Chi-Natooe-ek was the mother of Soft Feather. Warm Breeze took unto her the fair-haired Coural to be her mate. In his body ran the blood of a white trapper and that of Night Wind, perhaps the most famous of the Seers of our tribe from the land of the water that boils, for in her was the blood of Walira, a daughter of the Great Manitou and the swift Antelope of the Plains. With the union of Warm Breeze and the blood of Night Wind through Coural or Tuvantu-Wets as was his Indian name, the heritage of the Far Seers is twice deep within you. As I left the tribe for the love of a white man, my visions have slowed and are no longer as clear, but if they appear in you, be not afraid, for they are your heritage.

I feel that perhaps it will be through your daughter that they will run strong again many years in the future. I tell you this so that you might hold it close within, and understand why you are different from others, but I will not allow you to be scoffed at because of your heritage by those both white and red who no longer believe or understand. If you are reading this, it is because my time to cross the hanging road came before I could show you the way of the wind voice. Know always that I hold and love you deep within my spirit and heart. I will wait with joy the day of your birth.

By all the love that abides within me, your mother

Shaken by what she had just read, Nancy folded the letter and placed it gently back into the envelope before returning all of the papers to the box. She wondered what would have been different if Carrigan had read the letter before leaving for the mountains that night. Did he know the depth of his mother's love, or understand why she wished to protect him? How proud she must have been that he grew into the man he had become. Now Nancy understood why he always seemed so elemental to her, as natural as her very breath. Long ago she learned not to discount the Native American stories as mere myths, and she understood the forces that ran within Carrigan's soul. She wondered if he had foreseen her love for him, or the massive tree that would try to claim him in the draw beneath his cabin that stormy night.

One last item did Nancy hold within her hands before carefully closing the box. A long antler with a dry piece of rawhide wrapped carefully around the base intrigued her as she ran her hands along the smooth bone. Running the length of the horn were inscribed symbols carved in scrimshaw fashion. A few of these Nancy recognized, a bear, the sun, and what appeared to be an owl. The horn was unusual because no points branched off its length. Toward the sharpened tip dark brown stains swirled down the tip. It did not appear to be a weapon, but rather a charm or the story about someone, although Nancy's mind did at least question the brown stains and sharpened point that would pierce flesh easily. This too she replaced within the box.

Careful not to disturb anything else within the house, Nancy left quietly into the night, turning out the lights behind her. There would be time in coming days to return and learn more about the man she loved.

After she left the house that night, she knew everything was going to work out. She had returned many times during the last year. When she found out she was pregnant with Carrigan's children, she thought back on the letter she read from Carrigan's mother detailing her love for him and the predictions for his future. This was when she was sure, she carried a daughter in her womb, and that this child would be just as Melissa had predicted.

Missy would carry the gift and the burden of being able to float on the night wind and foretell events yet to pass. Nancy realized that it was her responsibility to raise the children according to their birthrights, and when the time was correct, she would make a pilgrimage to the Wind Rivers to introduce her children to their ancestors. There she could learn how to help them to fulfill their roles in the world around them. But for now, they were all hers to love and to hold; now she would teach them of their father's people and the love they were born into.

The twins fascinated Stephen from the moment they were born, and Nancy was thankful that he felt no resentment towards them. He understood the blood that ran within their veins came from her and Carrigan, but this made not the slightest difference to him, and he accepted them as full members of his family and life here in Wyoming.

Nancy pulled the big truck into Tracie's driveway, and Stephen raced ahead of her to knock on the door anxious to see his siblings. Nancy bundled the twins warmly in their blankets before buckling them securely in the car seats of the pickup. Tracie followed them outside, and just as Nancy was getting in, Tracie touched her slightly on the arm.

"I don't know if Carrigan ever told you this, but without him I don't know what would have happened to me. He was like a father that I never had. When I didn't place value in myself, he saw it there, and wouldn't let me go until I saw it also. He used to read to me and tell me stories from long ago about people that overcame their problems and made something of themselves. He talked to me of God and told me that I was God's creation and that I was beautiful and meant for great things. Other people looked down on Katie and called her a bastard, but never Carrigan. He always said, 'when you see yourself through your children's eyes, then you will know what joys life can bring.' I know that I'm rambling on, but I just wanted you to recognize if you need me to watch the babies anytime, anywhere, just call me."

"You're not rambling, and I know exactly what you mean," Nancy said, "he wouldn't let me go either, and now look at the fix I'm in. I'm just kidding," Nancy continued, afraid that Tracie might take her remark the wrong way. "The fix I'm in is a good one, one that I would die fighting for, before anyone took my children from me. You're right, when I look at the twins, I want to be more than I am, a better person. Kids have a way of doing that to you. I probably will call again, and thank you so much. Let me know when your college graduation ceremony is so we can attend, and think about us, we sure would like to hire you when you're done with school to work with our registered herd of mother cows."

Night by this time had succeeded in chasing any remnants of the daylight from the countryside, and the headlights carved a pathway through the evening. Glancing up into the darkening sky to the west, Nancy could see the stars starting their slow march through the heavens, and she smiled to herself as she checked out the constellations that Carrigan used to recite to her when they drove the long roads from rodeo to rodeo a million miles and years ago. Carrigan had called her Iris on that night, and she punched him, thinking he misspoke her name until laughingly he held both her small fists in one of his hands waiting for her to calm down.

"Iris," he said "was known as the mother of love. She was the Goddess of the rainbow, which was the bridge between heaven and earth. My father told me that she overcame Demeter, the Goddess of fields and grain, and coaxed Demeter out of her cave so that the land would become fruitful again, because Demeter was in mourning and would allow no green grass to grow.

In Genesis, angered by Yahweh's Flood, she removed the bridge from earth to heaven so He could not receive his sacrifices. When Yahweh promised to never flood the earth again, Iris replaced the rainbow.

The Native American's speak of Iris and call her "The "Daughterwind" because each spring new life is reborn upon the earth and the cycle continues. When a soul leaves this earth they walk the hanging road of stars, our milky way, to take their place in the heavens, watching over their families and loved ones. You're my Iris, my rainbow, and my bridge to eternity. Face it woman, I guess you're just stuck with me."

Nancy thought about how true Carrigan's predictions of long ago were. Stephen kept the twins entertained as Nancy drove the long ribbon of blacktop toward the ranch and home. Tomorrow would be a good day to sleep in, and she looked forward to the comfort of the ranch house and the bedroom with the large glass windows framing the Far Blue Mountains to the west. Just as she drove over the bridge across the Laramie River making its long trek to the Platte and onward to the Mississippi, her cell phone chirped, and Nancy smiled, already imagining who was calling her.

"Hello cowboy," she said, not waiting for an answer on the other end, "are you back from graduation. Have the bed all warmed up, I'm almost home."

Gertrude settled into a steady pace, secure in the knowledge that soon all of her family would be together again.

The End

Greg A. Garton Biography

Greg A. Garton is a Wyoming native born and bred. Living on a ranch in the Sybille Canyon of Wyoming, he received his early education, taught by his mother in a one-room schoolhouse. Summers were spent in other pastimes, hunting, hiking, and riding in the rugged terrain of the high mountain pastures. A voracious reader from an early age, Greg spent countless hours consuming all types of written work from the family library, including literary classics and adventure tales like Tarzan and Hopalong Cassidy. From these, a love of reading and story telling was born.

His K-12 education was completed at Wheatland, a small community in southeastern Wyoming, 70 miles north of Cheyenne, Wyoming, where he now teaches social studies, reading and basic skills to "at risk youth." Prior to teaching Greg completed an associates degree at Casper College in Political Science then finished his baccalaureate degree at the University of Wyoming, in Laramie. Throughout a variety of occupations including rancher, police officer, child abuse investigation, realtor, and schoolteacher, Greg has worked with all ages of young people, trying to show them the importance of the written word along with the beauty and significance of nature.

For the last twenty years Greg's major hobby has been the collection of early and rare works detailing the early history of Wyoming and the settlers and pioneers that came to this land of high mountains and broad plains, starting homes and families. He is currently at work writing the story of two brothers, his grandfather and great uncle, who homesteaded along the Laramie River adjacent to the mighty Two Bar Land and Cattle Company. Both brothers carved out a niche in Wyoming Territory rubbing shoulders with the famous and infamous characters of the time such as Tom Horn.

Printed in the United States
29476LVS00002B/37-279

9 781420 839425